WOMEN IN THE LABOUR MARKET IN CHANGING ECONOMIES

The International Union for the Scientific Study of Population Problems was set up in 1928, with Dr Raymond Pearl as President. At that time the Union's main purpose was to promote international scientific co-operation to study the various aspects of population problems, through national committees and through its members themselves. In 1947 the International Union for the Scientific Study of Population (IUSSP) was reconstituted into its present form.

It expanded its activities to:

- stimulate research on population
- develop interest in demographic matters among governments, national and international organizations, scientific bodies, and the general public
- foster relations between people involved in population studies
- disseminate scientific knowledge on population.

The principal ways through which the IUSSP currently achieves its aims are:

- organization of worldwide or regional conferences
- operations of Scientific Committees under the auspices of the Council
- organization of training courses
- publication of conference proceedings and committee reports.

Demography can be defined by its field of study and its analytical methods. Accordingly, it can be regarded as the scientific study of human populations primarily with respect to their size, their structure, and their development. For reasons which are related to the history of the discipline, the demographic method is essentially inductive: progress in knowledge results from the improvement of observation, the sophistication of measurement methods, and the search for regularities and stable factors leading to the formulation of explanatory models. In conclusion, the three objectives of demographic analysis are to describe, measure, and analyse.

International Studies in Demography is the outcome of an agreement concluded by the IUSSP and the Oxford University Press. The joint series reflects the broad range of the Union's activities; it is based on the seminars organized by the Union and important international meetings in the field of population and development. The Editorial Board of the series is comprised of:

Women in the Labour Market in Changing Economies: Demographic Issues

Edited by

BRÍGIDA GARCÍA
RICHARD ANKER
ANTONELLA PINNELLI

OXFORD
UNIVERSITY PRESS

This book has been printed digitally and produced in a standard specification in order to ensure its continuing availability

OXFORD
UNIVERSITY PRESS

Great Clarendon Street, Oxford OX2 6DP

Oxford University Press is a department of the University of Oxford. It furthers the University's objective of excellence in research, scholarship, and education by publishing worldwide in

Oxford New York

Auckland Cape Town Dar es Salaam Hong Kong Karachi Kuala Lumpur Madrid Melbourne Mexico City Nairobi New Delhi Shanghai Taipei Toronto

With offices in

Argentina Austria Brazil Chile Czech Republic France Greece Guatemala Hungary Italy Japan South Korea Poland Portugal Singapore Switzerland Thailand Turkey Ukraine Vietnam

Oxford is a registered trade mark of Oxford University Press in the UK and in certain other countries

Published in the United States by Oxford University Press Inc., New York

Oxford is a registered trade mark of Oxford University Press in the UK and in certain other countries

Published in the United States by Oxford University Press Inc., New York

Reprinted 2004

ISBN 0-19-926112-1

Contents

PART IV. INCREASING FEMINIZATION OF THE LABOUR FORCE: BALANCING WORK AND FAMILY

List of Contributors

Afsar, Rita, Bangladesh Institute of Development Studies, Dhaka, Bangladesh

Anan, Shen, Institute of Population and Development, Shanghai Academy of Social Sciences, Shanghai, China

Anker, Richard, International Labour Office, Geneva, Switzerland

Bardasi, Elena, University of Essex, United Kingdom

Beegle, Kathleen, The World Bank

Büchel, Felix, Max Planck Institute of Human Development, Berlin, Germany

Cerrutti, Marcela, Centro de Estudios de Población, Buenos Aires, Argentina

Clark, Robert L., North Carolina State University, USA

Cox, Amy G., RAND, Santa Monica, California, USA

Engelhardt, Henriette, Max Planck Institute of Human Development, Berlin, Germany

Feng, Wang, University of California at Irvine, USA

Festy, Patrick, Institute National d'Études Démographiques, Paris, France

Frankenberg, Elizabeth, University of California at Los Angeles, USA

Gallo, Gerardo, ISTAT (National Institute of Statistics) Rome, Italy

García, Brígida, El Colegio de México, México

Gornick, Janet C., Department of Political Science, Baruch College, City University of New York, USA

Grillo, Francesca, University La Sapienza, Rome, Italy

Hermsen, Joan, University of Missouri-Columbia, USA

Juárez, Lucía, University of Alabama at Birmingham, USA

Klerman, Jacob, RAND, Santa Monica, California, USA

Kortchagina, Irina, Institute of Socio-Economic Studies of Population, Russian Academy of Sciences, Russia

Kulczycki, Andrzej, University of Alabama at Birmingham, USA

Liang, Zai, State University of New York at Albany, USA

Mouratcheva, Olga, St. Petersburg State University of Economics and Finance, Russia

Pinnelli, Antonella, University La Sapienza, Rome, Italy

Por Chen, Yiu, Columbia University, USA

Prokofieva, Lidia, Institute of Socio-Economic Studies of Population, Russian Academy of Sciences, Russia

Stanfors, Maria, Lund University, Sweden

Strozza, Salvatore, University Federico II, Naples, Italy

Svensson, Lars, Lund University, Sweden

York, Anne, Meredith College, USA

Thomas, Duncan, University of California at Los Angeles, USA

List of Figures

List of Tables

PART I

BACKGROUND

1

Introduction

BRÍGIDA GARCÍA, RICHARD ANKER,
AND ANTONELLA PINNELLI

Women's increased participation and changing position in the workforce is one of the most significant transformations the world has experienced in recent decades. This is occurring in the context of major economic and labour market changes such as globalization, flexibilization, and informalization of production, high unemployment and underemployment in many countries, high rates of part-time and intermittent employment, economic insecurity, and the restructuring of economic systems. These new labour market conditions affect women's and men's demographic behaviour in complex, new ways that have not been adequately analysed or understood to date.

In view of a paucity of knowledge on this rapidly evolving situation, the Gender and Population Committee of IUSSP organized a seminar on 'Women in the Labour Market in Changing Economies: Demographic Issues'. The main objectives of this seminar, held in Rome in September, 1999, were to: (1) examine women's changing position and participation in the labour market in the context of major economic and labour market changes; (2) analyse how demographic conditions favour or hinder these transformations in the labour market; and (3) study the demographic consequences of rapid economic and labour market variations.

Papers for this seminar were wide ranging in terms of country and region of the world, discipline of authors (e.g. economists, demographers, historians, and sociologists), and subject area (e.g. family formation and dissolution, migration, labour markets, health, and reproductive behaviour). This helped meet one of the seminar's main aims of including a good representation of subject areas and changing economies in the developed world, the developing world and transition economies. A selection of the papers presented at the Rome Seminar are included in this book—12 country studies along with a study that offers a broad international perspective on women's participation in the labour market and occupational sex segregation.

In the case of developing regions, one chapter analyses the impact of export-oriented economic growth on the demand for women's labour in formal sector manufacturing and its consequences for demographic behaviour (Bangladesh garment industry); another chapter analyses employment transitions and adjustments during a major economic crisis (1998 Indonesian financial crisis); while other chapters deal with different types of labour market and demographic effects of structural adjustment and economic reform policies, such as the reduction of social expenditure, privatization and liberalization (Argentina and Egypt). As far as the developed countries of

North America and Europe are concerned, chapters are concerned with transformations underway in governmental and private service sectors and the extent to which this has led to an increase in part-time employment (e.g. Canada, Germany, Italy, the United States, and the United Kingdom), flexibility in working conditions and the segmentation of the labour markets, with mixed impacts on the welfare of women and families as well as on demographic behaviour (United States, Sweden, and Italy).

Regarding the rapid changes taking place in so-called transition economy countries, different analytical perspectives are represented in this book as these countries shift from centrally-planned to market economies. Some chapters focus on divorce (Russia) and single mothers (East and West Germany) and how difficult socio-economic and political conditions and the critical loss of job-related social benefits have affected women's and men's occupational careers and income levels at different stages of the life course. Two chapters deal with China, a country which has not only implemented significant market reforms but has also experienced rapid growth in non-agricultural sectors, and focus on the consequences of women and men's migration to urban areas and export-processing zones.

Studies in the book deal not only with changing economic systems, but also with social relations of gender, which influence the sexual division of labour and the distribution of resources between women and men. The cross-national analysis in Chapter 2 (Clark, York, and Anker) documents that there is a U-shaped relationship between female labour force participation rates in countries and national income per capita. At the same time, this chapter shows that social, cultural, and historical factors are more important than economic development in determining levels and patterns of occupational sex segregation. Women around the world remain responsible for childcare and domestic work and, in most countries are primarily socialized for marriage and motherhood, which invariably restricts their potential labour market activities outside the home. In addition, the sex stereotyping of occupations, which encourages the belief that certain types of work are inherently suitable or unsuitable for women, further restricts women's job opportunities and labour market alternatives to non-domestic work.

Chapters in this book indicate how women today are coping with social and cultural restrictions as well as major social and economic change, which affect both the supply and the demand for women's work—with varying consequences for their labour market participation and demographic behaviour. These case studies range from situations such as those of Bangladesh (Afsar) and Egypt (Kulczycki and Juárez) where residential female seclusion and a strong patriarchal ideology still prevail, to the recent severe economic disruptions in Indonesia (Thomas, Beegle, and Frankenberg), to Sweden (Stanfors and Svensson) with its policies designed to facilitate the combination of women's family and work roles, but where the labour market continues to be relatively highly segregated between men and women. Also included are chapters dealing with evolution of gender systems and labour markets in Russia (Festy, Kortchagina, Mouratcheva, and Prokofieva) and China, where socialist commitment to gender equality has progressively weakened as a result of the transition to market-oriented economies.

In the context outlined above, a number of demographic issues are explored. Three chapters are concerned with migration (Strozza, Gallo, and Grillo for Italy; Feng and Anan for Shanghai, China; Liang and Chen for Shenzhen, China). They contribute to the growing migration literature, which treats women as autonomous migrants and thus challenges the traditional assumption that women only migrate to follow other household members. These authors explore how labour market outcomes for women migrants depend not only on their human capital characteristics and the dynamics of labour markets in their places of origin or destination, but also on the types of disadvantages and discriminations women face when they are migrant labourers.

Several chapters in this book analyse family formation and dissolution, household composition, and contraceptive behaviour (Büchel and Engelhardt for West and East Germany; Stanfors and Svensson for Sweden; Festy, Kortchagina, Mouratcheva, and Prokofieva for Russia; Kulczycki, and Juárez for Egypt). These are considered both as factors that determine women's labour market participation and income levels, as well as demographic outcomes.

Marriage and conjugal union patterns, the percentage of women who never marry, number and age of children, birth spacing, and separation and divorce are interconnected with women's labour market responses and contributions to household budgets. This occurs both in societies that have experienced a decline in living standards (Cerrutti for Argentina), as well as in countries where opportunities have expanded (Büchel and Engelhardt for East and West Germany; Cox, Hermsen, and Klerman for the United States). Authors analyse the effect on women's labour force activity and disadvantaged labour market position when husbands and fathers in the household are absent and small children or older dependent adults are present (Bardasi and Gornick for part-time employed in five industrialized countries; Cerrutti for Argentina). Finally, some authors contribute to the important and controversial issue of how women's economic participation affects women's empowerment, taking a positive stand and offering examples of how increased earning power can contribute to changing women's lives in both economic and demographic spheres (Afsar for Bangladesh; Kulczycki and Juárez for Egypt).

ORGANIZATION OF THE BOOK

The organization of the book closely follows the main lines of interest and themes outlined above. In Part I, after this introduction, Robert L. Clark, Anne York, and Richard Anker, in their chapter 'Cross-national Analysis of Women in the Labour Market', provide an overview of women's position in the labour market around the world. In the first part of the chapter, the authors analyse levels, trends, and determinants of female labour force participation using data for over 100 countries. According to comparable ILO data, female participation rates decreased between 1970 and 1990 for women in the 15–19 age group by approximately 5 percentage points as women stayed in school longer in all parts of the world. In contrast, female participation rates increased by approximately 10 percentage points in the 1970–90 period for women 20–49. The authors then analyse the determinants of female labour force participation across countries using multiple regression techniques. A U-shaped relationship across countries is observed between women's participation and level of economic development for different age groups and points in time *ceteris paribus*. In the second part of the chapter, the authors analyse occupational sex segregation using two- and three-digit occupational data for 41 countries from around the world (with approximately 175 occupations per country) for 1970–90. High levels of occupational segregation by sex are found for in all regions of the world. What makes this situation especially detrimental for women is that women have more limited (and less valuable) opportunities as compared to men. The authors find that there are seven times as many 'male' occupations as 'female' occupations, and 'female' occupations tend to have lower pay and status as compared to 'male' occupations. The correspondence of occupational sex segregation with typical patriarchal values and sex stereotyping is found to be so strong that it leads the authors to conclude that socio-cultural values and sex stereotyping determine to a large extent which occupations are male-dominated and which are female-dominated.

Part II is specifically dedicated to the analysis of labour market and demographic effects of major economic and political change. It begins with the examination of the labour market effects of the 1998 financial crisis in Indonesia in the chapter 'Labour Market Transitions of Men and Women during an Economic Crisis: Evidence from Indonesia' by Duncan Thomas, Kathleen Beegle, and Elizabeth Frankenberg. As it is known, financial crises, and worsening labour markets, which accompany such crises, are recurring dangers at the beginning of the twenty-first century. The 1998 situation in Indonesia is analysed by the authors using a unique panel data set where the same households were interviewed just before and soon after this crisis. Contrary to expectations, they found that this financial collapse did not have much of an effect on unemployment or on overall employment levels (although there was a small increase in female labour force participation rates). Negative labour market effects were manifested in other ways. Real hourly wages fell by 40 per cent on average in the first year of the crisis. Labour turnover rates were very high and many workers shifted their employment status between private sector employee, self-employed, unpaid family worker, and government. According to the authors 'the picture which emerges is one of a remarkably flexible labour market, tremendous resilience of families in the face of a devastating crisis and of women playing a key role in supporting family income'. For example, approximately one-quarter of uneducated women left the labour market and a similar proportion joined the labour market between 1997 and 1998; in addition, 40 per cent of working women changed employment status between 1997 and 1998. The authors also emphasize one methodological implication of their findings, the importance of collecting information on self-employment and unpaid family work as well as on wage employment in order to understand how households adjust to and cope with crises situations.

Another type of rapidly changing economic and labour market situation is that of Bangladesh, which may provide an example where many poor women have benefited from globalization. One and a half million jobs have been created in the export-oriented garment industry over the past two decades, and women comprise 70 per cent of these workers (besides, ninety per cent of them are migrants coming from mostly functionally landless households). All this has taken place in a country where purdah is common, sex stereotyping is strong and labour market opportunities are very limited for women, especially poor women. Rita Afsar, in her chapter on 'Gender, Labour Market, and Demographic Change: a Case Study of Women's Entry into the Formal Manufacturing Sector in Bangladesh' uses qualitative and quantitative data to investigate consequences for women of garment sector jobs in terms of demographic behaviour, empowerment, and gender equality in the labour market. In terms of demographic outcomes, chapter 4 by Afsar finds that younger women who work in a garment factory generally delay marriage, and this together with income from work provides them with a degree of autonomy. Married female garment workers, however, continue to bear heavy workloads and abuse at home. In terms of labour market consequences, the picture is complex and mixed. On the one hand, high levels of occupational sex segregation are found in garment factories, with women much more likely to have lower skilled and lower paying jobs compared to men (repeating the cross-national findings of Clark *et al.*, chapter 2). On the other hand, garment jobs provide poor women with previously unthinkable independence and opportunity to earn money.

The two other chapters in this section analyse some of the consequences of one of the most important political events in the second half of the twentieth century, the fall of socialist states in places such as Russia and East Germany. Using household data, Felix Büchel and Henriette Engelhardt in their chapter on 'Missing the Partner and his Earnings: Income Situation and Labour Market Participation of Single Mothers in West and East Germany', estimate the effect on a person's relative income position of being in a single mother household compared to being in a two-parent household. This is done separately for former West and East Germany as well as for 1990 and 1997 (i.e. before and after the monetary, economic, and social reunification of Germany). The authors find that the well-known relationship whereby single mother households have much lower income per equivalent consumer as compared to two-parent households has remained stable over time. Major differences found between West and East Germany are that: (i) both single mother households as well as two-parent households with dependent children were relatively better off compared to other households in East Germany than they were in West Germany during socialist days; and (ii) the better relative income position in East Germany of households with dependent children has eroded between 1990–97. Since these descriptive results could be due to selectivity bias as single mothers and married mothers have different labour force participation rates, the authors also did a multivariate analysis using a Heckman approach to correct for selectivity bias. This methodological technique yields more consistent results. In both East and West Germany, the relative income position of single mother households is low even after controlling for social status and women's earnings. Among single mother households, never married women are worse off than separated or divorced women. Interestingly, these relationships are stable over time in both parts of Germany.

Finally, in their study on 'Divorce and Professional Careers in Russia during the Transition towards Market Economy', Patrick Festy, Irina Kortchagina, Olga

Mouratcheva, and Lidia Prokofieva, deal with gender differences in the careers of divorced persons, during marriage and after separation. Data comes from two retrospective surveys, carried out in 1993 and in 1998, a transition period in Russia when a great economic crisis unfolded, unemployment rose sharply and gender discrimination in the labour market widened. The main questions this paper addresses are: (i) when men are divorced, does this slow down their upward mobility in the labour market; and (ii) when women are divorced, do they continue losing ground compared to men? Results show that during married life, women's careers lag behind those of men. The presence of children does not explain this situation. Job segregation seems the main explanation, since women are concentrated in the least profitable sectors of the labour market, where professional and family life are easier to combine. Neither divorce nor marriage is found to have a noticeable impact on women's careers. In contrast, divorce is found to considerably slow down men's careers (especially when they do not remarry). Several factors contribute to help explain the lack of an effect of divorce or remarriage on women's careers: high female activity rates, a good alimony system and social policy that help lone mothers. Overall, the recent economic crisis has negatively affected all divorcees, especially increasing unemployment among men and causing women's careers to regress.

In Part III, authors focus on internal and international migratory movements of women and men. This includes Italy as the country of destination for migrants mainly from Eastern Europe and North Africa, and China, where important territorial mobility is taking place as a consequence of economic liberalization. In the chapter on 'Gender and the Labour Market among Immigrants in Some Italian Areas: the case of Moroccans, Former Yugoslavians, and Poles', Salvatore Strozza, Gerardo Gallo, and Francesca Grillo, analyse gender differences in the labour market among different immigrant communities in Italy. The quantitative information comes from official and survey data. A factor analysis, based on official data (residence permits) for 19 foreign communities, divides immigrant groups according to female and male participation in the labour market: there are communities with large differences between men and women (many women in these communities have migrated for family reunification reasons, and a large percentage are inactive or unemployed); communities where female activity rates and occupational sex segregation (e.g. many women are in domestic services) are very high; and communities where women's activity rate is high and their occupational structure is more similar to that of men. A sample survey was carried out in 1998 on several topics among three communities living in different areas: Moroccan to represent the first typology; and Polish and ex-Yugoslavian for the second typology. A regression model is used to analyse the determinants of earnings. Results show that women always earn less than men. However, in the Moroccan community, male–female differences in earnings remain even when human capital and sector of employment are taken into consideration, while in the Polish and ex-Yugoslavian communities differences in earnings can be attributed to a different sectoral structure of employment for women and men. A decomposition model of the gender wage gap confirms these results.

China's dual transformations of the past two decades, from a state planned to a market economy and from an agrarian to an industrial society, have resulted in an unprecedented number of female labour migrants in Chinese cities. Wang Feng and Shen Anan in their chapter on 'Double Jeopardy? Female Rural Migrant Labourers in Urban China, the Case of Shanghai', show that female labour migrants improve their economic well-being and increase their social mobility, but at the same time they find themselves not in one emerging market, but in two overlapping markets: one dominated by the capitalistic free market spirit and principles, and the other by socialist arrangements that still favour and protect the old urban establishment. The hierarchy of the Chinese urban labour market, therefore, consists of four layers: male urban workers, female urban workers, male migrant workers, and female migrant workers, in that order. Using Shanghai as a case study and sample survey data, the authors identify the determinants of income stratification for these subpopulations. They find that most of the observed gender and rural/urban difference in income is not due to female migrants' disadvantaged background since female rural migrants still earn less than the other groups after controlling for factors such as age, length of work per week, educational and occupational background. This net disadvantage is what the authors call 'double jeopardy' faced by female migrant labourers in the urban Chinese labour market.

Zai Liang and Yiu Por Chen offer another look at the gender differences in migration in China. They consider Shenzhen SEZ (Special Economic Zone). The major objectives of the SEZs are: technology transfers and capital investment, regional development and employment, foreign exchange earnings and export promotion, and management upgrading and training. Shenzen is a showcase of the so-called 'socialist market economy with Chinese characteristics': foreign investment has increased dramatically since 1979, along with the number of migrants, especially temporary migrants. The question addressed by the authors is: are gender differences reduced in this new economic environment; they use a 1 per cent sample from the 1990 China Population Census. Local residents in Shenzhen are compared with permanent immigrants and temporary immigrants; also migrants to Shenzhen from Guangdong (province where this city is located) are compared with residents in other parts of the province. A logistic regression model is used to estimate the determinants of the probability of being a permanent migrant (to get *hukou*), and multinomial logit models are used to estimate the determinants of being in a professional and managerial occupation or in a sales and services occupation instead of being in a lower level occupation (controlling for age, education, urban residence, and marital status). Results show that this migration process benefits women in some major aspects: as permanent migrants, women are more likely to be engaged in professional jobs (but mainly as accountants) than permanent migrant men, and in sales and service jobs compared to non-migrant women in Shenzhen. As temporary migrants, women do not have advantages compared to residents in Shenzhen, but do have a higher probability to be engaged in sales and service occupations compared to residents in other parts of the province. Moreover, women benefit more than men from higher education and consequently this reduces gender differences. The authors conclude that migration in the case of Shenzhen SEZ offers a message of limited optimism for women.

Part IV focuses on women's multiple roles and the search for a balance between work, marriage, and family. Chapters in this part of the book analyse the situation in North America (United States and Canada) and Western Europe, as well as in two developing countries (Argentina and Egypt). Amy G. Cox, Joan M. Hermsen, and Jacob A. Klerman, in their chapter on 'Economic Opportunities and the Transition to Marriage among Young Women in the United States' investigate the influence of economic opportunity on the transition to marriage among young American women. They hypothesize that women who live in areas with high levels of economic opportunity for women are more likely to delay marriage than women who live in areas with low opportunity. Individual level data are used from the 1979–94 waves of the NLSY (National Longitudinal Survey of Youth), which includes 3190 white, African Americans, and Latinas women ages 14–21 years in 1979. Contextual indicators of economic opportunity are estimated at the state level for each year of the analysis and attached to each individual record. Authors then use discrete time event history methods and logistic regression to model the log odds of women remaining unmarried. The explanatory variables are: women's and men's predicted earnings as contextual variables (women's predicted earnings to measure women's economic opportunities and men's predicted earnings to measure the quality of men in the marriage market), welfare benefit levels, education, current school enrolment, immigration status, pre-marital birth, employment experience, religion, employment aspirations, mother's education, and employment and whether raised in a single mother family. Results support the author's hypotheses: women delay marriage when they can expect to earn more, while individual level economic opportunity and the availability of higher earning men promote early marriage. These results confirm the need to consider economic opportunity both at the micro and at the macro level, both for men (as it is traditionally done) and for women.

Elena Bardasi and Janet C. Gornick, in their chapter on 'Women and Part-Time Employment: Workers' "Choices" and Wage Penalties in Five Industrialized Countries', use cross-nationally comparable micro-data from the Luxembourg Income Study to analyse patterns of part-time work and its consequences in five industrialized countries—Canada, Germany, Italy, the United Kingdom, and the United States—as of the middle 1990s. First, they investigate women's employment choices, specifically the three-option decision between non-employment, part-time employment, and full-time employment, with a focus on the household variables that shape those choices. Second, they analyse the direct economic consequences of part-time work for women, in the form of hourly pay penalties. Regression techniques as well as the Oaxaca decomposition of the wage differential are used. Regarding women's employment 'choices', as expected, both the presence and age of children are found to be crucial in nearly all cases. One of the most interesting findings is the strong and consistent downward pressure exerted by the presence of a non-wage earning adult in the home on women's labour market attachment. Finally, on the question of wage penalties, the authors report that part-time workers earn less per hour than full-time workers in all five countries studied. Controlling for measurable worker and job-related characteristics reduces the observed gap between different types of women's work in all countries, and only in Germany is there significant evidence of pay 'discrimination' directed at part-time workers relative to full-time workers.

The interactions between women's education, career opportunities, non-domestic work and fertility are explored for Sweden by Maria Stanfors and Lars Svensson in their chapter on 'Education, Career Opportunities, and Changing Patterns of Fertility: a Study of Women in the Labour Market in twentieth-century Sweden'. Using an economic-historical perspective, the authors base their study partly on analysis of aggregate time series for the twentieth century of official population statistics and partly on data from the 1992/1993 Swedish Family Survey. They find that while period fertility has fluctuated in Sweden during the twentieth century, cohort fertility has stayed roughly constant at around two children per woman. As women's economic status has changed and the education and work components of women's lives have increased, the age pattern of fertility has shifted towards older ages. However, higher education has not necessarily resulted in lower fertility, probably due to the fact that different groups of women with higher education have chosen larger or smaller families depending on career orientation and status. The cohorts of Swedish women born in the 1940s and early 1950s have been the ones marking a turning point. They were among the first to have a career throughout the life course. This cohort responded to economic, political, and institutional factors (e.g. tax reforms, extended parental leave, and the expansion of publicly provided child care), which increased the compatibility between work and family. Nevertheless, these reforms indirectly confirmed a traditional sexual division of labour in the market as well as in the home so that even today there is a high degree of occupational sex segregation in the Swedish labour market.

As far as the developing countries are concerned, women's family and labour market position is examined in Argentina and Egypt. Marcela Cerrutti in her chapter on 'Family, Quality of Jobs, and Female Labour Force Patterns in Buenos Aires, Argentina' investigates a relatively unexplored dimension of women's employment in Latin America, that is the determinants and consequences of short-term movements into and out of the labour force. The study is carried out in Buenos Aires, Argentina, at the beginning of the 1990's and combines quantitative and qualitative information (panel data from employment surveys and retrospective life histories). The main hypothesis of this study is that working intermittently negatively affects women's careers, since it prevents the accumulation of work experience, undermines promotions, and decreases the chances of obtaining other benefits such as social security and health insurance. Using regression techniques the author reaches the conclusion that intermittent employment arises from both the conflict in combining paid and domestic work as well as the nature of the labour opportunities available to women. The qualitative analysis drew attention to other factors that have a potential influence on women's labour force mobility, such as: the existence of labour force 'arrangements' between husbands and wives, the difficulties in obtaining affordable childcare, the lack of regular part-time white collar jobs in Argentina, the geographical segregation of job opportunities, and the impact of economic restructuring. Finally, another important factor, frequently pointed out by interviewees, was the detrimental effect of employers' practices which limit economic opportunities to married women with children, and in that way discriminate against them.

The last chapter in the book addresses the implications of women's work for their general well-being and empowerment, an issue which is not always clear and continues to be controversial. Andrej Kulczycki and Lucia Juárez, in their chapter on 'The Influence of Female Employment and Autonomy on Reproductive Behaviour in Egypt', offer new evidence on the type of relationship that exists between women's employment, autonomy, and contraceptive use in Egypt, a country where women have made gains in health and education but where they continue to lag far behind in economic and social participation, and decision making. Information from the 1995 Egyptian Demographic and Health Survey is used for a regression analysis study. Findings confirm that women's economic activity is important for modern contraceptive use (which is still moderate in Egypt). Regression results indicate, however, that rather than female labour force activity *per se* increasing modern contraceptives use, it is the interaction of employment status with the stage of family formation that helps explain this relationship. Working women tend to begin using modern contraception earlier in their marital lives than non-working women, suggesting that empowering women through work contributes to changes in contraceptive use and fertility behaviour in Egypt. Because this relationship is indirect, the authors argue that programmes which improve women's economic opportunity and security would have a beneficial impact on reproductive behaviour.

On the whole, this book offers a rich set of studies on the interaction between women's participation in the labour market and different demographic phenomena. The importance, range and depth of the issues covered indicate that women's changing position in the workforce is central for understanding labour market and demographic transformations taking place in both developed and developing countries, and that these relationships deserve closer consideration on the part of academics, other population professionals, and policy makers.

2

Cross-national Analysis of Women in the Labour Market

ROBERT L. CLARK, ANNE YORK, AND RICHARD ANKER

INTRODUCTION

Despite the continuing high levels of sexual inequality in the labour market, an increasing proportion of women joined the labour force and entered male-dominated occupations in the final decades of the twentieth century. This paper documents and explains recent levels, trends, and patterns in female labour force activity in both developed and developing countries. First, the chapter examines the increasing proportion of women who are in the labour force and how activity rates vary around the world along with economic development and the accompanying higher income and lower fertility. Second, the diffusion of women throughout the labour force is assessed based on recent evidence on occupational segregation by sex.

FEMALE LABOUR FORCE PARTICIPATION

Review of literature

There is some uncertainty over the nature of the relationship between economic development and female activity rates. Labour force data from most countries indicate that the activity rates of women have been increasing over time. However, research studies indicate that the relationship between economic development, as represented by rising income per capita, and the proportion of women who are in the labour force is non-linear.

As far back as 1965, J. N. Sinha (1965) hypothesized that a U-shaped relationship existed between female labour force activity and economic development. His analysis was based on Indian data and experience, as well as 1950 census data from the United Nations. Sinha noted that the employment gains of women in the emerging sectors of the economy are retarded by conditions of high male unemployment and underemployment that often occur in conjunction with the early stages of economic development.

In his classic book on the labour force in development, Durand (1975) provided further evidence of this U-shaped relationship. He argued that this pattern of labour force activity was the result of changes in women's employment opportunities and qualifications as economic development proceeds. Durand concluded that in the early stages of development, employment opportunities for women decline with the contraction of the agricultural sector and other primary industries where traditionally female participation rates are relatively high.

According to Durand's analysis, female participation rates eventually rise with economic development as women become better educated and the more modern industries and occupations become larger and more sympathetic to female workers. But this occurs only after an interim period (the bottom part of the U-shape), both because women are at a disadvantage in the newly developed labour market compared to men due to relatively low education and the relatively small size of employment opportunities in new industries and occupations.

The extent to which female activity rates follow this general pattern vary across countries depending on the degree of female employment in those sectors that are declining and those that are expanding. Durand reported that 'The expansion of the non-agricultural share in labour demand at the expense of agriculture makes for increasing opportunity for women in countries where the female share in non-agricultural employment is larger than in agriculture, as in Latin American countries, and for decreasing opportunity in the opposite case, as in the majority of South and East Asian countries'. Of course, cultural and religious norms also influence the ability of women to shift from agricultural and home employment into the industrialized sector. As well in many countries in recent decades, there has been a change in values and attitudes about the appropriateness of women working away from home, and this has contributed to a secular rise over time in female labour force participation rates.

The interaction of other aspects of development may also affect the change in female labour force activity. For young men, labour force activity rates tend to fall with economic development as increases in household income allow male teenagers to substitute increased years of education for reduced work. In contrast, the activity rates of young women may rise along with educational attainment as marriage and childbearing are delayed and the smaller family sizes are favourable to higher participation rates for women age 20–49.

In summary, Durand concluded that the decline in female activity rates in the early stages of economic development was well documented both in cross-sectional analysis and in changes within countries between censuses. He found less definitive support for the increase in activity rates at the later stages of development with some countries conforming to the predicted relationships and other countries deviating from the expected pattern.

Goldin (1995) provides a theoretical model and more recent empirical evidence of a U-shaped relationship between economic development and female labour force activity using national data from the 1980s for about 100 countries for women age 45–59. Her theoretical model is based on the assumption that there is a stigma attached to women entering the paid labour force in manual labour in a country's early stages of economic development that decreases women's labour force participation. Once a country has advanced enough that women's educational attainment is high, women can then enter non-manual labour jobs where less stigma is attached. The empirical results indicate a U-shaped relationship with regard to economic development when the natural log of per capita GDP or years of schooling for adult males are used as proxies for economic development. Other regression results show that a dominant factor positively related to labour force participation rates for women age 45–59 is the interaction of the per cent of the female labour force in the clerical sector and the years of schooling of adult women.

Outline of analysis

This study examines cross-sectional, country-level data on female labour force activity between 1970 and 1990 for countries at different levels of economic development using descriptive and regression analysis. It also analyses cross-country differences across the development spectrum using regression analysis for 1990.

Regression models are used to estimate the determinants of female labour force activity. The basic specification for age-specific activity rates is one where the national participation rate for women is related to the level of economic development as represented by per capita GNP and the total fertility rate. This latter explanatory variable partially represents the value of a woman's time in the home and in the market. Both of these variables are expected to have complex effects on female activity rates that vary with women's age, the stage of economic development of a country, and time period. In addition, regional dichotomous variables are included in the specification to capture the impact of cultural and religious norms on the proportion of women who are in the labour force.

Data description

To document and examine trends in the labour force activity of women between 1970 and 1990, we created a unique data file from several existing sources including the International Labour Office (ILO), the United Nations, and the World Bank. These data enable us to analyse the labour force activity of women aged 15–64. Women are divided into three age groups: 15–19, 20–49, and 50–64. This division allows us to examine the differential effects of national income and fertility on the labour force activity of women at different stages of the life cycle. The youngest age group represents an age when some women marry and begin to have children, while other women remain in school and delay marriage and child bearing. The age of marriage and of birth of first child vary by level of development and societal norms. Women age 20–49 are in the primary reproductive years and are most likely to have significant childcare responsibilities. Finally, women age 50–64 are in a post-reproductive and pre-retirement period when the responsibility for caring for small children is reduced.

National activity rate data for women in the three age categories come from ILO data tapes and ILO (1997). The ILO data report five-year labour force activity rates by sex. The number of economically active women are combined with population data in order to determine activity rates for the three age groups described above for

1970, 1980, and 1990. Throughout this chapter, average age-specific activity rates across countries are reported, that is, the average rates are not weighted by a country's population size.

The ILO data source covers all countries and territories with at least 200,000 inhabitants in mid-1990. They provide ILO estimates of female and male labour force activity rates which are said to be comparable across countries as well as across time for each country (ILO 1997). National estimates are based on censuses and sample surveys whenever these are available and adjusted when necessary to increase comparability. For countries where national data are not available, estimates are mainly based on data from neighbouring countries with similar social, cultural, and political characteristics. It should be noted that female participation rates were raised on an *ad hoc* basis for countries with a Muslin culture, since it was believed by the ILO staff that official statistics in such countries undercount many women working in agriculture (Denti and Ruhumuliaz 1995).

The level of economic development for a country is measured by per capita GNP from the World Bank's *World Tables of Economic and Social Indicators, 1950–1992.* The World Bank also sorts countries into low, middle, and high income categories based on national per capita GNP. The income ranges for 1990 are $610 or less in income per capita for low income countries, $611–7,620 income per capita for middle income countries, and above $7,620 income per capita for high income countries.

Fertility data are from the United Nations' *Demographic Indicators 1950–2050* and are given as the total fertility rate per woman for each country. In general, fertility rates are negatively related to per capita GNP and decline over time. The resulting data set includes 111 countries on which there is information on age-specific female activity rates, income per capita, and total fertility rates by women for 1970, 1980, and 1990.[1]

Trends in female activity rates: 1970–1990

Across regions and income levels, the data show that participation rates of women age 15–19 decreased from 1970 to 1990, while it generally increased for those in the older two age brackets. Table 2.1 shows the average female participation rate for the 111 countries included in the sample. For women aged 15–19, the participation rate decreased from 42.5 per cent in 1970 to 37.6 per cent in 1990 as increasing school enrollment in this age group had a substantial dampening effect on the proportion of young women in the labour force. A large gain in participation was observed for women aged 20–49 as their average activity rate increased from 48.5 per cent to 58.6 per cent, reflecting a world-wide labour market trend of increasing integration of women into national economies. Among women aged 50–64, the average activity rate rose moderately from 40.4 per cent to 43.4 per cent during these two decades, probably because of a secular increase in cohort participation rates over time.

[1] The 111 countries included in the analysis of female labour force activity represent 86.6 per cent of the female population age 15–64 in 1990, and their unweighted average labour force participation is 51.7 per cent as compared to 58 per cent for the other 66 countries with such data on the ILO data tape.

Table 2.1. *Descriptive Statistics for Female Labour Force Participation Rates by Level of Development, 1970–90*

Participation rates by age and year	All countries	Low	Middle	High
Age 15–19				
1970	42.5	57.0	30.9	46.9
1980	40.0	54.1	30.0	41.8
1990	37.6	52.1	28.7	36.3
Age 20–49				
1970	48.5	66.6	37.6	46.5
1980	53.8	66.4	42.8	59.7
1990	58.6	66.7	48.1	69.6
Age 50–64				
1970	40.4	60.2	31.0	32.8
1980	42.0	59.5	32.7	37.4
1990	43.4	59.3	34.2	41.0
Fertility rate				
1970	5.31	6.58	5.71	2.75
1980	4.70	6.36	4.91	2.00
1990	4.13	5.90	4.12	1.77

Number of observations is 111 when all countries are included. The number of low, middle, and high income countries are 34, 52, and 25, respectively.

Source: Author's calculations from UN and ILO data.

To examine further age-specific participation rates, countries in Table 2.1 are sorted into low-, middle-, and high-income groups based on their per capita gross national product (as defined by the World Bank). For each of the three years and three age groups, the U-shaped participation rate–income per capita relationship described earlier is observed. The activity rate for each age group declines with income per capita between low-income and middle-income group countries. Women in high income countries have higher participation rates than similar aged women in middle income countries. The U-shaped pattern of participation is illustrated by examining the data for 1990 for women aged 20–49. The participation rates for these women averaged 66.7 per cent in the low income countries, 48.1 per cent in the middle-income countries, and 69.6 per cent in the high income countries. Similar patterns are observed for the other two age groups in 1990 and for each of the three age groups in 1970 and 1980. Table 2.1 also shows that fertility rates have fallen both over time and over levels of economic development.

The U-shaped pattern of labour force activity can also be illustrated by plotting individual country observations reflecting the age-specific female activity rate and the natural log of per capita income. Figure 2.1 shows a scatter plot of the labour

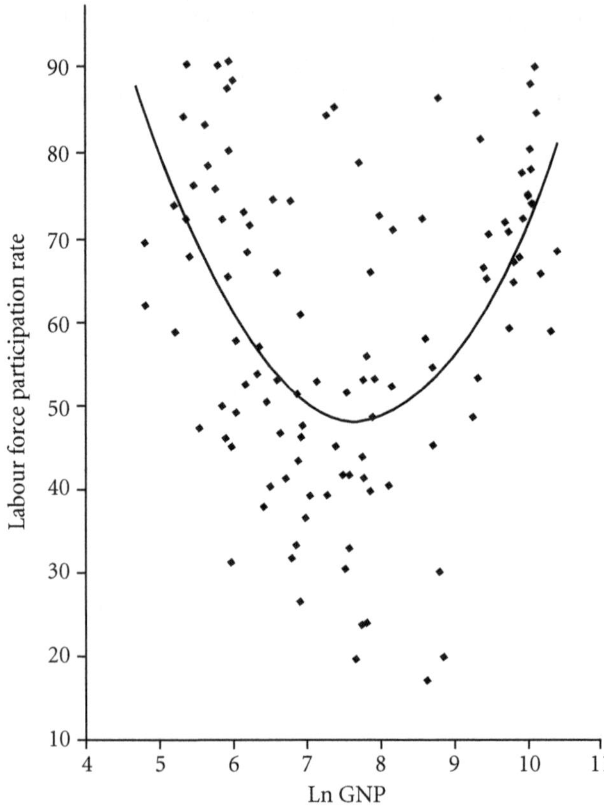

Figure 2.1. *Scatter Plot of Actual Labour Force Participation Rates of Women 20–49 and Natural Log Per Capita GNP in 1990*

force participation rate for all countries for women age 20–49 in 1990 against the natural log of per capita GNP.[2]

In general, the U-shaped participation–income curves shift up over time for women in the two older age categories between 1970 and 1990, but shift down over time for those age 15–19. Among women age 15–19, the average activity rate decreased 5 percentage points for the low income countries, 2 percentage points for the middle-income countries, and 10 percentage points for the high income countries from 1970 to 1990. For the women age 50–64, the activity rate for women in the low income category was mostly unchanged, while it increased by 3 percentage

[2] A quadratic regression line is fit to this data to illustrate the statistical relationship between these two variables. The regression line equation shown in the graph is: labour force participation= $311.02 - 68.774 * \ln \text{gnp} + 4.4859 * \ln \text{gnp}^2$. All coefficients are statistically significant at the 0.01 level of significance and this equation has an adjusted R^2 of 0.29. The natural log form of per capita GNP is used since GNP is a highly skewed variable.

points for those in the middle-income category, and 8 percentage points for those in the high-income category. A similar pattern is seen for the women age 20–49 with labour force participation rates remaining fairly constant across time for those in the low-income countries, however much greater increases are recorded for these women in middle- and high-income countries. The average activity rate in the middle-income countries increased by 10 percentage points, from 37.6 per cent to 48.1 per cent, and the rate for women in high-income countries rose by approximately 23 percentage points from 46.5 per cent to 69.6 per cent.

Table 2.2 shows that considerable variation in the age-specific activity rates prevails across geographical regions. For example, average 1990 participation rates for women aged 20–49 ranged from 40.3 per cent in the North Africa/Middle East region to 67.5 per cent in Europe/North America and 68.5 per cent in SubSaharan Africa. Among younger women, the average activity rates ranged from 24.6 per cent in Latin America/Caribbean to 53.6 per cent in SubSaharan Africa. For the women aged 50–64, the rates range from 31.6 per cent in Latin America/Caribbean to 62.6 per cent in SubSaharan Africa.

Over these two decades, activity rates have been largely unchanged in the African and Middle East regions, but increased rapidly for those age 20–49 and 50–64 in the

Table 2.2. *Female Participation Rates by Age and Region for 1970, 1980, and 1990*

Age and region	1970	1980	1990
Age 15–19	42.5	40.0	37.6
SubSaharan Africa	58.0	55.5	53.6
North Africa/Middle East	32.6	32.2	31.4
Asia/Oceania	46.1	43.6	39.7
Europe/North America+	44.0	40.1	34.7
Latin America/Caribbean	27.3	25.0	24.6
Age 20–49	48.5	53.8	58.6
SubSaharan Africa	69.9	68.8	68.5
North Africa/Middle East	37.4	38.5	40.3
Asia/Oceania	50.0	55.2	60.3
Europe/North America+	43.8	57.7	67.5
Latin America/Caribbean	34.3	41.4	48.9
Age 50–64	40.4	42.0	43.4
SubSaharan Africa	66.1	63.7	62.6
North Africa/Middle East	34.1	33.5	32.2
Asia/Oceania	38.8	41.1	44.0
Europe/North America+	29.8	36.4	39.4
Latin America/Caribbean	25.9	28.4	31.6

Number of countries in each region are: SubSaharan Africa—29, North Africa and Middle East—14, Asia and Oceania—18, Europe and North America—23, and Latin America and Caribbean—27.

+Israel is included in the Europe/North America region.

Source: Authors' calculations from UN and ILO data.

other three regions. For women aged 20–49, the activity rate in Europe/North America increased from 43.8 per cent in 1970 to 67.5 per cent in 1990, while rates in Asia/Oceania rose from 50.0 to 60.3 per cent and rates in Latin America/Caribbean increased from 34.3 to 48.9 per cent. In contrast, the activity rates for middle-aged women in North Africa/Middle East increased only from 37.4 to 40.3 per cent and rates in SubSaharan Africa decreased slightly from 69.9 to 68.5 per cent.

Determinants of female labour force activity

Activity rate equations for women aged 15–64 are estimated over the 111 countries to examine the effect that economic development, fertility, and regional differences have on the proportion of women who are in the labour force. Each country is treated as an observation, because we are interested in relationships within and across countries. The dependent variable is the national activity rate of women in the three age groups unweighted by population size. Explanatory variables include indicators of per capita income, the national total fertility rate, and dichotomous variables indicating the age category, year of the observation, and a country's region. This specification reflects basic economic theory of the allocation of time and the severe data limitations encountered when attempting to examine a large number of countries at all stages of economic development.

Rising per capita income and female activity rates

The primary objective of this analysis is to examine how the proportion of women who are in the labour force is related to the level of national income. Earlier studies have shown that the relationship between per capita income and labour force participation of women is nonlinear and U-shaped. The model shown in Table 2.3 combines data for 111 countries, the three age categories, and the three years of data. This model includes the quadratic form of the log of per capita GNP. The quadratic form of an independent variable allows for a turning point in its relationship with the dependent variable.

The analysis shows that the coefficients on the income variables are highly statistically significant. They indicate that income per capita has the predicted U-shape relationship with activity rates. The minimum point of the income–participation relationship is at a log income per capita of 8.245, corresponding to an income level of $3,808, which is approximately the mean income for the middle-income countries in this sample in 1990.

Fertility, region, and time period effects

The statistical analysis reported in Table 2.3 includes dichotomous variables indicating the various age groups for women. The results indicate the standard pattern that activity rates increase with age and then decline. The predicted rate for women aged 20–49 is 13.61 percentage points higher than that for women aged 15–19, while the rate for women 50–64 is only 2 percentage points higher than the youngest women and 11 percentage points lower than the middle-age group.

Table 2.3. *Regression of Female Labour Force Participation Rate for Pooled Data*

Variable	Coefficient	Standard error
Intercept	218.72*	11.36
Age 20–49	13.61*	1.15
Age 50–64	1.89***	1.15
Year 1980	9.15*	1.31
Year 1990	8.30*	1.37
Log GNP per capita	−44.69*	3.01
Log GNP squared	2.71*	0.21
Fertility rate	−2.39*	0.51
North Africa/Middle East	−9.07*	2.50
SubSaharan Africa	15.49*	2.40
Latin America/Caribbean	−9.12*	1.91
Asia/Oceania	−1.81	1.93
Adjusted $R^2 = 0.52$		
$N = 999$		

* Indicates significance at the 0.01 level.
*** Indicates significance at the 0.10 level.
N equals 999 as the pooled analysis includes three age groups (15–19, 20–49, and 50–64) and three years (1970, 1980, and 1990) for all countries.
The excluded class is 15–19 for age, 1970 for year and Europe/North America for region; therefore, age coefficients are deviations from 1970, and region coefficients are deviations from Europe/North America.

Source: Authors' calculations from UN and ILO data.

In this pooled regression, increases in fertility lower participation rates. An increase of one child per woman in the total fertility rate lowers the female participation rate by 2.4 percentage points. This result therefore implies that a decrease in the total fertility rate from the average in low-income countries to that in high-income countries (from 5.90 to 1.77) in 1990 is associated with an increase in the female participation rate of almost 10 percentage points, all else held constant.

Regional differences in participation rates are also evident, even though the pooled regression takes into consideration differences between regions in GNP per capita and total fertility rates. The omitted regional category is Europe/North America. North Africa/Middle East and Latin America/Caribbean have an average participation rate that is, 9 percentage points lower than the rate for the more developed region, *ceteris paribus*, while SubSaharan Africa has a rate that is 15 percentage points higher. These results may be due in part to the exclusion of certain explanatory variables from the specification used in Table 2.3. SubSaharan African countries have especially large agricultural sectors and female participation rates are known to be high in this sector as discussed in an earlier section. North African and Middle Eastern countries have lower participation rates as they are generally Muslim countries and female participation rates tend to be lower in such countries. The coefficient for the Asia/Oceania region is statistically insignificant, which is as expected since this region has similar levels of development as North America and Europe.

Finally, the results show that overall participation rates have increased since 1970 even after taking into consideration GNP per capita and fertility. The participation rates in both 1980 and 1990 are about 9 percentage points higher than in 1970 *ceteris paribus.* These results indicate that while there was an exogenous increase in participation rates between 1970 and 1980, the increase between 1980 and 1990 observed in Table 2.1 can be attributed to changes in income per capita and total fertility rates between 1980 and 1990.

Cross-sectional analysis for 1990

A further exploration of the relationship between female labour market participation and income per capita and fertility for each of the three age categories in 1990 is shown in Table 2.4. Activity rates for each age group are estimated using a quadratic transformation for the natural log of per capita GNP to again capture any turning

Table 2.4. *Cross-section Regression Analysis of Female Labour Force Participation Rates for 1990*

	Age 15–20	Age 20–49	Age 50–64
Intercept	255.08*	320.53*	284.20*
	(37.10)	(37.95)	(40.30)
Log GNP per capita	−53.97*	−65.02*	−63.28*
	(9.96)	(10.19)	(10.82)
Log GNP square	3.25*	4.10*	3.92*
	(0.66)	(0.68)	(0.72)
Fertility rate	−1.72	−4.68*	−0.14
	(1.40)	(1.43)	(1.52)
North Africa/Middle East	−1.26	−6.31	−7.29
	(6.83)	(6.98)	(7.41)
SubSaharan Africa	17.0**	20.19*	18.50*
	(6.82)	(6.97)	(7.40)
Latin America/Caribbean	−5.32	−1.00	−1.39
	(5.58)	(5.71)	(6.07)
Asia/Oceania	3.51	1.67	3.94
	(5.22)	(5.34)	(5.68)
Adjusted R^2	0.51	0.49	0.53
N	111	111	111

Standard errors are in parenthesis.

* Indicates significance at the 0.01 level.

** Indicates significance at the 0.05 level.

Excluded class for region is OECD; therefore, region coefficients are deviations from OECD.

Source: Authors' calculations from UN and ILO data.

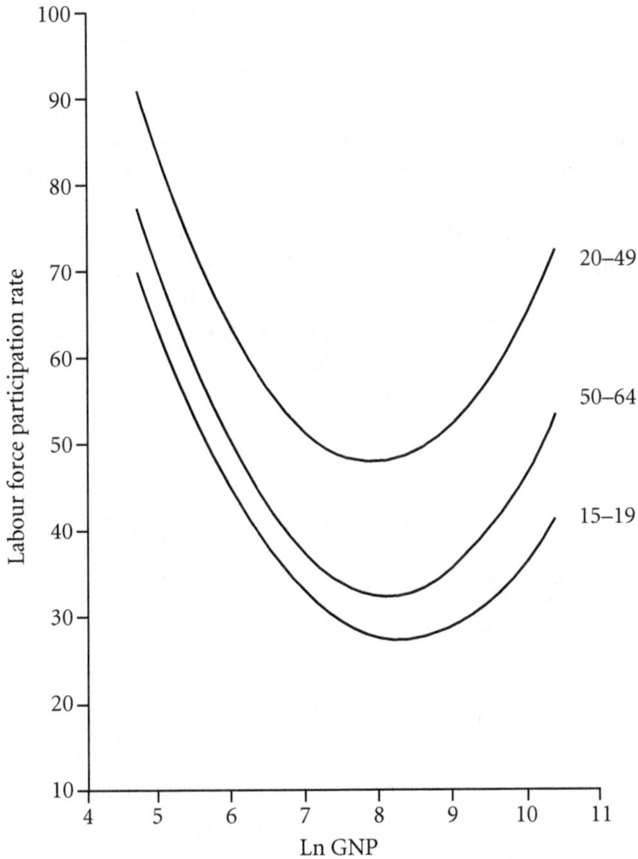

Figure 2.2. *Predicted Labour Force Participation Rates and Log of Per Capita GNP Based on Estimated Coefficients in Table 2.4*

point in this variable. The results for all age categories show that there is a statistically significant U-shaped relationship between income per capita and female labour force participation, even after taking into account other variables. The bottom of the U occurs at $4,000 for those age 15–19, at $2,800 for those age 20–49, and at $3,200 for those age 50–64. All three of these incomes are in the middle-income range as defined by the World Bank, which is $611–7,620 in per capita GNP in 1990.

Figure 2.2 shows a plot of the predicted labour force participation rate as a function of per capita GNP evaluated at the means of the other variables. As expected, women age 15–19 have the lowest participation rates while women age 20–49 have the highest.[3] Regressions that use the same variables as those in Table 2.4 but using

[3] A piecewise linear specification of the equations in Table 2.4 (not shown here) where linear regressions are estimated separately for low-, middle-, and high-income countries also shows statistically

1970 and 1980 data (not shown) also indicate the same statistically significant U-shape relationship between per capita income and female labour force participation.

Fertility is found to be negatively and significantly related to female labour force participation only for women age 20–49. There is no statistically significant relationship for the oldest and youngest women. These results provide strong support for the widely accepted view that fertility and family responsibility compete for women's time during their childbearing years and greater fertility leaves less opportunity for market work.

This analysis has confirmed the expected U-shape relationship between economic development and labour force activity rates for women found in earlier studies. The U-shaped pattern of labour force activity holds for women in three age groups and for three points in time. The next section discusses occupational segregation by sex and explores how occupational segregation is related to increasing female labour force participation rates, economic development, and the types of job opportunities available to women around the world.

OCCUPATIONAL SEX SEGREGATION

Occupational segregation by sex is pervasive in labour national economies throughout the world. Indeed, segregation of jobs by sex is one of the most important and enduring aspects of labour markets throughout the world.

High levels of occupational segregation by sex have important implications for women and men as well as for economic growth and efficiency. First, it creates a certain amount of labour market rigidity, since so many women are effectively excluded from 'male' occupations and so many men are effectively excluded from 'female' occupations. Second, occupational segregation affects the education and training of future generations, since decisions of parents, boys and girls are based in part on perceived labour market opportunities. This causes, in particular, an under-investment in female education and training. Third, limited labour market opportunities for women often reduce female labour force participation. Fourth, occupational segregation increases poverty rates, since 'female' occupations often have relatively low pay, as evidenced by the high incidence of poverty in female-headed households. Fifth, occupational sex segregation helps perpetuate gender stereotypes concerning appropriate roles for women, as well as female–male wage differentials.

The remainder of this chapter investigates the relationship between occupational sex segregation and the labour market focusing on the demographic and economic issues that are especially relevant for this book. The next two subsections describe the data and the statistical measures used in the analysis in subsequent subsections. The third subsection describes current levels in the world in occupational sex segregation. Next, the relationship between the level of occupational sex segregation and economic

significant changes in slope as income increases from the low to middle to high-income categories as defined by the World Bank. The slope of the income and participation relationship is highly negative for low-income countries, less negative for middle-income countries, and positive for high-income countries. Again, the U-shape is evident.

development in a country is investigated. The final subsection investigates the clear role played by typical sex stereotyping in society in determining which occupations are 'female' occupations and which occupations are 'male' occupations.

Data used in the occupation sex segregation analysis

Analysis in the remainder of this chapter is based on an ILO data set developed for measuring and studying occupational sex segregation. ILO requested national statistical offices to provide detailed occupational data at the two or three-digit level, along with the number of men and women in each occupation for 1970, 1980, and 1990. When data were unavailable for these years, statistical offices were requested to supply data for the closest available year. The most recent data-year for approximately one-half of the study countries is in the 1990s and approximately another 25 per cent between 1985 and 1989. Detailed occupational data are available for 41 countries including 17 OECD countries, 6 Middle East or North African countries, 4 Transition Economy countries in Europe, 7 Asian or Oceanic countries, and 7 Other Developing countries.

Approximately one-half of countries in the ILO data set have three-digit occupational data and the other half have two-digit occupational data. On average, there are 179 non-agricultural occupations per country and only four countries report data with fewer than 55 non-agricultural occupations. This data set is unique in this regard of having detailed occupational data for a number of countries.

It is important to note that the national data analysed below purposely exclude agricultural occupations. This exclusion is done in order to increase data comparability across countries, since the size and sex composition of agricultural occupations in national data are frequently inconsistent over time in the ILO data set. In addition, national classifications of agricultural occupations are typically very crude with very little disaggregation. This exclusion of the agricultural sector is also done for analytical reasons, since the determinants of occupational sex segregation in agricultural and non-agricultural occupations are quite different because of the relative importance of family female labour in agriculture.

Measuring occupational segregation

A number of different types of statistics can be used to measure occupational segregation. There are descriptive statistics, such as the extent to which women are over-or-under-represented in an occupation and the percentage of women to all workers in an occupation; indices which express in one number the extent to which male and female workers are equally distributed across occupations; extent to which workers are divided into gender-dominated occupations where the percentage of male or female workers is so high that these occupations could be considered to be 'male' or 'female' occupations; or specific occupations and the extent to which they are feminized. This paper relies on all four types of statistics noted above. It is important in any analysis of occupational segregation by sex to use more than one type of statistic, since each type provides a different perspective of the phenomenon.

The index used in this chapter is the index of dissimilarity (ID), which is by far the most commonly used index in the research literature on occupational segregation. ID has a minimum value of 0 and a maximum value of 1.0. The higher ID, the greater is occupational segregation by sex.[4]

The definition of male-dominated occupations used in this chapter is when the ratio of male to female workers in an occupation is at least 4 to 1, while the definition of female-dominated occupations is when there are at least four times as many female workers as male workers. Gender-dominated occupations are defined as the sum of female-dominated and male-dominated occupations.

It is well known that the level of occupational sex segregation observed is a function of the level of disaggregation in the occupational classification. The more dissagregated are occupational data, the greater is the observed level of occupational segregation. Analysis in Anker (1998) provides some indication of how strong this relationship is. It was found that ID rises on average from about 0.37 when based on typical one-digit non-agricultural data, to about 0.58 when based on typical two-digit non-agricultural data, and to about 0.64 when based on typical three-digit non-agricultural data. This sensitivity of ID (as well as other measures of occupational segregation) has two especially important implications for comparisons of occupational segregation across countries. First, one-digit data are not appropriate for analysing occupational segregation by sex. One-digit data simply hide too much of the occupational segregation by sex existing in the world. Second, cross-national comparisons of occupational segregation should be made for countries with similar levels of disaggregation in their occupational classifications.

In the light of the above points, this chapter uses two-and three-digit occupational data and adjusts observed levels of ID and percentages of workers in gender-dominated occupations to increase cross-national comparability by taking into consideration the number of occupations classified in each country. For example, observed segregation levels are decreased for countries such as the United Kingdom which has over 500 non-agricultural occupations in its classification, whereas observed levels are increased in countries such as Iran and Bulgaria which have less than 75 non-agricultural occupations in their classifications. This reordering is done for countries with three-digit data by reaggregating occupational data to the two-digit level when this is possible. Then for all countries in the ILO data set, the observed level of occupational segregation is adjusted to correspond to a typical classification with 75 non-agricultural occupations by using the mathematical relationship between the observed level of occupational sex segregation and the number of occupations classified estimated in Anker (1998).

Levels of occupational segregation by sex around the world

This subsection indicates levels of occupational sex segregation around the world based on data for 41 countries from Anker (1998) for five regions of the world

[4] The definition of the index of dissimilarity (ID) is one-half the summation over all occupations of the absolute difference between the proportion of all females (F_i/F) and the proportion of all males (M_i/M) in each occupation $ID = 1/2 \Sigma /F_i/F - M_j/M/$

(OECD; Transition Economies; Middle East and North Africa; Asia and Oceania, Other Developing) where national values have been adjusted to a classification with 75 non-agricultural occupations in order to increase cross-country comparability. The first part of the following discussion uses the adjusted index of dissimilarity (ID) as the measure of segregation, while the second part uses the adjusted percentage of male, female, and total non-agricultural workers which are in male, female, or gender-dominated occupations where at least 80 per cent of workers are either male or female (MDOM, FDOM, and TDOM). Results are shown in Table 2.5.

Adjusted national ID values indicate a high degree of occupational segregation in the world. The unweighted adjusted ID for the world is 0.58, and it exceeds 0.50 in 34 of the 41 countries included in the ILO. There are large regional differences, with regional averages ranging from 0.48 in Asia/Oceania, to 0.56 in OECD and Transition Economies, 0.64 in Other Developing countries, and 0.68 in Middle East/North Africa.

Adjusted ID tends to be fairly similar within each of the regions included in Table 2.5, as indicated by the fact that the standard deviations of adjusted ID values within all but the heterogeneous Other Developing Country region are much lower than the standard deviation for the world as a whole. A similar phenomenon occurs

Table 2.5. *Index of Dissimilarity (ID) and Percentage of Male, Female, and Total Non-Agricultural Labour Forces in Gender-Dominated Occupations by Region*

Region	ID	FDOM	MDOM	TDOM	% females in non-agri LF
OECD	0.56	35.8	57.6	53.0	41.5
Transition economies	0.56	32.2	53.7	48.9	42.2
Middle East & North Africa	0.68	9.5	84.9	77.2	14.8
Asia & Oceania	0.48	12.2	55.8	47.1	30.1
Other developing	0.64	46.7	63.1	63.5	41.2
Total	0.58	29.4	61.8	56.9	35.7

Notes: Data are for latest year in Anker (1998), usually around 1990.

Values are adjusted to a typical classification with 75 non-agricultural occupations.

Averages are unweighted averages of countries. The weighted (by population size) average for the world is 0.47. This is much smaller than the 0.58 shown in this table because the three most populous countries (China, India, and USA) have among the lowest adjusted IDs in the world at 0.36, 0.45, and 0.46, respectively.

Number of countries is 17 OECD, 4 Transition Economies, 6 Middle East and North Africa and Oceania, 7 Other Developing.

ID is index of dissimilarity. Values range from 0 to 1.0.

FDOM is percentage of female non-agricultural labour force in an occupation where at least 80 per cent of workers are women.

MDOM is percentage of male non-agricultural labour force in an occupation where at least 80 per cent of workers are men.

TDOM is percentage of total non-agricultural labour force in an occupation where at least 80 per cent of workers are either women or men.

Source: Richard Anker. (1998), *Gender and Jobs: Sex Segregation of Occupations in the World*, Geneva: ILO pp. 208–9.

within the OECD region, as standard deviations of adjusted ID are smaller within Scandinavia, North America, Other English-speaking, Western Europe, and Central Europe as compared to OECD as a whole. These results imply that social and cultural values, historical experiences, and legal systems play an important role in determining the extent to which labour markets are segregated between male and female workers.

The majority of men in the world work in a male-dominated occupation where they face little competition from women, as approximately 60 per cent of male non-agricultural workers are in a male-dominated occupation (MDOM). In contrast, only around 30 per cent of female non-agricultural workers are in a female-dominated occupation (FDOM). In addition of course, female-dominated occupations are less valuable than male-dominated occupations, since they tend to pay less and have lower status. A further indication of men's advantageous position in the labour market is the much greater choice available for men, as indicated by the fact that there are approximately seven times as many male-dominated occupations as female-dominated occupations.

There are major regional differences. Men in the Middle East and North Africa are in such a privileged position in the labour market that 85 per cent of male non-agricultural workers work in a male-dominated occupation, and on average, there are 72 male-dominated non-agricultural occupations for every female-dominated non-agricultural occupation in this region. In Asia/Oceania, FDOM is unusually small compared to MDOM. While the former is similar to the Middle East/North Africa, the latter is similar to OECD. In Other Developing countries, FDOM is unusually large, mainly due to women working in the informal sector such as petty traders and food processors.

Relationship between occupational segregation by sex and economic development

The present subsection investigates whether the level of occupational sex segregation is related to GDP per capita. Whereas earlier sections of this paper found a strong relationship across countries in the world between female labour force participation rates and income per capita, no relationship is found in the present subsection between economic development and level of occupational segregation by sex.

Figure 2.3 plots adjusted national ID values against GDP per capita, which is adjusted for purchasing power to increase comparability across countries. This scatter plot indicates that there is no relationship between the level of occupational sex segregation and the level of economic development. The statistical insignificance of this relationship is confirmed by regression analysis where GDP per capita is related to adjusted ID. This insignificant relationship remains even after the following explanatory variables are specified: regional binaries, per cent of the labour force in agriculture, adult female education level, and percentage of the non-agricultural labour force which is female (Anker 1998). These regression results confirm the importance of region in determining occupational segregation by sex, as regional binary variables by themselves account for over one-half of the variation across countries in occupational sex segregation (R^2 of 0.61 and adjusted R^2 of 0.56).

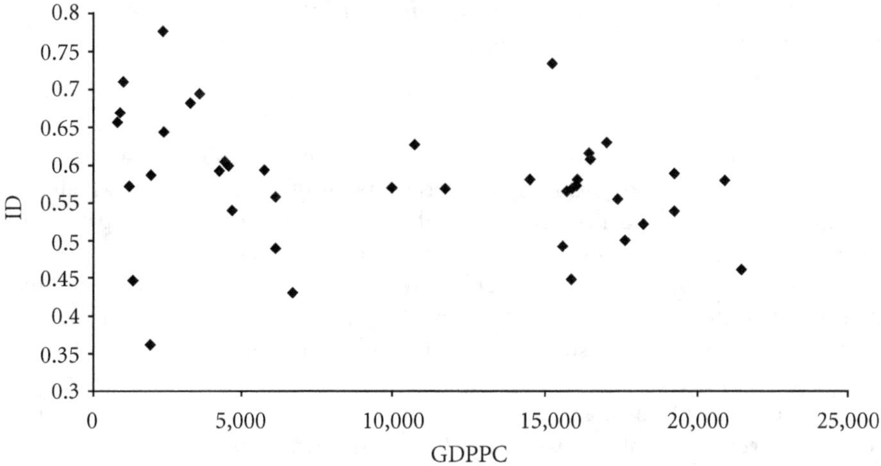

Figure 2.3. *Scatter Plot of Adjusted ID and Gross Domestic Product Per Capita (GDPPC)*
Note: To increase cross-national comparability, ID is adjusted to an occupational classification with 75 non-agricultural occupations; GDP per capita is adjusted for parity purchasing power.
Source: Anker (1998).

While there are possible explanations for this unexpected insignificant result for GDP per capita, it is necessary to accept the finding that social, cultural, and historical factors are very important, and indeed more important than economic development in determining levels and patterns of occupational sex segregation. On the other hand, the insignificant result for GDP per capita could be due, in part, to how occupations are classified and how occupational segregation is defined. First, even though the occupational data being analysed are much more disaggregated than in previous cross-national studies of occupational sex segregation, they are still somewhat crude for an economy. As a result, these discrimination measures may continue to hide substantial amounts of occupational sex segregation. This masking of segregation is especially likely in regards to vertical sex segregation (where men and women work in the same occupation but have quite different jobs in terms of pay, responsibility, and career opportunities). In some Asian countries such as Japan and Republic of Korea, for example, it is well known that men and women are slotted into different career paths in what are the same administrative and production occupations in the national classifications. A second possible explanation is that observers who expect a negative relationship with economic development may be in part unconsciously thinking of women's integration into the labour force, which is strongly related to economic development as demonstrated in the earlier part of this chapter.

Relationship between gender stereotyping and the specific types of occupations in which women (and men) are concentrated

Having established in previous subsections that social and cultural factors play an important role in determining the level of occupational segregation by sex in a country, the present subsection investigates the role which societal and cultural values and sex stereotypes play in determining the *specific* types of occupations in which men and women tend to be concentrated. It is demonstrated below how: (i) patriarchal societies, the subordinate position of women in society, and women's almost exclusive responsibility for housework and childcare create stereotypes of women and men that greatly affect labour market opportunities for women and men; and (ii) when sex stereotypes in society are transferred to the labour market (as they are of course), they greatly affect the types of occupations men and women are trained for, offered, and wish to enter. The fact that most sex stereotypes are incorrect, or are correct on average by only a small degree (e.g. while men are physically stronger than women on average, there is a large overlap in physical strength between men and women, with many women stronger than many men) does not detract from the important effects sex stereotypes have on labour market behaviour and outcomes. Perceptions and values are important. Also, small differences on average can have major effects.

Patriarchy and subordination of women means that women are generally considered to be 'better' than men at taking orders while men are considered better at giving orders; women are considered to be more willing to accept lower pay than men, as women are generally considered to be secondary workers with less need for income; women are considered to be physically weaker than men, and more fearful of physical danger; women are considered to be more honest and trustworthy than men; women are considered to be less able to do math and science than men. These stereotypes imply that women should be more likely than men to be in non-managerial and non-supervisory positions; work in the informal sector; work as bookkeepers, cashiers, receptionists, salespersons, and secretaries; and not be miners, policepersons, fire-fighters, engineers, architects, or construction workers.

Since women are responsible for household work and childcare in virtually all societies, they acquire (or are assumed to acquire) certain skills, experiences, and values. Therefore, in virtually all societies, women as compared to men are considered to be more skilled and experienced at household activities; have a more caring nature; have greater manual dexterity; are more willing to work at home and less willing to travel for work. These stereotypes increase the propensity for women to work in occupations such as nurse, social worker, ayah, maid, housekeeper, hairdresser, cook, launderer, and sewer, and decrease the propensity of women to work in occupations such as travelling salesmen and transport drivers.

Empirical evidence reported in Anker (1998) for the world and in Melkas and Anker (1998) for Nordic countries strongly supports gender explanations of occupational sex segregation and the above description of how patriarchy and gender stereotypes in society help determine which occupations become 'female' occupations and which occupations become 'male' occupations. Table 2.6 indicates the five largest female-dominated non-agricultural occupations (i.e. occupations where at least 80 per cent of workers are women) in terms of employment in 37 non-Transition Economy developing and developed countries. It is striking how few different occupations are included in Table 2.6—only 25 different occupations out of a possible 185 occupations (i.e. 5 times 37). Women's labour market opportunities in the world are very restricted indeed.

It is also striking how closely large female-dominated occupations in the world correspond to the gender stereotypes above. Thus, nurses and teachers are caring type occupations; maids, building caretakers, launderers, hairdressers, cooks, and caretakers are occupations which utilize housekeeping skills; sewers and spinners use housekeeping skills are low paid and are often home-based; salespersons, cashiers, and secretaries combine several stereotypes such as physical appearance, honesty, and lower pay.

There are also important regional differences. In the Middle East and North Africa, there are very few female-dominated occupations; only four appear in Table 2.6 (teacher, nurse, maid, and spinner/weaver). Women are virtually excluded from sales and other occupations where men and women have to interact in public. In Asia and Oceania, the largest female-dominated occupations are over-represented in production which reflects the use of cheap female labour in the export-oriented textile sector in this region (e.g. sewing machine operators, spinners, and weavers). In Other Developing countries, large female-dominated occupations tend to be concentrated in sales and services occupations, in part reflecting the importance of the informal sector in these countries.

Empirical evidence from around the world also indicate the extent to which women are excluded from occupational groups where sex stereotyping would imply that women should be less able and less interested to work. For example, men comprise over 80 per cent of workers on average in most countries in all of the following occupations investigated in Anker (1998) (with average percentage male always above 80 per cent).

Occupational groups	Gender distribution
Architects, engineers, and related technicians	34 of 35 countries (93% male)
Legislative officials and government administrators	22 of 31 countries (84% male)
Managers	27 of 34 countries (86% male)
Sales supervisors and buyers	13 of 33 countries (82% male)
Protective service workers	35 of 35 countries (96% male)
Production supervisors and general foremen	19 of 19 countries (94% male)
Tool-makers and blacksmiths	32 of 33 countries (96% male)
Bricklayers, carpenters, and other construction	34 of 34 countries (98% male)

Besides having very important implications for gender inequalities in the labour market, gender stereotyping also has very important demographic implications.

Table 2.6. *Five Largest Female-Dominated Non-Agricultural Occupations (in Terms of Number of Female Workers), by Major Occupational Group and Region*

Major occupational group	Region (no. of countries; % of countries in brackets)[d]					Occupations among five largest[a,b]	
	OECD	Asia/Pacific	ME	OD	Total	Occupational group	No. of countries
Professional/Technical	15 (18%)	5 (23%)	5 (71%)	0	25 (18%)	Nurses	22[c]
						Teachers	3
Administrative/Managerial	0	0	0	0	0		
Clerical	27 (33%)	3 (14%)	0	4 (15%)	34 (25%)	Stenographers, typist, and secretaries	24
						Bookkeepers, cashiers	6
						Other clerical	4
Sales	2 (2%)	0	0	3 (12%)	5 (4%)	Salespersons, shop assistants	3
						Miscellaneous	2
Services	31 (38%)	6 (27%)	1 (14%)	15 (58%)	53 (39%)	Maids and related workers	20
						Building caretakers	7
						Launderers, dry cleaners	5
						Hairdressers, barbers	6
						Cooks, waiters	4
						Caretakers	8
						Miscellaneous	3

Production	7 (9%)	8 (36%)	1 (14%)	4 (15%)	20 (14%)	Tailors, dressmakers, and sewers	11
						Spinners and weavers	3
						Miscellaneous	6[a]
Total	82 (100%)	22 (100%)	7 (100%)	26 (100%)	137 (100%)		

[a] Miscellaneous occupational groups consist of occupations which have only one country. Miscellaneous occupations are as follows: For sales: working proprietors in wholesale and retail trade (Ghana). For services: personal, apparel, and furnishing service (Canada); service workers n.e.c. (Luxembourg); working proprietors in catering and lodging (Ghana). For production; hosiers and shoemakers (Italy); food and beverage processors (Ghana); glass formers and potters (Ghana); package wrappers (Japan); paper and paper brand product makers (Fiji); production and related workers n.e.c. (Senegal).

[b] For expositional purposes, almost all occupations represented in this table are at the two-digit classification level in ISCO-68. Therefore, in compiling these data, judgment was used to bracket closely allied occupations from two-and-three-digit classifications for presentation in this table (but not for identifying important occupations to include here).

[c] For Sweden, the occupation included is health, nursing and veterinary work.

[d] Four countries have no female-dominated occupations; three have two female-dominated occupations; two have three female-dominated occupations; and seven have four female-dominated occupations.

Source: Richard Anker. (1998), *Gender and Jobs: Sex Segregation of Occupations in the World*, Geneva: ILO, p. 282.

It can lead to an underinvestment in female education and training due to lower labour market returns to education for women; this in turn will affect fertility, child mortality, and female age at marriage. It will also reduce female labour force participation, especially in the formal sector in developing countries, which will in turn again have demographic effects.

CONCLUSION

This chapter has examined female labour force participation rates and occupational segregation by sex across the world. Statistical analysis found that female participation rates are non-linearly related to income per capita, forming a U-shaped relationship. The independent effect of fertility on female labour force activity rates was also estimated, and the expected relationship between fertility and female labour market activity was found. Lower fertility rates typically result in higher female activity rates.

A detailed examination of country-specific employment patterns showed that occupational segregation by sex was widespread all across the development spectrum. Analysis indicated, however, that the level of occupational sex segregation is not related to the level of economic development as indicated by GDP per capita. In contrast, the level of occupational sex segregation was found to be significantly related to the country's region. It was also found that the occupations which are dominated by one sex to such an extent that they could be considered 'male' or 'female' occupations reflect patriarchal values and typical sex stereotypes in society. Results indicate how very important cultural and social values and historical experiences are in determining occupational sex segregation.

References

Anker, Richard. (1998), *Gender and Jobs: Sex Segregation of Occupations in the World*, Geneva: ILO.

Denti, E. and Ruhumuliza. (1996), 'Estimated rates of activity, 1950–1990,' in *Bulletin of Labour Statistics*, Geneva: ILO.

Durand, John. (1975), *The Labor Force in Economic Development*, Princeton, NJ: Princeton University Press.

Goldin, Claudia. (1995), 'The U-Shaped Female Labour Force Function in T. Paul Schultz (ed.) Economic Development and Economic History,' *Investment in Women's Human Capital*, Chicago: University of Chicago Press, pp. 61–90.

International Labour Office. (1997), *Economically Active Population*, 1950–2010, Geneva: ILO.

Melkas, H. and Anker, R. (1998), *Gender Equality and Occupational Segregation in Nordic Labour Markets*, Geneva: ILO.

Sinha, J. N. (1965), 'Dynamics of Female Participation in Economic Activity in a Developing Economy,' *United Nations World Population Conference*, Document WPC/285, Session A.5

PART II

LABOUR MARKET AND DEMOGRAPHIC EFFECTS OF MAJOR ECONOMIC AND POLITICAL CHANGE

3

Labour Market Transitions of Men and Women During an Economic Crisis: Evidence From Indonesia

DUNCAN THOMAS, KATHLEEN BEEGLE, AND ELIZABETH FRANKENBERG

INTRODUCTION

Indonesia is in the midst of a major financial, economic, and political crisis. The magnitude and unexpected nature of the crisis are particularly stunning when contrasted with the country's recent economic success. During the three decades prior to the crisis, Indonesia enjoyed sustained economic growth, accompanied by an impressive reduction in poverty, significant improvements in the health and human capital of the population and a shift in the structure of production away from agriculture towards higher paying manufacturing and service sector jobs. There are many ways one might summarize changes in the labour market; one often used metric is growth in hourly earnings which is likely to be related to changes in productivity. That growth has been dramatic. Real hourly earnings of the median female worker in the formal or market sector in 1997 was about twice that of the median female market sector worker a decade earlier; for men, real hourly earnings increased by about 50 per cent during this time (Smith *et al.* 2002).

In early 1998, Indonesia succumbed to the economic crisis that was sweeping South East Asia. Estimates that 5.4 million workers would be displaced by the crisis were accompanied by dire predictions of massive increases in unemployment (Feridhanusetyawan 1999; see also World Bank 1998, which estimated that 2 million workers had lost their jobs by April 1998 and predicted that number would double or triple by the end of 1998). Simply put, those predictions turned out to be wrong.

We are grateful to colleagues at RAND, Lembaga Demografi at the University of Indonesia, UCLA, and the Population Studies Centers in Indonesia who worked with us in the collection of the Indonesia Family Life Survey; we owe a special debt to Bondan Sikoki as well as Victoria Beard, Muda Saputra, James P. Smith, Cecep Sumantri, Wayan Suriastini and Graciela Teruel. Richard Anker made many very helpful comments and suggestions. This work has been supported by the National Institutes of Aging (NIA P01AG08291), the National Institute of Child Health and Human Development (NICHD 1R01HD33778, 5P50HD12639 and 5P01HD28372), the POLICY Project, the World Bank (East Asia Gender Program) and the World Health Organization.

The *Survei Amgkatan Kerja Nasional* (SAKERNAS), a labour market and income survey conducted annually by the Indonesian Government statistical bureau, *Badan Pusat Statistik* (BPS), is the primary source of employment data in Indonesia. According to those data, between August 1997, and August 1998, the male employment rate declined by about 1.5 per cent whereas female employment actually increased by about 0.8 per cent. The immediate effect of the crisis on employment has been rather small—a point that was made early in the crisis by Frankenberg *et al.* (1999) based on independent survey data collected in the Indonesia Family Life Survey (IFLS).

While overall levels of employment have held remarkably stable during the crisis, it would be premature to conclude that the labour market has not felt the upheavals that have reverberated through the economy and society. The drama of the crisis is reflected not in employment but in the collapse of real wages. Based on the 1997 and 1998 SAKERNAS, Smith *et al.* (2002) estimate that real hourly (market sector) wages in Indonesia declined by about 40 per cent during the first year of the crisis—offsetting almost all the growth in real hourly earnings of the prior decade for men and half the growth for women.[1] By this metric, the Indonesian crisis is of the same order of magnitude as the collapse of Soviet Russia in the 1980s and the Great Depression in the 1930s in the United States and dominates many of the more recent crises in Latin America and Asia (Fallon and Lucas 1999).

This study examines the immediate effects of the Indonesian crisis on labour market outcomes using two rounds of the IFLS, a longitudinal survey collected in 1997 and 1998. Attention is focussed on transitions in work and hourly earnings.

We begin by asking why the dire predictions of rampant unemployment were so off the mark. We show that the stability of employment aggregates mask considerable churning in the labour market. It is certainly true that many people lost jobs. But, what the predictions failed to consider was that there were also many people who got jobs. Exploiting the panel dimension of our data, we demonstrate that there was a good deal of movement *both* out of *and* into employment. We also show that there was substantial mobility between employment sectors among those who were working in both years. Mobility is particularly high for women.

On the face of it, it is difficult to draw inferences about the welfare consequences of this mobility. We turn, therefore, to income and present complementary evidence on changes in hourly earnings as the crisis unfolded. Special attention is paid to the distribution of these changes—across gender, sector of residence, and sector of work. The collapse in real wages documented in SAKERNAS is replicated in IFLS. In addition, unlike SAKERNAS, IFLS collects information on income from self employment. This turns out to be key. In rural areas, many of the self-employed are farmers; their real earnings declined very little on average making work in that sector considerably more attractive. This is especially true at the top of the earnings distribution.

[1] Similar estimates were reported by Frankenberg *et al.* (1999) and by Papanek and Handoko (1999) based on data sources other than SAKERNAS.

For some, the effect of the crisis was devastating: those that left the labour market, those that lost their jobs and took on much lower paying jobs, and those that stayed in the same job with much lower earnings. Some families benefitted from the flexibility of the labour market and exploited new opportunities—particularly those who were in the self-employed sector in 1997 or switched into that sector when the crisis began. There is evidence that a large number of women joined family businesses (which includes working on the family farm) and that they made a major contribution to mitigating the impact of the crisis on family incomes. The results provide yet another nail in the coffin of the argument that 'unpaid family workers' and income from self-employment should be ignored in labour force surveys.

DATA

The Indonesia Family Life Survey is a large-scale integrated socio-economic and health survey that collects extensive information on the lives of respondents, their households, their families, and the communities in which they live. These data have several features that make them particularly appropriate for understanding how the lives of Indonesians have changed as a result of the economic and political events surrounding the crisis of the late 1990s. We highlight these features briefly, then provide more detail about the study methodology below. For a fuller description of the survey, see Frankenberg and Thomas (1999).

First, the IFLS is a longitudinal survey. It is thus possible to compare labour market activities of individuals interviewed in late 1997 (IFLS2) with the activities of the *same* individuals one year later, in 1998 (IFLS2+). This is key for both understanding the nature of transitions that individuals have experienced during the crisis and for drawing inferences about who has been most deleteriously impacted by the crisis. Longitudinal surveys, however, have a potentially serious drawback: it is imperative that all respondents interviewed in one wave are re-interviewed in each follow-up. If they are not, it is very difficult to determine how much of changes observed between the waves are due to changes in the underlying population and how much is explained by changes in the composition of the sample. This is particularly germane in the context of the upheavals in Indonesia in 1998.

The IFLS was extremely successful in re-interviewing respondents. Of the 1,934 households interviewed in 1997 that were in the target sample for IFLS2+, 98.5 per cent were re-interviewed. Attrition bias is not likely to be an important concern for the analyses presented below (see Thomas, Frankenberg, and Smith 2001, for a detailed discussion of attrition in IFLS).

Second, as indicated in Fig. 3.1, the timing of the surveys provides an opportunity to examine the immediate effects of the crisis. The first wave of IFLS was conducted in 1993 and interviewed 7,224 households in 13 provinces in Indonesia; it is representative of about 83 per cent of the population. The second wave, IFLS2, was fielded four years later and interviews were completed with 94 per cent of all the original households (excluding those in which all members are known to have died).

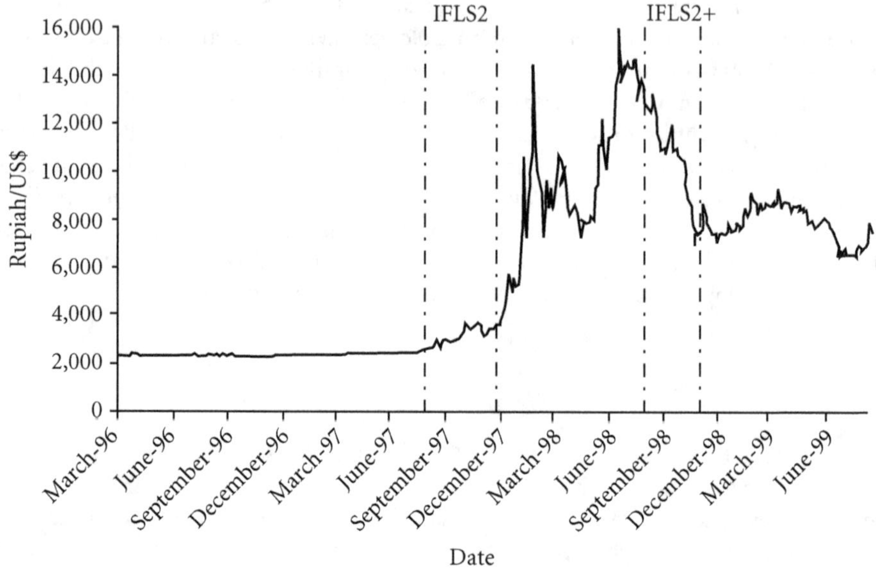

Figure 3.1. *Timing of the IFLS and Indonesian Exchange Rate*

Main fieldwork for the survey was conducted during the second half of 1997, just prior to the dramatic collapse of the rupiah in January 1998. IFLS2 was uniquely well-positioned to serve as a baseline for another interview with the same respondents, which would provide insights into the effects of Indonesia's economic crisis. Given the dearth of information on the crisis—and the fact that virtually nothing is known in the scientific literature about the immediate effects of crises on behaviour, we decided to return to the field a year later and field IFLS2+.

There was neither the time nor resources to mount a survey of the same magnitude as IFLS2 (which took more than two years to plan and test) and so a scaled down survey was administered which retained as much as possible from IFLS2. In IFLS2+, a 25 per cent subsample of the IFLS enumeration areas (EAs) were selected and all households who had lived in those EAs in 1993, including split-offs followed in 1997, were included in the target sample. The EAs were chosen to be representative of the entire IFLS sample.[2]

Third, the IFLS is rich in content. The depth of the IFLS is important because Indonesia's economic crisis has the potential to affect many different aspects of

[2] The sample was drawn in two stages. To reduce costs, 7 of the 13 IFLS provinces were revisited: 2 on Sumatra (North and South Sumatra), 3 on Java (DKI Jakarta, West and Central Java), West Nusa Tenggara, and South Kalimantan. These provinces span the full spectrum of socio-economic status and economic activity in the fuller IFLS sample. Second, within those provinces, we purposively drew 80 EAs with weighted probabilities to match the IFLS sample as closely as possible. The IFLS2+ sample achieves an efficiency of close to 80 per cent.

well-being and to provoke a variety of responses (see Frankenberg *et al.* 1999; Thomas *et al.* 2000, for some examples). With respect to this study, the IFLS instrument contains an extensive battery of questions regarding type of work, sector of work, hours of work, weeks worked, and earnings from work. A key difference between IFLS and many labour force surveys, including SAKERNAS, is the fact that questions are asked not only about earnings in the market or formal sector which pays a wage or a salary but questions are also asked about the earnings of the self-employed (net of their costs). Notwithstanding the fact that considerable effort was put into training interviewers to probe and help respondents estimate their income, it is important to recognize that self-employment earnings are likely to be measured with substantial noise. Nonetheless, those data turn out to be key for measuring the impact of the crisis and also for assessing the distribution of that impact.

Fourth, IFLS2+ was designed specifically to be comparable with IFLS2. Both studies were conducted as part of a collaboration between RAND, UCLA, and Lembaga Demografi (University of Indonesia). The instruments in the two waves are very similar; the fieldwork protocols are essentially the same and the IFLS2+ supervisors and interviewers were drawn from the pool that had conducted IFLS2.[3] While IFLS2 and IFLS2+ were conducted in the second half of 1997 and 1998, respectively, the IFLS2+ fieldwork was conducted over a shorter time period than IFLS2. Month-to-month variation in employment and earnings may contaminate our estimates. As we will show below, the magnitudes of the changes are such that this is not likely to be a serious concern.

In sum, in the IFLS data that are used here, the same respondents were interviewed twice, once just prior to the collapse of the rupiah in January 1998, and once during the crisis. By tracing the same respondent through this period of dramatic economic and political change, it is possible to provide some evidence on the immediate impact of the crisis.

One potential drawback of IFLS2/2+ is its limited geographic coverage of Indonesia. While the IFLS2/2+ sub-sample is intended to be representative of the entire IFLS sample (which is, in turn, representative of most of the Indonesian population), it is possible that because interviews are conducted in only 7 of the 26 provinces, IFLS2/2+ misses important spatial variation in the impact of the crisis. This argument has particular salience in view of the geographic diversity of the archipelago and the complexity of the crisis. Before directly addressing the issue of the representativeness of results in IFLS2/2+, a brief overview of the crisis as it pertains to labour markets is presented in the next section in order provide context for the empirical results which follow.

[3] IFLS2 and IFLS2+ did differ in that retrospective information about labour market activities stretching back several years collected in 1997 was not repeated in 1998. After repeating the questions that were used in 1997 about current labour activities, in 1998, respondents were asked to provided detail about labour market transitions during the previous twelve months.

BACKGROUND

The crisis in South East Asia began in Thailand in the middle of 1997. After coming under pressure for several months, in early 1998, the Indonesian rupiah collapsed. Over the space of a few days in January 1998, it fell from 4,000 per $US to 16,000. Although it subsequently recovered, it has remained very volatile. Whereas importers—and consumers of imported goods—were much worse off, exporters and export producers benefitted from the increase in the rupiah-denominated value of their output. The collapse of the rupiah was followed by very high inflation which was fuelled by a reduction in subsidies on rice, oil, and fuel. BPS estimates that in 1998, the consumer price index (CPI) rose by around 80 per cent, the price of rice rose by about 120 per cent. This imposed a heavy burden on consumers: rice, which is the main staple, accounted for around 20 per cent of the budget of the average Indonesian household in 1997 (Thomas *et al.* 2000). Net rice producers, in contrast, were relatively better off and it seems reasonable to suppose that rural landowners would have been protected from the worst effects of the crisis. That inference needs to be tempered since the drought associated with El Niño in 1997 seriously impacted parts of the Indonesian archipelago and agricultural output was affected, particularly in the eastern islands.

As the rupiah came under pressure, credit was tightened and interest rates rocketed with much of the banking sector being declared insolvent by the middle of 1998. The Indonesian government took control of a substantial fraction of the financial sector. Employment in that sector and in sectors that had borrowed heavily, such as construction, was severely curtailed. Employment in tourism also declined. As the relative price of food rose, so too did demand for labour in the agricultural sector (Smith *et al.* 2002).

Much has been written about the political upheavals and social unrest that has accompanied the economic crisis. That few have been left untouched by those events is an understatement.

With these sorts of facts in mind, some were quick to declare the crisis to have only affected the urban elites (Poppele *et al.* 1999). Given the multiple dimensions of the crisis, the fact that these dimensions are inter-related in complex ways, and that different sub-groups of the population likely responded to the crisis in different ways, it would seem that understanding the impact of the crisis would be feasible only with good empirical evidence. This paper seeks to provide some of that evidence, focussing attention on transitions in the labour market.

EVIDENCE

Before undertaking those analyses, we describe the basic facts on employment changes between 1997 and 1998. This description is also used as a vehicle to assess the representativeness of IFLS2/2+ sample by contrasting it with SAKERNAS which interviewed a cross-section of over 120,000 respondents in August 1997, and another cross-section in August 1998.

Employment rates

Table 3.1 contrasts 1997 and 1998 employment rates of males and females age 20 through 75 in 1997. In this chapter, employment is defined as working to produce either for sale or own consumption for at least one hour in the month prior to the survey. All employment rates are reported as fractions of the age-eligible population. Many people have more than one job: we focus on their main job—the one that takes up most of the respondent's time. We exclude domestic work done in one's own home and time spent raising one's own children. See Anker and Anker (1989) and Anker (1990) for good discussions of the issues surrounding the definition of work

Table 3.1. *Employment Rates and Sectoral Distribution of Workers. Comparison of SAKERNAS and IFLS Estimates. Males and Females Age 20–75 Years*

Sample (Data source)	Males		Females	
	1997 (1)	1998 (2)	1997 (3)	1998 (4)
A. All country (SAKERNAS)				
Worked				
1. in week prior to survey	88.9	87.9	51.2	52.7
2. in market sector	35.5	32.2	14.2	14.1
3. in self-employment	49.0	50.8	19.2	19.8
4. unpaid in family business	4.4	4.8	17.9	18.8
Sample size	76,023	57,051	79,803	59,628
B. IFLS2/2+ PROVINCES (SAKERNAS)				
Worked				
1. in week prior to survey	88.0	86.3	48.6	50.1
2. in market sector	38.7	35.0	15.3	15.5
3. in self-employment	46.0	47.6	18.2	18.8
4. unpaid in family business	3.3	3.7	15.1	15.9
Sample size	31,817	24,023	33,321	25,071
C. IFLS2/2+ PROVINCES (IFLS)				
Worked				
1. in week prior to survey	88.3	87.1	52.2	58.8
2. in market sector	40.7	39.4	15.4	16.7
3. in self-employment	43.7	43.7	23.7	24.4
4. unpaid in family business	4.0	4.0	13.1	17.7
Sample size	1,913	1,913	2,228	2,228

Notes: SAKERNAS (Survei Amgkatan Kerja Nasional) is annual national labour force survey conducted by Government of Indonesia. IFLS (Indonesia Family Life Survey) is an on-going longitudinal survey that was started in 1993 in 13 provinces of Indonesia. It is representative of 83% of the population of Indonesia at that time. IFLS2 was conducted in 1997. IFLS2+ was conducted in 1998 on a subsample of the IFLS respondents; 7 provinces are covered in the survey.

in surveys and Beneria (1999) and Mata Greenwood (1999) for recent reviews that pay particular attention to women's work.

Three sets of employment estimates are reported in Table 3.1. Panel A is based on SAKERNAS and includes all respondents in the survey; the estimates are representative of the entire country. Panel B is also based on SAKERNAS but is restricted to the seven IFLS2/2+ provinces. A comparison between panels A and B tells us whether changes in employment in Indonesia are different in the IFLS2/2+ provinces. The third set of estimates (sample C) are based on IFLS panel respondents who were interviewed in both 1997 and 1998.

We begin with men, in columns 1 and 2. The first row in each panel is the percentage of adults who were working (with or without pay) during the week prior to the survey. Slightly under 90 per cent of males were working in 1997; about 1–1.5 per cent fewer were working in 1998. The percentage of adults working in what we will refer to as the 'market' sector is in the second row. These are employees who earn a wage or salary; they are often called 'formal' sector workers and span both the private and public sectors. About one-third of men work in this sector—and there was about a 10 per cent reduction in labour demand for these workers between 1997 and 1998. The third panel presents estimates for the 'self-employed'—those who work for themselves or hire others to work for them. About half the male adult population works in this sector—and that fraction increased between 1997 and 1998. The final panel records the percentage of males who work in a family-owned business and are not paid a wage for their work. They account for a small proportion of 20–75 year old males.

The overwhelming impression emerging from Table 3.1 is that male employment rates, overall and within sectors, remained remarkably stable in Indonesia as the crisis unfolded. Comparing Panels A and B, we see that the differences between estimates for the whole country and those for the IFLS2/2+ provinces are extremely small; this is true if we focus on levels of employment or changes between 1997 and 1998. We conclude that restricting attention to only the IFLS2/2+ provinces will likely adequately reflect broader changes that have occurred throughout Indonesia. The differences between estimates based on SAKERNAS and IFLS are also small—at least in the context of the IFLS sample sizes (the differences are all within a 95 per cent confidence interval).

Turning to women, in columns 3 and 4, the picture that emerges is slightly different. About one-half of women were working in 1997 and, in contrast with men, that fraction *increased* as the crisis unfolded. The increase was concentrated among women entering self-employment and unpaid family work. Whereas the latter account for only about 5 per cent of the male workforce, unpaid family workers are an important component of the female workforce accounting for about one-third of female workers.

As is the case for men, the differences in the estimates between the entire country (Panel A) and the IFLS2/2+ provinces (Panel B) are very small. However, there is an important difference between the SAKERNAS and IFLS estimates (Panel C). Specifically, the estimated increase in female employment between 1997 and 1998 is much larger in IFLS. Although IFLS estimates higher rates of participation in all three employment sectors, the majority of the increase is due to a rise in unpaid family work between 1997 and 1998. SAKERNAS estimates a much smaller increase in this sector.

What explains this discrepancy? SAKERNAS and IFLS share the same conceptual definition of unpaid family work but take a different approach to measurement. Both surveys begin with the same lead-in question on whether, during the week prior to the survey, the respondent was working. In SAKERNAS, those who answer 'yes' are then asked the type of work they do, where family work is one option. The same screener question is asked in IFLS and those who answer 'yes' are asked about the type of work. The difference between SAKERNAS and IFLS lies in the treatment of those who answer 'no' to the screener question. In SAKERNAS, they are not asked any more questions about work. In IFLS, these respondents are asked a set of follow-up questions about whether they were on leave from work, whether they had worked for one hour for pay and, if they answer no to all these questions, they are explicitly asked whether they had worked in a family-owned business. Those who answered 'yes' to either the lead-in or to any of the follow-up questions are treated as working and they complete the employment module.

In principle, this additional probing in IFLS should elicit no more unpaid family workers than are reported in SAKERNAS. Korns (1996) compares the estimates of unpaid family work in each wave of SAKERNAS collected during the late 1980s and early 1990s. He reports large year-to-year fluctuations that are difficult to explain based on auxiliary knowledge of the labour market. He attributes the fluctuations mainly to measurement error that is associated with differences in interviewer training and supervision. Well-trained interviewers, he argues, will alert respondents to the fact that work includes unpaid work in the family business or on the family farm.

If the increase in family work reported in IFLS is because of the additional probing in that survey, the follow-up question about family work should have captured more positive responses in IFLS2+ relative to IFLS2. It did. In IFLS2, 1.8 per cent of female respondents who answer the question said they worked in a family business; in IFLS2+, 4.1 per cent of women answered affirmatively. This suggests that many of the women who entered the family business in 1998 would not ordinarily consider this activity as work in some traditional sense. We are inclined, therefore, to give more credence to the IFLS estimates of changes in employment rates of women (see Mata Greenwood 1999, for a more general discussion.)

In sum, as the Indonesian crisis unfolded, the fraction of adult males who were working remained remarkably stable, there was a slight increase in the faction of females working in the market and self-employed sectors and, according to IFLS, there was a more substantial increase in the fraction of women who were unpaid family workers. The picture that emerges is one of tremendous stability in overall employment rates. If we assume that there was not a large increase in the pool of people who were seeking work between 1997 and 1998, we would conclude that the dire predictions of a massive increase in unemployment were simply wrong.

Why were those predictions so far off base? It is possible that the stability of employment rates in 1997 and 1998 masks a good deal of change within the labour market. To fully examine that issue, we need longitudinal data that follows respondents as they move in or out of the labour force and across sectors. We focus, therefore, on IFLS.

Employment transitions

Table 3.2 presents employment transition matrices, which exploit the longitudinal dimension of IFLS; As can be seen from Panel A(1), 82 per cent of males were working in both 1997 and 1998 and 6 per cent were not working in either year. Over 6 per cent exited the labour force and 5 per cent entered. There is, apparently, a good deal of mobility in the labour market. Among women, the mobility is even greater: over one-quarter of the women working in 1998 were not working in 1997.

In an effort to determine whether the extent of turnover in the labour market varies across sub-populations, Panel B in Table 3.2, differentiates place of residence (in 1997) and level of education of the respondents. Among urban males, the better

Table 3.2. *Employment Transitions by Gender, Residence, and Level of Education, 1998*

	Not working	Working
A.		
Males		
1997		
Not working	6.3	5.4
Working	6.6	81.8
Females		
1997		
Not working	31.1	16.7
Working	10.1	42.1

	Urban		Rural	
	Not working	Working	Not working	Working
B. Residence				
Males				
No education				
1997				
Not working	5.7	7.6	5.0	4.3
Working	7.6	79.3	12.1	78.6
Some education				
1997				
Not working	9.9	7.2	3.4	3.9
Working	6.2	76.6	6.0	86.7
Females				
No education				
1997				
Not working	37.1	16.0	21.7	17.1
Working	5.7	41.1	16.6	44.6
Some education				
1997				
Not working	42.1	12.4	24.1	20.6
Working	6.4	39.1	11.5	43.8

Source: IFLS2/2+.

educated were slightly more likely to enter the labour market between 1997 and 1998 relative to exiting suggesting there was a slight upgrade in the level of education of the male workforce. In rural areas, there was a net decline in the fraction of males working and the exit rate was much higher for those with no education—one in seven left the labour force. The entry rate for the two education groups was very similar and so, as with urban males, the education of the rural male workforce increased between 1997 and 1998.

Labour market transition rates among rural women are even higher than for men. About one of every four women with no education who were working in 1997 left the labour force and an equal fraction entered the labour force in 1998. Among the better educated, the entry rate is about twice the exit rate and so, in 1998, one out of three working women were not working the year before. Again, there was an upgrade in the skill level of the workforce. The only exception to this pattern is among urban women, where the exit rate is about one-third the entry rate and women with no education are slightly more likely to have joined the labour force.

Taking the results for men and women together, it is clear that the stability of aggregate employment rates does mask considerable churning within the labour market between 1997 and 1998. Moreover, the nature of that churning differs substantially in the rural and urban sectors and the experience of males and females is quite different. Without knowledge about the amount of churning that normally takes place in the Indonesian labour market, it is difficult to draw welfare inferences based on these transition rates. However, to the extent that exits from the labour market between 1997 and 1998 were not voluntary, it would appear that in this dimension the rural poor bore a bigger share of the burden of the crisis.

Before taking up that issue, we delve a little more deeply into the labour market transitions. In addition to entry and exit into the labour force, workers may change the sector in which they work. Given the discussion of the nature of the crisis above, it seems plausible to suppose that workers will have shifted into those sectors that benefitted from the increase in the relative price of exports and food. Table 3.3 presents the sectoral distribution of the labour market transitions. In addition to self-employment and unpaid family labour, wage and salary workers are stratified into those in the private sector and those in the public or government sector.

Over 3 out of every 10 males and close to 4 out of every 10 females switched sectors between 1997 and 1998. Conditional on working in both years, the inter-sectoral mobility rate is about 25 per cent for both males and females. Job mobility is, of course, even higher.

Easily the most stable sector is government. Over 80 per cent of men and women who were working in the public sector in 1997, continued to work in that sector in 1998. The private market sector is quite different. Only about two-thirds of those in that sector in 1997 were still there in 1998. Three-quarters remained in self-employment.

About half the males who exited the private sector entered self-employment and vice-versa. Among men, there seems to be a good deal of movement between these sectors. About one-quarter of the switchers from both sectors exited the labour market while new entrants entered the private market and self-employment sectors at roughly the same rate.

Table 3.3. *Employment Transitions by Gender and Sector of Work, 1998*

1997	Not working	Private market	Government	Self-employed	Unpaid family labour	Σ
Males						
Not working	6.3	2.3	0.1	2.1	0.8	11.7
Private market	2.6	21.6	0.9	6.3	1.1	32.5
Government	0.4	1.2	6.4	0.3	0.0	8.2
Self-employed	3.1	6.0	0.2	33.5	0.8	43.7
Unpaid family labour	0.5	0.7	0.1	1.5	1.3	4.0
Σ	12.9	31.7	7.7	43.7	4.0	100.0

1997	Not working	Private market	Government	Self-employed	Unpaid family labour	Σ
Females						
Not working	31.1	3.9	0.0	6.3	6.5	47.8
Private market	2.3	7.7	0.4	1.3	1.3	12.9
Government	0.1	0.2	2.2	0.0	0.0	2.5
Self-employed	3.9	1.4	0.0	14.9	3.6	23.7
Unpaid family labour	3.8	0.9	0.0	2.0	6.4	13.1
Σ	41.2	14.1	2.6	24.4	17.7	100.0

Source: IFLS2/2+.

Among women, it is self-employment and unpaid family work that contributed the majority of exiters and also absorbed the vast majority of new entrants. Among those women who work in both years, transitions between these two sectors are far more common than between any other pairs suggesting considerable fluidity between them.

In fact, in many respects, the distinction between self-employment and unpaid family labour is artificial. It is convenient in a survey to designate a single individual in a household as the recipient of income from a family business in order to avoid double counting that income. From a conceptual perspective, however, it is not clear that the distinction among workers within a family has any substantive content, except, perhaps, when children are 'apprenticed' to one or both of their parents. To this point, we have maintained the distinction between self-employment and unpaid family work because of the difficulties associated with measurement of the latter highlighted above.

There is a good deal of mobility in the labour market in Indonesia. Did it increase at the time of the crisis? The first wave of IFLS was conducted in 1993 and so the hiatus between it and the second wave is four years. It is, therefore, not possible to compare transition rates between 1997 and 1998 with transition rates the year before with those data (obviously job mobility within four years is not informative about year-to-year mobility.) However, we can draw on two other sources of evidence. First, in 1997, respondents were asked about their work status one, two, and three years before the interview. The rates of entry and exit into the labour force between 1995 and 1996 and also between 1996 and 1997 are about one-quarter to one-third the rates recorded between 1997 and 1998. While it is certainly the case that transitions rates based on recall data are likely to under-estimate mobility (Sudman *et al.* 1996), it seems unlikely that the bias will be a factor of three or four. Second, qualitative work conducted early in the crisis, our own experience during the fieldwork and the local press all suggested that labour market mobility had increased at the time. The dire predictions of massive unemployment were presumably influenced by this sense of high rates of turnover.

It is rather more difficult to draw conclusions about the welfare consequences of these labour market transitions, at least among those who remained in the labour market during the turmoil of the late 1990s. There is, however, likely to be a closer tie between changes in income and changes in welfare. We turn, therefore, to an examination of the link between sectoral choice and labour market hourly earnings, focussing our attention on those people who were in the labour force in both years.

Hourly earnings

Table 3.4 provides the basic facts: median real hourly earnings of males and females collapsed by between 30 and 40 per cent in the first year of the crisis. This decline is nothing short of stunning. Given the evidence on aggregate employment rates described above, one might conclude that the attention given to unemployment and

Table 3.4. *Median Hourly Earnings 1997, 1998, and Change*

Workers	1997	1998	Change	% Change
Either 1997 or 1998				
Males	923	608	−315	−39
	[25]	[21]	[33]	[4]
Females	480	344	−136	−31
	[18]	[14]	[22]	[7]
Both 1997 and 1998				
Males	923	593	−330	−40
	[35]	[24]	[36]	[4]
Females	476	326	−150	−34
	[19]	[17]	[25]	[7]

Source: IFLS2/2+. Hourly earnings measured in rupiah. Deflated by Government of Indonesia province-specific consumer price index. Standard errors in parentheses.

calls for job creation through public works at the start of the crisis would seem to be misplaced. The drama of the crisis lies not in employment but in earnings.[4]

The upper panel of Table 3.4 is based on earnings of all people who work in either 1997 or 1998; the lower panel restricts attention to those who worked in both years. The differences between the estimates are small. We thus focus on the latter group as we explore the inter-sectoral distribution of the earnings declines in order to understand the nature of the employment transitions experienced by the Indonesian workforce.

To lay the groundwork, Table 3.5 provides estimates of the percentage difference in hourly earnings of workers in the government sector, self-employed sector, and private market. In line with the discussion above, unpaid family workers are treated as self-employed. Earnings from a family business is divided by the sum of the hours worked by all family members in that business to compute implied hourly earnings which is then attributed to all members. *Faut de mieux*, it is assumed that an hour of work by each family member is of equal value in the business.

We have estimated a series of regressions of (log) hourly earnings on sector of employment, controlling age, education, and province of residence. Models have been estimated separately for males and females living in urban and rural areas. Table 3.5 presents estimates of the premium (in percentage terms) associated with working in the government sector relative to the private market sector (in the first row of each panel) and the premium associated with being self-employed relative to a private market employee. These adjusted hourly earnings gaps are presented for workers in 1997 (in column 1), in 1998 (in column 2) and the change between the two years, estimated at the mean (in column 3). This is a measure of the 'shock' to hourly earnings for workers in each sector, relative to private employees. Because that shock may not be uniformly distributed, the last three columns report estimates of the (adjusted) change in the premium at the 25th, 75th, and 90th percentiles of the hourly earnings distribution based on quantile regressions.

For example, in 1997, holding age, education, and location of residence constant, urban males working in the Government sector earned 13 per cent more than those who were private employees (row 1, column 1); by 1998, that premium had increased to 31 per cent (row 1, column 2)—a rise of 18 per cent (row 1, column 3). Government workers at the top of the earnings distribution saw a slightly bigger increase in the gap (48 per cent, column 6), and those towards the bottom of the earnings distribution saw a smaller increase (25 per cent, column 4) although none of these differences is significant. We conclude that, among urban males, Government work was not only more secure but, by 1998, had become better remunerated than working in the private sector and that these benefits were enjoyed across the spectrum of jobs.

On average, rural males in the Government enjoyed a substantially higher premium in 1997 which persisted into 1998. At the mean, the change between 1997 and

[4] See Gunawan (1999) for a description of the public works program and Suryahadi *et al.* (1999) for an evaluation of the program. They conclude the program has neither expanded much nor is it particularly well targeted.

Table 3.5. *Regression Estimates of Changes in Inter-Sectoral Gaps in Log (Hourly Earnings)*

	Gap in 1997 (1)	Gap in 1998 (2)	Change at mean (3)	Change at percentile 25 (4)	75 (5)	90 (6)
Urban males						
Government	0.125	0.306	0.181	0.251	0.352	0.482
	[0.111]	[0.097]	[0.148]	[0.189]	[0.206]	[0.364]
Self-employed	0.017	0.237	0.220	0.026	0.070	0.728
	[0.108]	[0.115]	[0.157]	[0.222]	[0.219]	[0.321]
R^2	0.168	0.224	0.244	0.170	0.162	0.176
F	7.36	12.24	13.60			
Rural males						
Government	0.364	0.423	0.059	−0.093	0.314	0.612
	[0.156]	[0.143]	[0.212]	[0.267]	[0.319]	[0.481]
Self-employed	−0.570	0.046	0.615	0.295	0.896	1.508
	[0.127]	[0.095]	[0.159]	[0.229]	[0.256]	[0.337]
R^2	0.185	0.159	0.197	0.136	0.122	0.145
F	12.36	10.90	12.53			
Urban females	0.592	0.925	0.332	0.321	0.369	0.161
Government	[0.183]	[0.201]	[0.272]	[0.327]	[0.355]	[0.544]
Self-employed	0.297	0.583	0.286	0.112	0.319	0.776
	[0.152]	[0.164]	[0.224]	[0.261]	[0.330]	[0.434]
R^2	0.316	0.267	0.316	0.246	0.236	0.219
F	18.27	11.11	18.14			
Rural females						
Government	1.022	1.488	0.466	0.558	0.526	0.320
	[0.349]	[0.671]	[0.757]	[1.299]	[1.008]	[0.875]
Self-employed	0.004	0.457	0.453	0.595	0.431	1.269
	[0.182]	[0.178]	[0.255]	[0.332]	[0.358]	[0.554]
R^2	0.176	0.238	0.221	0.143	0.161	0.175
F	9.86	44.33	26.96			

Source: IFLS2/2+. Coefficient estimates are percentage hourly earnings differentials relative to working in private market sector. Self-employed includes unpaid family workers. Change in gap = gap in 1998-gap in 1997. Mean change estimated by OLS; changes at percentiles estimated by quantile regressions. Standard errors in brackets based on jackknife (for OLS) and bootstrap with 500 replications (for quantile regressions).

1998 was rather muted. Among Government executives, however, the gap between Government work and private sector worked increased substantially — by over 60 per cent (which is estimated very imprecisely and is not significant).

The public–private sector wage gap is considerably larger for females and it also rose between 1997 and 1998 although, like males, the change in the premium is not significant. A government job not only carried security but also considerably higher earnings in 1998: for example, holding age, education, and location constant, women in government jobs earned about twice their private sector counterparts.

The impact of the crisis on the private–public wage gap is small in contrast with changes in self-employment earnings. In 1997, urban males in self-employment earned, on average, the same as a private sector employee. By 1998, however, self-employment carried with it a 24 per cent premium. The benefits, however, accrued entirely at the top of the earnings distribution as indicated by the fact that at the 25th and 75th percentiles, employees and the self-employed took an equal hit in terms of hourly earnings.

In 1997, self-employment was a decidedly unattractive option for males in the rural sector: it carried a 60 per cent discount relative to being an employee. However, in 1998, that discount was entirely wiped out. While the increase in the relative attractiveness of self-employment is concentrated at the top of the earnings distribution, the benefits trickled down much further in the rural sector than among urban males.

It may be that the discount associated with self-employment in the rural sector in 1997 is a reflection of the drought and that earnings simply bounced back to their equilibrium in 1998. While this likely explains some of the difference, there are three reasons why we think that is not likely to be the entire story. First, we would expect to see the same pattern among rural female workers. We do not. In fact, in 1997, earnings of self-employed females and those who were private employees were identical. In 1998, like their male counterparts, earnings of female employees declined by about 50 per cent more than those of the self-employed. Second, as noted above, the drought did not affect the entire Indonesian archipelago equally: those areas that were more seriously affected by the drought did not enjoy a larger increase in the self-employment premium. Third, estimates of agricultural output indicate the impact of the drought was relatively small. For example, milled rice production was 3.4 per cent lower in 1998, relative to 1997 (and output then was 6 per cent higher then the average for the prior three years) (Bank Indonesia 1999).

Finally, urban females in self-employment earned more than private employees in 1997, the premium increased at the beginning of the crisis and, as with urban males, it was those at the top of the earnings distribution for whom self-employment became relatively more attractive.

Much of the limited evidence that exists on the effect of the crisis on incomes of Indonesians is based on only market sector wages (e.g. see ILO 1998; Feridhanusetyawan 1999; Papanek and Handoko 1999). Not only does that evidence overstate the magnitude of the crisis—since earnings in the market sector declined considerably more than among the self-employed (see also Skoufias and Surayahadi 1999, which examines the evolution of inequality using only wage incomes; those inferences are likely to be especially misleading). Studies based only on wage incomes also miss an important dimension of the likely response to the crisis: since self-employment became relatively more attractive during the crisis, particularly among the higher earners, we would expect people to have moved into that sector. This suggests a considerably more nuanced interpretation of the inter-sectoral mobility documented above. Specifically, the relatively skilled who moved out of the market into the self-employed sector were apparently able to mitigate the deleterious impact of the crisis on their earnings.

This idea is explored in detail in Table 3.6 which focusses on labour market transitions among respondents who were working in 1997 and 1998. Estimates of the percentage change in hourly earnings are reported for males and females who stayed in the same sector and for those who switched sectors. The first column in each panel reports the change for the average respondent; the remaining three columns report the change at the 25th, 75th, and 90th percentile which provides information on the marginal effect of the crisis across the distribution of skills.[5] Those transitions that were very infrequent are not included in the table.

The average urban male saw a large cut in his real hourly earnings—no matter what he did. However, at the bottom of the earnings distribution, those who stayed in the government sector saw an increase in their real wage. All other urban males with limited skills took a very deep cut—over 80 per cent among those who stayed in the private sector. Apparently the insurance associated with a government job is especially valuable among the poorest. At the top of the skill distribution, wages increased by about 30 per cent among those who stayed in the private sector and by around 60–70 per cent among those who were either in the self-employed sector or moved into that sector in 1998. Switchers from self-employment to the private sector fared much worse.

In the rural sector, the hourly earnings of the low-skilled male workers who stayed in the private sector were devastated: at the bottom quartile, wages declined by 90 per cent. By contrast, among those who moved into or stayed in the self-employment sector, real hourly earnings rose by about 50 per cent at the bottom quartile, doubled at the top quartile and increased by more than 150 per cent at the top decile. As with urban males, government jobs provided considerable income protection, particularly among the least skilled. Switching out of the private sector also construed benefits in terms of hourly earnings.

The evidence for females is remarkably similar although the effects are estimated with less precision. Those that were self-employed in 1997 and those that switched into self-employment were protected from the crisis relative to those that worked as private employees.

In our calculations, income from self-employment includes the return on assets such as land for farmers and equipment for businesses. Part of the apparent protection associated with working in self-employment may reflect an increase in the returns to these assets. Part of the protection may also reflect an increase in the return to entrepreneurship in which case one might expect it is the more entrepreneurial who have switched into self-employment during this time of uncertainty resulting in a re-sorting of skills across sectors of the economy. It is not possible to distinguish these mechanisms in the IFLS.

[5] Our working assumption is that workers at the top of the hourly earnings distribution will tend to be more skilled than workers at the bottom of the distribution.

Table 3.6. *Regression Estimates of Changes in Log (Real Hourly Earnings) and Inter-Sectoral Transitions*

	Urban, percentile				Rural, percentile			
	Mean	25	75	90	Mean	25	75	90
Males								
Stay in private market	−0.580	−0.839	−0.077	0.300	−0.842	−0.906	−0.107	0.310
	[0.060]	[0.054]	[0.053]	[0.080]	[0.113]	[0.262]	[0.110]	[0.235]
Stay in self-employment	−0.443	−0.235	0.360	0.710	−0.095	0.464	1.016	1.587
	[0.105]	[0.169]	[0.165]	[0.208]	[0.097]	[0.300]	[0.176]	[0.358]
Stay in government	−0.372	0.205	−0.024	−0.009	−0.528	0.982	−0.056	−0.183
	[0.081]	[0.089]	[0.105]	[0.175]	[0.104]	[0.279]	[0.137]	[0.267]
Private market to self-employment	−0.572	−0.664	0.504	0.639	−0.472	−0.125	0.764	1.985
	[0.267]	[0.478]	[0.287]	[0.349]	[0.279]	[0.544]	[0.383]	[0.700]
Self-employment to private market	−0.700	−0.495	−0.231	−0.079	−0.396	0.472	0.972	0.979
	[0.207]	[0.221]	[0.291]	[0.738]	[0.194]	[0.366]	[0.385]	[0.291]
Private market to government	−0.458	0.187	−0.131	−0.020	−0.079	1.079	−0.195	1.972
	[0.147]	[0.255]	[0.206]	[0.254]	[0.625]	[0.657]	[1.275]	[1.296]
Government to private market	−0.688	−1.073	0.242	0.628	−0.494	0.953	−0.167	−0.494
	[0.290]	[0.618]	[0.406]	[0.416]	[0.094]	[0.297]	[0.189]	[0.262]
Aggregate % change	−0.543	−0.930	−0.008	0.594	−0.504	−0.956	0.311	1.149
R^2	0.215	0.040	0.029	0.079	0.118	0.034	0.089	0.097
Females								
Stay in private market	−0.650	−0.889	−0.178	0.081	−0.615	−0.909	0.073	0.478
	[0.080]	[0.150]	[0.053]	[0.088]	[0.190]	[0.312]	[0.163]	[0.386]
Stay in self-employment	−0.314	−0.301	0.944	1.782	−0.213	0.037	0.565	0.986
	[0.154]	[0.239]	[0.319]	[0.256]	[0.099]	[0.366]	[0.196]	[0.502]

Stay in government	−0.403	0.229	0.099	0.165	−0.429	0.383	−0.222	−0.265
	[0.124]	[0.223]	[0.158]	[0.389]	[0.139]	[0.351]	[0.262]	[0.444]
Private market to	−0.504	−0.174	0.151	1.139	−0.628	−0.907	0.290	1.900
self-employment	[0.315]	[0.356]	[0.438]	[1.031]	[0.684]	[1.482]	[0.730]	[1.044]
Self-employment to	−0.656	−0.354	0.560	0.719	−0.918	−0.916	−0.006	0.718
private market	[0.373]	[0.595]	[0.595]	[0.667]	[0.446]	[0.616]	[0.738]	[0.675]
Aggregate % change	−0.478	−0.984	0.083	1.153	−0.397	−0.906	0.548	1.474
R^2	0.125	0.015	0.053	0.170	0.083	0.037	0.033	0.046

Source: IFLS2/2+. Change = log (real hourly earnings) in 1998—log (real hourly earnings) in 1997 for same respondent. Coefficients are interpreted as % changes. Changes at mean estimated by OLS; changes at percentiles estimated by quantile regressions. Standard errors in brackets estimated by jackknife (for mean) and bootstrap with 500 replications (for percentiles). Aggregate % change is change for all respondents in each gender and sector of residence sub-group calculated at mean and percentiles of distribution.

In complementary analyses, Smith *et al.* (2002) examine the effects of the crisis on family income. They show that the deleterious impact of the crisis was felt much more heavily among families at the bottom of the income distribution. For example, families whose incomes placed them at the top quartile of the distribution in 1997 saw a 20 per cent cut in their real incomes, independent of whether they lived in rural or urban areas. To be sure, this reduction is very large. However, those at the bottom quartile fared even worse: rural families had their real incomes cut by 30 per cent and urban dwellers suffered a 60 per cent decline in real family income in one year.

What were the sources of protection? We have shown that among higher income workers, income from self-employment was relatively resilient. This is particularly clear among rural households and likely reflects the fact that the relative price of food rose during the crisis, that many of the net food producers are self-employed and landowners tend to be among the better off in the rural sector. Among the rural poor, Smith *et al.* conclude that protection came from the contribution of 'unpaid family workers'. They draw the same conclusion in the urban sector except that it is relatively well-educated urban women who entered the labour market to work in the family business and so the incomes of those families were protected more than the incomes of the urban poor.

CONCLUSIONS

Predictions that the Indonesian crisis would be accompanied by massive unemployment were simply wrong. The drama of the crisis is not reflected in unemployment but rather in the devastation it has wreaked on earnings. On average, real hourly earnings declined by over 40 per cent between 1997 and 1998.

There has been considerable change in the structure of employment in Indonesia as evidenced by the high rates of turnover. Many males left the labour force and about the same number entered the labour force; many female workers exited the labour force but even more entered, and most of the new entrants worked in their own or the family business. There was also a good deal of shifting among sectors of employment. Some of that turnover reflects shifts in the relative attractiveness of different sectors. Specifically, there was a substantial tilt in favour of self-employment, particularly among those at the top of the income distribution. The picture that emerges is one of a remarkably flexible labour market, tremendous resilience of families in the face of a devastating crisis and of women playing a key role in supporting family income that would otherwise be drastically diminished because of huge cuts in real hourly earnings.

At a more general level, these results provide another compelling counter-example to two perennial arguments about the collection of data on labour market activities. First, collecting information on income from self-employment, including family enterprises, is not straightforward. However, ignoring income from self-employment would lead to seriously misleading inferences about the magnitude of the economic crisis in Indonesia, the distribution of the effects and the nature of individual and family responses to the crisis. Second, a key mechanism whereby families have mitigated the impact of the crisis on household income has been through an increase in the time allocated to the family business. It is women who have born the brunt of this re-allocation of time. Failure to collect information on so-called 'unpaid family workers' would completely miss this important fact.

References

Anker, R. and Anker, M. (1989), 'Measuring the Female Labour Force in Egypt', *International Labour Review*, 128(4): 511–20.

——(1990), 'Methodological Considerations in Measuring Women's Labor Force Activity in Developing Countries: The Case of Egypt', in I. Sirageldin, A. Sorkin, and R. Frank (eds), Female Labor Force Participation and Development, *Research in Human Capital and Development Series, Vol. 6*, Greenwich, Conn. and London: JAI Press, pp. 27–58.

Bank Indonesia. (1999), *Annual Report*, Jakarta: Bank Indonesia.

Beneria, L. (1999), 'The Enduring Debate Over Unpaid Labour', *International Labour Review*, 138(3): 287–309.

Fallon, P. and Lucas, R. E. B. (1999), 'Economic and Financial Crises: A Survey of the Evidence', forthcoming in *World Bank Research Observer*.

Feridhanusetyawan, T. (1999), 'The Impact of the Crisis on the Labor Market in Indonesia', Manilla: Asian Development Bank.

Frankenberg, E. and Thomas, D. (1999), 'Indonesia Family Life Survey: Study Design and Results from Waves 1 and 2', RAND DRU-2238/1-NIA/NICHD, Santa Monica, CA: RAND.

———— and Beegle, K. (1999), 'The Real Costs of Indonesia's Economic Crisis: Preliminary Findings from the Indonesia Family Life Surveys', RAND Labor and Population Working Paper 99-04, Santa Monica, CA.

Gunawan, A. (1999), 'Public works programs in Indonesia: What does recent experience tell us?', mimeo, LPEM-FEUI, University of Indonesia.

International Labour Organization (ILO). (1998), 'Employment Challenges of the Indonesian Economic Crisis', Report. Jakarta: ILO office.

Korns, A. (1996), 'Distinguishing Signal from Noise in Labor Force Data for Indonesia', Development Studies Project Research Paper #1. Jakarta: Bappenas/BPS.

Mata Greenwood, A. (1999), 'Gender Issues in Labour Statistics', *International Labour Review*, 138 (3): 273–86.

Papanek, G. and Handoko, B. S. (1999), 'The Impact on the Poor of Growth and Crisis: Evidence from Real Wage Data', Paper Presented at the Conference on The Economic Issues Facing the New Government. Jakarta, Indonesia.

Poppele, J., Sumarto, S., and Pritchett, L. (1999), 'Social Impacts of the Indonesian crisis: New data and Policy Implications', SMERU Report, Jakarta: World Bank.

Skoufias, E. and Suryahadi, A. (1999), 'Growth and crisis impacts on formal sector wages', SMERU Working Paper.

Smith, J. P., Thomas, D., Frankenberg, E., Beegle, K., and Teruel, G. (2002), 'Wages, employment and economic shocks: Evidence from Indonesia', *Journal of Population Economics*, 15: 161–93.

Sudman, S., Bradburn N., and Schwarz, N. (1996), *Thinking About Answers*, San Francisco: Josey-Bass.

Suryahadi, A., Suharso, Y., and Sumarto, S. (1999), 'Coverage and targeting in the Indonesian Social Safety Net programs', SMERU Working Paper, Jakarta: SMERU/World Bank.

Thomas, D., Frankenberg, E., and Smith, J. P. (2001). 'Lost but Not Forgotten: Attrition in the Indonesia Family Life Survey', *Journal of Human Resources*, Summer, 36.3: 556–92.

Thomas, D., Frankenberg, E., Beegle, K., and Teruel, G. (2000*b*). 'Household Budgets, Household Composition and the Crisis in Indonesia: Evidence from longitudinal Household Survey data', mimeo, Santa Monica, CA: RAND

World Bank. (1998), 'The Impact of the Crisis: Anecdotal Country Facts', Washington DC: World Bank.

4

Gender, Labour Market, and Demographic Change: A Case Study of Women's Entry into the Formal Manufacturing Sector in Bangladesh

RITA AFSAR

INTRODUCTION

Background and rationale

Bangladesh is one of the few countries which experienced women's entry into formal manufacturing sector without attaining universal level of primary education, and amidst the prevalent patriarchal values and ideology of sex segregation that govern gender relations in a conservative society.

Women have been experiencing some major changes in labour market in terms of nature of jobs and opportunities since last decade. Due to admission of increasing number of female workers to employment predominantly in garment and other small industries, the rate of female participation for all age groups have increased both in rural and urban areas. Moreover the growth rate of female labour force showed a steady increase over that of male labour force since mid-eighties. Among other things, rapid growth of Ready Made Garment (RMG) sector is one of the major contributing factors that causes a shift in women's predominantly home based to market-oriented economic activities since mid-eighties. From an insignificant level in 1975–80, RMG fetched nearly 53 per cent of the export earnings in 1995/96 (GOB 1996).[1] The uniqueness of this industry lies not in the fact that it is completely managed and owned by the private entrepreneurs, but that it has potential to change labour market context and women's position in the labour market, family and society at large, being dependent on the cheap labour of female migrants from rural areas.

Until to date, RMG sector employed 1.5 million labour force of which 90 per cent are migrants from rural areas and nearly 70 per cent are women (BGMEA 1998). The process of women's entry into global market directly or indirectly has profound impact on family, economy and society, and the roles of and relations between men and women. Very few studies focused on women's changing labour market context and its impact on their demographic behaviour and socio-economic roles (Afsar

[1] Government of Bangladesh (GOB) (1996), *Bangladesh Economic Review 1996*, Ministry of Finance, August.

2001; Zohir and Majumdar 1996). However, none of these studies addresses how demographic conditions favour or hinder women's changing position and participation in the labour market in the context of major economic and labour market changes and also socio-demographic consequences flowing from those changes. The paper would address all these issues.

Objectives

The broad objectives of the paper are to examine:

- Whether women's position and participation is changing in the labour market with the advent of RMG sector in a situation where there was limited employment opportunity for women and widespread gender stereotyping.
- Demographic and social-economic characteristics of women who get jobs in RMG and their position in the occupational hierarchy vis-a-vis their male counterparts.
- Implications of RMG jobs in terms of women's demographic behaviour, labour market gender equality, and empowerment.

Against the backdrop of change in labour demand and export oriented liberalization policy which caused massive increase in the employment of women in RMG factories in Bangladesh, the second section presents trends in women's position and participation in the labour market. This is followed by an analysis of socio-economic and demographic profile of women RMG workers, and their position in occupational hierarchy vis-a-vis their male counterparts, and if these are changing over time. The third section examines implications of RMG jobs for women in terms of demographic behaviour (e.g. fertility, contraception, and age at marriage), labour market gender equality (e.g. wages, occupations), and whether women and women's empowerment gain in the long-run from the availability of RMG jobs. The fourth section presents concluding remarks and policy implications in the context of demographic consequences of these major economic and labour market changes.

Data and methods

The study used a triangulation of both qualitative and quantitative methods of capturing multi-dimensions involved in the process of women's entry into formal manufacturing sectors and socio-economic and demographic changes that might have occurred as a consequence. It was not possible to get a list of workers disaggregated by gender and occupational category either through formal sources such as census of manufacturing industry published by Bangladesh Bureau of Statistics (BBS) or the list of RMG factories published by the Bangladesh Garment Manufacturers and Exporters Association (BGMEA). Hence, a non-government organization (NGO) called Unity Through Population Services (UTPS) that was working with around 100 RMG factories in Dhaka was approached for this purpose. As the author covered at least four types of samples viz., RMG factories, workers, employers of the selected RMG factories and relatives and/or neighbours of workers, a multi-stage random sampling procedure was adopted. It allowed the author to select her samples in sequential order and adopt judicious combination of quantitative and qualitative methods to generate more useful data than either method taken alone.

Sampling procedure and sample selection

It was decided to cover 15 per cent of the total RMG factories where UTPS had its program intervention at the initial stage[2] in the first phase given the budget and time frame. In order to have adequate geographic coverage of all factories, a systematic random sampling procedure was followed. Sample factories were also drawn proportionately from those areas where there is concentration of RMG factories in general. These factories are located in Dhaka and also adjacent areas where more than 90 per cent of the country's factories are located. Of the 14 factories studied, all but three are woven plant projects, preparing jackets and also shirts and pants for export to American and European markets. Sample RMG factories were established in the 1990s excepting two, which were founded in mid-1980s. The size of the sample factories varied between 200 and 400 workers with exception of two factories that employ nearly 700 workers. Of the total workers, a little over two-thirds are women and nearly a third are men and this is consistent with the author's earlier study of RMG workers (Afsar 2001).

It was decided to cover at least 15 per cent of the total respondents drawn from the sample factories in the second stage given the time and budgetary constraint. As a result, out of a total of 5,182 workers in 14 factories, 784 were drawn randomly representing 15 per cent of the total. Out of the 784 workers, 595 or nearly three-quarters are females, roughly corresponding proportional gender composition in each factory. It was not possible to draw an equal number of samples for male and female workers from each and every type occupation, because they are not equally represented in all categories[3]. Within each of these categories, however, the proportion of male and female workers drawn as 'operators' and 'helpers'[4] is roughly proportionate to the total number of male and female workers covered under the study. Nearly a fifth of the total male respondents also represent other categories as mentioned above. Of these respondents, 508 (72.8 per cent) were surveyed with the help of a structured questionnaire and the remaining 276 (27.8 per cent) were covered by FGD.

Methods of data collection

Survey questionnaire and focus group discussion guidelines were designed in advance to yield independent quantitative and qualitative research perspectives on the topics under investigation. FGD was held immediately after the survey and also

[2] UTPS started its activities largely since 1995. Mainly the factories where UTPS had less than one year of intervention were selected in order to have minimum bias from exogenous factors. It should be noted that in many of these factories UTPS had sent its medical team only once or is only at the preparatory stage of undertaking its activities.

[3] For a detailed discussion on gender segmentation in RMG sector see the Subsection on Women's Position in RMG vis-a-vis their male colleagues.

[4] See footnote at the bottom of Table 4.5 for classification of workers.

parallel to the survey fieldwork, with participants drawn from factory workers who are similar in their characteristics.

A survey was conducted to explore the socio-economic and demographic profiles of the workers, migration-related information, income, working hours and overtime, personal-hygiene- and water-sanitation-related information both in the community and factory.

In-depth interviews were conducted among management personnel, for example, Supervisor, Production manager, and Senior manager/General manager from each of the 14 sample factories, with the help of separate sets of schedules. Information generated from management related to type of productions and composition of the factory, changes in production, buyers, time schedule and employment patterns between 1996 and 1997, comparison between the performance of the male and female workers, difficulties they face, problems and prospects with regard to delivery of health services to workers and raising the productivity of the factory.

Each of the FGD consisted of 10–11 participants, one moderator and one note taker, and the discussion lasted approximately two hours. The composition of each group was homogeneous with respect to gender and age category. A total of 26 group discussions were conducted altogether. Generally one group-discussion was conducted from each sample factory and FGDs were evenly divided between male and female groups. In all, 14 FGDs were held, seven with male and seven with female groups from each of the sample factories. In addition, in two big factories where there were more than 700 workers, two more discussions were held to have greater representations from both male and female groups. Further, based on concentration of workers (with a minimum of 10 workers), 10 FGDs were conducted with relatives and neighbours of respondents in their community of residence. A uniform set of FGD guidelines was used for all sessions. The author herself was the moderator and maintained a relatively high level of control over discussion, introducing general issues from the guidelines for discussion and probing to ensure coverage of all essential points and to keep the conversation focussed. Finally, the preliminary findings from the analysis of survey data and FGD with the sample workers were shared to elicit suggestions and participation (including monetary contribution) of the owners of those factories, through informal discussion.

TRENDS IN WOMEN'S POSITION AND PARTICIPATION IN THE LABOUR MARKET

Introduction

Since 1974 certain notable changes have occurred in the labour force situation in Bangladesh. The total labour force is reported to have increased from 22 million to 41 million between 1974 and 1995/96, showing an annual growth rate of 3 per cent (exponential). What is more important to note is the remarkably high growth of female labour force. It grew sevenfold from 0.9 to 7.6 million registering 10.7 per cent annual growth rate, compared to 2.3 per cent growth rate for male labour force

Table 4.1. *Civilian Labour Force 10+ by Sex and Residence, 1974–1995/96 (Figures in Millions)*

Year	Bangladesh			Urban			Rural		
	Total	Male	Female	Total	Male	Female	Total	Male	Female
1995–96 LFS+	56.0	34.7	21.3	10.2	7.4	2.8	45.8	27.3	18.5
1995–96 LFS++	41.7	34.1	7.6	9.3	7.3	2.0	32.4	26.8	5.6
1984–85LFS	29.5	26.8	2.7	4.1	3.6	0.5	25.4	23.2	2.2
1974 Census*	21.9	21.0	0.9	2.1	2.0	0.1	19.8	19.0	0.8
Annual average growth rate of the labour force (%)									
1974–1984/85	2.9	2.4	10.9	6.7	5.8	16.1	2.5	1.9	10.1
1984/85–95/96	6.0	2.4	20.8	8.6	6.8	16.9	5.5	1.5	21.3
1984/85–95/96 (Usual definition)	3.2	2.2	9.9	7.7	6.6	13.4	2.2	1.3	8.9

+ From 1989, BBS employed extended definition to include 'any person aged 10 years and above who was either employed or unemployed during the reference period and who was engaged in household economic activities such as care of poultry and livestock, threshing, cleaning, boiling, drying, processing and preservation of foods etc. with or without pay or profit during the reference period is treated as economically active' (BBS 1996). Reference period is defined as the week preceding the day of enumeration.
++ According to the usual or conventional definition, any person aged 10 years and above who was either employed or unemployed during the reference period and any person of the same age putting in a minimum of one hour's work in family farms/enterprises for pay or profit during the reference period is considered economically active. Household economic activities are not considered as economic activities in the usual definition (BBS 1996). Although the extended definition of economic activity tried to cover 'all market production and certain types of non-market production including production and processing of primary products for own consumption, own account construction and production of fixed assets for own use' for the sake of comparability, we used usual definition of labour force to indicate trend.
* In the absence of labour force survey prior to 1980, the 1974 census data on economic participation was used. Although definition of economic activity was broadly similar but provided limited options to measure female labour force as it classified women only by their primary occupation in the reference week. As a result, the size of the female civilian labour force declined significantly from 2.6 million to 0.9 million between 1961 and 1974 (BBS 1977).

Source: Compiled and computed from BBS (1998: 20, 1996: XV–XVI).

during the same period (Table 4.1). Secondly, the growth (annual average growth rate) of female labour force is more rapid in urban (14.3 per cent) than rural areas.[5] One of the most important factors determining changes in the size of labour force is the sharp increase in the female labour force participation rate. Especially since the 1980s, there

[5] Note that official estimates suggests a substantial increase in female labour force participation in rural areas in 1995/96 and thus narrowing down the big gap in female participation rate between the two geographic units as found in other censuses (BBS 1996). However official sources are notorious for lack of consistency and methodological fallacies. Existing estimates from DHS data suggests around 10 per cent female participation rate in rural areas and a 16 per cent for urban areas (Mitra *et al.* 1994). This is consistent with the BIDS survey of 62 villages where Rahman *et al.* (1996) estimated rural female LFPR at 11 per cent. In their re-survey of same wards and similar cross-sections of slum and non-slum households in Dhaka city, Hossain *et al.* (1999) found that female LFPR increased from 16 to 26 per cent between 1991 and 1998.

was structural change in employment, with an emphasis on privatization and export-oriented growth—(which influenced demand for female labour)—fostered by the Multi Fibre Agreement (MFA) and Generalized System of Preference (GSP) to some extent.[6]

Growth of RMG sector and changes in women's position and participation in the labour market

Over time shifts in labour force between sectors revealed gradual declining trend of employment in the agricultural sector, whereas non-agricultural sector gained ascendancy. In 1974, more than 80 per cent of the female labour was absorbed in agriculture and community and personal services sector respectively (Table 4.2). By 1995/96, there was sharp decline in the relative size of the agricultural labour force both for men and women, and manufacturing sector emerged as an important source of female employment both in urban and rural area, particularly in the former. By way of contrast, there is slight decline in men's employment in the manufacturing sector in 1995/96 compared to 1974. In the 1990s, the average annual growth rate of the female labour force in the industrial sector was 16 per cent, nearly double the growth rate of 9 per cent in 1980s (World Bank 1997). The share of RMG employment in the total manufacturing sector increased from 2 to 30 per cent between 1981/82 and 1997/98 (Bhattacharya and Rahman 2000).

Background of migrant RMG workers

One of the most visible demographic changes in an underdeveloped society like Bangladesh, is the independent migration of female labour from rural to urban areas since mid-1980s with the advent of the RMG sector. In order to examine factors, which facilitate or constrain female labour migration, characteristics of female labour have been examined.

Migrant RMG women workers hailed from Central and South-Eastern districts of (nearly one-quarter each) Mymensingh and Barisal (nearly one-quarter), followed by Dhaka, Comilla, Faridpur (nearly one-tenth each) districts. Excepting Faridpur, male migrants also hailed largely from Barisal, followed by Mymensingh and Comilla and then Dhaka districts. Nearly half of the female migrants and two-fifths of their male counterparts originated from Dhaka division. Over time migrants of Dhaka slum and squatter settlements are also found to originate from those districts (Afsar 1995; CUS 1990; Majumdar *et al.* 1995).

[6] Under the present arrangement quota is imposed on Bangladeshi apparels in USA and Canada by virtue of which market access for Bangladesh is confined to thirty-one and nine product categories respectively for those two countries. It is now widely believed that the quota system has provided the country with a guaranteed market in both USA and Canada. Moreover there is also a big concern about the future of the Bangladesh's apparel sector in the context of total phase out of quota in 2005 under the WTO Agreement on Textiles and Clothing (ATC) (Bhattacharya and Rahman 2000).

Table 4.2. *Change in the Composition of the Labour Force by Major Industries, Gender, and Rural-Urban Residence of the Workforce, 1974 and 1996*

Major industries	1996 (%)				1974 (%)			
	Urban		Rural		Urban		Rural	
	Male	Female	Male	Female	Male	Female	Male	Female
Agriculture, forest, and fishery	12.3	9.7	64.9	49.0	14.7	7.8	86.0	81.2
Manufacturing	14.9	28.1	5.8	16.8	16.5	3.5	3.5	4.4
Electricity, gas, and water	0.6	0.3	0.2	0.1	0.2	—	—	—
Construction	3.9	0.8	2.5	1.2	0.9	0.1	0.1	—
Trade, hotel, and restaurants	29.4	6.6	13.3	6.1	17.6	2.5	2.5	0.8
Transport, storage, and construction	13.9	1.0	4.9	0.4	8.9	0.9	0.9	0.1
Finance, business, and services	1.9	0.5	0.2	0.1	2.0	0.4	0.1	—
Community and personal services	21.2	39.4	7.1	18.3	39.0	84.6	6.7	13.3
Household sector not adequately defined	1.6	13.4	1.0	7.9	—	—	—	—
All industries (%)	100	100	100	100	100	100	100	100

Note: Figures used for both 1974 and 1995/96 are the percentages derived from usual definition of economic activities for the sake of comparability. Please note that the total may not add up to 100 because of the rounding problem.

Source: Compiled and computed from BBS (1998: 20, 1996: XV–XVI).

Districts from where they migrate in the bulk are characterized by high population density although they do not represent the most impoverished districts (BBS 1996). Three-quarters of women migrants belonged to functionally landless households having 0.5 acres of cultivable land on an average. A half of the male migrants also came from the functionally landless families but slightly better economic background than women migrants (Fig. 4.1). Their families owned 0.8 acres of land on an average in the origin and they have higher educational attainment compared to female workers. In Bangladesh, seclusion of women was observed in the case of landed families only. For the large majority of landless families, women always contributed to family's income, whether directly through harvesting or indirectly through post-harvest and other income generating activities. What is important to note is the migration of many young women from the landless families to the capital city to earn a livelihood in the formal manufacturing sector. Daughters, sisters, and wives are increasingly assuming the role of the main bread-earner, which was hitherto considered to be a male prerogative.

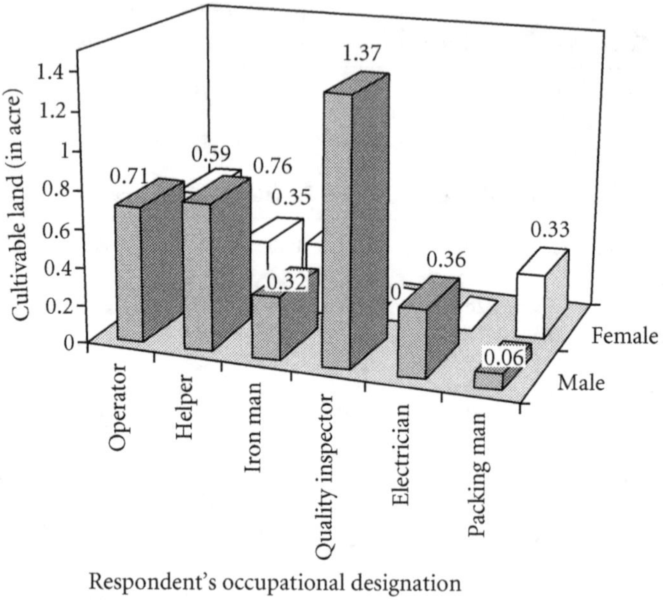

Figure 4.1. *Distribution of Respondents by Average Size of Cultivable Land Owned at Origin, Gender, and Current Occupation*

Source: Afsar (1998).

Age profile of the female labour force

Average age of a RMG worker is around 20 years and they are generally younger than their male counterparts at least by two years (Afsar 2001). Nearly three-quarters of the workers are between 15 and 24 years, and a half them are under 20 (Fig. 4.2). Studies conducted in the 1980s showed that women over 30 years constituted around a quarter and a third of the total women workers (Hossain *et al.* 1988; Unnayan Parishad 1980). It suggests that with the passage of time, more and more adolescent girls and young adults are joining the labour market, thereby defying *purdah* and cultural norms of sex segregation. Predominance of adolescents and young adults among female RMG workers was possible due to an informal and kinship dominated recruitment system and active assistance from social networks.[7] It also has important implications in terms of fertility and reproductive behaviour of the RMG workers, which will be discussed in the section on The Implications of RMG Jobs for Women.

[7] Nearly half of the migrant workers from RMG factories had been connected by blood to either employers or their agents. Moreover, 90 and 80 per cent of female and male migrant workers had family members and relatives in Dhaka who helped them in procurement of job and shelter, and provided necessary support in their settlement process (Afsar 2001).

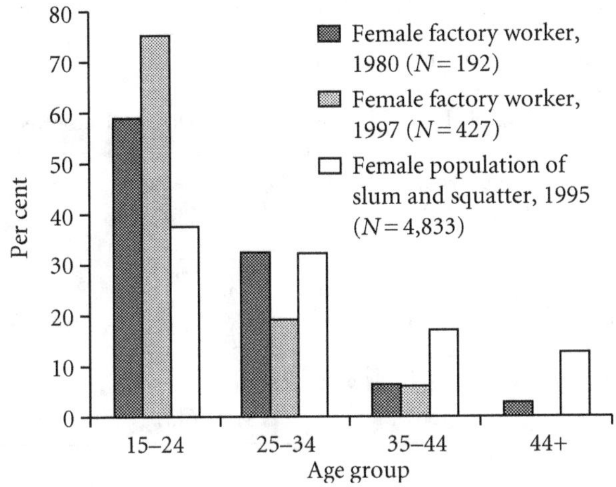

Figure 4.2. *Distribution of Female Factory Worker and Female Population of the Slum and Squatter Settlements by Age Group*

Source: Afsar (1998) for 1997; and Afsar (1997) for 1995; Unnayan Parishad (1988) for 1980.

Changes in the marital status of the female labour force

Pattern of independent migration by women suggests that increasingly, younger and currently unmarried women are migrating compared to 1980s, when migration was a strategy for survival by ever married women in their thirties. Among others, erosion of familial support and loss of male head (due to death, divorce or separation) were considered to be important factors behind women's independent migration in early 1980s or before (Rahman *et al.* 1996). Prior to the establishment of the RMG industries in Bangladesh, participation of currently unmarried women in the labour force was not only low, but also limited largely to the personal and community services. From her study of temporary migration of women to Dhaka city, the author found that the bulk of them were divorced (55 per cent) and nearly a third of them were unmarried and worked as the domestic servants in different boarding houses in Dhaka city (Afsar 1995). In contrast, Table 4.3 reveals that 71 per cent of the female respondents in garment factories were unmarried prior to migration.

Studies on RMG factories show that both married and unmarried women constituted nearly 90 per cent of the female labour force, and both categories of workers had almost equal representation in those factories (Afsar 2001; Zohir and Majumdar 1996). Some of the studies conducted in South Asia, characterized survival versus income maximization as dichotomous motives of married and unmarried migrants (Sardamani 1995; Teerink 1995). By way of contrast, nearly three-quarters of married women respondents from RMG factory in Bangladesh migrated for work related reasons, as opposed to nearly three-fifths of unmarried workers. Divorced and widow workers came exclusively for this purpose (Afsar 2001).

Table 4.3. *Distribution of Migrant Workers by Pre- and Post-Migration Marital Status, 1997 (%)*

Marital status prior to migration to Dhaka	Current marital status						
	Married		Unmarried		Divorced/deserted	All workers	
	Male (%)	Female (%)	Male (%)	Female (%)	Female (%)	Male (%)	Female (%)
Married	100.0	69.1	—	5.1	25.8	2.8	24.8
Unmarried	15.7	34.9	84.3	62.2	2.9	97.2	71.3
Widow/divorced/ deserted	—	13.3	—	—	86.7	—	3.8
All workers (%)	18.1	42.6	81.9	45.6	11.8	100.0	100.0
(No.)	(13)	(166)	(56)	(178)	(46)	(72)	(390)

Source: Afsar (1998).

Table 4.3 shows that five per cent of female respondents, who declared themselves married prior to migration, reported that they were unmarried at the time of interview. Clearly, it suggests an attempt to hide broken marriages. If those respondents were added, those who declared to be abandoned would increase to 13 per cent. Compared to their pre-migration situation, those female respondents who reported incidence of broken marriages after migration, has increased to four-fold. Moreover, of those who declared themselves currently divorced/widowed, nearly a quarter was married at the time of migration. However, it should be interpreted with caution. This is because at the time of migration only a quarter of female respondents were married and hence, there is a possibility of sampling fluctuation because of the small sample size under the category.

Table 4.4 suggests that the proportion of never married adolescent women is almost the same for the study and the women in general. However, the inconsistency between the two groups arises with regard to both currently married and abandoned women. The magnitude of divorced/widow/deserted women is significantly higher in sample population than is the case with Bangladeshi women in general. Particularly, at 25+ age, the proportion of such women reaches nearly thirty per cent, which is almost double than their age-cohort of mainstream female population in Bangladesh, although it should be noted that divorce/desertion is much higher among low-income groups than the overall population, and women, who join RMG predominantly represent this income group.

During FGD, with women workers from several factories in Dhaka City, marital instability emerged as one of the important reasons for some young women to join in garment factories. They told the author that the spread of garment factories in Dhaka City is both a bane and boon to them. It has generated opportunities for poor young women from rural areas to earn cash income, which entices both married and unmarried young men towards them. Thus, more than a third of the unmarried migrants female workers got married after migration to Dhaka City. By way of contrast, more than a quarter of married women, who were divorced or deserted by their husband after migration in this process, are now working in the RMG factories to earn cash income.

Table 4.4. *Marital Status by Gender and Age-Group for the Study Population and Sample Population from Health and Demographic Survey, 1998*

Age-group	Current marital status							
	Never married (%)		Currently married (%)		Widowed/divorced/ separated (%)		All (No.)	
	Male	Female	Male	Female	Male	Female	Male	Female
BBS, 1998								
<15	98.7	98.1	1.2	1.8	0.1	0.0	4,989	4,824
15–19	96.8	71.8	3.1	27.1	0.2	1.1	3,797	3,621
20–24	74.6	18.7	25.0	78.6	2.7	2.7	2,856	3,520
25–39	16.9	2.7	78.2	93.1	4.2	4.2	7,976	8,272
Afsar, 1998b								
<15	100.0	88.9	—	11.1	—	—	2	18
15–19	94.4	70.0	5.6	25.5	—	4.5	36	200
20–24	89.3	23.3	10.7	63.1	—	13.6	28	103
25–39	33.3	5.7	66.7	65.1	—	29.2	15	106

Source: Afsar (1998), BBS (1998).

Changing educational status of the female labour force

Conducting survey in 1990, Zohir and Majumdar (1996) found that nearly two-thirds of the formal RMG workers were either illiterate (29 per cent) or had up to primary level of education (34.5 per cent). Excepting nearly a tenth of the remaining workers, who had post secondary level of education, others (27 per cent) were educated up to secondary level (ranging from class VI to Class X). A substantial deterioration in the stock of female workers was noted by the author in 1997 (Afsar 2001) who found that illiterate and up to primary level women constituted 80 per cent of the RMG workers, resulting in subsequent squeeze at the secondary and post-secondary level (Fig. 4.3). In the case of male workers, however, the proportion of illiterate workers remained constant (at one-tenth) between 1991 and 1997, whilst there is a decline at the post secondary level from 36 to 21 per cent during the same reference period. As illiteracy is highly correlated with poverty, it suggests greater participation of poorer women migrant in the RMG factories than before.

Women's position in RMG vis-a-vis their male colleagues

Review of literature and observation suggest that women workers predominated in the unskilled and some skilled categories in both RMG and other manufacturing industries, and men in the management, supervisory and also special skilled categories such as cutters.[8] It is important to examine if with the passage of time, the gender composition of

[8] Zohir and Majumdar (1996) found 11 per cent of the workers were female in the cutting section. It is generally argued that cutting needs special skills, experience and strong physique to handle heavy machine. Sewing on the other hand, had been traditionally performed by women and employers show explicit preference for women because of dexterity that might be associated with nimble fingers of girls.

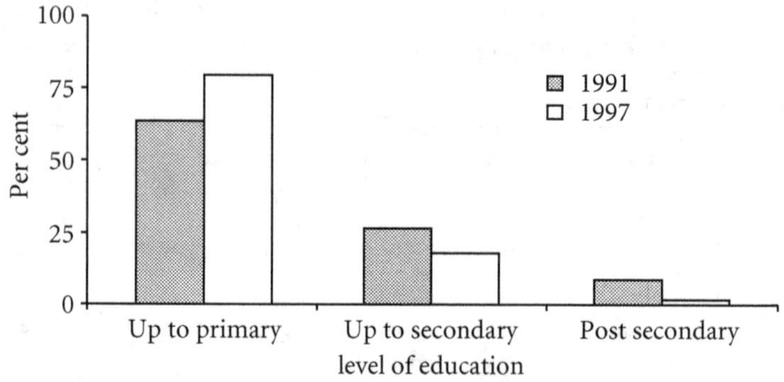

Figure 4.3. *Changing Educational Status of the Female Workers of the RMG Factory*
Source: Zohir and Majumder 1996 ($N = 295$), Afsar 1998 ($N = 427$).

different sections in RMG factory is changing. The author found earlier in 1996 and 1997 studies, that managerial, supervisory and technical jobs such as Production Manager, Quality Controller, Mechanic, Electrician, Cutter, etc. remained almost exclusively male dominated. However, women are now involved in ironing along with men, which was not common in the early 1990s (Zohir and Majumdar 1996).

Another important change that occurred is the substantial decline in the proportion of unskilled production workers and subsequent increase at skilled category with longer stay in Dhaka city (Table 4.5). A comparison between recent and long-term migrants by their occupational status reveals that unskilled production workers fell by half, in the case of long-term migrants.[9] Such transformation is more dramatic for male workers because with longer stay in Dhaka City, the gap between the skilled and the unskilled male workers widened more rapidly than their female counterpart. For example, among recent migrants, unskilled male workers constituted 25 per cent, which declines to 12 per cent in the case of long-term migrants. It is also important to note that women have fewer opportunities for promotion after being machine operators compared to their male colleagues.[10]

Nearly three-quarters of men and seven out of ten women respondents had informal training in their work in the garment factory. Given that there is almost no formal place for skill development training for garment work, young men and women often learn machine operation from the workplace, with the help of their relatives, friends, and other co-workers. Once they acquire that skill, they can bargain for better salary and absorption as a skilled operator in the same or other factories. Thus, 84 and 70 per cent of women and men respectively, who had informal training, are currently working as operators. Compared to skilled operators, very few unskilled production workers, one out

[9] Long-term migrants are defined as those who were not born in Dhaka City but migrated here between 1981 and 1991. Recent migrants are those who were not born in Dhaka City but migrated during the last five years taking the year of survey (i.e. 1997).

[10] Gender implication of occupational hierarchy has been discussed in detail in section on Background.

Table 4.5 *Distribution of Respondents by Gender, Current Occupation, and Migration Status, 1997*

Current designation	Non-migrant[a]				Long-term migrant[b]				Recent migrant[c]				All			
	Male		Female		Male		Female		Male		Female		Male		Female	
	No.	(%)	No.	(%)	No.	(%)	No.	(%)	No.	(%)	No.	(%)	No.	(%)	No.	(%)
Skilled operator[1]	5	55.6	33	89.2	18	72.0	91	77.1	22	46.8	167	67.4	45	55.6	336	78.7
Unskilled production worker[2]	3	33.3	4	10.8	3	12.0	26	22.0	12	25.5	103	37.8	18	22.2	133	31.1
Iron-man/woman[3]	—	—	—	—	2	8.0	1	0.9	1	2.1	1	0.4	3	3.7	2	0.5
Packer[4]	—	—	—	—	—	—	—	—	9	19.1	1	0.40	1	1.5	1	0.2
Quality inspector[5]	—	—	—	—	2	8.0	—	—	—	—	—	—	11	13.6	—	—
Electrician[6]	—	—	—	—	—	—	—	—	2	40.3	—	—	2	2.5	—	—
Mech. in Charge[6]	1	11.1	—	—	—	—	—	—	—	—	—	—	1	1.2	—	—
All	9	11.1	37	8.7	25	30.9	118	27.7	47	58.0	272	63.7	81	100	427	100

[1] Skilled operator or operator: Those who can operate a sewing machine. Here generally women predominate.

[2] Unskilled production workers or helpers: Generally three categories of unskilled workers are found in RMG factories. These are cutting helpers, sewing helpers, and finishing helpers. Women predominate in the last two categories and men in the first category.

[3] Iron-man/woman: Skilled in ironing finished products.

[4] Packers: Skilled in packaging and cartoning work.

[5] Quality Inspectors/controller: Largely male dominated and requires secondary level education and experience. A quality inspector/controller inspects each and every finished goods.

[6] Electrician/Mechanic in charge: Technically skilled staff who are recruited to provide technical support. Male workers exclusively dominate this category.

[a] Long-term migrant: Those who are not born in Dhaka city but migrated here between 1981 and 1991.

[b] Recent migrant: Those who are not born in Dhaka city but migrated here between 1992 and 1997.

[c] Non-Migrant: Born in Dhaka city and/or migrated here before 1981.

Source: Afsar (1998).

of every seven, had prior training. As a result, turnover is very high in RMG factories, which can be substantiated from average length of service in the sample factories. On average, female and male workers had been associated with their factories for 2.4 and 1.8 years. The average length is the least for unskilled production workers (1.5 and 1 year, respectively for women and men), who are more prone to job changes than other categories of workers. Generally, men are less stable than women. This is obvious given their higher level of education, lesser household responsibilities and more options in the labour market, compared to the female workers. Often being first generation workers, women working in garment factories have to surmount tremendous hardship in a predominately sex-segregated society, which will be discussed later.

IMPLICATIONS OF RMG JOBS FOR WOMEN

Demographic behaviour

Fertility and contraception

Considering entrance of younger women in RMG sector, adolescent fertility is compared with Bangladesh Demographic and Health Survey (BDHS) data and other surveys on RMG workers (e.g. Zohir and Mujumdar 1996). The BDHS data indicate that more than one-quarter of ever-married women aged between 15 and 19 years have given birth to a child. The figure comes down to more than a fifth and a tenth respectively in the case of the same age cohorts in RMG factories in 1991 and 1997 (Table 4.6). Given higher incidence of dissolution of marriage among RMG workers than women in general which might have influenced child-bearing statistics, comparison was also made with currently married women. Here too, unlike 90 per cent of women who have had more than one child by their early twenties, three-fifths of their age-cohorts in RMG factories reported to have no child at all. Obviously, this brings up the whole issue of contraception.

Table 4.6. *Child Bearing by Ever-Married and Currently Married Women Workers, by Age Group, 1997 and 1993–94*

Age group	Children per worker/women (average)			Women with no children (%)		
	BDHS data, Mitra *et al.* (1994)	Zohir and Majumder (1996)	Afsar (1998*b*)	BDHS data, Mitra *et al.* (1994)	Zohir and Majumder (1996)	Afsar (1998*b*)
Ever-married women						
<15	—	0.0	0.0	0.0	100.0	100.0
15–19	0.3	0.2	0.1	72.6	77.4	90.0
20–24	1.4	0.9	0.6	22.3	41.7	57.0
Currently married women						
15–19	0.6	—	1.0	44.5	—	90.2
20–24	1.6	—	1.3	10.5	—	60.0

Source: Mitra *et al.* (1994), Zohir and Majumder (1996), Afsar (1998).

More than 80 per cent of the currently married women reported to rely on pills as a means to control unwanted pregnancy. The Pill is the most popular method in Bangladesh as it accounts for nearly two-thirds of total modern contraceptive use in the country (BBS 1998). Remarkably higher scale of use of pills by currently married women of RMG industries suggests a high level of awareness and adoption by them. Since in RMG factories female workers hardly enjoy paid maternity leave, they take necessary protection to prevent unwanted or untimely pregnancy.

It is also important to note that the onus of using contraceptive lies largely with married women as very few men used condoms and very few women were aware of the importance of condoms as a means to ensure safe sex. While conducting FGD, it was observed that a large number of married women respondents do not consider it appropriate to ask their husbands for condoms because it might jeopardize their marital relation and also husband might suspect their fidelity. Others feel that men had an upper hand in this regard as they could marry and desert women at any time in a patriarchal society. It suggests that the male-female disparities and role differentiations are deeply rooted in the minds of men and women through the socialization process which is too powerful in Bangladesh to be challenged by first generation of the female migrant labourers.

Plans for marriage

In order to assess if a RMG job is helping female workers to delay marriage, currently unmarried workers were asked about their plans for marriage. Two out of every five currently unmarried garment factory workers wanted to defer their marriage until they could save enough money. However, a marked gender gap with regard to their marriage plans can be observed (Fig. 4.4). Majority of male workers (56 per cent) as opposed to one-seventh of women workers from garment factory wanted to defer their marriage for that reason. The bulk of the female garment factory workers (three-quarters), on the contrary, were waiting for their parents to find a suitable groom for them.

Considering the complex web of social and cultural forces in Bangladesh, the relevant question at this stage for first generation migrants, is whether they defer

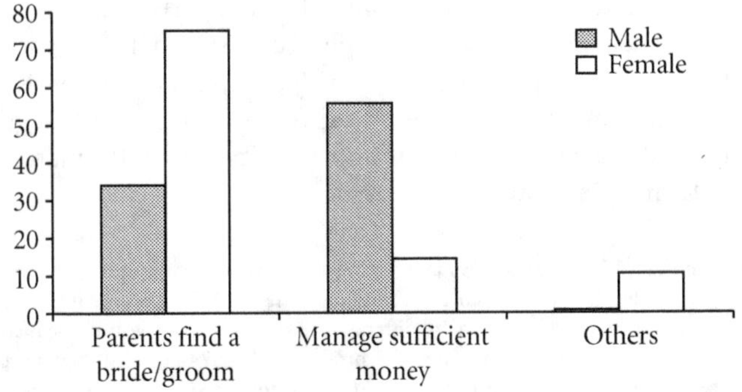

Figure 4.4. *Distribution of the Currently Unmarried Garment Factory Workers by their Plans to Get Married and Gender*

Source: Afsar (1998).

marriage to generate some more savings or surrender to their parent's choice in selecting their marriage partners.[11]

Women's independent migration: an enabling factor in women's economic participation

Traditionally, it was not considered appropriate for girls and women to work outside home for wages in Bangladesh. Although prior to 1990s, studies on internal migration seldom dwell on women as an independent category of migrants, one could observe a clear shift in the women's development literature between 1970 and 1990. Whilst womens *Bari* (home compound) based post-harvest activities assumed the central place in the literature of the 1970s (Cain *et al.* 1979; Ellickson 1975; Macarthy 1978), from early eighties, women's involvement in road construction, maintenance and repair became the dominant theme (Ann-Lisbet 1984; Marum 1981). On the other hand, emergence of women as factory workers has become the main focus of attention in the late 1980s and continued even in the 1990s (Afsar 2001; Hossain *et al.* 1988; Zohir and Majumdar 1966). In their study on RMG factory workers in 1990, Zohir and Majumdar (1996) found that migrants constituted three-quarters of the total workers and higher proportion male workers were migrants as compared to female workers in those factories.[12] By way of contrast the author's studies in 1996 and 1997, reveal that the proportion of migrant constituted more than 90 per cent of the total workers in the RMG industries, and there is no gender based divergence in this regard. The labour composition of other manufacturing industries is split fifty–fifty between migrant and non-migrant workers. Obviously, it suggests predominance of migrant workers in the RMG sector, compared to other manufacturing industry, mainly as a result of cheaper labour from rural than urban areas. This is supported from the authors interview with the former president of BGMEA who admitted that migrants from rural areas were preferred by employers over local female labourers of Dhaka, because the latter has greater aspiration and bargaining power than the former.

One visible impact of independent women's migration is a declining trend in the sex ratio of metropolitan cities in general and Dhaka in particular. Sex ratio obtained for Dhaka city dwellers declined substantially from 150 to 105 between 1961 and 1993–94. As the younger group (15–34), who predominate among RMG workers largely live in urban poor agglomeration, the drop in sex ratio for this group is more remarkable: from 103 to 65 between 1991 and 1996 in slum and squatter settlements of Dhaka city (Afsar 1999; Thwin *et al.* 1996).

[11] Bangladesh Demographic and Health Survey data (1994) reveal that about 60 per cent of Bangladeshi women were married by the time they reach 15 years. The same data also show that urban women marry later than their rural counterparts, with an overall difference of more than one year in the median age at marriage among women (15.4 versus 14.3, respectively) (Mitra *et al.* 1994: 74–5). Had they not been employed, they might have been married off without much consideration for the suitable groom. Hence, the employment opportunities generated by the RMG sector for the young migrant rural women provided them with some time to be away from the load of domestic responsibility either in parental or in-law's house.

[12] Composition of male workers showed preponderance of migrants (83 per cent) over non-migrants (17 per cent). By way of contrast, they found 30 per cent of non-migrant women in RMG factories.

Migration and urban adaptation

The literature on rural to urban migration in developing countries describes migrants adjustment to urban life as a problematic process (Goldscheider 1983). Their adjustment is heavily influenced by two basic tasks: obtaining a suitable job and finding accommodation (Afsar 2000). Considering the fact that generally RMG workers have had information about their job at destination, it is important to focus on their housing and adjustment process with regard to living arrangement. This is particularly important since RMG factories started purely with profit motive and Dhaka city (which houses more than 90 per cent of the RMG factories) remained largely ill equipped to house female migrants and respond to their needs.

With increasing independent migration by women, who come predominantly to work in export-oriented RMG factories, new types of families such as branch families, single member families are emerging.[13] It is interesting to observe that, a quarter and a third of male and female garment factory workers, respectively live in branch and single member families, including a few, who live in mess or boarding houses. Given the existing negative attitude on the single women earners and lack of low-cost housing or hostel facilities for them, and also highly insecure situation in terms of law and order, branch families emerged to fill up this gap. Nonetheless conventional family remained quite widespread as three-quarters of RMG female migrants live either in their own nuclear units or as a member of the extended family nexus.

The bulk of these workers live in low rental accommodations and even after spending almost half of their wage, they have to share 2/3 latrines and 5/6 gas burners with 10/15 families as cost-saving strategy because houses equipped with all basic amenities for the private use of a single family, are not within the reach of their budget. Heavy work pressure and environmental pollution both at home and in the workplace, and low and irregular payment of salary[14] make women more susceptible to morbidity than their male counterparts. During FGD sessions, women workers reported that the continuous work of ten hours on an average in the factory, the burden of household chores, and the extra efforts required to cope with precarious living conditions made them more vulnerable. Under the circumstances, a few cases of return migration were reported by the friends and neighbours of the respondents' communities. Those who went back to village of origin did so when they became disabled or because of prolonged sickness as a result of diarrhoeal diseases or jaundice.

Health and survival outcomes including the threats of STD, AIDS/HIV

Incidence of diseases is quite widespread among garment factory workers. More than two out of every five women, as opposed to a quarter of their male colleagues were

[13] Branch family can be defined as a family without a married couple but essentially consists of two or more adult members related by blood such as more than one sister, sisters and brothers, mother and daughter or aunt and niece, in sub-let arrangements.

[14] In most of the factories, workers did neither get their wages nor payment for overtime work at regular intervals.

reported to be sick in the month preceding the survey (Table 4.7). It is also important to note that propensity to become sick increases with the age of female workers. No such clear-cut correlation could be observed in the case of their male colleagues. Heavy work burden of ever-marred married women and limited availability of familial support at domestic front can be put forward to explain the positive correlation between age and sickness found for female RMG workers.

Management personnel observed very high frequency of jaundice and they cited some cases where TB infected workers were sacked. Even a recently published WHO sponsored report showed high risk of TB infection for the population of Bangladesh. It is suspected that over half of all Bangladeshis are already infected with TB bacteria (Kabir 1997). More than a tenth suffer from water borne diseases such as diarrhoea, jaundice, typhoid, etc. Almost similar proportion of female workers suffered from pains and aches of different parts of the body and another 10 per cent complained about general weakness. Diseases suffered by men, on the other hand, could be classified into five major

Table 4.7. *Distribution of Respondents Who Were Sick Last Week and Last Month by Sex and Types of Diseases Suffered, 1997*

Diseases/Health problems	Male				Female			
	Last week		Last month		Last week		Last month	
	No.	%	No.	%	No.	%	No.	%
Fever	11	52.3	11	52.3	54	44.6	85	47.2
Headache	—	—	1	4.8	17	14.0	12	6.7
Diarrhoea/dysentery	1	4.8	2	9.5	7	5.8	13	7.2
Weakness	5	23.8	1	4.8	8	6.6	21	11.7
Jaundice	—	—	3	14.2	4	3.3	6	3.3
Gastro-enteritis	—	—	—	—	2	1.7	5	2.8
Breathing problem/asthma	—	—	—	—	1	0.8	1	0.5
Typhoid	—	—	—	—	1	0.8	1	0.5
Conjunctivitis	—	—	—	—	2	1.7	2	1.1
Caugh/cold	—	—	1	4.8	7	5.8	8	4.5
Stomach ache/body pain/chest pain	2	9.5	1	4.8	13	10.7	15	8.3
Skin disease	—	—	—	—	2	1.7	3	1.7
General accident	1	4.8	—	—	2	1.7	3	1.7
Others*	1	4.8	1	4.8	1	0.8	5	2.8
Total number of sick respondents	21	100.0	21	100.0	121	100.0	180	100.0
Sick respondents as proportion of the total respondents	81	25.9	81	25.9	427	28.3	427	42.3

* Others include menstrual problem/leucorrhoea, dental problem, pox/measles, bleeding from nose.
Source: Afsar (1998).

Despite a strong *'purdah'* culture, one in every five workers, irrespective of gender, admitted to have acquaintance with some of the co-workers, suffering from STD.[15] A half and a third of those female and male workers also know about the sources, from where those patients seek treatment. However, during the FGD session, it was observed that some of female workers did not have a clear idea about symptoms of STD and a large majority were not aware of the ways through which AIDS is generally transmitted from one to the other person. After FGD session in Gemy garments, one of the FGD respondents approached the author and disclosed that her husband has a swollen penis with occasional discharge of pus. Her husband is a truck driver, who recently acquitted from jail, told his wife that he got this problem in jail because of maltreatment by the jail authority. The wife also believed his story because of lack of knowledge about STD.

categories. These are fever and headache, water borne diseases, general weakness, pains and aches, and general accident. Although not the same, to a great extent both male and female workers suffer from common water, environment, and occupational problems.

All women workers irrespective of age, marital status, education, and current designation unequivocally expressed their need to learn about AIDS and STD.[16]

Labour market gender equality

Wage level and the scope for upward mobility are generally considered to be important indicators for labour market gender equality. Table 4.8 suggests two important patterns. One, income of both men and women increases with longer stay in Dhaka City. Second, gender based wage differential also increase with longer stay in Dhaka City. As a result the gap between men and women widens. Question arises why and how it happens? In order to answer these questions, opportunities for upward mobility of male and female workers by average duration in the same factory and their gross salary by occupational categories were examined. Average duration in the same factory is 1.8 and 2.4 years for men and women, respectively. From second year onwards, men start bargaining for better-paid job either in the same or other factories. As they have higher level of education and greater mobility than their female colleagues, oftentimes they do not stay in the same factory before the completion of second year. Among those who stay, many of them are subsequently absorbed at technical and managerial levels.

Table 4.9 for example, shows clearly that even at entry point where women enter mainly as unskilled production workers and operators, one out of seven men enters as a supervisor or technician. With increase in experience, men often capture technical

[15] Here, illness is often associated with bad omen and people learn more to hide than disclose their diseases, particularly, if it relates to reproductive organs.

[16] They wanted to know about symptoms, ways through which it spreads, and more importantly, preventive measures. Although their male colleagues were found to be better equipped in terms of knowledge of those dreadful diseases, they also wanted to know about the preventive measures. Even friends, neighbours and relatives of the respondents demanded detailed information about STD and AIDS/HIV at the community level. Hence, sex education becomes a necessity for the RMG workers, irrespective of sex.

Table 4.8. *Distribution of Respondents by Average Gross Take Home Income, Average Duration in the Same Factory, and Average Hours of Work, 1997*

Respondents' categories/gender	Number	Average working hours (yesterday)	Average gross take home income (monthly)	Average wage/ month	Average wage rate/ hour[a]	Average duration in the same factory
		Hours	Taka	Taka	Taka	Years
Non-migrant	46	8.2	1,908.01	1,555.43	7.5	3.4
Male	9	6.2	2,252.78	1,961.11	9.4	1.2
Female	37	8.9	1,824.15 (0.81)	1,456.76	7.0	4.0
Long-term migrant	143	9.4	1,725.99	1,346.26	6.5	3.0
Male	25	9.2	1,937.86	1,594.60	7.7	2.3
Female	118	9.5	1,680.50 (0.87)	1,293.64	6.2	3.1
Recent migrant	319	9.9	1,531.19	1,147.68	5.5	1.8
Male	47	8.9	1,683.69	1,304.26	6.3	1.4
Female	272	10.1	1,504.85 (0.89)	1,120.62	5.4	1.9

Figures in parenthesis are the ratio of female earnings to male earnings.

[a] Wage rates have been calculated on the basis of 26 working days a month and 8 working hours a day.

Source: Afsar (1998).

Table 4.9. *Percentage Distribution of RMG Workers by Current Occupation, Gender, and Duration in the Sample Factory, 1997*

Duration in the sample factory (years)	Male	Female	Helper		Operator		Others[1]	
			Male	Female	Male	Female	Male	Female
1	52	203	34.6	48.3	50.0	50.7	15.3	1.0
2	15	80	—	22.5	86.7	77.5	13.3	—
3	7	60	—	18.3	42.9	80.0	57.2	1.7
4	4	23	—	4.3	—	95.7	100.0	—
5+	3	60	—	8.3	100.0	91.7	—	—

[1] Others include quality control inspector, iron-man/woman, packer, and technician.

Source: Afsar (1998).

and managerial categories. By way of contrast, women's mobility is largely limited to machine operation. Small proportions of women are found as supervisors and at technical and managerial level. A large number of women also drop out from the middle of the second year onwards. However, whilst many of them continue as skilled machine operators in other factories, it is assumed that some of them do not continue mainly due to health related reasons. The above situation explains how the

Table 4.10. *Distribution of Respondents by Current Occupation, Gender, and Information on their Inputs and Earnings, 1997*

Current designation/ gender	No.	Average working hours (yesterday)	Average overtime hours (last month)	Average wage earned (last month) Taka	Average overtime earned (last month) Taka	Average gross take home income (last month) Taka	Average wage rate/ hr.[a] Taka/hour Taka
Operator	336	—	—	(0.95)	(1.00)	(1.03)	—
Male	45	7.42	78.92	1,507.0	476.26	1,810.5	7.2
Female	291	9.56	70.43	1,433.5	476.68	1,860.7	6.9
Helper	151	—	—	(0.73)	(0.66)	(0.75)	—
Male	18	10.59	106.38	933.33	448.77	1,289.7	4.5
Female	133	10.44	81.87	681.28	296.56	964.8	3.3
Iron-man/woman	5	—	—	(1.22)	(1.08)	(1.12)	—
Male	3	12.00	97.50	1,183.3	425.00	1,701.7	5.7
Female	2	10.25	96.00	1,450.0	460.00	1,988.4	6.9
Electrician							
Male	2	3.00	75.00	2,150.0	250.00	2,312.5	10.3
Quality	11						
Inspector							
Male	11	11.25	110.56	1,350.0	727.75	1,933.4	6.7
Packer	2	—	—	(0.5)	(0.98)	(0.65)	—
Male	1	—	102.00	1,400.0	612.00	2,070.3	6.7
Female	1	12	245.00	700.0	600.00	1,345	3.4
Mechanic							
Male	1	13.00	—	6,500.00	—	6,500.0	31.25
All	508	—	—	(0.84)	(0.83)	(0.89)	—
Male	81	8.64	89.77	1,422.4	505.04	1,780.9	6.8
Female	427	9.86	74.74	1,197.6	417.76	1,581.1	5.7

Figures in parenthesis are the ratio of female's earning to male's earning.

[a] The wage rates per hour have been calculated on the basis of 26 working days and 8 working hours a day.

Source: Afsar (1998).

gender gap widens in the case of gross take home income of the male and female workers with longer stay. Data presented in Table 4.10 help to explain the situation further.

It shows that a skilled female operator earns slightly more than her male counterparts. As there is significantly higher prevalence skilled female than male operators among recent migrants compared to either long-term migrants or non-migrants, the gender based wage gap is narrower in this category.[17]

[17] Yet it persists because more than a quarter of male recent migrants occupied the post of quality control inspectors and electrician, whose salary is much higher than the skilled machine operators. Similarly, the presence of one mechanic-in-charge who earns Taka 6,500 per month exacerbates gender based wage differential among non-migrants.

Based on her poverty level income estimates, the author found that more than 80 per cent of women as opposed to 90 per cent of male RMG workers earn an income which is above the poverty threshold on a per capita basis (Afsar 2000).[18] However, more than half of the unskilled production workers still earns below poverty line income. In all fairness to RMG factories, it could be said that from a situation of absolute poverty having no income of their own, a large majority of women are now earning above poverty line income. Had they not migrated they would have remained either unemployed or under-employed or unpaid family helpers and only a few might have been working as wage labourers.

Women's empowerment

Review of literature suggests contrasting views on the impact of factory work on women's empowerment. Positivists believe that factory work has benefited women in number of ways. Workers are provided with better wages and more stable economic opportunity compared to women who were previously engaged as unpaid family helpers, or even when they worked for wages in the markets, their wages and working conditions were much inferior to factory employment (Foo and Lim 1989; Lim 1983). By virtue of entry into formal manufacturing sector, women gain economic power and more freedom in selecting spouses and delaying marriage, temporary escape from parental control and the burden of household chores, and opportunity to broaden their life chances.

Structuralist on the other hand, view factory work as another way of female subordination to the market economy and private capital. Confinement of the female labourers to semi-skilled or unskilled job categories, high gender differential in the wage, long hours of work, poor working and environmental conditions, and ban on trade union activities are highlighted as evidence of exploitation of female labour by the twin system of capitalism and patriarchy (Goonatilake and Goonaskera 1988; Mather 1985).

In the Bangladeshi context, the impact of factory work on women's empowerment is often contradictory and even complex, which cannot fit in the straitjacket of either gains or losses. Survey data reveal that 55 per cent of male and 42 per cent of female workers considered themselves as the 'principal bread-earner'. This is unthinkable for an illiterate or semi-literate and unskilled rural woman from landless households, who seldom gets such recognition, despite her ceaseless efforts to augment income and save expenditure of the family.

Women's entry into RMG factory has provided opportunities for selecting partner, having dates and room for pre and extra marital relationship although in a limited scale. In a sex segregated society like Bangladesh, where poor and illiterate or semi-literate women hardly encounter strange men in their occupations, working with male co-workers by the young migrant women and living in a less controlled environment, give them an opportunity to mix with opposite sex. As a result, marriage between

[18] Poverty line income was estimated at Taka 992 (per capita per month) taking into account the cost of living and that urban poor households spend around 60 per cent on food. A RMG factory worker who earns below this level, was identified as moderately poor.

co-workers of the garment factory has been found common during focus group discussion and in-depth interview sessions. Also, it was learnt that some unskilled female production workers were involved in a pre and extra-marital sex with co-workers or those who are placed slightly up in the hierarchy for small gifts of cash or upward mobility.

Paradoxically, women workers also complained that taking the advantage of their economic hardship, male co-workers, technical and even some managerial staff, make false promises of marriage or even promotion. However, once they establish sexual relationship, male partners often do not continue or stick to that relationship. Citing those incidences, female garment factory workers regretted that their male colleagues treat them as 'garment', which is used for sometime and then thrown away with the changing trend in fashion. Side by side, the threat of sexual harassment in the factory and outside is also not uncommon. Community based FGDs revealed many instances of threat of *Mastaans* (muscle men) and other forms of sexual abuses/ harassment faced by female garment factory workers. Eve teasing on the road and the cases of kidnapping of the female garment factory workers are not rare.

> In Kalapani area, a young girl was kidnapped by the 'mastaans' while coming home alone at around 10 o'clock at night. Next morning, they left her in the same place after raping her. She was badly injured and was under treatment for some time. After her recovery, she felt too embarrassed to work in the same garment factory and live in the same area. Hence, she left the factory and the area. They also cited another rape case in Madhya Badda, the eastern fringe of Dhaka city. Mechanics and electricians were identified as the major sources of sexual harassment within the factory by the male respondents in the most of the FGDs conducted in the sample factories. They cited a case of Rahima, an operator in one of the sample factories, who approached the mechanic for a needle in the same factory. The mechanic, Mr. Akram was surrounded by other co-workers. He first tried to embrace her forcefully, when failed, as Rahima moved backward briskly and fell down he bite her breast and invited her to go for a movie. Whilst his friends started condemning him publicly for his failure to embrace her, Rahima managed to escape from the evildoers.

Fear of losing the job and bringing disrepute to chastity, which is highly valued in this patriarchal society act as a silencer on the part of the violated women.[19] Apart from the human rights implication, the threat of health hazards, including STD and AIDS looms large for female workers.[20]

At domestic front, migrant women of RMG factories are continuously waging war against want, adversities, deprivations and insecurity, towards achieving a better future. As regards workload, married working women who live with their husbands at the place destination are in a more disadvantageous position than the unmarried co-workers, who usually live in branch families. Nearly 80 per cent of the married

[19] There are numerous case studies of women who were beaten, murdered or driven to suicide because of the dishonour that rape or illegitimate pregnancy brought upon their family (Fauveau and Blanchet 1989).

[20] Sexual assaults can cause physical injury and profound emotional trauma. Survivors of rape incident also run the risk of becoming pregnant or contracting STD, including AIDS.

women workers manage household chores by themselves as opposed to 13 per cent of their male spouse and 28 per cent of the unmarried women workers.

To manage the heavy workload, often the married women are late to reach the factory which results in salary cut. Some husbands also beat their wives, if they do not get their food ready after returning from factory. By way of contrast, husbands often come late at night and are not bound either to offer explanation or hand over their salary to their wives. Some of them establish extra-marital relations and abandon their first wives. Thus by and large, factory work has neither relieved the married women from the burden of domestic chores nor from physical violence or verbal abuse, which is a common feature in most part of this region. The question of the patriarchal control over women's chastity is a complex one to address. However, it might not be difficult to comprehend that had the women got the basic amenities at the doorstep, low-cost housing and safe and cheap transportation facility, they would have been at least released from undue burden of domestic chores to a great extent.

CONCLUSION AND POLICY OPTIONS

Since 1980s some major economic and demographic changes occurred that affected women's position in the labour market, family and society at large. There was structural change in employment in response to structural adjustment and globalization among other factors, and subsequent emphasis on privatization and export oriented growth, which influenced demand for female labour. Growth of RMG sector was particularly instrumental in this regard. Elsewhere the author wrote (Afsar 2000):

> Growth of RMG sector in Bangladesh has lead to at least two important socio-economic changes in Bangladesh apart from its recognized role as the major foreign exchange earner. First, it enhanced women's mobility defying *purdah* and geographical barriers and thus visibalizing women's economic participation and contribution to the family and the national economy at large. Second, it led to poverty alleviation to a great extent by creating employment opportunity for rural poor predominantly from landless families. From no income of their own, 80 percent of the women workers earn above poverty threshold income.

The study shows clearly that rural women are migrating to city in quest for economic independence and human dignity, and they show high resilience in coping with severe challenges in labour market and living environment. Considering that profitability of the RMG sector entirely derives from the value added by the labour of its women workers, it is important to raise productivity of these women. Productivity can be raised most effectively when it is combined with justice and fair play instead of the current practice of imposing physically more exhausting work and longer hours of work on these women. Hence it is recommended that women workers should be given equity share in the enterprise where they work. Simultaneously, tax rebate can be offered to those entrepreneurs who provide both in the job training and advanced training facilities outside the factory in collaboration with government and NGOs. Government must provide low-cost housing to RMG workers with the help of private sector and bank loan and cheap and safe transportation facilities. During the FGD and informal interview sessions with workers, they demanded more secured shelter and provision for better infrastructure to meet the demand of basic needs through formal sources. They wanted both the government and the factory owners to provide shelter and NGOs along with Dhaka City Corporation to cater to the water-sanitation problem. Policy makers should give priority to the installation of a hygienic sanitation and sewerage system as well as improvising ways for the distribution of clean water for the low income and poor agglomeration in Dhaka city.

Considering the human rights implications and the threat of health hazards, including STD and AIDS, it is important to have sex education and awareness programme for women workers about their reproductive rights. It is recommended that all factories should have health intervention programmes for workers particularly, women and it should include STD and HIV treatment and prevention. Sex education should be introduced both within the factory and in the school curriculum at the secondary level. Simultaneously, it must address gender inequality, reproductive and sexual rights and the political and economic context within which poor women risk exposure to HIV. It is also recommended that with the help of NGOs the RMG factories must provide health insurance and primary and preventive health services on a regular basis. Each factory should have a medical team consisted of a female and a male doctor. They must visit the factory for periodic check-up and vaccination against dreadful diseases such as Hepatitis B. Factories must have the provision for safe drinking water and canteen facilities to provide subsidized food to the workers to minimize work burden of female labour and the risk of water borne diseases.

Finally the big challenge is the future of the low-skilled/low-waged labour force, particularly female labour with the phasing out of MFA and elimination of quotas. There is obviously no straightforward answer. Even under the existing situation there is serious doubt as to whether female workers can continue with the RMG sector for around 10 years given the precarious working and living conditions. Whilst measures to spread women's secondary education can hardly be overemphasized, keeping in mind the need for backward linkages to back up RMG sector it is important to provide technical training to women in textile, dying and knitwear that are linked to RMG production. However it is argued that RMG output is largely demand driven and that of technology as well as in-house capacity continue to remain mostly supply driven and there is poor supply of trained technical hands (Rahman 1998). Hence, it is important to embark on a policy package that aimed at 'encouraging skill development, facilitating technology transfer and raising productivity level of the workers' in order to 'translate Bangladesh's comparative advantage into competitive strength' (Bhattacharya and Rahman 2000).

References

Afsar, R. (1995), 'Causes, Consequences and Challenges of Rural-Urban Migration in Bangladesh', Ph.D. Thesis. University of Adelaide.

—— (1997), '*Onus of Poverty on Women in the Poorer Settlements of Dhaka City*', paper presented at the National Committee on Women and Poverty. Dhaka: Women for Women.

—— (1998), '*Working and Living Conditions of Female Garment Factory Workers and the Threat of Health Hazard including STD/AIDS/HIV*', A Report Prepared for Disability and AIDS Control Unit. Dhaka: ACTIONAID Bangladesh.

—— (1999), '*Mapping Urbanization and Urban Change for the Twentieth Century: The Case of Bangladesh*', A case study prepared under 'Better Understanding of Urban Change', IIED: London and Dhaka: BIDS, Mimeo.

—— (2000), '*Female Labour Migration and Urban Adaptation*', paper presented at the National Seminar on Growth of Garments Industry in Bangladesh: Economic and Social Dimensions. Dhaka: BIDS and OXFAM.

—— (2001), 'Sociological Implications of Female Labour Migration in Bangladesh', in Rehman Sobhan and Nasreen Khundker (eds), *Globalization and Gender: Changing Patterns of Women's Employment in Bangladesh*. Dhaka: Centre for Policy Dialogue and University Press Limited.

Ann-Lisbet, A. (1984), '*Social Acceptability and Economic Viability of Women's Programme under the Maintenance Component of Noakhali Integrated Development Project*', BIDS/CDR Research Centre. Mimeo: Dhaka.

Bangladesh Bureau of Statistics (BBS) (1977), *Bangladesh National Population Census Report 1974*, National Volume. Ministry of Planning: Government of the Peoples' Republic of Bangladesh.

—— (1984), *Bangladesh Population Census 1981: Analytical Findings and National Tables*. Ministry of Planning: Government of the Peoples' Republic of Bangladesh.

—— (1996), *Report on Labour Force Survey 1995–96*, Ministry of Planning: Government of the Peoples' Republic of Bangladesh.

—— (1998*a*), *Report on Household Expenditure Survey 1995–96*, Ministry of Planning: Government of the Peoples' Republic of Bangladesh.

—— (1998*b*), *Population, Health, Social and Household Environment Statistics, 1996*. Ministry of Planning: Government of the Peoples' Republic of Bangladesh.

Bangladesh Garments Manufacture and Exporters' Association (BGMEA) (1998), Report. Dhaka: Export Promotion Bureau.

Bhattacharya, D. and Rahman, M. (2000), *Bangladesh's Apparel Sector: Growth Trends and the Post_MFA Challenges*. A Paper Presented to the National Seminar on Growth of Garment Industry in Bangladesh: Economic and Social Dimensions. Dhaka: BIDS and OXFAM, Bangladesh.

Cain, M., Khanam, S. R., and Nahar, S. (1979), *Class Patriarchy and the Structure of Women's Work in Rural Bangladesh*. Working Paper No. 43. Centre for Policy Study: The Population Council.

CUS (Center for Urban Studies) (1990). The Urban Poor in Bangladesh, vol 1, Comprehensive Summary Report, Dhaka University, Dhaka, Center for Urban Studies.

Ellickson, J. (1975), 'Rural Women: A Field Survey', Dhaka: Women for Women.

Faureau, V., and Blanchet, T. (1989). "Deaths from injuries and induced abortion among rural Bangladeshi Women", *Social Science* and *Medicine*, 29: 1121–27.

Foo, G. H. C. and Lim, L. Y. C. (1989), 'Poverty Ideology and Women Export Factory Workers in South-East Asia', in Haleh Afshar and Bina Agarwal (eds.), *Women, Poverty and Ideology in Asia: Contradictory Pressures, Uneasy Resolutions*. London: Macmillan, 212–33.

Goldscheider, C. (1983), 'The Adjustment of Migrants in Large Cities of Less Developed Countries: Some Comparative Observations', In C. Goldscheider (ed.), *Urban Migrants in Developing Nations: Patterns and Problems of Adjustment*, Boulder, Co: Westview Press.

Goonatilake, H. and Goonesekera, S. (1988), 'Industrialization and Women Workers in Sri Lanka, Working Conditions inside and outside the Investment Promotion Zone', in Noeleen Heyzer (ed.), *Daughters in Industry. Kuala Lumpur*: Asian and Pacific Development Centre.

Government of Bangladesh (GOB) (1996), *Bangladesh Economic Review 1996*, Ministry of Finance. Dhaka.

Hossain, H., Jahan, R., and Sobhan, S. (1988), *Gender Differential in the Field of Legal and Economic Conditions of Industrial Workers*. BILIA (Mimeo).

Hossain, M., Afsar, R., and Bose, M. (1999), *Growth and Distribution of Income and Incidence of Poverty in Dhaka City*. Revised Version of a Paper Presented for the Workshop on Changes and Determinants of Urban Poverty. Grameen Trust: Grameen Bank, Dhaka.

Kabir (1997), *The Daily Star Dhaka*. November 25.

Lim, L. Y. C. (1983), 'Capitalism, Imperialism and Patriarchy: The Dilemma of Third-World Women Workers in Multinational Factories', in June Nash and Maria Patricia, Fernandez-Kelly (eds.), *Women, Men and the International Division of Labour*. Albany: State University of New York Press, 70–91.

MacCarthy, F. (1978), *The Status and Conditions of Women in Bangladesh*. Planning and Development Division, Ministry of Agriculture and Forest: Government of the Peoples' Republic of Bangladesh.

Majumdar, P. P., Mahmud, S., and Afsar, R. (1995), *The Squatters of Dhaka City: Dynamism in the Life of Agargaon Squatters*. Dhaka: University Press Limited.

Marum, M. E. (1981), *Women in Food for Work in Bangladesh*. Dhaka: USAID.

Mather, C. (1985), 'Rather than Make Trouble, its Better Just to Leave: Behind the Lack of Industrial Strait in the Tangerang Region of West Java', in H. Afshar (ed.), *Women Word and Ideology in the Third World*. London and New York: Tavistock Publications.

Mitra, S. N., Ali, M. N., Islam, S., Cross, A. R., and Saha, T. (1994), *Bangladesh Demographic and Health Survey, 1993–94*. Calverton, Maryland: National Institute of Population Research and Training (NIPORT), Mitra and Associates, and Macro International Inc.

Rahman, H. Z., Hossain, M., and Sen, B. (1996), *1987–94 Dynamics of Rural Poverty in Bangladesh*. Final Report. Dhaka: Bangladesh Institute of Development Studies (Mimeo).

Rahman, M. (1998), *Harnessing Competition through Enhancement of Technological Capability: A Study of Export-Oriented Apparels Sector of Bangladesh*. Dhaka: Bangladesh Institute of Development Studies (Mimeo).

Saradamoni, K. (1995), 'Crisis in the Fishing Industry and Women's Migration: The Case of Kerala', in Loes Schenk-Sandbergen (ed.), *Women and Seasonal Labour Migration, Indo-Dutch Studies on Development Alternatives-16*. New Delhi/Thousand Oaks/London: Sage Publications, 55–209.

Teerink, R. (1995), 'Migration and its Impact on Khandeshi Women in the Sugarcane Harvest', in Loes Schenk-Sandbergen (ed.), *Women and Seasonal Labour Migration, Indo-Dutch Studies on Development Alternatives-16*. New Delhi/Thousand Oaks/London: Sage Publications, 210–300.

Thwin, A.A., Islam, Ataharul, M., Baqui, A. Hel, Reinke, W. A., and Black, R. E. (1996), *Health and Demographic Profile of the Urban Population of Bangladesh: An Analysis of Selected Indicators*', Special Research Report No. 47, MCH-FP Extension Project (Urban), Health and Population Extension Division, Dhaka: International Centre for Diarrhoeal Disease Research, Bangladesh.

Unnayan Parishad (1980), *Survey of Female Industrial Workers in and around Dhaka*. Dhaka (Mimeo).

World Bank (1996), *Bangladesh: Labour Market Policies for Higher Employment*. Dhaka: University Press Limited.

World Bank (1997), *World Development Report 1997: The State in a Changing World*. New York: Oxford University Press.

Zohir, S. C. and Majumder, P. P. (1996), *Garment Workers in Bangladesh: Economic, Social and Health Condition*. Research Monograph No. 18. Dhaka: Bangladesh Institute of Development Studies.

5

Missing the Partner and His Earnings: Income Situation and Labour Market Participation of Single Mothers in West and East Germany

FELIX BÜCHEL AND HENRIETTE ENGELHARDT

INTRODUCTION

The number of single parent families has risen very rapidly in Germany in recent years.[1] Several studies for West Germany show substantial differences in the economic well-being of single parents compared to families where both parents are present (e.g. DIW Wochenbericht 1993; McFate *et al.* 1995; Roll 1992; Ruspini 1998). Habich and Krause (1997: 524) found a rapidly increasing poverty rate for West German single parents within a short time period.[2]

A low income situation of single parent families seems mainly to be a problem of single mothers. Studies based on West German and on English data find that single fathers experience less likely poverty than single mothers (Burghes 1993; Neubauer 1993).[3] The basic explanation for this finding is the well-known worse labour market position for women than for men.[4] Furthermore, low income in many single mother households is caused by mothers' generally disadvantaged position in the labour market, for example,

[1] The number of single parents living together with children up to age 18 increased in West Germany from 701,000 persons in year 1972 to 1,164,000 in year 1995 (=15.7 per cent of all households having children of this age). Most of them (about 66 per cent) live in one-child families. In East Germany (1995) lived 538,000 single parent households (=25.9 per cent, all numbers: Statistisches Bundesamt 1997: 33f.). In East Germany (1982) there existed 358,000 single parent households living with children up to 18 years (Deutscher Bundestag 1998: 502).

[2] The poverty rate grew from 36.2 per cent in 1990 to 42.4 per cent in 1995. Comparative analysis consistently find that the proportion of single parent families that face poverty is substantially higher in Germany than in most other Western industrialized countries (McFate *et al.* 1995; Neubauer 1993; Roll 1992).

[3] Furthermore, among single mothers there is a substantial difference in the risk of low income depending on the family status. Especially unmarried single mothers more often face poverty than do married, divorced or widowed women because substantial financial transfers from the child's father are the least likely in this group (Burghes 1993; Neubauer 1989; Sørensen 1994).

[4] Differences in mean ages between mothers and fathers could play an additional role in this context.

due to time restrictions and a lack of occupational experience due to child care periods. Concerning single mothers, Büchel and Weißhuhn (1997) have shown that single mothers work in jobs for which they are overqualified more often than the average. An economic explanation for this phenomenon is financial needs or budget constraints which often force single mothers to minimize job search time.[5] Another important cause of the economic woes of many single mother households are higher costs of living when the parents are separated or divorced because of running two households and likely lower economic support when the father does not share the same household with the children (Sørensen 1994: 174).

Thus, there are three main causes of the poor economic position of many single mother families: Firstly, women's (and especially mothers') relatively low wages; secondly, the lack of economic support from a partner; and thirdly, a relatively great need for income. Concerning the first two factors, the increasing German unemployment rate in the last decade have not only weakened women's earnings potential but also the financial support from former husbands.

A highly particular development of single parents' social situation is given in East Germany. The different social and family political context in the former GDR had a clear positive impact on the relative standard of living of single mothers. Although they got neither financial support from the government nor from their former husbands, the legal conditions (e.g. protection against wrongful dismissal for single parents with a child under age 3) and special supports for childcare made it possible for most single mothers, at least for those with only one child, to be financially independent (DIW Wochenbericht 1990; Großmann and Huth 1993, 1995) for the US see Kimmel 1995.[6] In the transition from a planned economy to a market oriented economy, the labour market participation rate of women dropped dramatically. This development was accompanied by a substantial spread of the income distribution: Between 1990 and 1995 the Gini coefficient for the net income increased from 0.18 to 0.22 (Frick *et al.* 1997: 507). As a consequence, the relative income position of single parent households which traditionally show incomes at the lower end of the income distribution became worse over time (Dathe 1995).[7]

Although the low-income situation and high poverty rates for single mothers are well known, much less is known about details, or determinants, respectively, of their relative income position. The few existing studies remain on a very general level. They especially do not indicate the isolated effect of a missing partner for the relative income position. Therefore, the 'net' effect of being a single parent of the relative income position is still unknown. Reducing this information gap is a major aim of this contribution. Furthermore, previous studies do not control for the different labour supply or labour participation behaviour of mothers with respect to their specific

[5] For an overview about labour supply of single mothers see Staat and Wagenhals (1996).

[6] Nevertheless, the standard of living of single parent families in 1990 was (with 80 per cent of the average per capita income) clearly below that of two-parent families (DIW Wochenbericht 1993).

[7] Habich and Krause (1997: 524) found only 16.1 per cent of single parents living in poverty in 1990, this rate increased to 35.5 per cent by 1995.

family situation. This seems to be crucial because the relative income position as well as the female labour supply behaviour is determined by the household structure which gives women the opportunity or the restriction to stay at home or to work.[8]

In this paper we analyse the relative income position of single mothers in comparison to two-parent families with similar age structure of children. Because female labour supply is crucial for the income situation especially in single mother households (Solera 1999), we will set a special focus on the female labour participation behaviour in the household context. In doing so, we compare the effects of the determinants in East and West Germany as well as their development in the 1990s because of the different labour market dynamics, and, in East Germany, the change from a socialist system to a market oriented corporatist welfare state.

In the next section we briefly describe the data used in the empirical analysis. The first part of the empirical analysis consists of a comparison of the relative income position and poverty of two-parent households and single mothers with dependent children. This is followed by a multivariate examination of the effect sizes of the determinants on the relative income position. After having interpreted the empirical results, the paper ends with a short discussion of the findings.

DATA AND METHODS

Database

The empirical analysis is based on representative data from the German Socioeconomic Panel (GSOEP), conducted by the German Institute for Economic Research (DIW) in Berlin. This ongoing survey was started in 1984, when about 6,000 households were interviewed. Additional information on these households is collected annually with a broadly similar questionnaire. Household information, mainly on income and household structure, is obtained by interviewing the head of household. Additional detailed information on persons living in the household comes from interviewing all household members aged 16 years and older. This person-related data contains information on educational attainment, labour market participation, health condition, among other issues. An East German subsample of more than 2,000 households was added in 1990. The specific advantage of this additional sample is that it was collected in spring, that is, before the monetary, economic, and social reunion of Germany. The East German restructuring process, especially in the labour market, was not really started at this point in time, which means that the 1990 East German interview covers more or less the existing GDR social reality (for more details on the GSOEP, see Wagner *et al.* 1993 or, more specifically, Projektgruppe Panel 1995).

[8] From an econometric point of view, disregarding labour participation causes biased estimates for the effects on the relative income position, because the error term of the relative household income position equation is very likely to be correlated with the error term of the labour supply equation (e.g. Greene 1993).

Points of observation and general case selection

We analyse the economic situation of single parent households in 1990 and 1997—the most recent available wave of GSOEP at this moment—for West and East Germany separately.[9] This approach leads to four separate analyses whose results are discussed in relation to each other. We exclude some few single father households.[10] In addition, we exclude non-German single mothers from our analysis because of the very different social situation of foreigner households compared to German ones.

Selection of single mother households

The classification of single parent households is not a trivial task (e.g. Rendall 1997; Ruspini 1998). A wealthy 70-year-old woman living together with her unemployed 40-year-old son or daughter could define herself, if she considers herself to be the head of household, as a single mother. However, beyond this subjective assessment, this specific social situation would not fit the image of a classic single mother situation (e.g. Fox Folk 1996). Entering an age limit criterion for children obviously makes sense. In addition to that, the economic status of children living in the household must be taken into account. The question is how (financially) dependent children are. In Germany, the majority of young persons start an apprenticeship at age 16 and earn at least some money which can ease the financial situation of the household they live in. Therefore, we consider in our analysis female heads of household living without a partner only to be single mothers if they live together with at least one child aged 15 years or younger. Our data enables us to distinguish this group in the multivariate analysis according to the family status of the female head, differentiating never married women, women who are divorced or living separately, and widows. It is expected that the financial situation of these subgroups varies strongly because of additional income sources, such as child support and alimony from the children's father, or income from inheritances. Additionally, we use the number of children in our analysis to control for further heterogeneity among single mother households.

Selection of reference group

Our aim is to compare the economic situation of single mother households with those of married parent family households. After the specific categorization of the single mothers group, a comparison with the whole German married parent family population would not make much sense because age structure of adults would differ significantly between those two groups. Therefore, to increase comparability, we use

[9] The distinction between West and East Germany is made by place of interview. Note that within this approach the West German sample contains former East Germans who migrated to West Germany, and vice versa.

[10] Among the 1,163,000 single parent households with at least one child up to age 18 in West Germany of 1995, only 133,000 had a male head (Statistisches Bundesamt 1997: 33f.)

the same case selection rule as applied to single mother households: restricting the married parent family group to those couples living together with at least one child aged 15 years or younger.[11] For the same reason, we disregard households in which three or more generations live. Our joint sample of households with dependent children results in the following number of cases (in parentheses: *n* of single mother households): West Germany 1990: 895 (66); 1997: 935 (95); East Germany 1990: 919 (75); 1997: 512 (64).

Second level of comparison: the entire household population

Comparing the relative income position of single mother households with that of the reference group of married parent families with at least one dependent child is the first dimension in analysing the income situation of single mother households in a relative approach. However, a comparison with this specific reference group is only one part of the story. Another level of comparison is that of the whole society. This comparison makes sense in a longitudinal (1990–1997) or a comparative (West versus East Germany) approach. In other words: The question is not only how much a missing male adult affects the income situation of a family, but also whether the relative income position of single mother families in the society is different between West and East Germany, and whether this relative position changes substantially over time. This aspect is considered when constructing our relative income measures.

Measuring the economic situation of household

Our income measure is based on net monthly household income. This measure including transfers and excluding taxes is then transformed into an equivalent household income to adjust for economies of scale related to different household structures, or family sizes, respectively. We use the following weights: 1.0 for head of household; 0.7 for household members aged 16 or older; 0.5 for household members aged 15 or younger. This equivalent scale is similar to the one formerly used by the OECD and very close to a scale Faik (1997) considered to be the most valid one within the wide range of scales developed in the literature.[12]

[11] Unmarried partners with children are included; this form of living is of growing importance in Germany and—in general—no longer causing a stigma effect for concerned children. For better readability, we keep the expression 'married parent family' to identify all two generation households with two adult partners regardless of their legal marital status. Because we are more interested in the economic effect of a missing male adult in the household than in social familial behaviour, we also include into the reference group those households where the male adult is a permanent partner of the female adult, but not necessarily the natural father of all children living in the household.

[12] It is obvious that results are substantially influenced by the choice of a specific equivalent scale. This should be taken into account when interpreting the results. However, this problem can not be avoided in income analyses dealing with different household types. Nevertheless, it is crucial to use equivalent measures as standardized as possible to facilitate the comparability of results (which was done in this contribution).

Measuring the relative income position of household

A major problem comparing incomes at several points in time is that of changes in prices and earnings. This aspect causes problems when comparing West and East Germany because of different developments in this field, and, especially, when analysing incomes in East Germany over time: Incomes in East Germany in 1990 were reported in GDR Marks and in subsequent years (after the monetary union in June 1990) in Deutsche Marks. To avoid methodological problems with this respect, we use relative income position measures in our analysis. In this approach, the equivalent income of a specific household is related to the mean of the overall equivalent household income distribution in 1990 or 1997, respectively. Due to the very different income distributions in West and East Germany, this mean is calculated separately per year for both parts of Germany. Therefore, we obtain for each household a relative income position measure that indicates what percentage of median equivalent household income the individual equivalent household income makes (gained from the whole GSOEP household population, per year and region).[13]

Descriptive analysis

In a first descriptive step, we compare the relative income position of single mother families with that of married parent families, differentiating by number of children in the household. This is done separately for West and East Germany, and for both regions for 1990 and 1997. For each group, we present the group specific median of net equivalent household income as a percentage of the median of the overall net equivalent household income distribution per region (West or East Germany) and year (Table 5.1).

Multivariate analysis

In a second step, we use the median related relative income position of households as a dependent variable in OLS models. Single mother households and married parent families with dependent children are jointly analysed, but models are separately estimated by year of observation and region. The main interesting question is how the missing male adult affects the income situation. This effect is determined by the terms of interaction 'number of kids * family structure' where we distinguish between number of children in married parent family households, those in single mother households whose head was never married, and those in single mother households in which the head is divorced or living separately.[14] This approach requires a control for the characteristics of the female adult in the household as precisely as possible. Therefore, we control not only for female earnings, but also for

[13] Median related relative household income position in one specific year = (individual net equivalent household income/median of overall distribution of net equivalent household incomes per region in specific year) * 100.

[14] Due to limitations in number of cases, we have to pool divorced single mothers and those living separated. In Germany, the latter status usually is a preliminary step to divorce. Couples living separated for occupational reasons are not expected to report this specific family status in surveys.

Table 5.1. *Median Related Relative Income Position of Households with Dependent Children, West and East Germany, 1990 and 1997, by Household Structure*

		1990	1997	Diff.
West Germany				
1 kid	Married parent family	94 ($n = 311$)	95 ($n = 319$)	+1
	Single mother family	69 ($n = 30$)	70 ($n = 49$)	+1
	Diff.	−25	−25	
2 or more kids	Married parent family	84 ($n = 518$)	85 ($n = 521$)	+1
	Single mother family	66 ($n = 36$)	69 ($n = 46$)	+3
	Diff.	−18	−16	
East Germany				
1 kid	Married parent family	105 ($n = 306$)	99 ($n = 154$)	−6
	Single mother family	84 ($n = 46$)	84 ($n = 32$)	0
	Diff.	−21	−15	
2 or more kids	Married parent family	90 ($n = 538$)	81 ($n = 326$)	−9
	Single mother family	67 ($n = 29$)	63 ($n = 30$)	−4
	Diff.	−23	−18	

Note: All results are weighted.

Only households with at least one child aged 15 years or younger living in household. West Germany: only households whose head is of German nationality. Some few single father households are excluded.

Median Related Relative Income Position: group specific median of (Net equivalent monthly household income/Overall median net equivalent monthly household income) * 100. Equivalent scale: 1.0 for head of household; 0.7 for household members aged 16 or older; 0.5 for household members aged 15 or younger. Overall median incomes are calculated separately for West and East Germany, by year.

N of kids: total number of children in household, regardless of age.

'Married Parent Family': two adult partners living in household. 'Single Mother Family': female head of household, no partner living in household.

Source: Own calculations from GSOEP.

age and education.[15] This information should be taken as proxy for the earnings potential of existing male partners in married parent families, taking into consideration that education and age of partners correlate highly positively, and that mainly those two variables determine the earnings potential of husbands. Finally, we control for income differences caused by the location's population density using data-protected regional information (Appendix Table 5.A2).[16] Covariate means are presented in Appendix Table 5.A1.

To enhance the quality of our multivariate analysis, we take into account that the main control covariate, female earnings, is strongly affected by different labour supply behaviour of single and married mothers. Reacting to this selectivity problem,

[15] 'Low Education' = without vocational degree. 'High Education' = Fachhochschule and University degree (in East Germany also including GDR Fachschule degree). Note that the variable 'low education' is omitted in the East German models due to a small number of cases of unskilled people in East Germany.

[16] The authors would like to thank the SOEP administration and the data protection administrator of the DIW for giving special permission to use this information.

Table 5.2. *Estimates of Determinants of Relative Income Position*[a] *of Households With Dependent Children, West and East Germany, 1990 and 1997 (Selection Model After Heckman Correction Controlling for Female Labour Supply Behaviour)*

Household characteristics	West Germany		East Germany	
	1990 Coef. (Std. err.)	1997 Coef. (Std. err.)	1990 Coef. (Std. err.)	1997 Coef. (Std. err.)
Constant	75.366**	74.964**	75.606**	85.425**
	(6.575)	(6.502)	(3.878)	(7.525)
Living in city with	2.173	2.444	9.974**	8.243**
>100,000 inhabitants	(2.710)	(2.628)	(1.601)	(3.093)
Female adult with	−10.687**	−8.810**	—	—
low education	(2.897)	(2.856)	—	—
Female adult with	23.116**	23.235**	12.152**	21.115**
high education	(4.956)	(4.121)	(1.554)	(3.049)
Female adult: age	0.896**	0.914**	0.770**	0.436(*)
	(0.182)	(0.187)	(0.122)	(0.227)
Female adult: earnings[b]	0.006**	0.009**	0.013**	0.005**
	(0.002)	(0.002)	(0.002)	(0.002)
N of kids in complete	−7.969**	−9.040**	−10.852**	−13.690**
family household	(1.456)	(1.328)	(.961)	(1.831)
N of kids in single mother	−24.858*	−26.148**	−24.485**	−29.305**
household (never married)	(11.504)	(6.146)	(2.842)	(4.503)
N of kids in single mother	−18.593**	−20.714**	−20.246**	−19.786**
HH (divorced or separated)	(2.799)	(2.441)	(2.000)	(3.188)
(Lambda)	13.088**	10.594**	13.477**	18.472**
	(2.170)	(1.862)	(1.611)	(2.420)
n of cases	846	870	832	512
F value	31.3**	42.3**	90.9**	49.2**
R^2 adj:	0.24	0.30	0.46	0.43
Dep. mean (unweighted)	94.1	95.8	97.6	90.4

** $p < 0.01$; *: $p < 0.05$; (*): $p < 0.06$.

— The variable 'low education' is omitted in the East German models due to a small number of cases of unskilled people in East Germany (reference category is 'low' or 'intermediate' education). Only households with at least one child aged 15 years or younger living in household. Only households interviewed in West Germany whose head is of German nationality. Some few single father households and some single mother households with widowed head are excluded.

[a] Dependent Variable = (Individual net equivalent monthly household income/Median net equivalent monthly household income) * 100. Equivalent scale: 1.0 for head of household; 0.7 for household members aged 16 or older; 0.5 for household members aged 15 or younger. Median incomes are calculated separately for West and East Germany, by year.

[b] Net monthly earnings.

Source: Own calculations from GSOEP.

we re-run the models applying a Heckman correction (Table 5.2).[17] The pre-step labour supply Probit estimation controls for location population density as a proxy for restrictions at the labour demand side, educational level, age and age squared, health status[18], and additional household income[19] as a proxy for the financial need of female labour activities. The existence of children as an indicator for time restrictions in female labour supply is controlled in form of terms of interaction (number of children * parental situation: single mother yes/no). The latter differentiation is made on the assumption that single mothers have a higher labour market participation regardless of additional household income than mothers living together with a partner. As in the standard OLS model, the effect of the differential situation of single mothers compared with married parent families is completely drawn on the interacted children effect. Again, this approach was chosen because of the expectation that the major distinction in the social situation between single and married mothers is not merely determined by just being a single mother, but mainly by being a single mother with one or more children, and that the effect of the existence of these children makes the major social difference (DiPrete and McManus 1999). A documentation of these Probit results is reported in Appendix Table 5.A3.

EMPIRICAL RESULTS

Descriptive results

Table 5.1 shows descriptive measures on the relative income position of single mother and married parent households with dependent children. This is done for families with one and two or more children, West and East Germany, and for the observation years 1990 and 1997, separately.

In West Germany, households with children show below-average income positions compared to all West German households (relative income positions below 100). Single mother households do much worse than married parent families, this difference being especially large in one child households. From 1990 to 1997, there was little change in income relations between single mother and married parent families. In addition to that, all measures remain rather stable over time.

A very different picture emerges in East Germany. Married parent families with just one child have had an atypically privileged relative income position in East German society during socialist rule (1990). Single mother households are worse off than married parent families in East Germany just as in West Germany. However, in GDR times, the income position of single mother households with only one child was much better than in West Germany. This situation holds over time. This

[17] For details of this procedure see Greene (1997).

[18] Health status in the GSOEP data is asked in various forms. Unfortunately, the 1990 interview only contains information about satisfaction with health status (scale from 0 ['absolutely dissatisfied'] to 10 ['absolutely satisfied'] which is not the most valid indicator for health. Nevertheless, to make the 1990 and 1997 models as comparable as possible, we still chose this measure. Poor health status is stated for answers 0–4.

[19] Monthly net household income minus monthly net earnings of female adult in household.

remarkable result could be explained by an ongoing much higher female labour market participation in East than in West Germany which is—among other factors—still supported by better opportunities for childcare.

The gap between the relative income positions of single mother and married parent households in East Germany becomes closer during the transformation process. Nevertheless, East German single mothers with two or more children end up with the lowest income position among all distinguished socio-economic groups in West and East Germany at any time of observation: They are severely affected by the rapidly spreading East German income distribution after reunification, which makes low income people relatively poorer than at times of a most levelled income distribution (Frick *et al.* 1997).[20]

Multivariate results from the standard model

The results discussed above neglect heterogeneity in the analysed groups. For this reason, OLS models were run to control for important measures of the households, especially concerning labour market participation of mothers and proxies for the socio-economic background of the household in the form of age and educational level of mothers. In addition, we can now distinguish between children growing up in single mother households whose mother was never married and those whose mothers are divorced or living separately from the children's father.[21] Results for this OLS analysis are shown in Appendix Table 5.A2 (for final results after correction for heterogeneity, see Table 5.2).

At first glance, the resulting pattern shows a striking similarity between West and East Germany regardless of the time of observation: The missing male breadwinner causes severe reductions in the relative income position even when controlling for social status and earnings of women. Among the single mother households, those with a head who was never married are substantially worse off than those who are living separated or divorced. This result shows that the first group has much lower opportunities to be financially supported by the children's father. Again, the similarity of East German results to the situation in the GDR and that in 1997, when a most different welfare system has been established, is surprising.

In West German married parent families with dependent children, every additional child causes a reduction of about 8 per cent in the relative income position. In East Germany, this value is somewhat higher. In both parts of Germany, the isolated negative effects of the number of children on the relative income position have become somewhat stronger over time. The isolated negative income effect seen in single mother households is much higher and keeps rather stable regardless of region and time of observation: minus 25–28 per cent per additional child in single mother

[20] Note, however, that in our approach we are not able to consider changes in institutional regulations over time which could affect our results. Especially in the former GDR, a system of substantial non-monetary benefits was influencing individual well-being; the allowance for these benefits varied strongly between different socio-economic groups.

[21] We dropped some few widowed single mothers because of a low number of cases and their most specific income situation which can mainly be influenced by income from inheritances.

households in which the mother was never married, and minus 19–21 per cent in those households with a separated or divorced female head.

In both regions of Germany, the positive correlation between the higher education of mothers and relative income position has risen over time. In West Germany, we can observe a growing gap between low- and medium- educated women and highly-educated women. As expected, additional earnings of mothers lead to a better relative income position.[22]

Within this quite levelled pattern over region and time, two effects show rather 'strange' results. First, the formerly highly significant effect of living in an East German city on the relative income position has disappeared over time. The same happens with the age effect of East German mothers, which is even more surprising. Why should a formerly strong effect which can be observed also at both points of time in West Germany, suddenly disappear? The positive correlation between the ages of husbands and wives should be existent in today's East Germany as well as the positive effect on husbands' age on earnings. One possible explanation could be that the high unemployment rates in East Germany could diminish this effect, which does not seem very plausible. Another explanation could be that the determinants of labour supply of single and married mothers show substantial differences and have probably changed substantially in East Germany during the restructuring process. If this were true, a comparison between the 1990 and 1997 results would lead to misinterpretations as well as to an isolated interpretation of time-specific results because of selectivity effects in female labour market behaviour which cause biased results (e.g. Greene 1993).

To avoid this methodological problem, we ran a selection model controlling for these differences within a Heckman approach (Heckman 1979). For that purpose, we estimated first labour market participation functions for all women living together with dependent children, focusing mainly on their household situation. The results presented in Appendix Table 5.A3 are of minor interest for our analysis. Nevertheless, some aspects should be mentioned. As expected, labour market participation is highest for women of middle age. The higher the additional household income (earnings of husband or income from fortune), the lower the probability of gainful employment. Women with poor health tend to have lower, those with better education, a higher participation rate. However, a remarkable result of this study is that educational attainment did not influence female labour supply behaviour in the former GDR. This finding is obviously driven by the typically very high labour market participation of women in socialist economies. The main result of this step of analysis is that the number of children in married parent families reduces labour market participation of mothers significantly, regardless of region or observation time. Contrary to this finding, the number of children in single mother households did not significantly affect the labour participation of their mothers. An explanation is that these mothers were forced to accept second-best job offers because of financial needs. An outlier of this pattern is found for the current East German situation. One can only speculate

[22] Note that the untypical high effect in East Germany, 1990, is caused by a very low earnings level at this time.

about this finding. One possible explanation is that the German welfare system allows non-working East German single mothers to 'survive' via public transfers. Their financial situation, compared to the West German situation, is somewhat easier to handle because of the still substantially lower costs of living. Another, probably more reasonable, explanation could focus on restrictions on the labour demand side, overlapped by discrimination effects: If there are no jobs available, those having time constraints due to familial restrictions are the least likely to find an appropriate job.

Entering the information gleaned from this preliminary step into our selection models, we find the results presented in Table 5.2.

The selection corrected results are most similar to those shown in our standard models listed in Appendix Table 5.A2, with two remarkable exceptions. The non-significant effect of population density on relative income position in East Germany of 1997 disappears; now the effect turns out to be highly significant. In addition to that, the most unexpected missing significance of the age variable for the same population now comes at least very close to a .05 significance line. Overall, the results become much more plausible than found in the standard model. This finding signals that unobserved selectivity in social science models can severely affect the quality of results and their interpretation.[23]

SUMMARY AND CONCLUSIONS

In West Germany, the relative income position of single mother households is much lower than for married parent families. From 1990 to 1997, there was little change in income relations between single mothers and married parent family household. Similarly in East Germany, single mother households are worse off than married parent families. East German single mother households with one child only, however, are much better off than comparable households in West Germany. On the other hand, the relative income position of East German single mother households with two or more children is the worst among all analysed socio-economic groups: they are some of the very losers of the rapidly spreading East German income distribution after reunification.

Results from our models indicate that a missing male breadwinner causes severe reductions in the family's relative income position in both East and West Germany, even when controlling for social status and earnings of women. The results remain surprisingly stable between West and East Germany and over time. Furthermore, the family status of single mothers together with transfer payments determine the relative income position. Among single mothers, those that never married are substantially worse off than those

[23] Controlling for selectivity caused by different labour supply behaviour of single and married mothers, the positive effect of higher education and age on the relative income position is growing, and that found for female earnings is diminished. On the other hand, the negative effect caused by rising number of children in married parent families has risen, but is still far away from the striking negative effect resulting from children living in single mother households. Finally, the estimated effect of the selection variable is of interest itself. The significant positive effect indicates, however, that the error terms between the equation of the relative income position and the labour market participation equation are positively correlated. Thus, for those working women the probit estimation results indicate a low probability to work, the estimates of the relative income position are unexpected high, which is most plausible. Therefore, the estimated relative income position of mothers is upwardly biased without taking into account their labour supply behaviour.

who are living separated or divorced. Every additional child living in a married parent family lowers the net equivalent income position in West Germany by about 8–9 per cent and by 11–14 per cent in East Germany. We observed higher negative income impacts for children living with a single mother who was never married (minus 25–29 per cent per child). A similar, but somewhat lower effect is seen in cases of children living with a divorced or separated mother, who has better chances to receive at least some private transfers from the father of her children (minus 19–21 per cent).

A re-estimation of our models that took account of the very different labour supply behaviour of single and married mothers and controlled for this selectivity using a Heckman approach provided us with a result pattern which is much more plausible than the one gained with the uncorrected model. Not controlling for this selectivity problem mainly causes an overestimation of the mothers' earnings effect and an underestimation of mothers' educational background on the relative household income position of their households. Consequently, misinterpreting the real size of the effects of these crucial socio-economic status measures could negatively affect the effectiveness of social, labour market, and educational policies to secure the economic well-being of families with dependent children.

Appendix

Table 5.A1. *Unweighted Means of Covariates Used in Tables 5.2 and 5.A2*

	West Germany		East Germany	
	1990	1997	1990	1997
Living in city with >100,000 inhabitants	0.279	0.245	0.285	0.237
Female adult with low education	0.236	0.193	—	—
Female adult with high education	0.078	0.088	0.382	0.363
Female adult: age	35.304	36.305	33.172	35.724
Female adult: age ** 2/100	12.942	12.884	11.421	13.143
Female adult: Poor health status	0.104	0.105	0.117	0.121
Female adult: Additional household income[a]	3.228	3.981	1.207	2.645
Female adult: earnings[b]	576.478	754.840	710.565	1290.103
N of kids in complete family households	1.768	1.720	1.641	1.656
N of kids in single mother household (never married)	0.012	0.024	0.038	0.054
N of kids in single mother HH (divorced or separated)	0.099	0.130	0.072	0.119

[a] (Net monthly household income–net monthly earnings of woman)/1000.
[b] Net monthly earnings.
— The variable 'low education' is omitted in the East German models due to a small number of cases of unskilled people in East Germany (reference category is 'low' or 'intermediate' education).

Source: Own calculations from GSOEP.

Table 5.A2. *Estimates of Determinants of Relative Income Position*[a] *of Households with Dependent Children, West and East Germany, 1990 and 1997 OLS (Standard Model)*

Household Characteristics	West Germany		East Germany	
	1990 Coef. (Std. err.)	1997 Coef. (Std. err.)	1990 Coef. (Std. err.)	1997 Coef. (Std. err.)
Constant	72.985**	76.835**	75.143**	88.011**
	(6.691)	(6.604)	(4.031)	(7.919)
Living in city with	1.661	2.724	9.091**	5.231
>100,000 inhabitants	(2.769)	(2.668)	(1.655)	(3.215)
Female adult with	−10.901**	−7.918**	—	—
low education	(2.957)	(2.901)	—	—
Female adult with	15.580**	19.602**	9.284**	13.947**
high education	(4.903)	(4.139)	(1.578)	(3.052)
Female adult: age	0.764**	0.702**	0.502**	0.054
	(0.184)	(0.186)	(0.122)	(0.233)
Female adult: earnings[b]	0.015**	0.015**	0.026**	0.013**
	(0.002)	(0.002)	(0.002)	(0.001)
N of kids in complete	−6.505**	−7.957**	−9.955**	−11.547**
family household	(1.470)	(1.337)	(.987)	(1.904)
N of kids in single mother	−28.428*	−27.511**	−26.001**	−25.377**
household (never married)	(11.748)	(6.249)	(2.952)	(4.714)
N of kids in single mother	−19.371**	−21.113**	−20.261**	−19.069**
HH (divorced or separated)	(2.856)	(2.481)	(2.080)	(3.252)
n of cases	847	874	834	514
F value	29.2**	42.2**	86.6**	43.6**
R^2 adj:	0.21	0.27	0.42	0.37
Dep. Mean (unweighted)	94.0	95.6	97.6	90.3
Dep. Mean (weighted)	94.9	97.8	97.9	88.5

** $p<0.01$; * $p<0.05$.

— The variable 'low education' is omitted in the East German models due to a small number of cases of unskilled people in East Germany (reference category is 'low' or 'intermediate' education).

Only households with at least one child aged 15 years or younger living in household. Only households interviewed in West Germany whose head is of German nationality. Some few single father households and some single mother households with widowed head are excluded.

[a] (Individual net equivalent monthly household income/Median net equivalent monthly household income) * 100. Equivalent scale: 1.0 for head of household; 0.7 for household members aged 16 or older; 0.5 for household members aged 15 or younger. Median incomes are calculated separately for West and East Germany, by year.

[b] Net monthly earnings.

Source: Own calculations from GSOEP.

Table 5.A3. *Estimates of Determinants of Female Labour Supply Behaviour*[a] *in Households with Dependent Children, West and East Germany, 1990 and 1997, Probit (Results Later Used in Heckman Correction)*

Household Characteristics	West Germany		East Germany	
	1990 Coef. (Std. err.)	1997 Coef. (Std. err.)	1990 Coef. (Std. err.)	1997 Coef. (Std. err.)
Constant	−3.268**	−5.012**	−4.678**	−5.093**
	(.962)	(1.212)	(1.238)	(1.578)
Living in city with	0.007	−0.031	0.183	0.409*
>100,000 inhabitants	(0.109)	(0.106)	(0.145)	(0.162)
Low education	0.009	−0.076	—	—
	(0.110)	(0.117)	—	—
High education	0.287+	0.296+	−0.001	0.854**
	(0.171)	(0.163)	(0.132)	(0.153)
Age	0.201**	0.263**	0.371**	0.375**
	(0.054)	(0.066)	(0.077)	(0.090)
Age**2/100	−0.251**	−0.281**	−0.409**	−0.436**
	(0.072)	(0.087)	(0.114)	(0.123)
Poor health status	−0.065	−0.295*	−0.369*	−0.631**
	(0.148)	(0.145)	(0.178)	(0.197)
Additional household	−0.160**	−0.149**	−1.149**	−0.330**
income[b]	(0.033)	(0.027)	(0.128)	(0.048)
N of kids in complete	−0.145*	−0.136*	−0.151+	−0.379**
family household	(0.057)	(0.056)	(0.086)	(0.099)
N of kids in single mother	−0.089	−0.017	−0.233	−0.560**
household	(0.104)	(0.097)	(0.176)	(0.149)
n of cases	846	870	832	512
Chi2	58.4**	108.6*	210.6**	167.0**
Dep. Mean (unweighted)	0.435	0.450	0.839	0.646

** $p<0.01$; * $p<0.05$; + $p<0.10$.

— The variable 'low education' is omitted in the East German models due to a small number of cases of unskilled people in East Germany (reference category is 'low' or 'intermediate' education).

Only households with at least one child aged 15 years or younger living in household. Only households interviewed in West Germany whose head is of German nationality. Some few single father households and some single mother households with widowed head are excluded.

[a] Dependent Variable: Female adult in household is working at least regularly part-time (1 = yes; 0 = not working or irregularly part-time employed).

[b] (Net monthly household income—net monthly earnings of woman)/1,000.

Source: Own calculations from GSOEP.

References

Anker, R. (1997), 'Theories of Occupational Segregation by Sex: An Overview', *International Labour Review, 136*: 315–39.

Büchel, F. and Weißhuhn, G. (1997), 'Unter Wert verkauft—Ausbildungsinadäquate Beschäftigung von Frauen in West- und Ostdeutschland: Arbeitsbedingungen und sozio-ökonomische Bestimmungsgründe. Gutachten im Auftrag des Bundesministeriums für Bildung, Wissenschaft, Forschung und Technologie', Bonn. Bielefeld: Bertelsmann.

Burghes, L. (1993), *One-parent Families. Policy Options for the 1990s*, London: Family Policy Studies Centre.

Dathe, D. (1995), 'Zur Einkommenslage ausgewählter Haushaltstypen in den neuen Bundesländern', in H. Betram, S. Hradil and G. Kleinhenz (eds), *Sozialer und demographischer Wandel in den neuen Bundesländern*, Berlin: Akademie Verlag, 71–100.

Deutscher Bundestag, Referat Öffentlichkeitsarbeit (1998), 'Zweiter Zwischenbericht der Enquete-Kommission "Demographischer Wandel". Herausforderungen unserer älter werdenden Gesellschaft an den einzelnen und die Politik', Bonn: Deutscher Bundestag, Referat Öffentlichkeitsarbeit.

DiPrete, T. and McManus, P. A. (1999), 'The Sensitivity of Family Income to Changes in Family Structure and Job Change in the United States and Germany', *Vierteljahrshefte zur Wirtschaftsforschung, 68*: 171–76.

DIW Wochenbericht (1990), 'Die ökonomische Situation von Alleinerziehenden in der DDR und der Bundesrepublik Deutschland in den 80er Jahren', *Deutsches Institut für Wirtschaftsforschung, Wochenbericht* 42/90: 598–603.

—— (1993), 'Einkommensverteilung und Einkommenszufriedenheit in ostdeutschen Privathaushalten', *Deutsches Institut für Wirtschaftsforschung, Wochenbericht* 6/90.

Faik, J. (1997), 'Institutionelle Äquivalenzskalen als Basis von Verteilungsanalyzen—Eine Modifizierung der Sozialhilfeskala', 13–42 in I. Becker and R. Hauser (eds) *Einkommensverteilung und Armut. Deutschland auf dem Weg zur Vierfünftel-Gesellschaft?* Frankfurt a. M./New York: Campus.

Fox Folk, K. (1996), 'Single Mothers in Various Living Arrangements: Differences in Economic and Time Resources', *American Journal of Economics and Sociology, 55*: 277–92.

Frick, J., Krause P., and Wagner, G. (1997), 'Einkommensverteilung' in Statistisches Bundesamt (ed.), Datenreport 1997—Zahlen und Fakten über die Bundesrepublik Deutschland. Schriftenreihe des Statistischen Bundesamtes, Band 340, Bonn, 502–14.

Greene, W. (1993), *Econometric Analysis*, New York: MacMillan.

Großmann, H. and Huth, S. (1993), 'Alleinerziehende Frauen berichten. Erfahrungen einer Ost-West vergleichenden Untersuchung', in A. Diezinger, H. Kitzer, I. Anker, I. Bingel, E. Hass, and Odierna, S. (eds), *Erfahrung mit Methode. Wege sozialwissenschaftlicher Frauenforschung*, Freiburg: Kore, 219–42.

—— and Huth, S. (1995), 'Sozialhilfeabhängigkeit Alleinerziehender als Folge des gesellschaftlichen Umbruchs', in H. Betram, S. Hradil and G. Kleinhenz (eds), *Sozialer und demographischer Wandel in den neuen Bundesländern*, Berlin: Akademie Verlag, 159–87.

Habich, R. and Krause, P. (1997), 'Armut. in Statistisches Bundesamt' (ed.), Datenreport 1997—Zahlen und Fakten über die Bundesrepublik Deutschland, Schriftenreihe des Statistischen Bundesamtes, Band 340, Bonn, 515–25.

Heckman, James, J. (1979), 'Sample Selection as a Specification Error', *Econometrica, 42*: 153–62

Kamerman, S. and Kahn, A. (1993) 'Income Transfers and Mother-only Families in Eight Countries', *Social Service Review, 57*: 448–64.

Kimmel, J. (1995), 'The Effectiveness of Child-Care Subsidies in Encouraging the Welfare-to-Work Transition of Low-Income Single Mothers', *The American Economic Review, Papers and Proceedings, 85*: 271–75.

McFate, K., Smeeding, T., and Rainwater, T. (1995), 'Markets and states: Poverty trends and transfer system effectiveness in the 1980s', in K. McFate *et al.* (eds), *Poverty, Inequity and the Future of Social Policy*. New York: Russel Sage Foundations, 29–66.

Neubauer, E. (1993), 'Alleinerziehende als Zielgruppe der Familienpolitik', in E. Neubauer, C. Dienel, and M. Lohkamp-Himmighofen (eds.), Zwölf Wege der Familienpolitik in der EG, Bd. 1. Stuttgart: Metzler, 405–35.

Projektgruppe Panel (1995), 'Das Sozio-oekonomische Panel (SOEP) im Jahre 1994', *Vierteljahrshefte zur Wirtschaftsforschung, 64*: 5–15.

Rendall, M. S. (1997), 'Identifying and Misidentifying Single Mothers in the Panel Study of Income Dynamics', *The Journal of Human Resources, 33*: 596–610.

Roll, J. (1992), 'Single Parent Families in the Economic Community', Report to the European Commission, London: European Family and Social Policy Unit.

Ruspini, E. (1998), 'Living on the Poverty Line. Single Mothers' Poverty in Belgium, Germany, Great Britain, Italy, and Sweden. A Comparative, Dynamic, Gender-friendly Analysis', paper presented at the GSOEP98 Conference in Berlin.

Solera, Cristina (1999), 'Income Transfers and Support for Mothers' Employment: The Link to Family Poverty Risks. A Comparison between Italy, Sweden and the U.K', paper presented at the LIS Conference 'Child Well-Being in Rich and Transition Countries: Are Children in Growing Danger of Social Exclusion?', Luxembourg, October 1–2, 1999.

Sørensen, A. (1994), 'Women's Economic Risk and the Economic Position of Single Mothers', *European Sociological Review 10*: 173–88.

—— and Trappe, H. (1995), 'The Persistence of Gender Inequality in Earnings in the German Democratic Republic', *American Sociological Review 60*: 398–406.

Staat, M. and Wagenhals, G. (1996), 'Single mothers: A review', *Journal of Population Economics, 9*: 131–40.

Statistisches Bundesamt (1997), Datenreport 1997. Zahlung und Fakten über die Bundesrepublik Deutschland, Bonn: Bundeszentrale für politische Bildung.

Trappe, H. and Rosenfeld, R. A. (1999), 'How do children matter? A comparison of gender earnings inequality for young adults in the former East Germany and the former West Germany'. In: T. van der Lippe and L. van Dijk (eds), *Women's Employment in a Comparative Perspective: Integrating Micro and Macro Approaches*, New York: Aldine de Gruyter.

Wagner, S. (1996), 'Einelternfamilien in Grossbritannien und Deutschland: Struktureller Rahmen und Lebensverhältnisse', *Zeitschrift für Familienforschung, 8*: 46–78.

Wagner, G., Burkhauser, R. V., and Behringer, F. (1993), 'The English Language Public Use File of the German Socioeconomic Panel', *Journal of Human Resources, 28*: 429–33.

6

Divorce and Professional Careers in Russia During the Transition Towards Market Economy

PATRICK FESTY, IRINA KORTCHAGINA, OLGA MOURATCHEVA, AND LIDIA PROKOFIEVA

Russian society has for decades shown a blend of archaism and modernism which contrasts with the industrialized countries of the West. The modern features include women's very high educational achievements and their systematic participation in the labour force, as well as an exceptionally high divorce level which was reached long before Sweden, Great Britain, or other countries followed suit. These elements are brought together in the present study, in which men's and women's career patterns during married life, then after a divorce, are compared, and the implications of the economic and political upheavals of the 1990s are investigated.

WOMEN'S ACTIVITY IN RUSSIA: THE CHANGES DURING THE TRANSITION PERIOD

The ongoing transition from a State-driven economy to a market economy has profound implications for Russian society at large. Prior to the reforms, the economic system was totally dominated by the public sector and there was zero unemployment. The State policy privileged qualifications for women and encouraged them to work. In the late 1980s, the proportion gainfully employed or students among working-age women as well as men was 90 per cent. And in 1989 46 per cent of working women had a higher or middle technical level of education versus only 34 per cent of men.[1] Women were used to leading two lives at once, professional and domestic (surveys reported that working women spent an average of 40 hours a week on household chores and childcare). The lack of services to lighten the family burden meant that most women could not compete seriously with men in the labour market. A *de facto* professional segregation existed, with women opting for jobs that left them time and strength to perform their domestic tasks. These jobs were generally in education, the health service, trade, light industry or textiles, the sectors offering the lowest wages and the dimmest career prospects (Babaeva 1996; Grouzdeva and Tchertichina 1983; Rochin 1996).

[1] The 1989 census results: *Goskomstat Rossii* [Russian State Statistics Committee], (1995), *Sozialnaya sfera Rossii* [Russian Social Sphere], Statistical data.

Table 6.1. *Employment Status of the Working-age Population in Russia, 1993–98 (%)*

	Total	Men	Women
1993			
Gainfully employed	76.6	78.2	74.8
Unemployed	4.2	4.3	4.2
Students (full-time)	5.0	3.8	6.2
Retirement or disablement pensioners	8.2	8.7	7.8
Other (incl. housewives)	6.0	5.0	7.0
Total	100.0	100.0	100.0
(Population, thousands)	(83,700)	(43,500)	(40,200)
1998			
Gainfully employed	65.7	67.7	63.5
Unemployed	9.8	10.1	9.4
Students (full-time)	9.4	9.2	9.8
Retirement and disablement pensioners	4.7	6.1	3.1
Other (incl. housewives)	10.4	6.9	14.2
Total	100.0	100.0	100.0
(Population, thousands)	(83,655)	(43,695)	(39,960)

Source: Surveys of Russian population on the Problem of Employment in October 1993, October 1998 (Goskomstat Rossii; methodology of ILO).

When the reforms were introduced in the early 1990s, Russian society and labour structure underwent drastic changes, with the emergence of a private sector and the creation of new forms of gainful activity. The economic crisis disrupted a number of State-run concerns, so that official unemployment came on the scene, or cutbacks in work hours or unpaid leave. Men, first, began looking for side work (which was often deskilled) in the private sector or the underground economy. But in the absence of the conditions required for the creation of small private or mixed firms to absorb this manpower, unemployment has continued to grow. In the Employment Survey conducted in August 1999, only 6 per cent of working women and 8 per cent of working men were not employees (0.6 per cent of women and 1.2 per cent of men were workers on own account).

Between 1993 and 1998, the years our two surveys were conducted (see further), the proportions of working-age men and women in gainful employment dropped by more than ten percentage points (Table 6.1). The rise in official unemployment only accounts for part of this figure: the student populations have also grown, a classic response in times of crisis when continuing to study becomes an alternative to unemployment. The observed increase in the proportion of housewives may also be a form of unemployment in disguise: women who have lost their job take longer than men to find another one (50 per cent wait for more than a year[2]), and some, disheartened, stop looking for work and become homemakers.

[2] Survey on the Problems of Employment, Moscow, *Goskomstat Rossii*, August 1999, p. 59.

In addition, heightened discrimination against women in the workplace has widened the salary gap between men and women. When the prestige and remunerations of a particular sector (such as banking and insurance) are enhanced by the market economy, women specialists are replaced by men: women held 85.8 per cent of jobs in this sector in 1992, but only 71.4 per cent in 1998.[3]

THE RUSSIAN FAMILY: FROM TRADITION TO CRISIS

Russian family life is marked by an apparent contradiction: marriage is popular and divorce is frequent. This can no doubt be explained by a third element, the extended family, which cocoons the couple and their children in a dense network of presences and solidarities formed by parents, grandparents, aunts, uncles, cousins and so on.

Marriage in Russia was very early and very frequent until the 1990s: 95 per cent of the population got married, at age 20–22 on average for women and 23–24 for men (Avdeev and Monnier 1996). This is in keeping with a longstanding division between Eastern Europe and Western Europe, separated by a line running from Saint Petersburg (Leningrad) to Trieste. In France under the Ancien Régime, for instance, men did not marry until the eldest son had inherited, by his father's death, the land he needed to set up a family. The radically different system of exploitation and inheritance in Russia meant that nothing prevented early marriage (Avdeev *et al.* 1999). One generation did not take over from another, but different generations coexisted. Son did not follow father, but collaborated with him, and by marrying he could increase the manpower needed on the farm. In the extended family, the generations pooled their resources, without any competition or rivalry over succession. Early marriage knitted successive generations together, with the younger members marrying while the older ones were still alive and wedded. So this dense family network both resulted from and encouraged early marriage. In more recent history, the land has lost this role of estate on which reproduction hinged. The housing shortage has replaced land capacity restrictions. The interweaving of generations has become coresidence in the same house or flat. Today, more than half of young couples spend some of their first years of married life cohabiting in their parents' or in-laws' home. And more generally, exchanges of goods, services or money within the family have helped improve the young couple's well-being in a sometimes difficult economic and material environment (Gessat-Anstett 1999).

Since the Second World War, this early marriage pattern has gone together with a high frequency of divorce. As early as the mid-1960s—10 years ahead of Scandinavia, for instance—divorce became a straightforward procedure in the Soviet Union, and one marriage in three ended this way. An upturn in the 1970s and 1980s has brought the proportion to one in two today; an estimated 60 per cent of urban marriages now break down. The personal and social consequences of such widespread divorce are made bearable by the support given to divorcees and their children by the family

[3] The Economic Yearbook of the Russian Federation, *Moscow, Goskomstat Rossii*, 1999, p. 116.

network. Their drop in living standards is often softened by material aid from kin, notably when they do not remarry. Since lone mothers have some social advantages, it is more often men who turn to their parents for refuge after they have left their conjugal home. In addition, the presence of grandparents provides young children with the stability of an extended family that continues to pass on its values and behaviours; this is important at a time when the nuclear family breaks down (Eliseeva *et al.* 1999).

The Russian family system has undergone deep changes since 1990, concomitant with the radical transformation of the political, economic, and social environment. Births and marriages have fallen while the proportion of births to unmarried parents has grown, suddenly echoing the trends previously recorded in Western Europe (Avdeer and Monnier 1999).

The transfer of housing property from the State to the occupiers has had little impact, in the short term, on the population's living conditions. It has merely permitted the emergence of a market in which some goods are exchanged at exorbitant prices—at least in the cities—, thereby intensifying the housing shortage and the inequalities. The role of the extended family may be slightly enhanced in terms of assistance provided to young couples and divorcees. But the end of the system of government housing attributions has closed the door on the possibility young couples had of obtaining their own home after a number of years spent living with their elders. After acting in favour of marriage, which was a necessary condition for couples to obtain a dwelling of their own, the housing shortage now acts rather as a deterrent and encourages cohabitation instead. Marriage, insofar as it represents a wager on the future, is thus declining, while divorce is not.

But the day-to-day material or financial support provided by the family is another matter. The crisis of the 1990s, which culminated in 1998, has curbed the generosity on which transfers between generations depend. The sudden drop in incomes, in contrast with the slow erosion of the housing stock, was immediately felt by all. No generation has escaped the consequences, and the parents' capacity to help their adult children has been reduced at the same time as the latter's needs have become more acute (Eliseeva *et al.* 1999).

The economic crisis that is accompanying Russia's transition towards a market economy may well be undermining the foundations on which its society has stood for centuries.

PROFESSIONAL MOBILITY, DIVORCE, AND ECONOMIC CRISIS IN RUSSIA

In the context of a State-run economy where male and female labour resources were utilized in full (or at least paid as if they were) and a strong family solidarity rallied round couples throughout their children's upbringing years, the interactions between family and working life were stated in quite different terms from those generally found in the West. Even today, the adjusting factor in the West is essentially mothers' participation rates, by number and age of children, family type (two- or single-parent), the requirements of the economy, social mores, the support provided by family and social solidarity. In the Soviet Union, where both men and women were continuously employed, it was their professional mobility that played this role and revealed gender inequalities in the family burden borne by husbands and wives.

For these reasons, the contribution of family studies conducted in the West is often limited for understanding the mechanisms at play in the Soviet family and its relationship with the labour market. We shall, however, refer to three approaches. The first is based on the concept that gains and losses linked to marital and family life are unequally shared by men and women. According to T. Parsons (Parsons 1949), wives take on the responsibilities of home and offspring *so that* their husbands can enable the family to benefit from the higher income they derive from their work; less radical, Dex (1987) and Waite (1980) show that husbands and wives do not have the same career mobility at the different stages of the family cycle and that, overall, women's upward mobility only brings them back to their starting level, whereas men's upward mobility is generally continuous and cumulative. A second approach, which also refers to Parsons' functionalism, is based on the interactions between spouses: competition within the family leads women to hold back their careers, or risk divorce (Philliber and Vannoy-Hiller 1990), while the preference for homogamy and the pooling of resources within the couple lead careers to move in parallel, with too much divergence being a factor of marriage breakdown (Hornung and McCullough 1981). Having examined the situation in the European Union member states, Smits *et al.* (1996) conclude that the first mechanism predominates in families with lower socio-economic status and the second one in families with high socio-economic status. Third and last, men's and women's very unequal participation in the different sectors of the economy and in top positions, together with discrepancies in salaries, lead to a hypothesis of gender discrimination, based on the economic theories of human capital or labour market segmentation or on sociocultural theories. Anker (1997) demonstrates the contribution of the latter, by establishing a close correlation between the most predominantly female professions and the common stereotypes about women's qualities.

We shall consequently analyse our survey material to verify whether, during their married life, men's and women's professional careers run in parallel or to men's advantage, whether there is a correlation between the two careers, whether the division of family responsibilities can explain any divergences between men's and women's careers or whether there is a broader-based mechanism of gender discrimination. However, we have chosen to focus our study on the history of divorced couples before and after their separation, so that this separation becomes revealing of how the marriage functioned: the responses of spouses looking back on their marriage will throw light on why they chose to accept or reject married life, and their living conditions after the breakdown will reflect the consequences of their decision. We shall add to the above verifications, therefore, those resulting from a comparison of careers (of same men and women) during and after marriage, to evaluate the weight of the union by measuring the impact of its breakdown.

Even less than marriage, has the impact of marriage breakdown been the object of observations and theorizations that might provide a framework for analysing the situation in Russia. Only divorce-related changes in living standards have been studied in recent years. Divorce is a factor of impoverishment. Once separated, both former spouses experience a drop in living standards, and this is more acute for women than for men. The divorcees who remain single are durably affected by this regression, while those who form a new union recover the level they had when they were married. This pattern satisfies a simple logic: living as a twosome (or more, if there are children) permits 'scale economies' and gives each spouse a higher standard of living than if they were on their own. Transfers between former spouses (alimony) and the different state allowances contribute only modestly to making up the loss (Duncan and Hoffmann 1985; Festy 1990; McManus and Diprete 1999).

Change in living standards after a separation is related to the work patterns investigated in the present study. The questions that were relevant within marriage can again be asked, but sometimes inversely. Now that men are deprived of the protection marriage gave them, is their upward mobility slowed down? Do women, having an even heavier family burden than before, continue to lose ground to men or do they benefit from official discrimination in their favour?

Our survey design (see below) is such that the impact of divorce and the impact of the economic and political upheavals that have shaken Russia since 1990 knit together in the inquiry. To what extent does the transition towards a free market economy, like the transition to a new life after marriage, modify professional careers? Does marital breakdown create groups that are more fragile and less able to face up to the consequences of the economic crisis? And finally, the question underlying all the rest, are men and women affected differently?

THE DATA

Two retrospective surveys on divorcees were taken in Russia, with the objective of studying the impact of separation on men's and women's living conditions. A range of variables was selected to encompass the situations of both spouses, their relationships with one other and with their families, at time of marriage, of separation and of survey. Biographical data were gathered on successive unions, birth and outcome of children, residential history, own or spouse's professional career.

The first survey, taken in 1993, concerned 1,215 women who had divorced between 1975 and 1993, and the second, in 1998, concerned 1,249 men who had divorced between 1986 and 1998. The survey design used the same stratified random sampling procedure in both cases. Six strata were defined by divorce level and one town or city was selected in each; within this same sampling frame, a probability sample of divorced women, in 1993, and men, in 1998, was drawn. After weighting, the sample provided a satisfactory scale model of the urban population of 'European' Russia. Thus, *we are not dealing with pairs of ex-spouses*, but with separate samples of divorced men and women; however, respondents were interviewed about former spouse's life in the same terms as about their own. In addition, the sampling procedure provided two samples that matched but for three points:

- the sample of women covered 18 divorce years and the sample of men only 12 years (we consequently reduced the female sample to 867 women who had divorced in the last 12 years);
- the two surveys were taken five years apart; this is a lot in a context of rapid change (in particular recent years), but little for times of slow change (the past, the surveys being retrospective);
- only women present in 1993 and men present in 1998 in the town where they had divorced were interviewed (but information was collected on ex-wives and ex-husbands, even when they had emigrated).

Taking these reservations into account, when we compared men's and women's responses concerning their own and their spouse's professional mobility, the consistency was generally good. Most of the weaknesses concerned the post-divorce period (after 1993 for women, 1998 for men), owing to lack of information on former spouses. But for the period of married life before the divorce, men's and women's answers tended to tally.

To estimate the level and direction of the spouses' socio-occupational mobility during and after marriage, we constructed an indicator taking into account changes in educational achievement, occupation, position, industry, and career breaks. On this basis, four types of career profile were defined:

(1) Downwardly mobile
(2) Level
(3) Slightly upwardly mobile
(4) Strongly upwardly mobile.

The category was determined essentially by changes in educational attainments and qualifications, on the one hand, and job responsibility, on the other. Unemployment or women's career breaks were considered as downward mobility, as was deskilling: a highly qualified expert (with higher education—a works engineer, for instance) had a manual or service job (car salesman or repairs worker).

A level career is when there was no progress in educational attainment or job responsibility, or when a change of industry or occupation had maintained the same level of qualification.

A career is upwardly mobile when, during or after marriage, the person had completed a cycle of higher education or progressed at work to become a company manager or head clerk, etc., or when a manual worker had entered the highly skilled category.

DIVORCE, A FACTOR OF PROFESSIONAL MOBILITY?

Work experience plays an important role in professional mobility, for men and women alike. The longer the marriage had lasted before the separation, the greater

Table 6.2. *Men's Professional Mobility During Marriage, by Duration 1998 Survey (percentage)*

Mobility	Marriage duration (years)			
	0–4	5–9	10–14	15+
(1) Downward	10.4	16.1	13.5	8.8
(2) Level	66.7	48.2	38.0	30.4
(3) Slightly upward	12.0	14.7	25.3	31.3
(4) Strongly upward	10.9	21.0	23.1	29.5
Total	100.0	100.0	100.0	100.0
(*n*)	(442)	(353)	(229)	(217)
Net mobility: (3 + 4) − 1	+12.5	+19.6	+34.9	+52.0

Source: Own calculations based on Survey of Russian population on the Problem of Employment in October 1998 (Goskomstat Rossii; methodology of ILO).

the progress reported. The difference between the cases of upward mobility (slight or strong) and downward mobility among men whose marriage had lasted less than five years was 12.5 per cent (Table 6.2); this rises to 19.6 per cent at 5–9 years, 34.9 per cent at 10–14 years and 52 per cent at durations of 15 years or more.

To measure the impact of divorce on professional mobility, it is necessary to consider same working-life durations, and compare persons who have and have not divorced within a same lapse of time. We chose not to take non-divorced married couples as reference population, since people who remain married and those who eventually divorce do not become different just at time of divorce, but may differ throughout married life and sometimes even earlier. The discrepancies between the two groups may thus prove insurmountable, whatever the level of *ceteris paribus*; they are less revealing of the impact of divorce than of its selective nature. Instead, therefore, we selected as reference population a sub-group of divorcees, those whose divorce did not occur until they had been married for 10–19 years. Their professional careers between marriage and the eve of their divorce will be compared to those of people who, within the same lapse of time, experienced marriage, divorce and a post-divorce period up to survey. When we considered a lapse of less than ten years, very few respondents had already experienced marriage, divorce and post-divorce, and above twenty years, we found very few of our future divorcees were still married.

Among the persons already divorced at time of survey, we distinguish between those living in a new union and those living singly. This will allow us to verify whether a new union re-establishes the 'partnership effects' or whether it defines a specific sub-group of divorcees.

The gender comparison underlying this study will require only a minimum number of statistical controls, since divorced men and divorced women form two paired groups, whether it is a question of former spouses, as described by the other spouse in 1993 or 1998, or of the two samples of men and women which are independent but representative of the same population. Whenever possible, we shall match spouses' answers from one survey or the other (almost indiscriminately). But even

Table 6.3. *Inactivity at Time of Marriage and 10–19 Years Later, by Marital Status at Latter Date (1993)*

Inactivity		**Marital status**		
		Still married	**Already divorced***	
			In a new union	**Single**
At time of marriage	Women	20.9% (230)	28.6% (147)	22.1% (285)
	Men	10.4% (230)	18.4% (125)	16.3% (307)
10–19 years later	Women	2.6% (230)	10.2% (147)	5.6% (285)
	Men	4.4% (230)	4.0% (125)	7.5% (307)

* In 1993, the men 'in a new union' are those reported by their former spouse as having had this intention.
Source: Own calculations based on Survey of Russian population on the Problem of Employment in October 1993 (Goskomstat Rossii; methodology of ILO).

when it proves necessary to compare men's responses in 1998 and women's responses in 1993, it will be superfluous to enter socio-economic attributes for the comparison to be relevant.

Women's career profiles, when measured under the same conditions as those of men, are shown to differ substantially from men's. The same can be said of the impact divorce has on these profiles. When they got married, more than 20 per cent of the women were economically inactive, that is, between six and ten percentage points more than men (Table 6.3). This is above all an age effect, since most of this inactivity is related to education. Indeed, Russians marry early, and those who marry earliest are particularly prone to divorce.

The situation 10–19 years on is very different. Men are more often inactive[4] than women in two of the situations out of three. The differences are not significant, but they highlight the particularity of divorcees who have formed a new union: only 4.0 per cent of men were inactive vs 10.2 per cent of women. Divorced women living with a new partner are far more likely to be inactive than other women.

Another clear gender differential is that women who were working when they married *and* 10–19 years later have often made less progress in their careers than men (Table 6.4). There is little difference in this respect between the women who were married throughout the period and those who had experienced marriage, divorce and post-divorce, or between divorced women living with or without a new partner. By contrast, there is a cleavage between men still married and those already divorced. It is as though divorce put a brake on men's upward mobility, but had little or no impact on women.

To be more exact, there is much less upward mobility among men who remain single after a divorce, whereas the impact of divorce is slight on men who enter a new union. This pattern is not found among women: those who remain single after a divorce are as likely to progress as those who have not yet divorced. The careers of

[4] The term 'inactive' is taken here in the broader sense, to include unemployment (it encompasses all categories in Table 6.1 except 'gainfully employed').

Table 6.4. *Net Mobility During the 10–19 Years Following Marriage. Men and Women who were Working at Beginning and End of this Period, by Marital Status at End (1993)*

Gender	Marital status		
	Still married	Already divorced*	
		In a new union	Single
Women	+19.0% (179)	+15.6% (83)	+19.9% (212)
Men	+37.2% (196)	+31.8% (66)	+20.8% (148)

* The men 'in a new union' are those reported by their former spouse as having had this intention.
Source: Own calculations based on Survey of Russian population on the Problem of Employment in October 1993 (Goskomstat Rossii; methodology of ILO).

still married and divorced-repartnered women lag far behind those of men in the corresponding situations, but not the careers of divorcees remaining on their own. Thus, men's advantage concerns those who have spent most time in a union (with wife or new partner).

The information reported by men in 1998 on former spouse's career confirm these observations. During the economic crisis, women's careers have been curtailed in the same proportion as men's and the gender gap remains the same. As previously, women's mobility is not greatly affected by marital status. A comparison of the situations in 1993 and 1998 will be made at the end of this study.

In short, divorce and in particular remaining single after a divorce does not handicap women's careers in the same way as men's. On the other hand, men's careers are more upwardly mobile than women's during marriage and when a new union follows the divorce.

We shall now explore this last point and investigate the possibility that married life slows down women's careers by removing them for a time from the labour market, thereby jeopardizing their chances of promotion. We shall also investigate why men who remain single after a divorce form a group apart, all the more visibly so in 1998 because of the economic crisis.

IS WOMEN'S CAREER LAG DUE TO THEIR FAMILY RESPONSIBILITIES?

Men's careers move up as their marriage moves on. We have seen that the longer the marriage had lasted before the separation, the more likely men were to have experienced upward rather than downward mobility. The pattern is different for women: their mobility is similar to men's when the divorce occurred within five years of marriage (+10.2 per cent) but there is then little variation whether the marriage lasted 5–9, 10–14, or 15+ years (+29 or +30 per cent). Women's careers thus appear to stagnate after ten years marriage (Table 6.5).

Table 6.5. *Net Mobility Between Marriage and Separation, by Marriage Duration*

Duration (years)	Men (1998)	Women (1993)
0–4	+12.5% (442)	+10.2% (312)
5–9	+19.6% (353)	+28.7% (279)
10–14	+34.9% (229)	+28.6% (136)
15+	+52.0% (217)	+31.7% (164)

Source: Surveys of Russian population on the Problem of Employment in October 1993, October 1998 (Goskomstat Rossii; methodology of ILO).

Table 6.6. *Distribution of Spouses by Professional Mobility During Marriage (1998)*

Husband's mobility	Wife's mobility				
	Downward	Level	Slightly upward	Strongly upward	Total
(a) Duration of marriage: 0–9 years; n = 780					
Downward	2.9	6.2	1.7	1.9	12.7
Level	6.3	42.7	4.4	5.0	58.3
Slightly upward	2.1	7.8	1.5	2.1	13.5
Strongly upward	1.8	7.9	2.1	3.7	15.5
Total	13.1	64.6	9.6	12.7	100.0
(b) Duration of marriage: 10+ years; n = 433					
Downward	3.0	4.6	2.3	1.2	11.1
Level	6.9	18.0	4.4	5.3	34.6
Slightly upward	7.9	10.6	4.6	4.6	27.7
Strongly upward	3.5	9.0	3.9	10.2	26.6
Total	21.2	42.3	15.2	21.3	100.0

Source: Own calculations based on Survey of Russian population on the Problem of Employment in October 1998 (Goskomstat Rossii; methodology of ILO).

The information provided by respondents on their own *and their former spouse's* career allows us to compare the mobility of husbands and wives and measure any widening of the gap in the course of marriage.

In marriages dissolved within 10 years, men's and women's career profiles are very similar (Table 6.6(a)). Globally, men's careers move a little more frequently upward than women's and a little less frequently downward or with no change. In addition, there is a strong correlation between the spouses' careers. For instance, if we compare women whose careers regressed to those whose careers progressed sharply, the former's husbands (13.1 in Table 6.6(a)) show a barely more positive than negative mobility (3.9 versus 2.9), while the latter's husbands (12.7) show a more often positive and much more rarely negative trend (5.8 versus 1.9). Very generally speaking, and including the intermediate situations, the more favourable the wife's career profile, the more favourable the husband's.

This does not mean there are no divergences, but they are more or less equally distributed between advantages in favour of husbands and advantages in favour of wives, with the former being slightly more frequent. In 28 per cent of cases, men's careers had made more progress (above the diagonal in Table 6.6(a)), while in 21.3 per cent of cases the opposite was true (below the diagonal). The situations of pronounced disparity between husband and wife (a downward or level career versus a slightly or strongly upward career, shaded in the table) are only 11.8 per cent in favour of men and 8.6 per cent in favour of women.

Beyond the tenth year of marriage, such symmetry and correlation between men's and women's careers becomes obscured (Table 6.6(b)). In all, 54.3 per cent of men have moved ahead and 11.1 per cent have regressed, compared to 36.5 per cent and 21.2 per cent of women. Also, the correlations between husband's and wife's career are not so clear. It is true that men's careers fare better when their wife's career is strongly upward, but there is virtually no difference between the other situations: whether the wife's career is downward, level or slightly upward, men progress on average in much the same way.

Husbands' careers surpass wives' much more frequently than in the shorter marriages: 41.8 versus 28 per cent (above the diagonal), while the contrary is roughly as frequent, 22.4 versus 21.3 per cent (below the diagonal). The greatest differential in favour of men (shaded) now represents 20.4 per cent compared to 11.8 per cent in marriages not exceeding 10 years. The information collected from women in 1993 confirmed these findings: from the shortest to the longest marriage durations, the proportion of husbands who had moved far ahead in their careers increased almost twofold, whereas the cases where the wife had moved ahead remained almost constant.

Might career gaps between spouses be a factor of divorce, and consequently be over-represented in our surveys of divorcees?

Beyond the fact that surveys restricted to divorcees are inappropriate to measure divorce *factors*, none of our findings points in this direction. The divorced men questioned in 1998 about their own and their former spouse's dissatisfaction with partner's career, provided very similar responses whatever the career gap (15–20 per cent reported personal dissatisfaction, whether their wife's career was above, below or on a par with their own, while 31–35 per cent reported spouse dissatisfaction in the same situations).

Furthermore, household survey findings suggest that the curtailing of women's careers is not limited to divorcees but is a much more general problem of gender discrimination. In two household surveys taken in 1980 and 1989 in Taganrog, one of the towns which provided our samples of divorcees, the career disparities between men and women still married after 20 years echoed those in Table 6.6(b): in 1980, men had much better careers in 25.7 per cent of couples, and women in only 11.7 per cent (in 1989, the proportions were 21.3 and 5.0 per cent, respectively) (Prokofieva 1985, 1991).

The most plausible hypothesis would appear to be that family responsibilities slow down mother's careers during married life, whether the marriage continues or ends in divorce.

In fact, the presence of children has a notable impact on women's careers during the early years of marriage (Table 6.7). Between marriage and divorce (occurring

Table 6.7. *Women's Activity at Time of Marriage and Separation by Marriage Duration and Family Size (1993)*

Women's activity	Marriage duration (years)			
	0–5		6+	
	Childless	1 child or more	1 child	2+ children
(1) active at time of marriage	67.6%	74.4%	78.0%	77.3%
(2) and active at separation	61.6%	53.3%	75.5%	74.3%
(1)–(2)/(1)	0.09%	0.28%	0.03%	0.04%
(*n*)	(99)	(289)	(278)	(198)

Source: Own calculations based on Survey of Russian population on the Problem of Employment in October 1993 (Goskomstat Rossii; methodology of ILO).

Table 6.8. *Women's Activity at Time of Marriage and of Separation by Marriage Duration and Age of Youngest Child (1993)*

Women's activity	Marriage duration (years)			
	0–5		6+	
	Age of youngest child			
	0.2	3–6	0.2	3–6
(1) active at time of marriage	71.9%	78.6%	75.7%	70.9%
(2) and active at separation	41.0%	73.8%	62.2%	68.2%
(1)–(2)/(1)	0.43%	0.06%	0.18%	0.04%
(*n*)	(178)	(103)	(37)	(151)

Source: Own calculations based on Survey of Russian population on the Problem of Employment in October 1993 (Goskomstat Rossii; methodology of ILO).

within five years), 28 per cent of previously active women who started a family stopped working; of those who remained childless, only 9 per cent did so. At longer marriage durations, the distinction between mothers and non-mothers becomes meaningless, since the latter account for only 4 per cent of future divorcees. Family size is more pertinent, but there is no significant difference between mothers-of-one and mothers-of-two-or-more. Thus, childcare affects women's activity in early marriage, but this effect subsequently disappears.

This might be an effect of children's age, since they are obviously younger in short-lived marriages and older in those that have lasted. But women's activity rates by age of youngest child only go part way to confirming this hypothesis (Table 6.8). In marriages that lasted less than 6 years, 43 per cent of mothers of under-3s had stopped work, versus only 6 per cent of mothers with older children (3–6). In the

Table 6.9. *Mobility Between Marriage and Separation of Women Working at Time of Marriage by Marriage Duration and Family Size (1993)*

Mobility	Marriage duration (years)			
	0–5		6+	
	Childless	1 child or more	1 child	2+ children
(1) Downward	10.5%	13.5%	12.0%	16.3%
(2) Level	74.6%	72.1%	57.6%	53.6%
(3) Upward	14.9%	14.4%	30.4%	30.1%
(3) − (1)	**+4.4%**	**+0.9%**	**+18.4%**	**+13.8%**
(*n*)	(67)	(215)	(217)	(153)

Source: Own calculations based on Survey of Russian population on the Problem of Employment in October 1993 (Goskomstat Rossii; methodology of ILO).

longer-lasting marriages, the contrast remains but is less sharp: 18 per cent of mothers of infants versus 4 per cent of mothers with older children.

The presence of fewer infants of younger ages cannot explain, therefore, on its own that the family burden weighs less heavily on women's activity in the longer-lasting marriages. The marriage duration is *per se* an independent factor in women's activity. This conclusion is confirmed by the fact that the association between age of youngest child and mother's labour force participation is very different once the divorce has taken place: 0–12 years after the separation, 79 per cent of mothers of under-3s[5] have left work, compared to 11 per cent of mothers of 3–6-year-olds.[6] Far higher than when the marriage was still ongoing, even when it was a short one, these proportions underline how differently a same family burden can weigh at different stages in the family cycle.

It is hardly surprising, therefore, that the professional mobility of women who were already in the labour force when they got married is not much affected by the presence and number of children, however long the marriage lasted (Table 6.9). In short-lived marriages, the upward mobility of childless women is 4.4 per cent in excess of downward mobility, while the difference is 0.9 among mothers. In longer-lasting marriages, the excess is 18.4 per cent for mothers-of-one and 13.8 per cent for mothers-of-two-or-more. The family burden effect takes second place to the marriage duration effect. Likewise, after divorce, women's career profiles are not affected by family size.

Even if there is clearly an effect of familial factors on married women's careers, this is not *the* explanation for the divergences between husband's and wife's career profiles. The stagnation observed in women's careers after 10 years marriage, while their husbands continued to progress, does not tie in with this explanation. It can be argued that a gender discrimination weighs upon women's jobs and slows down their progress once they reach the higher rungs of the professional ladder.

[5] At time of separation.

[6] Data not tabulated here.

A REGRESSION MODEL FOR MOBILITY DURING MARRIAGE

The associations noted so far between the professional mobility of former spouses and a number of intuitively selected variables, needed next to be tested in a more elaborate statistical model capable of isolating the role of each factor independently of the others. A multiple regression analysis was performed to model a relationship of the form $y_{x_1x_2\ldots x_k} = f\ (x_1,x_2,\ldots,x_k)$, where y measures professional mobility between marriage and separation and x_i ($i = 1, 2,\ldots, k$) the independent variables liable to explain the different y values found in our samples. The model was applied to the 1993 female sample and the 1998 male sample data relative to respondents and their former spouses (Table 6.10). This enabled us to collate the information provided by two different respondents and to compare, as we have done systematically so far, the situations of men and women (Tables 6.11 and 6.12).

Table 6.10. *Description of the Variables Entered in the Regression Model**

Dependent variable	Job adequated to qualifications
Career profile	No
Downward	Yes
Level	Work hours
Slightly upward	A few hours a week
Strongly upward	Part-time
Independent variables, socio-economic	Full-time
Educational level	*Independent variables, familial*
Primary	Living with parents
Vocational	Throughout marriage
Secondary	Part of marriage
Technical	None of marriage
Higher	Dwelling at time of separation
Change in educational level	Temporary dwelling
No	Room in communal dwelling
Yes	Dwelling shared with parents
Occupational status	Independent dwelling
Unemployed	Cocaregiver support
Military service	No
Student	Yes
Manual worker	Birth of child(ren)
Clerical or sales	No
Middle-level	Yes
Trade	New conjugal status
Managerial	Married
Sector	Cohabiting
Public enterprise	Single
Private enterprise	Alimony
Independent employer	No
Own-account	Yes

* and in the model for mobility after divorce (Table 6.16).

Table 6.11. *Regression Estimates for Men's Careers from Marriage to Separation*

Independent variables	1993	1998
Socio-economic variables		
Level of education	0.235***	0.155***
Change in educational level	0.239***	0.73***
Occupational status at marriage	−0.267***	−0.278***
Sector at time of separation	0.235***	0.328***
Spouse's career		
Wife's career	0.16***	0.117***
Familial variables		
Living with parents	0.142***	0.173***
Dwelling at time of separation	0.045**	0.04**
Cocaregiver support	0.167**	n.s.
Birth of child(ren)	0.275*	n.s.
Duration variables		
Age at separation	0.026***	0.026***
Constant	2.245***	1.504***
Summary statistics		
R^2	0.308	0.306
F (significance level)	46.65 (0.00)	48.90 (0.00)
n	1,026	1,197

*** $p<0.01$; ** $p<0.05$; * $p<0.10$; n.s.: nonsignificant.

Source: Surveys of Russian population on the Problem of Employment in October 1993, October 1998 (Goskomstat Rossii; methodology of ILO).

There is remarkable consistency between the findings of the two surveys as derived from respondent's or spouse's answers, whether we consider the summary statistic R^2 or individual regression coefficients.

Two types of variables—socio-economic and familial—are associated with men's and women's professional mobility during marriage. Multiple regression allows each explanatory variable to be measured independently after the action of all others has been taken into account.

The socio-economic variables form a compact group traditionally associated with career patterns. Their impact is in most cases very similar for women and men. For instance, the higher the level of education, the more positive the professional mobility. Continuing to study during marriage also leads to a notable gain in terms of social position. These effects are not unusual in the industrial world, nor is the association between occupational status at time of marriage and subsequent promotion: the higher the starting level, the more limited the upward mobility will be.

The relationship is no doubt an inverse one between professional mobility and the extent to which women felt their job matched their qualifications: the fit was closest for careers that had progressed most since marriage (the woman's appreciation being

Table 6.12. *Regression Estimates for Women's Careers from Marriage to Separation*

Independent variables	1993	1998
Socio-economic variables		
Level of education	0.152***	0.187***
Change in educational level	0.749***	n.a.
Occupational status at marriage	−0.391***	−0.220***
Sector at time of marriage	−0.235***	n.s.
Sector at time of separation	n.s.	0.353***
Job adequated to qualifications	0.239***	n.a.
Spouse's career		
Husband's career	0.129***	0.111***
Familial variables		
Living with parents	n.s.	0.025***
Cocaregiver support	0.114**	n.s.
Duration variables		
Age of youngest child at separation	0.026	0.026***
Constant	3.34***	2.96***
Summary statistics		
R^2	0.345	0.309
F (significance level)	62.89 (0.00)	85.07 (0.00)
n	954	989

*** $p < 0.01$; ** $p < 0.05$; * $p < 0.10$; n.s.: nonsignificant; n.a.: data not available.

Source: Surveys of Russian population on the Problem of Employment in October 1993, October 1998 (Goskomstat Rossii; methodology of ILO).

made *a posteriori*, at time of survey). This association only concerns women, since only women were asked this question, in 1993.

This set of relationships between career and socio-economic status forms a backcloth against which the other variables stand out. First, the association between spouses' careers which is revealed by both surveys: in 1993, by the women's responses concerning themselves and their ex-husbands, and in 1998 by men's responses concerning themselves and their ex-wives. This confirms one of the hypotheses presented in the introduction, referring to homogamy and the pooling of resources within marriage. Simple cross-tabulations have demonstrated, however, that the correlation is strong at short marriage durations but becomes toned down in longer unions.

The familial variables form another group but which is much less compact than the previous one, and less evenly balanced by gender. For men, living with parents during marriage is associated with lesser upward mobility, as though having their own home were a spur to getting their career off the ground; this is confirmed, though less strongly, by the correlation with dwelling type at time of separation. An association is also found between women's careers and duration of cohabitation with parents, but it is an inverse one: the longer the cohabitation had lasted, the more positive the effect. This no doubt reflects the support provided by parents' presence, freeing their daughter for professional activity. Backing this up is the positive effect of having a cocaregiver—someone to share the childminding—but this effect is neither systematic (it is found in one survey only) nor very significant.

It is thus confirmed that, once the socio-economic factors and the association between men's and women's careers have been taken into account, the familial variables, and particularly the responsibilities of motherhood, have relatively little effect on women's careers. The strongest impact is that of age of youngest child at time of separation: older children made mothers more likely to have an upward career. In fact, this indicates a familial effect and a duration effect, with younger children indicating shorter marriages and therefore less time to achieve promotion. For men, the latter point is revealed better by their own age at separation.

PROFESSIONAL MOBILITY AND REMARRIAGE[7]

At time of survey, that is, up to 12 years after their divorce, 30 per cent of women respondents were living in a new union and 70 per cent were living alone—in the sense of without a partner, though generally with children. The proportions were quite different for men: 52 per cent had formed a new union while only 48 per cent were alone, without a partner and most often without children. In other words, remarriage is much more frequent among divorced men than among divorced women.

These different remarriage patterns are associated with different career profiles. Women who remarry make less career progress than those who stay single (i.e., without a partner) after a divorce. The divergence is slight, however: the 1993 survey found a net mobility (upward minus downward) of 6.3 points for the former and 8.9 for the latter. The situation is the opposite for men and the differences go much deeper. Aggravated by the economic crisis culminating at time of male survey in 1998, net mobility was negative for men—more regressions than promotions—and amounted to—3.3 points for those in a new union and—16.1 for those remaining single, a spectacular recession.

How should such gender asymmetry in the relationship between conjugal status and career profile following a divorce be interpreted? Does it mean that living together is more profitable to some than to others, or does a given career profile affect the remarriage odds?

Before their divorce, those men who were going to stay single were already laggards careerwise (Table 6.13). In an economic context that was far better than it would be after their divorce, the future singles had a net mobility of +18.7 (difference between promotions and regressions), which fell far behind the achievements of those who would marry again (+31.9). Thus, their poorer post-divorce performance was bespoken by their poorer performance during marriage. In contrast, there is no trace of any difference in women's careers during marriage between future single and future remarried.

[7] For convenience, 'remarriage' is used here to denote new unions, whether marriages or cohabitational unions.

Table 6.13. *Men's and Women's Net Mobility During Marriage According to Subsequent Conjugal Status*

Gender	Conjugal status	
	Will form a new union	Will stay single
Men (1998 survey)	+31.9%	+18.7%
(*n*)	(643)	(598)
Women (1993 survey)	+24.2%	+22.1%
(*n*)	(268)	(618)

Source: Surveys of Russian population on the Problem of Employment in October 1993, October 1998 (Goskomstat Rossii; methodology of ILO).

Table 6.14. *Men's and Women's Net Mobility after Separation by New Conjugal Status and Mobility During Marriage*

Men (1998 survey) %			Women (1993 survey) %		
Mobility during marriage	New union	Single	Mobility during marriage	New union	Single
Downward	+16.9	+24.9	Downward	+22.6	+14.3
Level	−2.0	−14.4	Level	+7.1	+5.8
Upward	−3.1	−18.2	Upward	+5.3	+7.0

Source: Surveys of Russian population on the Problem of Employment in October 1993, October 1998 (Goskomstat Rossii; methodology of ILO).

Table 6.15. *Proportions of Men and Women who Remarried after a Divorce, by Career Profile During Marriage*

Men (1998 survey)			Women (1993 survey)		
Mobility during marriage	*n*	Proportion remarried %	Mobility during marriage	*n*	Proportion remarried %
Downward	60/153	39.2	Downward	31/108	28.7
Level	318/618	51.5	Level	141/468	30.1
Upward	265/470	56.4	Upward	96/310	31.0

Source: Surveys of Russian population on the Problem of Employment in October 1993, October 1998 (Goskomstat Rossii; methodology of ILO).

This does not mean, however, that men, but not women, duplicated after their divorce their previous career profile. Whatever their new conjugal situation, the same pattern is observed: men whose careers had regressed during marriage progressed afterwards, and those whose careers had moved forward or stagnated during marriage subsequently regressed (Table 6.14).

The relationship becomes clearer when we consider the frequency of remarriage by career profile during marriage (Table 6.15). Almost 54 per cent of men whose careers had been stable or moved upward were remarried, versus only 39 per cent of those whose careers had moved down. While there is little difference between level, slightly upward and strongly upward mobility, there is a sharp contrast with regard to downward mobility. It is these downsliders, who are under-represented among the new husbands and over-represented among the men remaining single, who explain the difference between the two groups. Among divorced women, on the contrary, there is no association between past career and new partnership: the frequency of remarriage is the same whatever the type of career profile.

For a same career history, divorced men then diverge clearly according to whether they remarry or remain single. The selective role of remarriage, which tends to frown on unemployed divorcees, plays a minor part compared to the handicap that living alone appears to represent for working men.[8]

A REGRESSION MODEL FOR MOBILITY AFTER DIVORCE

As previously for the study of professional mobility within marriage, a regression model was fitted to the survey data to measure the effect of each variable on men's and women's careers, independently of the action of the other variables.[9] The models proved even more sensitive to the information coverage than the cross-tabulations presented earlier. The frequency of 'don't knows' in response to questions on former spouse's situation at time of survey led us to consider only the information concerning respondents themselves: women in 1993 and men in 1998 (Table 6.16). The effects of the economic crisis on divorced men and women respectively will, therefore, be addressed in the next section.

The economic determinants again form a compact group that is decisive for explaining career differentials after divorce. This is all the truer for women, in part because some variables relative to present job (adequated to qualifications, work hours) were only collected in the survey on women. For the main part, the socioeconomic factors of women's careers continue after the divorce with no notable discontinuity. Level of education remains a positively discriminating factor: the higher it was, the more marked the progressions. Occupational status at separation correlates negatively, since women who were in the least favourable position at time of divorce held a greater potential for improvement. The pattern is somewhat different for men: education has no significant effect, while the impact of occupational status at survey more than offsets the symmetrical effect of status at separation among women. The economic crisis is no doubt much more patent in the men's survey, taken five years after the women's. The weight of the recent changes and the vast inequalities they

[8] We have reinforced the conclusion by an analysis of some of the possible factors for marriage selection: age at divorce, number of children born before divorce and alcoholism. None of them proved to be possible explanations. More details on these points in Festy et Prokofieva, 2000.

[9] See Table 6.10 for a description of the variables.

Table 6.16. *Regression Estimates for Men's and Women's Careers after Divorce*

Independent variables	Women, 1993	Men, 1998
Socio-economic variables		
Educational level	0.147***	
Occupational status at separation	−0.293***	
Occupational status at survey		0.507***
Sector at time of separation	−0.152***	
Sector at time of survey		0.32***
Job adequated to qualifications	0.155***	
Work hours	0.136***	
Familial variables		
New conjugal status		−0.164***
Age at separation		−0.022***
Alimony	−0.266***	
Constant	3.32***	2.96***
Summary statistics		
R^2	0.162	0.248
F (significance level)	28.19 (0.00)	82.05 (0.00)
n	934	1,185

*** $p<0.01$; ** $p<0.05$; * $p<0.10$.

Source: Surveys of Russian population on the Problem of Employment in October 1993, October 1998 (Goskomstat Rossii; methodology of ILO).

have engendered in Russian society make the characteristics at survey more meaningful than those at divorce for describing professional mobility in the interval.

Faced with this consistent set of socio-economic variables, the role of the familial variables is even less visible than during marriage[10]. The only significant effect, for women, concerns alimony payments, which is no doubt as much a socioeconomic as a familial factor. Women who received no alimony after their divorce made more headway in their careers, either because this situation led them to take on a greater workload (as suggested by the correlation with work hours) or because a lighter family burden made them more available for promotion (but the number of children in mother's custody is not a factor of mobility after divorce). The variables affecting men's careers are very different; they are the more classic age at time of separation and new conjugal status. The younger the men were when they divorced, the more upwardly mobile their careers afterwards, a trend which is no doubt accentuated by the economic crisis. And those who entered a new union were more liable to move ahead than those who remained single.

[10] Ages and durations have no significant impact, in particular because duration since divorce is limited to a 0–12 year range. In the previous model, there was more variability since duration from marriage to divorce was not controlled for, even if in fact ages at separation proved to be more active than durations themselves.

The latter point is, therefore, confirmed to be an essential factor of divergence between men's and women's careers after divorce: whether men remarry or not is decisive for their careers, while this element is not significant for women. The findings concerning the post-divorce period square with those relative to marriage: the familial variables again play only a minor role in women's professional careers, thus wrong-footing our hypotheses. And living in a partner relationship is observed to be far more important for men's careers than for women's.

THE ROLE OF THE ECONOMIC CRISIS

The economic crisis which had been creeping on for a long time suddenly escalated in the mid-1990s. To capture its effects, it was necessary to compare the situations described by men in 1998 to those reported by women five years earlier. A degree of uncertainty remains concerning information reported on current situation of former spouse.

To standardize the career profiles as reported in the two surveys, we selected those with a duration of 10–19 years since marriage, during which time the separation had occurred. We focus on two elements likely to have been affected by the crisis: activity at time of survey and professional mobility of workers between marriage and survey (Table 6.17).

From 1993 to 1998, the proportions of men and women currently jobless have risen substantially. In three cases out of four, the increase was six or seven percentage points, comparable to that measured in Table 6.1. The men who have stayed single

Table 6.17. *Inactivity at Survey and Net Mobility Between Marriage and Survey (10–19 Years Duration), by Conjugal Status*

Inactivity and mobility		Conjugal status at survey*	
		In a new union	Single
Inactivity at time of survey			
1993 survey	Women	10.2% (147)	5.6% (285)
	Men	4.0% (125)	7.5% (307)
1998 survey	Women	16.1% (162)	12.4% (153)
	Men	10.8% (325)	22.8% (264)
Net mobility from marriage to survey (men and women working at both dates)			
1993 survey	Women	+15.6% (83)	+19.9% (212)
	Men	+31.8% (66)	+20.8% (148)
1998 survey	Women	−8.4% (95)	−11.6% (95)
	Men	+21.2% (274)	+10.6% (180)

* In 1993, the men 'in a new union' are those reported by their former spouse as having had this intention.

Source: Surveys of Russian population on the Problem of Employment in October 1993, October 1998 (Goskomstat Rossii; methodology of ILO).

after their divorce are more sharply hit than those who have remarried. The position of the former, who were disadvantaged even before the crisis, has deteriorated and almost one out of four is now jobless. Women, in comparison, have been relatively spared.

The female high-activity model is apparently withstanding the economic crisis and growing unemployment. Women continue to participate actively in the labour force, especially when they do not have the material support of a new husband and are bringing up their children unaided. For those living with a partner, we have seen that having a family only slightly modifies their participation; in 1998, as before the crisis, they are scarcely more often inactive than remarried men or single women. The disguised unemployment in the form of housewives, suggested by the national data in Table 6.1, does not really concern divorced women, particularly those remaining single.

The men who have stayed single have been hit particularly hard by joblessness, which has risen threefold in this group compared to five years earlier. Their economic frailty was already perceived in their ex-spouse's responses in 1993, but, enhanced by the crisis, it is now expressed by a sharp rise in unemployment: no doubt these men are particularly poorly equipped to adapt to such a different economic order. Also, fewer men than women do not remarry after a divorce, which implies a more rigorous negative selection.

The unemployment born of the economic crisis does not discriminate between divorced men and divorced women, but accentuates, to the detriment of single men, a process that was already visible earlier. By contrast, the careers of those divorcees who have managed to keep a job have evolved very differently for men and women (Table 6.17). Men's careers have slowed down, but continue to progress; those who have not remarried continue to lag behind those who have, and the gap remains around ten points, as in 1993. In the same interval, the brakes have been slammed on women's careers: instead of predominantly upward, as they were only five years earlier (+15 or +20 points), they have now regressed to a negative mobility of a full 10 points. The difference between remarried and single divorcees is still nonsignificant: whatever path they have chosen, divorced women have been hit head on by the economic crisis.

During this crisis, the activity and unemployment rates of divorced men have evolved differently depending on whether or not they have formed a new union, indicating the persistence of a conjugal effect on their professional lives. In parallel, the careers of divorcees who have stayed in work reflect the same gender discrimination previously noted during marriage, but no new association with conjugal status. Thus, the economic crisis accentuates trends which already existed but does not reveal any new factors at play.

The sensitivity of men's activity to the economic situation contrasts with women's relative protection. Notably, single women—generally lone mothers—have not suffered the spectacular setbacks of single men, who are far more often living alone or back with their parents.

However, the women who have kept their jobs have experienced a greater deterioration of their working conditions than men. Already lagging behind before the crisis, their careers have regressed in 1998 to an extent that is in no way comparable to men's. The disparities between men's and women's careers have been strikingly accentuated by the slump.

CONCLUSION

Two surveys on divorcees taken in 1993 and 1998 provide the material for studying men's and women's professional careers during the family cycle, from marriage to separation, then from separation to survey. The second survey, in which the respondents were men, captured the situation when Russia was in the throes of its economic and financial crisis.

Throughout their family history, women participate in the workforce almost as much as men: slightly less when they marry because, being younger than their husbands, they are more often still students; often more after a divorce, especially in 1998 since divorced men have fallen victim to the crisis more than women. This full activity, barely modified by the transition towards a market economy, has been a permanent feature of Russian women since the Soviet era; it is *a fortiori* the case of divorced women who are lone mothers bringing up a family on their own.

During married life, women's careers lag behind those of men. The hypothesis of an interaction between husband's and wife's careers is confirmed in part: there is a correlation between the two mobilities, but disparity between them is not apparently a decisive factor of marriage breakdown. Neither does the presence of children explain women's lesser performance. The conclusion seems to be rather a segregation that keeps women confined to the least profitable sectors of activity, where the jobs make professional and family life easier to combine.

Divorce has no notable impact on women's careers, but it considerably slows down those of men who remain partnerless. Outside of the context of a marriage, and the protection it affords to them, men lose their professional advantage over women. Divorce thus brings into focus the foundations of marriage and shows exactly what men give up when they turn their backs on married life. These mechanisms are no doubt more visible in Russia than elsewhere because several factors contribute to easing the consequences of divorce for women: first, almost all women work; second, the alimony system transfers a substantial share of the former husband's earnings to the divorcee for child custody; and third, Russian social policy has always privileged lone mothers.

The recent economic crisis has hit all divorcees, increasing unemployment among men, especially when they have not remarried, and causing women's careers to regress. Far from inverting the associations that existed, the slump has maintained them and amplified their effects. The traditional lifejackets have been floated to avoid sinking in financial straits. The family network has, more than ever, rallied round to erect a rampart against poverty, and the remnants of the social policy in favour of lone mothers have cushioned the worst of the shocks.

References

Anker (1997), 'Richard, Ségrégation professionnelle hommes-femmes: les théories en présence', *Revue Internationale du Travail*, 136 (automne 1997), 371–96.

Avdeev (2000), 'Alexandre and Alain Monnier, La nuptialité russe: une complexité méconnue, *Population*, juillet-octobre 1999; and in English, 'Marriage in Russia: A complex phenomenon poorly understood', *Population: An English Selection*, 12.

Avdeev, Alexandre and Alain Monnier (1996), '*Mouvement de la population de la Russie 1959–1994: Tableaux démographiques*', INED (*Données Statistiques*, n° 1).

——, Alain Blum and Irina Troitskaia (1999), 'La nuptialité en Russie avant la réforme de 1861 (une étude sur trois villages de la région de Moscou)', European Population Conference, The Hague, September.

Babaeva, L. (1996), 'Women and Social Change in Russia: Work, Politics, Everyday life', Moscow: Russian Science Foundation (in Russian).

Dex, S. (1987), *Women's Occupational Mobility*, London: MacMillan.

Duncan, J. G. and Hoffmann, D. (1985), 'Economic Consequences of Marital Instability', in M. David and T. Smeeding (eds), *Horizontal Equity, Uncertainty and Well-Being*, Chicago: University of Chicago.

Eliseeva, Irina, Patrick Festy and Lidia Prokofieva (1999), 'The Impact of Divorce on the Mobilisation of Family Network in Russia', Congrès de l'Association européenne de sociologie, Amsterdam, août.

Festy, Patrick (1990), 'Mobilité résidentielle des femmes séparées: une étape dans le cycle familial', in *Stratégies résidentielles*, INED, 231–52 (*Congrès et Colloques* n° 2).

——et Lidia Prokofieva (2000), 'Nombre d'enfants et autres dimensions familiales de la mobilité professionnelle en Russie', Colloque de l'AIDELF, Byblos, October, 10p.

Gessat-Anstett, Élisabeth (1999), 'Du collectif au communautaire. À propos des réseaux familiaux dans la Russie post-soviétique', *L'Homme*, October.

Grouzdeva, E. and Tchertichina, E. (1983), 'Work and Everyday Life for Soviet women', Moscow: *Politisdat* (in Russian).

Hornung, C. A. and McCullough, B. C. (1981), Status Relationships in Dual-Employment Marriages', *Journal of Marriage and the Family*, 43: 125–41.

McManus, P. A. and Diprete, T. A. (1999). 'Does Union Dissolution Hurt Men's Standard of Living? An Analysis of Recent Conditions and Possible Trends', *Population Association of America* Annual Meeting, New York, March, 29p.

Parsons, T. (1949), 'The social structure of the family', in R. Anshen (ed.), *The family: Its functions and destiny*, New York: Harper, 173–201.

Philliber, W. W. and Vannoy-Hiller, D. V. (1990), 'The Effect of Husband's Occupational Attainment on the Wife's Achievement', *Journal of Marriage and the Family*, 52: 323–29.

Prokofieva, L. (1985), 'Life Cycle of Families and Incomes', in *Family and Well-being*, Moscow: Mysle, 36–49 (in Russian).

——(1991), 'Socio-economic Status of Families in Certain Life Cycle Stages', in *Well-being of the People: Trends and Prospects*', Moscow: Nauka, 119–37 (in Russian).

Rotchin S. (1996), 'Women's Activity in the Transition Economy in Russia, Moscow: Moscow State University (in Russian).

Smits, J., Ultee, W., and Lammers, J. (1996), 'Effects of Occupational Status Differences Between Spouses on the Wife's Labor Force Participation and Occupational Achievement: Findings from 12 European Countries', *Journal of Marriage and the Family*, 58(February): 101–15.

Waite, L. J. (1980), 'Working Wives and the Family Life Cycle', *American Journal of Sociology*, 86: 272–94.

PART III

MIGRATION AND LABOUR MARKET CHANGES FOR WOMEN AND MEN

7

Gender and the Labour Market among Immigrants in Some Italian Areas: The Case of Moroccans, Former Yugoslavians, and Poles

SALVATORE STROZZA, GERARDO GALLO, AND FRANCESCA GRILLO

REFERENCE FRAMEWORK AND AIMS

In recent years, interest in female migration (United Nations 1994, 1995) and in its economic consequences (Makinwa and Afolayan 1995; Vicarelli 1992, 1994*b*) has increased. This is a new issue, since traditional research on international migrations focused only on male migration (Schoeni 1998; Tapinos 1995), due to lack of data (Lim 1995; Lodigiani 1994; UN Secretariat 1995; Vicarelli 1992; Zlotnick 1995) and because it was assumed that women migrated mainly for family reunification reasons, and it was thought that female migration would not affect economies. Foreign women were not considered as part of the economic system in receiving countries, due to the limited number of immigrant women and the fewer possibilities for their participation in the regular labour market (UN Secretariat 1995). In many countries with immigrant communities, data has contradicted the numerical inferiority of women (ISTAT 1998; United Nations 1995). Migration is perceived as one of the elements that changes the condition of women (UN Secretariat 1995) and relationships between genders (Makinwa and Afolayan 1995), especially when, after migration, women enter into the labour market (Zlotnik 1993).

In order to analyse the condition of foreign immigrant women, several aspects must be examined. Participation in the labour market, occupation, and wages seem to be the most outstanding aspects, even though they may not be exhaustive. With reference to the destination countries, two main research lines can be identified. The first one is focused on the analysis of differences in the participation in the labour

The general layout of this paper was jointly agreed by the authors. Salvatore Strozza is the author of the second and fourth sections Gerardo Gallo of third section and Francesca Grillo of first section. The last section is contributed by Salvatore Strozza and Gerardo Gallo. The authors are grateful to various anonymous referees for their helpful comments. They would also like to express their appreciation and gratitude to Antonella Pinnelli for her supervision of the preliminary and subsequent versions of the paper. Of course, full responsibility for all errors and shortcomings rests entirely with the authors.

market and in the earnings of immigrant women and native-born women (Long 1980; Reimers 1984, 1985) and, within communities of immigrant women, separated by country of origin (Duleep and Sanders 1993; MacPherson and Stewart 1989; Schoeni 1998). The second one is oriented to examine the gender differences among immigrants as regards their participation in the labour market, their occupations, professional mobility (Powers and Seltzer 1998), and earnings (Borjas and Tienda 1993).

Immigration to Italy

Starting in the second half of the 1970s, and despite being a traditional emigration area, Italy has acquired a new role in the scenario of international migrations, and has become the destination of migrants from less developed countries (LDCs). From the beginning, foreign migration has acquired specific features: no immigrant community has significantly predominated (Cacciani *et al.* 1998; Istat 1998) and this heterogeneity of citizenship has been combined with broad differences in gender among migrant communities (Casacchia and Strozza 1995). There are some mainly male communities (i.e. those from North-Africa) while others are mainly female (i.e. from the Philippines, Cape Verde, and Poland). This is a new element, differing from previous migratory patterns in Europe, but one that is present also in other regions (Hugo 1999). In Italy, some immigrant communities are composed mainly of women (i.e. the Philippine community), who inaugurated the migration process and were then followed by men from the same community (Barsotti and Lecchini 1995; Bonifazi 1998; Campani 1990; Casacchia and Natale 1993; Lodigiani 1994; Raffaele 1992).

There are differences by gender as well as differences by citizenship and areas of employment in Italy (Casacchia and Natale 1993; Strozza 1995, 1996). In fact, men have wider employment opportunities in Italian industry, while women mainly meet the labour demand from households. While in some North-European countries (especially in France, Germany, United Kingdom, and the Netherlands) immigrant women are even employed in some industrial sectors (i.e. food and textiles) (Boyd 1995; Schoorl 1995; Tapinos 1995), foreign women in Italy are mainly employed in the domestic service sector,[1] and have more recently been engaged in personal care assistance, that is, looking after children and the elderly (Natale and Strozza 1997). In fact, immigrant women arriving in Italy with the support of a network established by women from their own country or through religious organizations (Raffaele 1992), are likely to find a job easily due to the high labour demand for household assistance.[2] In any case, in the first phase of the immigration process this specific labour demand is an advantage for women, since it provides more stable conditions, although in the

[1] Few immigrant women are employed in manufacturing activities (Lodigiani 1994), and some come to Italy to work in illegal entertainment activities (Raffaele 1992).

[2] The employment of immigrant women meets the actual (or status) needs of the higher middle class in Italy (Raffaele 1992; Vicarelli 1994*b*; Giudici 1997), as they fulfil typically female roles that are now becoming more available due to the greater participation in the labour market of Italian women and to shortfalls in the welfare system.

long-term it may hinder professional mobility and consequently the integration process (Natale and Strozza 1997).

Therefore, employment segregation and low professional mobility seem to characterize the employment of foreign women in Italy as well, since Italy has become a receiving country. Adopting a simplified scheme to analyse the conditions of immigrant women and men, it could be very important to identify the foreign communities in Italy according to the prevalence of labour or family reunion immigration, even though we also have to consider the case of asylum seekers and refugees (i.e. the Former Yugoslavians). In fact, a hypothesis can be made to evaluate if the reasons of immigration may influence labour market participation, employment sectors, and earning differences by gender.

Aims and organization of the research

This article discusses labour force participation, employment integration, and earning determinants for men and women immigrants in Italy. First of all, the overall number and the activity status of legal foreigners in Italy will be analysed by main country of citizenship and gender (Second Section). On the basis of official data available and through multivariate analysis, the gender differences in the registered labour force participation, regular employment access, and the official occupational structure will be examined for the main immigrant communities. This section of the chapter will provide a general framework of reference that will allow for indications to be drawn on the representation of the communities on which an in-depth study will be carried out in the following sections. In fact, gender differences, either on participation in the labour market and sectoral distribution of employment or on the level and determinants of earning, will be focused on three foreign communities in Italy: Moroccans, Former Yugoslavians, and Poles. As to wage differences, the following elements will be analysed: the determinants of weekly earnings, the measure of differentials, and the assessment of their causes. In the fifth section, a summary will be made of the most important results and some final remarks will be made.

GENDER DIFFERENCES IN REGULAR WORK PARTICIPATION OF LEGAL FOREIGNERS IN ITALY

Gender differences in the legal foreign presence in Italy

Official data allow for the outlining by gender and citizenship[3] of the number and participation in the labour market of foreign immigrants in Italy. The following information is used: data supplied by the Ministry of the Interior on permits to stay, revised

[3] In this entire paper, citizenship is used as an identification variable for the foreign communities, even if such variables present some limitations, mainly connected with the presence of important differences pertaining to ethnic groups (this is the case for Former Yugoslavians and Albanians). Besides, the Former Yugoslavians are considered as a whole, without taking into account the present political situation in which the Former Yugoslavia is divided into more than one nation. This is because the data available only allow for an approximate division among the actual different nationalities.

by ISTAT (1998, 1999), data supplied by Ministry of Labour on new employees and on non-EU citizens registered on the official unemployment lists as well as National Security data on people employed in the domestic service sector. These statistics are based on administrative surveys and only refer to legal foreigners and regular employment.[4]

At the end of 1991, there were 650,000 legal foreigners in Italy, of which 475,000 from LDCs and Eastern Europe countries[5] (Table 7.1). The growth in the numbers of legal foreigners between 1992 and 1995 was mainly due to the increase in foreigners from Eastern Europe, particularly to permits to stay granted for humanitarian reasons as *de facto* refugees, to people from the Former Yugoslavia (Table 7.1). The amnesty established by the Dini decree (Legislative decree 485/95) and ensuing modifications on 19 November 1995 and 30 March 1996, allowed about 250 thousand illegal foreigners to legalize their status. The number of legal foreigners increased, and by the end of 1997 it exceeded 1 million people, of which 800,000 came from LDCs and Eastern European countries (Table 7.1).

The gender structure of legal foreigners shows a greater number of men and remarkable differences by geographical area, and even greater differences by citizenship (Table 7.1). Immigrants from Africa, especially those coming from the Mediterranean coast, Eastern Europe, and Asia (except Eastern Asia) record a larger proportion of men, which slightly decreased in the 1990s, due to migrants arriving to join their immediate families. On the contrary, women clearly prevail among immigrants from MDCs, Eastern Asia, and South America (Table 7.1).

The largest foreign female community is from the Philippines. Early settlement took place in the late 1970s, and at the beginning of the 1990s its number was larger than any other foreign community. In 1991 it numbered almost 25,000 people and about 40,000 in 1997 (Table 7.1). From the very beginning, this labour migration was characterized by the prevalence of women, although this partly decreased in the past years (about 67 per cent) due to the arrival of husbands or other male members of the household, who were employed in the same occupational sector as women. It is a labour migration where women play a key role, as they migrate first and thus ease the ensuing migration and integration of the other male members in the labour market, showing a different trend from the usual, where men were the first to migrate.[6] Until the mid-eighties, researchers most of all analysed this community, as well as the community from Cape Verde (Barsotti 1989; Barsotti and Lecchini 1988, 1995; Birindelli 1986; Campus *et al.* 1988), while in recent years the following communities acquired some importance: immigrants from Peru (especially after the 1995–96 amnesty) and a large number of women was recorded from Poland (more than 15,000), greatly exceeding numbers of men (in both communities, women represent two- thirds of the population). In absolute values, women from Morocco

[4] For further information on illegal foreigners and irregular work see estimates in literature (ISTAT 1991; Natale 1990; Natale and Strozza 1997; Reyneri 1998*a*,*b*; Blangiardo 1998; Strozza 1999).

[5] The number of permits to stay can be used to estimate the number of legal adults in Italy (Natale and Strozza 1997), since minors do not usually have their own permit to stay, but are usually included in that of an adult relative (ISTAT 1991).

[6] For more details on main Philippine migration flows of domestic workers, see Hugo (1999).

Table 7.1. *Permits to Stay by Gender and Area of Origin (Citizenship). Italy, 31st December 1991, 1995, and 1997. Absolute Figures and Percentage of Women*

Area of origin/ Citizenship[a]	Total			Women			% of women		
	1991	1995	1997	1991	1995	1997	1991	1995	1997
Total	648,935	729,159	1, 022,896	259,050	344,539	458,613	39.9	47.3	44.8
MDCs	172,186	199,231	212,112	102,390	120,520	127,865	59.5	60.5	60.3
LDCs and East Europe	476,749	529,928	810,784	156,660	224,019	330,748	32.9	42.3	40.8
European Union	100,404	122,185	135,207	59,049	72,957	80,274	58.8	59.7	59.4
Other MDCs	71,782	77,046	76,905	43,341	47,563	47,591	60.4	61.7	61.9
Eastern Europe	86,471	152,473	226,387	33,124	68,553	99,378	38.3	45.0	43.9
North Africa	147,954	131,298	200,067	15,353	27,504	41,342	10.4	20.9	20.7
Rest of Africa	79,577	74,649	110,681	27,762	30,720	42,729	34.9	41.2	38.6
Eastern Asia	59,526	60,835	102,125	34,956	37,723	60,259	58.7	62.0	59.0
Rest of Asia	53,148	53,723	85,068	13,331	19,057	25,560	25.1	35.5	30.0
Latin America	50,073	56,950	86,456	32,134	40,462	61,480	64.2	71.0	71.1
Philippines	36,316	36,007	57,312	24,407	25,162	38,574	67.2	69.9	67.3
Morocco	83,292	81,247	122,230	8,180	17,660	27,960	9.8	21.7	22.9
Former Yugoslavia	26,727	73,538	73,492	9,911	26,001	27,271	37.1	35.4	37.1
Albania	24,886	30,183	72,551	3,504	9,882	22,264	14.1	32.7	30.7
Peru	5,022	8,001	22,996	3,201	5,762	16,006	63.7	72.0	69.6
China	15,776	16,200	35,310	6,283	7,262	15,738	39.8	44.8	44.6
Poland	12,139	13,955	22,938	6,757	9,059	15,486	55.7	64.9	67.5
Romania	8,250	14,212	28,796	4,786	9,850	15,301	58.0	69.3	53.1
Brazil	10,953	12,985	16,193	7,513	9,569	11,852	68.6	73.7	73.2
Sri Lanka	12,144	16,010	24,841	3,758	6,878	9,939	30.9	43.0	40.0

[a] The first 10 largest foreign communities are listed, foreigners are from LDCs and are ranked by permits to stay granted to women, valid as of the end of 1997.

Source: Our processing of Ministry of Interior data, revised by ISTAT (1998, 1999).

and Former Yugoslavia exceed the number of 25,000. There are now more than 20,000 women from Albania and more than 15,000 Chinese women (Table 7.1). Thus, these last foreign communities, despite a large predominance of men (Table 7.1), count a very remarkable number of women in comparison with other foreign communities. Therefore, this large number of women plays an important and specific role in the labour market and in the integration process, even when taking into consideration their distinctive migration patterns not exclusively oriented to family reunification.

A synthesis of some labour market indicators by foreign community and gender

A general framework of reference on the characteristics of participation in the labour market according to gender of the main immigrant communities will be based on nine indicators (see Table 7.2) based on available data from official sources (Ministry of the Interior, Ministry of Labour and National Security). These data are related to legal foreigners and their regular employment. The selected indicators represent the following aspects: participation in the labour market, which is identified by the proportion of labour permits to stay (as an estimate of activity rate), the unemployment rate and also the presence index for family reasons; the capability to access to work, defined by the rates of new employees distinctly for the three geographical divisions of the country (Northern, Central, and Southern Italian areas); employment characteristics as the index of concentration in urban areas, the proportion of workers in the domestic service sector and the proportion of self-employed (see Table 7.2).

Nineteen foreign communities were examined, broken down by gender. The nine basic indicators were constructed for these 38 statistical units (19 communities for each gender). In outlining the information, factorial analyses were used with a principal component method which allows for summarizing a set of quantitative information to find out a smaller number of factors, linear combinations of the initial indicators, with minimum loss of information (Johnson and Wichers 1992; Halli and Rao 1990).The application of the factorial analysis[7] has led to the discovery of three significant factors, with eigenvalue greater than one, which account for more than 70 per cent of total variability (see last two rows of Table 7.2). The meaning of the factors was determined through correlation between indicators and factors (factor loadings) considering, for each factor, only indicators with greater correlation with factors themselves. In Table 7.2 the correlation values of the correlation between the elementary indicators and the three factors extracted from the analyses are shown.

The first factor represents the *participation in the labour market*. Table 7.2 shows that it is positively correlated to the activity rate (0.918) and rate of new employees in Northern Italy (0.581). At the same time, it is negatively correlated to the presence index for family reasons (−0.954) and to the unemployment rate (−0.813). The statistical units can be represented on a plane constituted by a couple of factors. As an example, therefore, when moving the first factorial axis from the left to the right, communities can be identified

[7] Indicators were standardized and factors were extracted after rotation (varimax procedure).

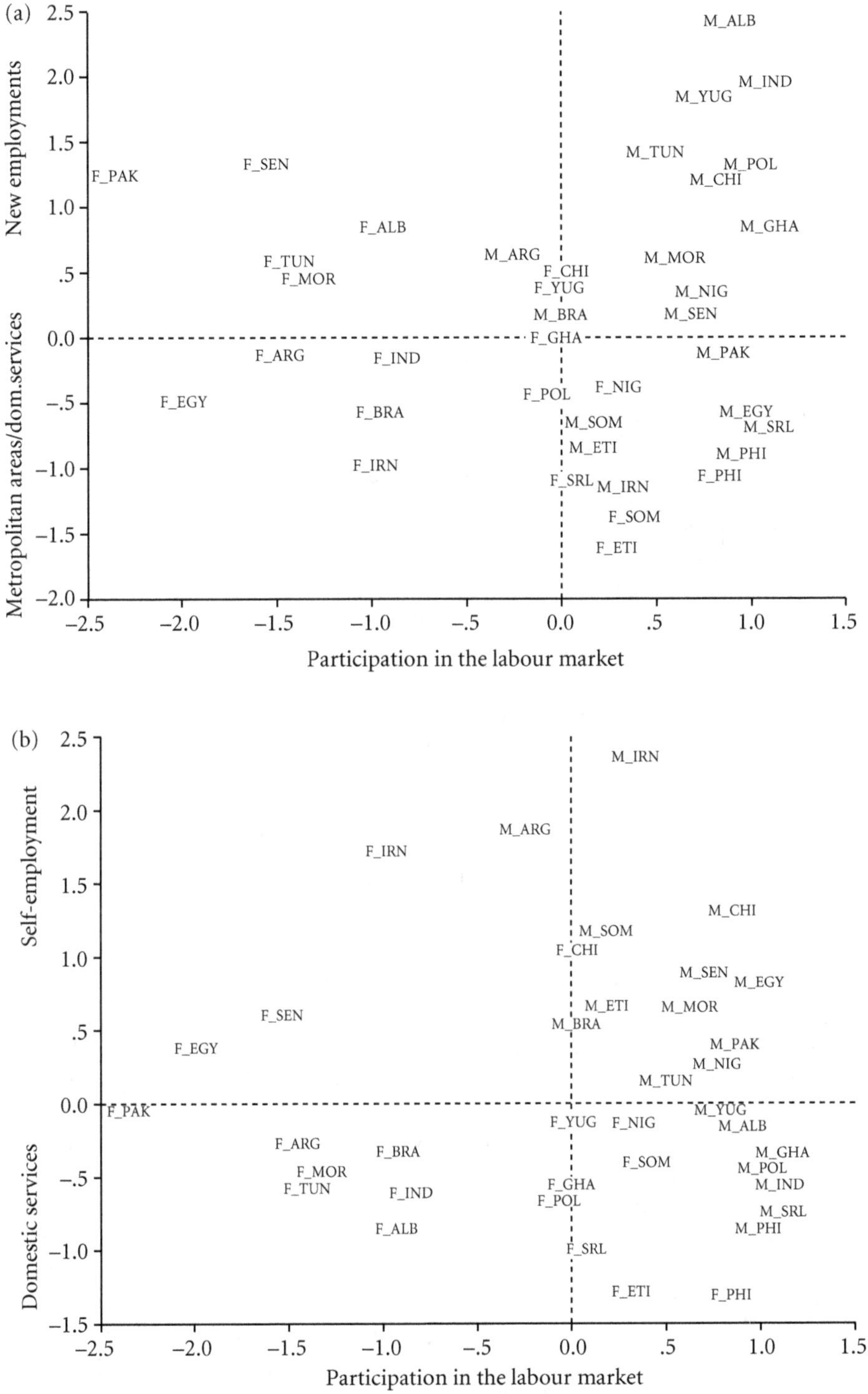

Figure 7.1. *Projection of Units (Foreign Countries by Gender) on Factorial Axes. (a) First Factorial Plane (b) First and Third Factor*

Table 7.2. *Factor Loadings of Indicators on Labour Market, Concerning Foreign Communities (Varimax Rotation)*

Indicators	Factors		
	1	2	3
Presence index for family reasons (family permit to stay per 100 permits to stay).	−0.954	0.019	−0.053
Activity rate (labour permit to stay per 100 permits to stay) per 100 labour permits to stay).	0.918	0.033	0.012
Unemployment rate (foreigners registered in the unemployment lists.	−0.813	0.091	0.137
Rate of new employees in Northern Italy (new employees in the North per 100 labour permits in the North).	0.581	0.542	−0.299
Rate of new employees in Central Italy (new employees in the Centre per 100 labour permits in the Centre).	0.135	0.754	0.066
Index of metropolitan concentration (percentage of permits to stay in the 12 metropolitan provinces).	0.113	−0.706	0.047
Rate of new employees in Southern Italy (new employees in the South per 100 labour permits in the South).	−0.079	0.658	0.055
Proportion of self-employed (self-employment permits to stay per 100 labour permits to stay).	−0.187	−0.105	0.889
Proportion of employees in the domestic service sector (employees in domestic service per 100 labour permits to stay).	−0.206	−0.556	−0.670
Variance (%)	31.8	23.6	15.1
Cumulate variance (%)	31.8	55.4	70.5

Source: Our processing of Ministry of Interior data, revised by ISTAT (1998, 1999), Ministry of Labour and National Security (INPS)

which present a progressively wider labour supply and lower official unemployment (see Fig. 7.1a). The second factor is positively correlated to the rates of new employees in each Italian geographical division (i.e. 0.754 in Central Italy, 0.658 in Southern Italy, and 0.542 in Northern Italy), and negatively correlated to the index of metropolitan concentration (−0.706) and the proportion of employed in the domestic services (−0.556) (Table 7.2), the two variables being correlated because domestic work is the typical employment of immigrants in the big cities. It is important to underline that high levels of new employment rates could be related to more regular opportunities of work, but also to a short tenure of regular employment (especially in the sectors of agriculture, constructions, and food) that means several entries in employment per year for the same worker. The negative correlation between index of metropolitan concentration and work in domestic services on one side and the rates of new employees on the other side is due to the recent scarcity of new regular opportunities of foreign labour in the larger urban contexts where employment of immigrants has been mainly represented by the domestic service sector. The third factor is positively correlated with the proportion of self-employed (0.889) and negatively with the proportion of employees in the domestic service sector (−0.670).

Therefore, on the third factorial axis there is a contrast of communities with a larger proportion of self-employed, located on the positive side, with communities having predominant paid employment in the domestic service sector, located on the negative side (see Fig. 7.1b).

The statistical units (communities by gender) are shown on the first factorial plane (Fig. 7.1(a)) and on the plan composed by the first and third axes (Fig. 7.1(b)). Each statistical unit is identified by a label indicating gender and citizenship.

Observation of the two factorial planes shows firstly a marked contrast across the first axis between the male component of communities, who emigrate in search of work, with the female component of many female communities who emigrate for family reunification reasons and therefore include a high percentage of the inactive and unemployed. These women come from Pakistan, India, Iran, Albania, Egypt, Tunisia, Morocco, Senegal, Argentina, and Brazil. The female component of other communities are to be found in correspondence with the positive values of the first factor (high rates of activity), and negative values in the second (metropolitan areas and the domestic service sector), or in the third (employees in the domestic services) and are therefore closer to the corresponding male community (Former Yugoslavians, Poles, Ghanians, Nigerians, Ethiopians, Somalis, Sinhalese, and Philippines).

The distance between the male and female component in the same community shows the type and dimension of gender differences. If the male and female units are close, there are few gender differences, whereas when the units are distant, there are gender differences with respect to the indicators summarized by the factorial axes. For example, in the case of Pakistan immigrants, there is a notable distance between men and women, mainly due to the scarce participation of females in the labour market. Also for Moroccans, and for other North-African communities, a great distance is shown between the two sexes as regards participation in the labour market. For the Former Yugoslavians and for Poles, the distance between men and women is small, because women's participation in the labour market is rather high, and differences in gender are scarce as regards status in employment, with the result that the majority are paid employees (Fig. 7.1(b)). Rather different, however, remains the intensity of new employees (entry and re-entry in regular work), which is greater for males, who are to be found on the positive side of the second axis. In the case of Chinese, both the male and female component are to be found within the same quadrant (the first quadrant), showing a small distance, a sign that there is not a great gender difference both in access to the labour market and type of work. This is due to the fact that Chinese men and women migrate to Italy with the support of their household and community and work in established trade activities and restaurants (Favaro 1991). Finally, Philippine people remain the most extreme case among the communities characterized by female labour migration. For that community, the coordinates of the male component and those for females result as being almost the same on all three axes, indicating a remarkable gender equality. In many cases, Philippine women migrated before their men, which eased their arrival and participation in the labour market. For this reason, men are mainly employed in the same employment sector as women, that is, domestic services.

In the following sections, attention will be focused on some foreign communities, from which the availability of micro-data on immigrants coming from some North-African and Eastern Europe countries allows us to analyse thoroughly the principal aspects of gender differences in labour market integration (labour force participation, employment characteristics, and earnings). The examined communities are those of Morocco, the Former Yugoslavia, and Poland, which although succeeding in covering different typologies identified through the multivariate analysis, do not explain all the different situations emerging from the analysis. Specifically, the concentration of the sample survey on communities coming from geographical areas nearest to Italy does not allow for investigation of a subject of great interest such as of Philippine migration. Naturally, such limitations must not be ignored when considering the overall results and the whole picture.

ACCESS TO THE LABOUR MARKET OF MOROCCAN, FORMER YUGOSLAVIAN, AND POLE IMMIGRANTS

Data

The analysis is based on data from a sample survey on 'Labour market integration, earnings and remittances of foreign immigrants'.[8] It was carried out between mid-December 1997 and the end of July 1998 on immigrants coming from some Eastern European countries (Former Yugoslavia, Albania, Poland, and Romania) and from a North African country (Morocco). Foreign individuals[9] have been interviewed in three Italian regions (in Veneto in the provinces of Treviso, Verona, and Vicenza; in Campania in the commune of Napoli and in the province of Caserta; in Lazio in the commune of Rome).[10] On the basis of a very detailed questionnaire, mainly composed of multiple choice questions, it examined the following key items: labour market participation, economic behaviour (income, consumption, and savings) and, above all, formation and transfer of remittances of immigrants. In addition, information on social and demographic characteristics, migration histories, migration plans, family condition, and households of interviewed foreigners have been also collected. This survey aimed at gathering information on legal and illegal foreigners, as the latter are not usually recorded by official surveys. The sample was obtained from a method based on places and centres where foreign people gather (Blangiardo 1993, 1996; Migliorati 1997). For each community, distinctly by region of survey, the sample units were weighted to consider the number of attended meeting centres and the number of attending people (see Blangiardo 1996). Moreover, to use jointly the sampled units of

[8] This survey, headed by Marcello Natale and coordinated by Salvatore Strozza, was part of a research funded by Rome University 'La Sapienza' on 'International migrations and capital movements in Europe', which has been directed by Eugenio Sonnino and Nicola Acocella.

[9] A foreign immigrant is defined in the sample survey as someone who is a 'foreign citizen'.

[10] Marcello Natale directed this survey and Salvatore Strozza was the activity co-ordinator. It formed part of a research financed by Rome University 'La Sapienza' on 'Capital movements and migrations of people in Europe', directed by Eugenio Sonnino and Nicola Acocella.

the three regions, a second weighting system was implemented so as to consider the number of foreigners coming from each community in the three regions examined. Again, for each immigrant interviewed, a weight was given that was obtained by multiplying values from the first and the second weighting system.[11]

In this analysis, we consider only the communities of Moroccans, Former Yugoslavians, and Poles, for which the number of collected interviews (765, 264, and 411, respectively) provides a comparative analysis by gender. For each community, the structure by gender and age groups of the legal sub-sample (holding valid permit to stay) was similar to the whole population of legal foreign immigrants (see Giovannelli 1999).

Labour force participation and occupational status

The analysis of activity status before emigration and at the time of interview shows some interesting elements, especially on gender differences. With reference to employment conditions before emigration, the male communities of the three immigrant groups show a roughly similar employment structure (Table 7.3). Although less than women, the proportion of male immigrants not economically active is somewhat high, with percentages ranging from 13 per cent of Poles to 22 per cent of Former Yugoslavians. These last male communities are more likely to be employed than Moroccans, who record 57 per cent of employed individuals, while for Poles and Former Yugoslavians the proportion of employed is 62 and 68 per cent, respectively. Among immigrant women, greater differences could be observed in the labour force participation. Whereas the Pole communities recorded the highest proportion of employment (about 60 per cent), Moroccan women accounted for a very low proportion (less than 15 per cent) due to a significantly high percentage who is not economically active (almost 70 per cent), while the proportion of women in employment coming from Former Yugoslavia can be placed in an intermediate position (about 40 per cent). Therefore, analysis on the activity status and employment structure bring out remarkable differences among the foreign women examined. Moreover, it seems that women have a lower probability of gaining entry into the labour force of their country of origin. In general, the condition of women before migration has to be related, on the one hand, to the economic characteristics of their home countries, and on the other hand, to the social and cultural rules which are in force in the same countries (Golini *et al.* 1999). In fact, it is well-known that the figures showing the participation rate of women in the labour force have been somewhat higher for Communist countries such as Poland and Former Yugoslavia. In Morocco, on the contrary, women are generally considered to suffer particular disadvantages as regards their entry into the labour force, because they are limited by cultural norms (Saint-Blancat 1995; Schmidt di

[11] For further information on the formal aspects of the second weighting system (the territorial weighting system) see recent researches (Moretti and Strozza 1997; Natale and Strozza 1997). More detailed information on the construction of the first and second weighting system for this survey can be found in Chapter 3 of the dissertation by Giovannelli (1999).

Table 7.3. *Activity Status Before Emigration and at the Time of Interview (Current Activity Status) and Duration of Unemployment by Gender of Moroccans, Former Yugoslavians, and Poles Interviewed in Some Italian areas in 1998. Absolute Values and Percentages*

Activity status and duration of unemployment	Moroccans			Former Yugoslavians			Poles		
	Women	Men	Total	Women	Men	Total	Women	Men	Total
Number of observations (absolute values)	120	645	765	93	171	264	258	153	410
Activity status before emigration (%)									
Employed	14.7	56.8	50.5	39.1	62.6	54.4	59.7	68.4	62.7
Unemployed	17.2	22.4	21.5	17.4	15.8	16.3	18.6	18.4	18.8
Not economically active	68.1	20.8	28.0	43.5	21.6	29.3	21.7	13.2	18.5
Current activity status in Italy[a] (%)									
Employed	57.5	69.1	67.3	71.9	85.9	81.0	86.8	79.3	84.0
Unemployed	6.3	22.0	19.6	3.2	11.7	8.7	3.0	12.2	6.5
Seeking employment for the first time in Italy	6.9	6.0	6.1	3.0	2.4	2.6	3.6	5.9	4.4
Not economically active	29.3	2.9	7.0	21.9	0.0	7.7	6.6	2.6	5.1
Length of unemployment (%)									
Less than 4 months	28.6	54.2	53.0	33.0	65.0	60.8	57.2	94.1	84.0
More than 4 months	71.4	45.8	47.0	67.0	35.0	39.2	42.8	5.9	16.0

[a] Chi-Square: Moroccans: 113.7; Former Yugoslavians: 43.4; Poles: 17.3. Contingency coefficient: Moroccans: 0.36; Former Yugoslavians: 0.38; Poles: 0.20.

Source: Our processing of sample survey data on 'Labour market integration, earnings and remittances of foreign immigrants' (University of Rome "La Sapienza).

Friedberg and Saint-Blancat 1998). Nevertheless, it should be observed that employment conditions of the Former Yugoslavians have to be related to the political-economical instability which has been determined by the ethnic conflicts, giving rise to a large number of de facto asylum seekers and refugees. Participating in the labour force does not constitute a prime incentive for them to emigrate.

With regard to the current active status, important new facts are emerging. Firstly, a lower proportion of current inactive women is recorded. Moreover, women participate more than men in the labour force (except Moroccans), and women record lower unemployment rates, even if they are affected by long-term unemployment (Table 7.3). Differences by citizenship are recorded, especially if Moroccan and Pole women are compared. Moroccan women record the highest inactivity rate (about 30 per cent) and proportion of the unemployed (about 13 per cent, of which 6.3 per cent unemployed and 6.6 per cent seeking work for the first time in Italy), with a long-term unemployment (more than 70 per cent have been unemployed for more than 4 months); Pole women record the largest participation in the labour market (87 per cent are employed) with a very low proportion of unemployed (about 6.6 per cent).

This is in agreement with the literature in which has been remarked that Pole women have a short-term labour migration pattern. They are ready to accept very hard working conditions (often working night and day) and, when they return to their country, they leave their jobs to other newly-arrived female compatriots, extending the migration chain (i.e. De Filippo 1994). On the other hand, Muslim female workers come to Italy to join their husbands, and their participation in the labour market is scarce, as in Italy they also maintain their typical traditional Muslim roles. Only few immigrant women work and they only participate occasionally in the labour market, in ways which do not affect their roles as wives and mothers. (Schmidt di Friedberg and Saint-Blancat 1998).

Moroccan women resulted as being inactive for the greater part before emigration (Table 7.3). It has to be noted, however, the way in which Moroccan women, presenting a current activity status very dissimilar to their male counterpart (see the values for the contingency coefficient[12] in the footnote to Table 7.3), are, among the women interviewed, those who, following a migratory experience, have recorded a very remarkable transition from conditions of inactivity towards actual participation in the labour market.

There is a strong relation between sectors of economic activity and gender (see Table 7.4). In particular, women from Poland and Former Yugoslavia are usually employed in the domestic service sector as maids, but they also care for the elderly and sick (on the whole, more than 80 per cent and almost 50 per cent, respectively). The domestic service and trade employ almost the same proportion (about 35 per cent) of Moroccan women. Manufacturing activities employ about 16 per cent of Moroccan women and more than 22 per cent of women from Former Yugoslavia (Table 7.4).

[12] It is a chi-square-based measure that ranges from 0 to 1 and minimizes the influence of the sample size and degree of freedom. The higher the value of the coefficient, the larger is the association between the variables.

Table 7.4. *Branch of Economic Activity and Status in Employment by Gender of Employed Moroccan, Former Yugoslavians, and Pole Immigrants Interviewed in Some Italian Areas in 1998. Percentage Values*

Branch of economic activity and status in employment	Moroccans			Former Yugoslavians			Poles		
	Women	Men	Total	Women	Men	Total	Women	Men	Total
Absolute values	68	448	521	67	147	214	223	121	344
Branch of economic activity[a] (%)									
Agriculture	2.9	13.8	12.9	—	8.2	5.6	0.4	5.8	2.3
Constructions	—	9.2	7.5	—	23.1	15.9	—	46.3	16.3
Industry	16.2	34.2	31.7	22.4	33.3	29.9	2.2	17.4	7.5
Trade	35.3	25.4	26.9	13.4	14.3	14.0	7.2	6.6	7.0
Domestic services	33.8	0.7	5.3	47.8	—	15.0	83.9	6.6	56.8
Other services	11.8	16.7	15.7	16.4	21.1	19.6	6.3	17.4	10.1
Status in employment (%)									
Self-employment	10.4	25.1	23.2	4.5	9.5	7.5	2.7	14.1	6.5
Paid employment	89.6	74.9	76.8	95.5	90.5	92.5	97.3	85.9	93.5

[a] Chi-Square: Moroccans: 149.7; Former Yugoslavians: 93.6; Poles: 228.6; Contingency coefficient: Moroccans: 0.47; Former Yugoslavians: 0.55; Poles: 0.63. Index of dissimilarity: Moroccans: 43.0%; Former Yugoslavians: 47.8%; Poles: 78.0%.

Source: Our processing of sample survey data on 'Labour market integration, earnings and remittances of foreign immingrants' (University of Rome "La Sapienza").

The structure by sector for male employment is compounded and very different from that of women (see in the note of Table 7.4 the high values of contingency coefficient and index of dissimilarity, especially for Poles and Former Yugoslavians). Industry employs about 43 per cent of Moroccans, 56 per cent of Former Yugoslavians and 64 per cent of Poles (Table 7.4). In particular, construction employs about 46 per cent of Pole immigrants and more than 20 per cent of immigrants from Former Yugoslavia as well as more than 30 per cent of immigrants from Morocco and Former Yugoslavia are employed in industry (Table 7.4). Moroccans are characterized also by their employment in the primary sector (about 14 per cent), which has a lower global weight than other sectors, and in trade (more than 25 per cent), in particular as pedlars (see Table 7.4).

Status in employment is another gender-differentiating element (Table 7.4). Women are usually paid employees, while there is a significant proportion of self-employed men, especially Moroccans (25 per cent) and Poles (about 14 per cent). Many Moroccans are pedlars though they do not have regular permits to stay (illegal presence in Italy) or are irregularly employed. Self-employed Poles work mainly in the construction sector and they are in the same irregular conditions as Moroccans with regard to their permits to stay and employment.

This outline shows better conditions for women as regards access to employment, at least in the case of Poland and Former Yugoslavia for which women record very high employment rates. They usually work as maids and almost 50 per cent of them live with their employer and they are often on duty both night and day. They seldom work under a regular labour contract, so they are usually irregularly employed. In some case, they work on a daily or hourly basis, and usually with more than one employer (Natale and Strozza 1997). Nevertheless, even if fewer difficulties in their participation in the labour market are recorded, their employment opportunities are limited to the domestic service sector. In other words, employment segregation seems to characterize job opportunities for immigrant women.

WAGE DIFFERENCES BY GENDER AMONG MOROCCAN, FORMER YUGOSLAVIAN, AND POLE IMMIGRANTS

Regression model

Earnings represent another important issue in the analysis of gender differences in participation in the labour market. In the three communities examined, when the survey was carried out, the average weekly earning of employed women was lower than men. In fact, male Moroccan immigrants earned an average weekly wage of 355,000 lire and females 310,000 lire; for Former Yugoslavians the figures were 411,000 and 300,000 lire, respectively; while for Poles it was about 395,000 lire for males and 272,000 lire for females.

A typical *statistical earning function* (Mincer 1974) adjusted for foreign immigrants (see Chiswick 1978; Borjas 1985; Phillips and Massey 1999) was used to analyse earning determinants and assess the importance and causes of gender differences.

People who at the time of the survey were in employment, without making any distinction between employees and self employed were considered.[13] The natural logarithm of weekly earnings[14] (LNW) is a linear function of some independent variables, continuous or dummy, and have regard to the characteristics of the individual or his working activity. The variables included take into consideration some important factors influencing individual earnings (see Table 7.5).

The individual life cycle phase has been synthesized with two continuous variables: age at the time of the survey (AGE) and the number of relatives living in Italy (RELATIVES). The life cycle phase influences the number and the relationship between workers and not inside the family, affecting their economic needs and therefore the need for adequate work (Stark 1991). Such variables constitute, together with the dummy on gender (WOMEN), the main demographic characteristics of the interviewees.

With regard to the migratory aspects, only one variable dummy has been introduced concerning *the juridical condition of presence in Italy* (LEGAL) which appears, in general to play an important role in the formation of earnings (Chiswich 1984; Bailey 1985; Massey 1987; Borjas and Tienda 1993; Baldacci *et al.* 1999).

The *human capital* of immigrants is expressed by the number of years of study carried out successfully in their country (YSCHOOL), the level of knowledge of the Italian language (ITALIAN) and the number of years worked in Italy (JOBEXPIT). In fact, is it well known that a greater experience on the employment market and a better knowledge of the language of the receiving country generally render foreign workers more productive, and therefore more interesting to local employers, leading to more stable employment and higher salaries (Donato *et al.* 1992; Donato and Massey 1993). Moreover, it is to be supposed that such requirements are absolutely necessary when initiating and implementing self-employement successfully. It also has to be added that the variable for the number of years worked in Italy from the beginning of the professional history of the interviewee, has been given preference over the actual presence since migration took place, because this variable seems better able to express the experience acquired on the labour market in the receiving country.

[13] Such a choice was determined by two lines of reasoning: on the one hand self-employed were too few, with the exception of the Moroccans, to allow for an in-depth study of this category, but they were not excluded from the analysis so as not to reduce the number, already limited by a shortage of available cases; on the other hand, the foreigners who declared themselves as being *self-employed* were in many cases very similar to employees, often being pedlars in various distribution networks for products controlled by other people—often Italians, or by immigrants carrying out marginal activities while waiting to find a job.

[14] The use of logarithms of wage has two different explanations. On the one hand, from a theoretical point of view, a statistical model can be derived from a general human capital equation, which links the number of years of schooling s, to the earning level w, given the rate of return on schooling investment r through the following equation, normalizing to one level of income for people with no education: $w = \exp(rs)$. This exponential function can be transformed into the following linear form: $\ln w = rs + u$, where u is a random error term, that allows for a direct estimation of the rate of return on education investment. On the other hand the use of logarithm at the left hand side of the earning function is due to possible heteroskedastic error distribution which can lead to biased parameter estimates. If one assumes that the distribution of wage rates has a very high degree of dispersion, logarithmic transformation can, at least partially, cope with this problem.

Table 7.5. *Means of Variables Used in the Analysis of Wages Earned by Employed*[a] *Moroccan, Former Yugoslavian and Pole Immigrants Interviewed in Some Italian Areas in 1998*

Label of variable	Type of variable	Definition	Moroccans	Former Yugoslavians	Poles
WAGE	Cont.	Weekly earnings (in Lire)	349, 019	376, 769	314, 229
LNW	Cont.	Natural logarithm of weekly earnings	12.662	12.736	12.562
WOMEN	Dummy	Women	0.131	0.309	0.658
AGE	Cont.	Age when survey was carried out	33.867	31.345	32.590
RELATIVES	Cont.	Number of other household members	1.053	1.647	0.655
LEGAL	Dummy	With valid permit to stay	0.768	0.893	0.424
YSCHOOL	Cont.	Years of successful schooling in the country of origin	9.297	11.307	12.390
ITALIAN[b]	Cont.	Proficiency in Italian	0.553	0.702	0.602
JOBEXPIT	Cont.	Years employed in Italy	4.973	4.793	2.847
STABWORK	Dummy	Employed in current job for more than one year	0.746	0.839	0.589
DEPENDENT	Dummy	Employee	0.771	0.925	0.941
AGRICUL	Dummy	Employed in Agriculture	0.127	0.055	0.022
CONSTRUCT	Dummy	Employed in Construction	0.078	0.161	0.159
MANUFACT	Dummy	Employed in other sectors of Industry	0.322	0.299	0.077
DISTRSEC	Dummy	Employed in Trade	0.260	0.142	0.071
HOUSESERV	Dummy	Employed in the Domestic Service sector	0.050	0.151	0.575
CAMPANIA	Dummy	Employed in Campania	0.328	0.000	0.285
VENETO	Dummy	Employed in Veneto	0.439	0.510	0.000
HOURS	Cont.	Hours worked per week	46.537	45.179	48.465
LNHOUR	Cont.	Natural logarithm of hours worked per week	3.784	3.727	3.791
WORKACCOM	Dummy	Free accommodation in place of employment	0.048	0.087	0.319

[a] The employed who declared their earnings for the last week or last month were excluded.

[b] A quantitative variable was constructed, and for each skill the maximum score was 3, the minimum being 0. Scores were assigned on the basis of interviewee self-assessment (very good, fairly good, poor, none) of the proficiency in Italian, with reference to four basic skills: listening, speaking, reading and writing. The highest score of each interviewee was divided by 12 which is the maximum score (three out of the four skills).

Source: Our processing of sample survey data on 'Labour market integration, earnings and remittances of foreign immigrants' (University of Rome "La Sapienza").

The characteristics of the main working activity, whose importance has been brought to light also through some recent contributions on immigration in Italy (Venturini and Villosio 1998; Baldacci *et al.* 1999), are expressed through work stability (STABWORK), a dummy variable that takes on value one when the current work is carried out uninterruptedly for more than 1 year, the status in employment (DEPENDENT), economic sector of employment (five dummy variables) AGRICUL, CONSTRUCT, MANIFACT, DISTRSEC, and HOUSESERV) and the region of employment (two dummy variables: CAMPANIA and VENETO). The *dummy variables* over the territory were added to include the income variability due to the differing living costs in the geographic areas under consideration[15] as well as to analyse the different possibilities to access local labour market. These dummy variables allow the metropolitan area of Rome to be separated from the other areas covered by the survey. The distinction between urban and rural areas is, for the major part, assumed from the addition of dummy variables on the employment sectors.

A natural logarithm for weekly hours worked was introduced (LNHOURS) as well as a dummy variable to indicate free accommodation in the place of employment (WORKACCOM). The last variable was required since interviewees only declared their monetary weekly wages and other kinds of compensation were not included (especially accommodation in the employer's home). This is a most important aspect as the majority of maids lives with their employers. Table 7.5 shows further information on explanatory variables and related average figures divided into the three communities examined. The general income function to be estimated is represented by the following equation:

$$\begin{aligned}\mathrm{LNW_i} = \alpha &+ \beta_1 \cdot \mathrm{WOMEN_i} + \beta_2 \cdot \mathrm{AGE_i} + \beta_3 \cdot \mathrm{RELATIVES_i} + \beta_4 \cdot \mathrm{LEGAL_i} \\ &+ \beta_5 \cdot \mathrm{YSCHOOL_i} + \beta_6 \cdot \mathrm{ITALIAN_i} + \beta_7 \cdot \mathrm{JOBEXPIT_i} + \beta_8 \cdot \mathrm{STABWORK_i} \\ &+ \beta_9 \cdot \mathrm{DEPENDENT_i} + \beta_{10} \cdot \mathrm{AGRICUL_i} + \beta_{11} \cdot \mathrm{CONSTRUC_i} \\ &+ \beta_{12} \cdot \mathrm{MANIFACT_i} + \beta_{13} \cdot \mathrm{DISTRSEC_i} + \beta_{14} \cdot \mathrm{HOUSESERV_i} \\ &+ \beta_{15} \cdot \mathrm{CAMPANIA_i} + \beta_{16} \cdot \mathrm{VENETO_i} + \beta_{17} \cdot \mathrm{LNHOURS_i} \\ &+ \beta_{18} \cdot \mathrm{WORKACCOM_i} + u_i \qquad (1)\end{aligned}$$

where u_i is a random error term.

Several problems arise when estimating eqn (1) with the usual OLS method.[16] The most relevant problem with earnings data is *sample selectivity* (Goldenberger 1981;

[15] The geographical dummy variables help us to consider the economic differences among the areas where immigrants live. Alternative solutions are: to divide average weekly wage by a cost-of-living index for place of residence (Reimers 1983); to introduce some macro-variables on territorial labour market conditions (Phillips and Massey 1999).

[16] First of all, omitted variable bias can affect parameter estimates if individual abilities are not considered; in this case an instrumental variables estimator is more appropriate if the number of instruments is sufficiently high (at least equal to the number of covariates). A second problem with OLS estimates is that residuals could show a heteroskedastic distribution even after the logarithmic transformation of the dependent variable. In this case a feasible GLS estimator should be adopted in order to have efficient estimates and a corrected test of hypothesis. Moreover variables representing latent concepts as human capital could be incorrectly measured, biasing ordinary estimates.

Greene 1981). This problem arises when the wage function has to be estimated by using a sub-sample of data where the units of observation have a positive value for the dependent variable. Excluding the non-working part of the sample, a selection of the sample is identified, making the mean of the residual distribution different from zero and correlated to the independent variables. To cope with this problem, causing OLS estimates to be inconsistent and downward biased, several methods have been proposed (Heckman 1976, 1979). Among them Olsen (1980) and suggests a two-step procedure to handle sample selection bias: in the first step a linear probability model is applied to the whole sample, where the dependent variable is a dummy taking positive values for the units that have a positive wage and zero value elsewhere (Maddala 1996). The predicted values of the OLS estimates of this model are then transformed, subtracting one to each unit (SELECT) and the new variable is used in the wage function model confined to the sample with positive earnings. Therefore this variable has to be added in eqn (1). When this two-step procedure is used, OLS estimates become consistent and can be more reliable than the ordinary estimates, especially when the sample is large enough.

The explanatory variables of the linear probability model with a dummy dependent variable assuming values, one for employed and zero otherwise are the following: age when the survey is carried out; years of successful schooling in the country of origin; proficiency in Italian; years since migration; number of other household members; marital status (a dummy variable for married people); a dummy variable for children under 14; two dummy variables for the occupational status in the country of origin (one for employed and the other for unemployed with reference to other conditions); a dummy variable to identify migrants for economic reasons; two dummy variables to specify how migration was carried out (singly, without help, with the help of other household members). The reference mode is Aother helps@; two dummy variables for the region of residence (one for Campania and one for Veneto with Lazio as reference mode).

Estimated earnings functions

Two different models were examined for each community: one with and one without dummy variables applying to the economic sector of employment, to assess their statistical importance and changes in value as well as the importance of the gender regression coefficient (Table 7.6). The models proposed explain rather efficiently the process of earning determination (at worst, the R^2 value is slightly lower than 0.5), even though a part of the variability captured by the estimated function concerns the natural logarithm of hours worked weekly.

In both models, gender differences in earnings do exist, and are disadvantageous for women, but they are significant only for the Moroccan and Pole communities according to the first model, that is, controlling the demographic characteristics, the human capital and the work characteristics, while for the second model they are significant only among the Moroccan community, that is, also controlling the activity sectors (Table 7.6). More specifically in the first model, if conditions are the same, women

Table 7.6. *Olsen Two-step Estimates of Effect of Selected Variables on Log Weekly Wages Earned by Moroccan, Former Yugoslavian, and Pole Immigrants Interviewed in Some Italian Areas in 1998*

Variable	Moroccans				Former Yugoslavians				Poles			
	Model 1		Model 2		Model 1		Model 2		Model 1		Model 2	
	B	SE	B	SE	B	SE	B	SE	B	SE	B	SE
WOMEN	−0.304[c]	0.052	−0.163[c]	0.060	−0.090	0.071	0.052	0.076	−0.218[c]	0.043	−0.055	0.063
AGE	0.006[b]	0.003	0.007[b]	0.003	0.006	0.004	0.005	0.004	0.003	0.002	0.004[a]	0.002
RELATIVES	0.055[c]	0.013	0.050[c]	0.012	−0.014	0.013	−0.009	0.012	0.028[a]	0.017	0.026	0.017
LEGAL	0.083[a]	0.045	0.094[b]	0.045	0.371[c]	0.086	0.350[c]	0.084	0.024	0.042	0.030	0.042
YSCHOOL	0.003	0.004	0.004	0.004	−0.008	0.014	−0.002	0.013	0.021[c]	0.007	0.023[c]	0.007
ITALIAN	0.167	0.104	0.189[a]	0.104	−0.019	0.153	−0.067	0.148	0.037	0.109	0.045	0.111
JOBEXPIT	0.003	0.005	0.004	0.005	0.010	0.009	0.017[a]	0.009	0.009	0.011	0.009	0.011
STABWORK	0.168[c]	0.039	0.139[c]	0.039	−0.007	0.067	−0.009	0.063	0.165[c]	0.046	0.156[c]	0.045
DEPENDENT	0.057	0.039	−0.055	0.048	−0.081	0.105	−0.105	0.104	−0.089	0.079	−0.126	0.080
AGRICUL	—	—	0.149[b]	0.064	—	—	−0.292[c]	0.112	—	—	0.235[a]	0.129
CONSTRUC	—	—	0.124[a]	0.069	—	—	0.082	0.078	—	—	0.203[c]	0.076
MANUFACT	—	—	0.089[a]	0.049	—	—	0.035	0.067	—	—	0.163[a]	0.086
DISTRSEC	—	—	−0.062	0.052	—	—	−0.257[c]	0.081	—	—	−0.070	0.087
HOUSESERV	—	—	−0.238[c]	0.087	—	—	−0.325[c]	0.100	—	—	−0.049	0.073
CAMPANIA	−0.414[c]	0.047	−0.430[c]	0.048	—	—	—	—	−0.301[c]	0.044	−0.288[c]	0.044
VENETO	0.119[c]	0.043	0.114[b]	0.045	−0.025	0.053	−0.126[b]	0.055	—	—	—	—
LNHOURS	0.408[c]	0.045	0.385[c]	0.046	0.553[c]	0.054	0.516[c]	0.054	0.289[c]	0.042	0.288[c]	0.042
WORKACCOM	−0.004	0.069	0.048	0.071	−0.303[c]	0.087	−0.207[b]	0.088	−0.166[c]	0.047	−0.149[c]	0.049
SELECT	−0.124	0.146	−0.146	0.143	0.805[c]	0.303	0.738[b]	0.293	0.062	0.245	0.016	0.247
Constant	10.580[c]	0.293	10.658[c]	0.292	10.490[c]	0.350	10.699[c]	0.347	11.298[c]	0.246	11.159[c]	0.250
R^2 (Adjusted)	0.522		0.543		0.554		0.605		0.464		0.482	
Standard Error	0.323		0.316		0.328		0.308		0.3105		0.305	
F	38.775		31.343		21.139		18.910		23.329		18.360	
N[d]	484		484		210		210		335		335	
Test of differences between the two models	$F_{5,464} = 5.409$[c]				$F_{5,191} = 6.020$[c]				$F_{5,316} = 3.273$[c]			

[a] Significant at the 10% level.
[b] Significant at the 5% level.
[c] Significant at the 1% level.
[d] Weighted figures approximate to unit.

Source: Our processing of sample survey data on 'Labour market integration, earnings and remittances of foreign immigrants' (University of Rome "La Sapienza").

have a lower LNW than men by 0.304 (wages lower by 26.2 per cent)[17] for Moroccans and 0.218 (wages lower by 19.6 per cent) for Poles (Table 7.6). The introduction of dummy variables for the sector of employment (model 2) is statistically important to the three communities examined,[18] as shown by test F (see last row of Table 7.6). But while among the Moroccan community women continue to have a 15 per cent lower income than men, among the Pole community, as has been said, the gender differences are no longer significant. In fact, people employed in the trade and domestic service sectors have a lower intercept (negative regression coefficient) as regards reference mode (other services) and lower than people employed in agriculture and industry, who have a positive regression coefficient (Table 7.6). The disadvantage of immigrant women can be partly determined by their employment in the domestic service sector where earnings are lower than in other economic sectors. Moreover, for Poles and Former Yugoslavians, the wage function is affected by WORKACCOM, standing for compensation in kind, represented by accommodation, especially for women. For these two communities, therefore, forms of compensation other than monetary are relevant, above all for women with a steady job in the domestic sector.

With regard to the other explanatory variables, the wage functions of the three communities examined show remarkable differences. The coefficient of the selection variable is statistically significant only for Former Yugoslavians. Among variables related to human capital, the extent of proficiency in Italian (ITALIAN) is positively reflected on earnings for Moroccans, while for Poles the years of schooling (YSCHOOL) represent a very significant statistical coefficient. Previous jobs in Italy (JOBEXPIT) are not so important as wage determinants. Only in the case of Former Yugoslavians does it seem to bear any relevance. On the contrary, stability of employment has great importance (STABWORK), and it is shown by the dummy variable representing employment for more than one year in the position held when the survey was carried out (Table 7.6).

In fact, referring to the Moroccan and Pole communities, working experience in Italy does not appear to be important, while great relevance is shown by current job stability. This could depend on the often precarious and sometimes occasional nature of working experiences undergone in Italy, above all for illegal immigrants.[19] Legal residence in Italy is particularly important for Former Yugoslavians, while among variables related to previous job, the geographical area where employment is found is highly significant (Table 7.6).

For each of the three examined communities, the earning function was estimated for the subgroups of men and women, using only two dummy variables with reference to sector of employment[20] (Table 7.7). The selection variable, which has been

[17] In an OLS regression equation in which the outcome is the natural log of wages, the percentage effect on wage of a dummy variable is derived from the formula (e-1)100 (Halvorsen and Palmquist, 1979).

[18] The null hypothesis that there is no difference between model 2 and model 1 is rejected, the confidence level for Moroccans being 99 per cent, and Former Yugoslavians and Poles, 95 per cent.

[19] Therefore the question has to be asked as to what role can be played, during the different phases of the individual migratory cycle, mobility of work and stability of employment in improving the working situation for foreigners. The results of this analysis appear to be that current job stability is the variable connected to migration-specific human capital that has a more positive impact than others on received income.

[20] One takes together agriculture and industry, and the other trade and the domestic service sector; reference is always Another services.

Table 7.7. *Olsen Two-Step Estimates of Effect of Selected Variables on Log Weekly Wages Earned by Moroccan, Former Yugoslavian, and Pole Immigrants According by Gender. Foreigners Interviewed in Some Italian Areas in 1998*

Variable	Moroccans				Former Yugoslavians				Poles			
	Women B	SE	Men B	SE	Women B	SE	Men B	SE	Women B	SE	Men B	SE
AGE	0.015[a]	0.008	0.004	0.003	0.008	0.006	0.004	0.005	0.002	0.002	0.007	0.005
RELATIVES	0.055	0.036	0.039[c]	0.015	−0.109[a]	0.060	0.005	0.014	−0.012	0.021	0.067[a]	0.038
LEGAL	−0.172	0.179	0.102[b]	0.047	−0.009	0.250	0.349[c]	0.092	0.033	0.045	0.056	0.083
YSCHOOL	0.001	0.011	0.004	0.004	0.028	0.018	0.008	0.014	0.020[c]	0.007	0.024	0.015
ITALIAN	0.706[a]	0.358	0.127	0.108	0.485	0.498	0.174	0.145	−0.170	0.107	0.365	0.221
JOBEXPIT	0.024	0.015	0.004	0.005	0.015	0.022	0.004	0.009	0.000	0.012	0.015	0.025
STABWORK	−0.015	0.105	0.141[c]	0.042	0.218	0.155	−0.035	0.074	0.158[c]	0.045	0.094	0.107
DEPENDENT	−0.393[b]	0.158	−0.043	0.050	−0.766[c]	0.255	0.005	0.122	−0.381[c]	0.119	−0.029	0.121
AGRIND[e]	−0.228	0.146	0.124[b]	0.050	0.109	0.163	−0.016	0.067	−0.057	0.128	0.221[b]	0.105
DISTRHOUSE[f]	−0.303[b]	0.134	−0.045	0.055	−0.136	0.147	−0.399[c]	0.097	−0.120	0.079	−0.091	0.133
CAMPANIA	−0.360[b]	0.146	−0.410[c]	0.051	—	—	—	—	−0.291[c]	0.047	−0.365[c]	0.101
VENETO	0.160	0.109	0.134[c]	0.048	0.207	0.157	−0.102[a]	0.059	—	—	—	—
LNHOURS	0.493[c]	0.099	0.359[c]	0.054	0.389[c]	0.099	0.564[c]	0.076	0.226[c]	0.042	0.453[c]	0.104
WORKACCOM	0.133	0.164	0.032	0.076	−0.408[c]	0.140	−0.155	0.132	−0.202[c]	0.046	−0.066	0.127
SELECT	−0.811[b]	0.349	−0.060	0.138	−0.122	0.549	0.206	0.241	0.270	0.231	−0.282	0.431
Constant	10.081[c]	0.504	10.884[c]	0.333	10.833[c]	0.571	10.207[c]	0.395	11.982[c]	0.282	10.071[c]	0.543
R^2 (Adjusted)	0.746	—	0.520	—	0.581	—	0.536	—	0.424	—	0.451	—
Standard Error	0.252	—	0.318	—	0.335	—	0.296	—	0.253	—	0.371	—
F	13.276	—	31.374	—	7.451	—	12.922	—	12.664	—	7.578	—
N[d]	63	—	421	—	65	—	144	—	222	—	112	—
Chow-test male and between female models		$F_{16,452} = 2.758^c$				$F_{15,180} = 1.828^b$				$F_{15,305} = 2.146^c$		

[a] Significant at the 10% level.
[b] Significant at the 5% level.
[c] Significant at the 1% level.
[d] Weighted figures approximate to unity.
[e] Agriculture, construction and industry included.
[f] Trade and domestic service sector included.

Source: Our processing of sample survey data on 'Labour market integration, earnings and remittances of foreign immigrants' (University of Rome "La Sapienza").

discussed in the subsection on the regression model, shows a regression coefficient statistically significant only for Moroccan women. The negative sign of the coefficient indicates that unemployed women have unobserved characteristics that would have yielded lower earnings if they had worked in Italy. Large differences are shown in the earning function estimated for men and women in these three communities, especially if the sign and significance of regression coefficients are examined (Table 7.7). There are not many variables which have the same influence on the wages of the two genders: only 'living in Campania' and 'longer working hours' have the same sign for both men and women. The former has always a negative influence while the latter always exerts a positive influence on earnings. With regard to the other variables, in at least two out of the three communities, women earn less if they are paid employees[21] and if they are provided with accommodation by their employers. Men earn more if they have a larger family in Italy, are legal immigrants and work in industry or the agricultural sector. Other variables which have an important significance for women, even if only for one of the three communities, are: age, language proficiency, and stability of employment. These all have a positive impact on income, as opposed to being paid employee and employed in trade or in the domestic service sector which have a negative impact on earnings. The Former Yugoslavian community is the one for which fewer variables influence the earning of both men and women.

Chow tests show that individual earning functions are statistically different for men and women among Moroccans and Poles (the significance is rather high: $p < 0.01$), whereas for Former Yugoslavians, the null hypothesis is accepted for the same level of statistical significance, that is, that there is no difference in regression equations of earning levels for men and women (see last row of Table 7.7).

The results emerging from the regression analysis can be summarized in the following way. Among the income determinants, special relevance is assumed by the variables relative to the characteristics of working activities carried out (longer hours, sector of employment, region where employed, and job stability). More self-evident and differentiated greatly by community appears to be the role of the variables regarding human capital and life cycle. Particularly interesting from the point of view of working aims is the role played by gender, a role that presents some differences among the communities under consideration. Women in the Moroccan community, taking all other conditions as equal, have an income significantly lower than that of the men, also when the sector of employment is included in the regression model, a sign that the reasons for discrimination go beyond those merely structural. On the contrary, among the Former Yugoslavians there does not exist, all other conditions being equal, gender differences in the amount of income received. Instead, for the Pole community, the regression coefficient for gender loses its significance with the introduction of dummy variables on employment sectors. This means that for this community the income difference between males and female depends mainly on a different sectoral

[21] As to women, status in employment is important for all three communities. The negative sign of the regression coefficient seems to demonstrate, all other conditions being equal, the very small number of self-employed women who have reached a level of substantial economic improvement.

structure of employment (different occupational structure by employment sector). The application of distinct models for males and females has allowed important differences in gender in the functions of earning to be brought to light. These findings encourage us to try to carry out a deeper analysis of the key factors in determining income differentials by gender.

Decomposition of the wage gap between men and women

A conventional procedure of decomposition suggested by Oaxaca (1973) and Blinder (1973) can be used to analyse the impact of different variables on wage differences among men and women workers. For each foreign community the separate estimated earnings eqn (1), that can be expressed in compact manner for male immigrants as $\ln W_i^m = \alpha_i^m + \sum_j \beta_{ij}^m \cdot X_{ij}^m + u_i^m$ and for female immigrants as $\ln W_i^w = \alpha_i^w + \sum_j \beta_{ij}^w \cdot X_{ij}^w + u_i^w$, can be used to decompose the difference in wage levels. Assuming the average values of the variables in the two examined groups, the wage difference among foreign immigrated men and women can be decomposed as follows:

$$\begin{aligned}\overline{\ln W^m} - \overline{\ln W^w} &= \alpha^m + \sum_j \beta_j^m \cdot \overline{X}_j^m - \alpha^w - \sum_j \beta_j^w \cdot \overline{X}_j^w \\ &= (\alpha^m - \alpha^w) + \sum_j (\beta_j^m - \beta_j^w) \cdot \overline{X}_j^w + \sum_j \beta_j^m \cdot (\overline{X}_j^m - \overline{X}_j^w) \qquad (2)\end{aligned}$$

where the difference of the natural logarithm of wage for men and women immigrant workers $(\overline{\ln W^m} - \overline{\ln W^w})$ can be decomposed into two factors: one is linked to the socio-economic differences in the individuals of the two sub-samples EQN $(\sum_j \beta_j^m \cdot (\overline{X}_j^m - \overline{X}_j^w))$; the other is given by a residual factor. First and second term of right-hand side (rhs) of eqn (2) represent the part of the earnings gap not explained by the different worker characteristics considered in the regression. This unexplained part of the earning gap can be seen as a measure of 'discrimination'.[22] This formula is largely used when analysing wage differences by gender and/or ethnic groups, and it should be assumed that the wage structure that would prevail in the absence of discrimination is more likely to be closer to the wage function for men rather than to the wage function for women.[23] Different solutions were suggested to consider the sample selection bias in the context of labour market discrimination (Reimers 1983; Miller 1987).

[22] The component identified as discrimination contains unexplained differences in constant terms. In other words, the residual is a mixture of discrimination and other omitted influences (Jones 1983). Thus, the unexplained section should be assumed as 'discrimination' if it does not include unspecified differences in production characteristics.

[23] In other papers (see Reimers 1983; Cotton 1988) the use was suggested of unobserved non-discriminatory wage structure (β^*) a mean of OLS wage regression coefficients assigning equal weight to both groups ($\beta^* = 0.5 \cdot (\beta^m + \beta^w)$) or a weighted mean ($\beta^* = f^m \cdot \beta^m + f^m \cdot \beta^w$). The results emerging from the adoption of these other solutions are similar to those shown.

Table 7.8 shows the summary results of the decomposition analysis, where the importance of each of the explanatory variable is also estimated separately. First of all, it is to be noted how the observed earning gap by gender becomes progressively wider passing from the Moroccan to the Pole communities, and then on to the community of Former Yugoslavians. Log wage gender differential is 0.166 for Moroccans, 0.328 for the Poles and 0.361 for the Former Yugoslavians[24] (shown on the second-last row of Table 7.8). Among Moroccans, out of total earning differentials between men and women (0.166 log wage in favour of men), 0.041 should be the log wage in favour of women due to their more productive endowments and working conditions. Consequently 0.208 is the log wage differential due to structural differences in their wage function. Thus, the remaining differentials (0.208 of log wage) are the result of unexplained variables in favour of men. In other words, if female Moroccan workers were to be rewarded for their labour market skills and work characteristics at the same rate as male Moroccan workers,[25] the earnings differentials between the two groups would be at least completely reduced. It has to be underlined how the human capital, the branch's structure of employment and the strong efforts made in terms of weekly working hours justify the wage differential in favour of males (positive values in the endowments column on Table 6.8). But this disadvantage for females appears to be more than compensated by the demographic characteristics, legal presence, and, above all, by the territorial distribution resulting as being more favourable for women than for men (negative values in the endowments column of Table 7.8). In other words, women succeed in compensating the disadvantage of having less human capital (education, knowledge of the Italian language, and working experience in Italy), an unfavourable structure by sector of employment (greater presence in the trade and domestic services sectors) and the lesser number of average hours worked weekly, with an average much higher age, a greater number of family members living together,[26] a lesser illegal component and a stronger presence in Veneto and Lazio, two regions where income is higher.

With regard to Former Yugoslavians and Poles, the earning gap is mainly determined by individual aspects and characteristics of employment. In fact, among

[24] The minor differences in income by gender between the Moroccans depend on the fact that this community has the lowest average income for men, and the highest among the women. This last circumstance basically seems to be tied to the strong selection made by Moroccan women in their participation in the employment market, also previously shown by the significance of the regression coefficient for the selection variable.

[25] Employed Moroccan women have a slightly higher average age than that of Moroccan men. They usually have legal residence permits and a greater work stability. For the most part, other characteristics are similar to those for men.

[26] The regression coefficient related to the variable for families living together, even not having any significant statistical import, does have, contrary to expectations, a positive sign. A sign, therefore, different from that recorded for the women in the other two communities. Thus the greater number of families recorded among the Moroccan women instead of explaining a part of the wage differential by gender, would appear to constitute a factor that should determine greater earnings for women with respect to men in the same community.

Table 7.8. *Decomposition of Wage Differentials between Men and Women for Moroccan, Former Yugoslavian, and Pole Immigrants Interviewed in some Italian Areas in 1998*

Variable	Moroccans			Former Yogoslavians			Poles		
	Total	Endowments[a]	Coefficients[b]	Total	Endowments[a]	Coefficients[b]	Total	Endowments[a]	Coefficients[b]
AGE	−0.378	−0.002	−0.376	−0.134	0.002	−0.136	0.143	−0.015	0.158
RELATIVES	−0.078	−0.045	−0.033	0.162	0.002	0.161	0.065	0.023	0.042
LEGAL	0.236	−0.021	0.257	0.316	−0.020	0.336	0.009	−0.002	0.010
YSCHOOL	0.032	0.008	0.024	−0.244	−0.008	−0.236	0.039	−0.020	0.060
ITALIAN	−0.295	0.005	−0.300	−0.250	−0.014	−0.236	0.320	−0.006	0.326
JOBEXPIT	−0.089	0.002	−0.091	−0.041	0.004	−0.045	0.045	0.003	0.042
STABWORK	0.116	−0.004	0.120	−0.216	0.001	−0.217	−0.024	0.011	−0.035
DEPENDENT	0.320	0.006	0.314	0.744	0.000	0.744	0.346	0.003	0.343
AGRIND	0.114	0.047	0.067	−0.035	−0.007	−0.028	0.157	0.149	0.008
DISTRHOUSE	0.197	0.019	0.178	0.029	0.193	−0.164	0.097	0.070	0.027
CAMPANIA	−0.124	−0.120	−0.003	—	—	—	0.023	0.048	−0.024
VENETO	−0.026	−0.013	−0.014	−0.161	0.003	−0.164	—	—	—
LNHOURS	−0.395	0.083	−0.478	0.785	0.168	0.617	0.862	0.000	0.862
WORKACCOM	−0.007	−0.001	−0.006	0.067	0.021	0.046	0.080	0.022	0.059
SELECT	−0.260	−0.006	−0.254	−0.037	0.005	−0.042	0.078	0.012	0.066
Constant	0.803	0.000	0.803	−0.626	0.000	−0.626	−1.911	0.000	−1.911
Total contribution									
Absolute values	0.166	−0.041	0.208	0.361	0.351	0.010	0.328	0.298	0.031
Percentage values	100.0	−24.9	124.9	100.0	97.2	2.8	100.0	90.6	9.4

[a] Third component of rhs of eqn (2)
[b] First and second term of rhs of eqn (2).

Source: Our processing of sample survey data on 'Labour market integration, earnings and remittances of foreign immigrants' (University of Rome "La Sapienza").

Former Yugoslavians, about 97 per cent of wage differential is due to less productive endowments and only 3 per cent to differences in their wage function. For Poles they are about 91 and 9 per cent respectively (Table 7.8). For the first community 0.186 of a total of 0.351 log wage difference by gender (corresponding to 51.6 per cent) is due to structure by sector of employment and for the second one 0.219 of a total of 0.298 log wage difference (corresponding to 66.7 per cent) (Table 7.8). Therefore, it should be pointed out that the structure by sector of employment is the basic and central element to understand the gender wage differences for Former Yugoslavians and especially for Poles.[27] This is an additional evidence of how this division of employment for immigrant women in this community, mainly employed in the domestic service sector, represents the principal element in determining the lowest average income for women, compared with that of their male counterpart.

The Moroccan case should be further discussed: Moroccan women have a lower labour market participation rate than women from the other two foreign communities. Those employed who are a selected group, have a lower observed earning differential with men than the women from the other two communities with their male counterpart. But the earning gap for Moroccan women is not explained by the individual and employment characteristics by gender differences.[28] This perhaps depends firstly on the strongly aggregated nature shown in the organization of employment categories, possibly concealing differences in the employment sector and in the jobs carried out. This explains, at least in part, the different wages by gender. In addition, and not to be ignored, could perhaps be the subordinate situations encountered in the search for jobs and when carrying out the work of a male fellow national, specially a husband, in the case of Moroccan women. Besides, even the same work opportunity could result as being just integrative to that of the male, in such way contributing to the family budget without providing any conflict from the cultural viewpoint and ensuring, at the same time, the completion of domestic duties.

Despite the changing of female condition of life in Morocco, we have to consider that women in their country of origin show a low rate of labour participation and are relegated to unskilled activities. Moreover Moroccan women, in many cases, still have a subordinate role in migratory processes (Campani 2000), as highlighted also in the first section. The employment of Moroccan women is supposed to be an extension of their domestic behaviour and a further help to their family (Giannini 1994). According to Campani (2000), the work outside household is scarcely important in

[27] In the case of the Former Yugoslavians a role not to be considered as secondary is played also by the lower number of average hours worked by the women. Instead, in the case of the Poles, a role which cannot be ignored has to be assigned to the different territorial distribution. In fact, Pole women have a stronger proportion of presence in Campania, particularly in the commune of Naples, than that recorded for males. In this area particularly, the wages are less. For both communities a certain relevance is ultimately assumed by a significant presence among the women of forms of non-monetary compensation (Table 7.8).

[28] Basically it has to be remembered that the number of interviews available is quite restricted, above all when looking at the problem of employed women at the time of the survey. Therefore, we need to consider the results obtained with a certain caution, while awaiting further evidence from broader surveys.

the building of female identity of Moroccan immigrant women. Their opportunity of emancipation is concentrated especially within the family relations (Campani 2000).

These are structural characteristics which the data do not succeed in bringing to light, and cultural reasons can therefore also explain the persistence of differences in earnings between the two genders, all other characteristics being equal.

SUMMARY OF RESULTS AND CONCLUDING REMARKS

Foreign immigration to Italy is characterized, just as in other Southern Europe countries experiencing new waves of immigration, by the presence of a broad spectrum of foreign communities with different structures according to gender. This fact is mainly due to different adopted migration patterns and early stages of the migratory process.

There are communities (e.g. those from Pakistan, Senegal, Morocco, Egypt, Tunisia, India, and Iran) characterized by strong gender differences because the female component migrated prevalently to join immediate family members. These show a low participation in the labour market and high unemployment rates, while the male component is characterized by a high rate of regular employment. Other communities (Former Yugoslavia, Poland, Ghana, Nigeria, Ethiopia, Somalia, Sri Lana, and the Philippines) show less distance between the male and female components due to the scarce differences in gender as to work opportunities. Other communities show gender differences both as regards capability to find a job as well as status in employment because the women result as being almost exclusively paid employees in the domestic service sector. Only in the case of the Philippine community there is a notable gender equality. In many cases, Philippine women migrated before the men, and were able to ease their arrival and participation in the labour market. For this reason, men are mainly employed in the same occupational sector as women, that is, the domestic service sector.

Gender differences were assessed as to participation in the labour market and earnings by typology of migration. For the three communities considered (Moroccans, former Yugoslavians, and Poles), the proportion of regular and non-regular employed foreigners was determined through a sample survey. Among Moroccans, immigrants' earnings are largely determined by gender rather than by sector of employment. The observed wage gap for Moroccan women is smaller than in other communities but is not explained by the different characteristics by gender. A hypothesis has been made that this depends on access to the labour market, totally controlled by the male component. Among Poles and Former Yugoslavian communities, women seem to earn less than men because they are more frequently paid in kind, often benefiting from free accommodation in their place of employment, and due to the fact that their work is restricted to the domestic service sector, characterized by lower wages.

Therefore, in Italy, the pattern of participation in the labour market of immigrant women is determined not only by their citizenship, but also by the reasons behind their migration and therefore the role played by women in the migratory process. Our findings show that for communities where the women migrated mainly for reasons of family reunification, their reduced participation in the labour market could be characterized by an employment structure by sector similar to men and by a wage gap between the sexes that could be due to economic discrimination. The high participation in the labour market of women migrating in search of work, is often characterized by employment and geographical segregation, implicating a larger wage gap.

This aspect has been clearly brought out also in some recent contributions regarding foreign immigration in North America. As highlighted by Powers and Seltzer (1998), gender-related employment segregation could be one of the most important issues for the integration process of women from some immigrant communities. This aspect especially concerns the foreign communities mainly working in the domestic service sector. Up to now they have recorded a reduced professional mobility, and different employment possibilities have been mainly limited to working hours in the domestic service sector, often changing over from 'night and day' duties to working on a daily or hourly basis. The meagre possibilities for socio-professional improvement could represent a risk in the integration process if exclusion becomes permanent with a division in the labour market which could become structural and cause more powerful social tensions.

References

Bailey, T. (1985), 'The Influence of Legal Status on the Labour Market Impact of Immigration', *International Migration Review*, 19: 220–38.

Baldacci, E., Inglese, L., and Strozza, S. (1999), 'Determinants of Foreign Workers' Wages in Two Italian Regions with High Illegal Immigration', *Labour*, 13(3): 675–709.

Barsotti, O. (ed.) (1989), *La presenza straniera in Italia. Il caso della Toscana*. Milano: F. Angeli.

—— and Lecchini, L. (1988), 'Caratteristiche demografiche ed economico-sociali della presenza straniera in Toscana'. *Studi Emigrazione—Etudes Migrations*, 91–2: 382–8.

—— —— (1995), 'The Experience of Filipino Female Migrants in Italy', in United Nations, *International Migration Policies and the Status of Female Migrants*, 153–62.

Berndt, E. R. (1991), *The Practice of Econometrics*, Massachusetts: Addison Wesley.

Birindelli, A. M. (1986), 'L'immigrazione straniera a Roma: problemi ed esperienze della prima fase dell'indagine'. *Studi Emigrazione—Etudes Migrations*, 82–3: 391–402.

Blangiardo G. C. (1993), 'Una nuova metodologia del campionamento per le indagini sulla presenza straniera', in Di Comite L., De Candia M. (eds), *I fenomeni migratori nel bacino mediterraneo*. Quaderni n. 6, Dipartimento per lo studio delle società mediterranee. Bari: Cacucci Editore: 27–44.

—— (1996), 'Il campionamento per centri o ambienti di aggregazione nelle indagini sulla presenza straniera', in *Studi in onore di G. Landenna*, Milano, Giuffrè: 13–30.

—— (1998), 'Relazione di sintesi sugli aspetti quantitativi della presenza straniera irregolare', in Presidenza del Consiglio dei Ministri, *Relazione sulla presenza straniera in Italia e sulle situazioni di irregolarità*, Gazzetta Ufficiale, 15 September 1998: 62–74.

Blinder, A. (1973), 'Wage Discrimination: Reduced Form and Structural Estimates', *Journal of Human Resources*, 8(4): 436–55.

Bonifazi, C. (1998), *Immigrazione straniera in Italia*, Bologna: Il Mulino.

Borjas, G. J. (1985), 'Assimilation, Changes in Cohort Quality and the Earnings of Immigrants'. *Journal of Labor Economics*, 3: 463–89.

——and Tienda, M. (1993), 'The Employment and Wages of Legalized Immigrants'. *International Migration Review*, 27(3): 712–47.

Boyd, M. (1995), 'Migration Regulations and Sex Selective Outcomes in Developed Countries, in United Nations', *International Migration Policies and the Status of Female Migrants*: 83–98.

Cacciani, I., Casacchia, O., Diana, P., and Strozza, S. (1998), 'Production systems, local labour market and geographical distribution of some immigrant communities in Italy: initial empirical evidence', paper presented at Conference on International Migration: Challenges for European Populations, EAPS, Bari, June 25–27.

Campani, G. (1990), 'Donne immigrate in Italia', in Cocchi G. (ed.), *Stranieri in Italia*, Bologna: Misure/Materiali di Ricerca dell'Istituto Cattaneo, 3–16.

——(2000), *Genere, etnia e classe. Migrazioni al femminile tra esclusione e identità*, Pisa: Edizioni ETS.

Campus, A., Maffenini, W., and Blangiardo, G. C. (1988), 'La presenza straniera nell'area milanese: osservazioni e scelte per l'impostazione di una nuova ricerca', *Studi Emigrazione—Etudes Migrations*, 82–3: 380–6.

Casacchia, O. and Natale, L. (1993), '*Female immigrant and labour market in Italy*', paper presented at Cicred.

——and Strozza, S. (1995), 'Il livello di integrazione socio-economica degli immigrati stranieri: un quadro di riferimento', in SIS, *Continuità e discontinuità nei processi demografici. L'Italia nella transizione demografica*. Rubettino: 553–60.

Chiswick, B. R. (1978), 'The effect of Americanisation on the Earnings of Foreign-Born Men', *Journal of Political Economics*, 86(5): 897–921.

——(1984), 'Illegal Alien in the United States Labor Market: Analysis of occupational Attainment and Earnings', *International Migration Review*, 18(3): 714–32.

Cotton, J. (1988), 'On the Decomposition of Wage Differentials'. *Review of Economics and Statistics*, 70: 236–43.

De Filippo, E. (1994), 'Le lavoratrici 'giorno e notte', in Vicarelli, G. (ed.), *Le mani invisibili. La vita e il lavoro delle donne immigrate*, Ediesse, 65–72.

Donato, K. M., Durand, J., and Massey, D. S. (1992), 'Changing conditions in the US labor market. Effects of the Immigration Reform and Control Act of 1986', *Population Research and Policy Review*, 11: 93–115.

Donato, K. M. and Massey D. S. (1993), 'Effects of the Immigration Reform and Control Act on the Wages of Mexican Migrants', *Social Science Quarterly*, 74: 523–41.

Duleep, H. O. and Sanders, S. (1993), 'The Decision to Work by Married Immigrant Women', *Industrial and Labor Relations Review*, 46(4): 677–90.

Favaro, G. (1991), 'Le donne immigrate: progetti, vissuti e strategie d'inserimento', in Favaro G. and Tognetti Bordogna M. (eds), *Donne dal mondo. Strategie migratorie al femminile.* Guerini e Associati.

Giannini, M. (1994), 'Donne del Sud', in Vicarelli, G. (ed.), *Le mani invisibili. La vita e il lavoro delle donne immigrate*, Roma: Ediesse.

Giovannelli, R. (1999), 'Caratteristiche e comportamento economico degli stranieri immigrati', Degree thesis in Scienze Statistiche Demografiche e Sociali, Università di Roma 'La Sapienza'.

Giudici, C. (1997), 'Les femmes face au projet migratoire', *Studi Emigrazione—Migration Studies*, XXXIV, 127: 467–85.

Goldenberger, A. S. (1981), 'Linear Regression After Selection', *Journal of Econometrics* 15(3): 293–318.

Golini, A., Strozza, S., and Gallo, G. (1999), 'Population trends and migratory pressure in the European Economic Area and the Euro-Middle East-Africa Region', paper presented to the IV Italy—Germany Forum, Milan: Istituto di Studi Politici Internazionali (ISPI).

Grasso, M. (1994), *Donne senza confini. Immigrate in Italia tra marginalità e emancipazione*, Torino: L'Harmattan Italia.

Greene, W. H. (1981), 'On the Asymptotic Bias of the Ordinary Least Squares Estimator'. *Econometrica*, 49(2): 505–13.

Halli, S. S. and Rao, K. V. (1990), *Advanced Techniques of Population Analysis*, New York and London: Plenum Press.

Halvorsen, R. and Palmquist, R. (1979), 'The Interpretation of Dummy Variables in Semilogarithmic Equation', *American Economic Review*, 70(3): 474–5.

Heckman, J. (1976), 'The Common Structure of Statistical Models of Truncation, Sample Selection and Limited Dependent Variables and a Simple Estimator for Such Models', *Annals of Economic and Social Measurement*, 5(4): S11–S44.

—— (1979), 'Sample Selection Bias as a Specification Error'. *Econometrica*, 47(1): 153–61.

Hugo, G. (1999), 'Gender and Migration in Asian Countries', in Pinnelli, A. (ed.), *Gender in Population Studies*, Liège: IUSSP.

ISTAT (1991), *Gli immigrati presenti in Italia. Una stima per l'anno 1989*. Note e relazioni n. 1. Roma.

—— (1998), *La presenza straniera in Italia negli anni '90*. Informazioni n. 61. Roma.

—— (1999), *La presenza straniera in Italia: caratteristiche demografiche*. Informazioni n. 6. Roma.

Johnson, R. A. and Wichern, D. W. (1992), *Applied Multivariate Statistical Analysis*, Englewood Cliffs: Prentice-Hall International, Inc.

Jones, F. L. (1983), 'On Decomposing the Wage Gaps: A Critical Comment on Blinder's Method', *Journal of Human Resources*, 18: 126–30.

Kofman, E. (1999), 'Female "Birds of Passage" a Decade Later: Gender and Immigration in the European Union', *International Migration Review*, 33(2): 269–99.

Lim, L.L (1995), 'The Status of Women in International Migration, in United Nations. *International Migration Policies and the Status of Female Migrants*, : 29–55.

Lodigiani, R. (1994), 'Donne migranti e reti informali'. *Studi Emigrazione—Etudes Migratons*, 115: 494–505.

Long, J. E. (1980), 'The Effects of Americanization on Earnings: Some Evidence for Women'. *The Journal of Political Economy*, 88(3): 620–9.

MacPherson, D. A. and Stewart, J. B. (1989), 'The Labor Force Participation and Earnings Profiles of Married Female Immigrants', *Quarterly Review Economic Business*, 29(3): 57–72.

Maddala, M. (1996), *Introduction to Econometrics*, New York: Prentice Hall.

Makinwa, P. and Afolayan, A. A. (1995), 'Migration and Women's Status in SubSaharan Africa', in Makinwa, P. and Jensen, A. M. (eds), *Women's Position and Demographic Change in Sub-Saharan Africa*. Liège: IUSSP, 253–69.

Massey, D. S. (1987), 'Do Undocumented Migrants Earn Lower Wages than Legal Immigrants? New Evidence from Mexico', *International Migration Review*, 21(2): 236–74.

Migliorati, S. (1997), 'Alcune considerazioni sul campionamento per centri', *Statistica Applicata*, 9(3): 369–86.

Miller, P. W. (1987), 'Gender Differences in Observed and Offered Wages in Canada, 1980', *Canadian Journal of Economics*, 20: 225–44.

Mincer, J. (1974), *Schooling, Experience and Earnings*, New York: Columbia University Press for NBER.

Moretti, E. and Strozza, S. (1996), 'L'esperienza italiana delle due indagini coordinate sulla presenza straniera in Italia: obiettivi, contributi metodologici, difficoltà', *Rivista Italiana di Economia, Demografia e Statistica*, L (2): 357–94.

Natale, M. (1990), 'L'immigrazione straniera in Italia: consistenza, caratteristiche, prospettive', *Polis*, IV (1): 5–40.

Natale, M. and Strozza, S. (1997), *Gli immigrati stranieri in Italia. Quanti sono, chi sono, come vivono?* Bari: Cacucci Editore.

Oaxaca, R. (1973), 'Male-Female Wage Differentials in Urban Labour Market', *International Economic Review*, 14(3): 693–709.

Olsen, R. J. (1980), 'A Least Squares Correction for Selectivity Bias'. *Econometrica*, 48(7): 1815–30.

Phillips, J. A. and Massey, D. S. (1999), 'The New Labor Market: Immigrants and Wages After IRCA'. *Demography*, 36(2): 233–46.

Powers, M. G. and Seltzer, W. (1998), 'Occupational Status and Mobility Among Undocumented Immigrants by Gender'. *International Migration Review*, 32(1): 21–55.

Raffaele, G. (1992), 'Le immigrate extracomunitarie in Italia'. *Studi Emigrazione—Etudes Migrations*, 106: 194–225.

Reimers, C.W. (1983), 'Labor Market Discrimination against Hispanic and Black Men'. *Review of Economics and Statistics*, 65: 570–9.

—— (1984), 'Sources of the Family Income Differences among Hispanics, Blacks and White Non-Hispanics'. *American Journal of Sociology*, 89(4): 889–903.

—— (1985), 'Cultural Differences in Labor Force Participation Among Married Women'. *American Economic Review*, Papers and Proceedings, 75(2): 251–5.

Reyneri, E. (1998*a*), 'Immigrazione ed economia sommersa', *Stato e Mercato*, 53: 287–317.

—— (1998*b*), 'The Role of Underground Economy in Irregular Migration to Italy: Cause or Effects', *Journal of Ethnic and Migration Studies*, 24(2): 313–31.

Saint-Blancat, C. (1995), *L'islam della diaspora*, Roma: Ed. Lavoro.

Schmidt di Friedberg, O. and Saint-Blancat, C. (1998), 'L'immigration au féminin: les femmes marocaines en Italie du nord. Une recherche en Vénétie', *Studi Emigrazione—Migration Studies*, 131: 483–97.

Schoeni, R. (1998), 'Labor Market Outcomes of Immigrant Women in the United States: 1970 to 1990', *International Migration Review*, 32(1): 56–77.

Schoorl, J. J. (1995), 'Comparing the position of Moroccan and Turkish Women in the Netherlands and in the Countries of Origin', in United Nations, *International Migration Policies and the Status of Female Migrants*: 131–52.

Shamsuddin, A. F. M. (1998), 'The double-negative effect on the earnings of foreign-born females in Canada', *Applied Economics*, 30(9): 1187–99.

Stark, O. (1991), *The Migration of Labor*, Cambridge, MA: Clackwell Publishers.

Strozza, S. (1995), 'I lavoratori extracomunitari in Italia: un esame della letteratura ed un tentativo di verifica di alcune ipotesi', *Studi Emigrazione—Etudes Migrations*, 119: 457–90.

—— (1996), 'Migrations internationales, desequilibres demographiques et economies irregulieres', in Colajanni, A. and Maffioli, D. (eds), *Gens de la mediterranee*, Rome: Ricerca e Cooperazione: 29–56.

—— (1999), 'Foreign immigrants in Italy: estimates of legal and illegal presence', mimeo.

Tapinos, G. P. (1995), 'Female Migration and the Status of Foreign Women in France' in United Nations, *International Migration Policies and the Status of Female Migrants*, 99–115.

United Nations (1994), *The Migration of Women. Methodological Issues in the Measurement and Analysis of Internal and International Migration*, Santo Domingo: U.N.-INSTRAW.

United Nations (1995), *International Migration Policies and the Status of Female Migrants*, Proceedings of the United Nations Expert Group Meeting on International Migration Policies and the Status of Female Migrants. San Miniato, Italy, March 28–31, 1990.

United Nations Secretariat (1995), 'The International Migration of Women: An Overview' in *International Migration Policies and the Status of Female Migrants*, Proceedings of the United Nations Expert Group Meeting on International Migration Policies and the Status of Female Migrants. San Miniato, Italy, March, 28–31 1990.

Venturini, A. and Villosio, C. (1998), 'Foreign workers in Italy: are they assimilating to Natives? Are they competing against Natives? An Analysis by the SSA dataset', paper presented at the Conference on 'Flussi migratori: cause ed effetti', Napoli: Istituto Universitario Navale.

Vicarelli, G. (1992), 'Emigrazioni e mercato del lavoro: differenze di genere'. *Sociologia del lavoro*, 47–48: 56–77.

—— (1994*a*), 'Immigrazioni al femminile', in Vicarelli, G. (ed.), *Le mani invisibili. La vita e il lavoro delle donne immigrate*, Roma: Ediesse: 10–24.

—— (1994*b*), 'L'economia della vita quotidiana', in Vicarelli, G. (ed.), *Le mani invisibili. La vita e il lavoro delle donne immigrate*, Roma: Ediesse: 26–39.

Zlotnick, H. (1993), 'Discussion note', Meeting on the Economic Roles of Migrant Women, Cicred, June 16–18.

—— (1995), 'The South-to-North Migration of Women', *International Migration Review*, 29(1), Spring: 229–54.

8

Double Jeopardy? Female Rural Migrant Labourers in Urban China, The Case of Shanghai

WANG FENG AND SHEN ANAN

Two fundamental economic and social transformations of the past two decades are redefining the lives of Chinese women simultaneously. One transformation involves an economic transformation characterized by a shift from a centrally planned economy to a market-oriented economy. The other is a transition from a predominantly agrarian economy to an industrial and post-industrial economy.

As a result of the first transformation, China's state dominance and control over the economy has been weakened drastically during the past two decades. Between 1978 and 1993, for instance, the share of retail sales in China that was under the government's fixed prices declined from 97 to 5 per cent, whereas the share under market or 'guidance' prices rose from 3 to 95 per cent (Naughton 1995: 14). The state has also lost its dominance in industrial production. The share of total value of industrial output by state-owned enterprises dropped from 78 per cent in 1978 (Naughton 1995: 14) to 55 per cent in 1990 and to 28.5 per cent in 1998 (SSB 1999: 9). At the same time, the share produced by private- and foreign-owned enterprises rose from non-existent to 10 per cent in 1990 and 37.8 per cent in 1998 (SSB 1999: 9). Private- and foreign-owned enterprises, in other words, have exceeded the state-owned sector in industrial production.

A most suitable measure to gauge the second transformation is the share of the labour force employed in agriculture. During the first two decades of China's industrialization prior to the recent forms, the gross value of industrial output rose by sixteen-fold between 1952 and 1978 (SSB 1984: 12). This rise, however, was not accompanied by a corresponding labour force transfer from agriculture to industries. In fact, the absolute number of labourers employed in agriculture increased by more than 60 per cent, from 173.2 million in 1952 to 283.1 million in 1978 (SSB 1995: 83). The early phase of China's industrialization under socialism, therefore, was achieved in the absence of labour transfer both from agriculture and from the countryside. Such a pattern of growth, exacerbated by a fast population growth rate in the 1960s and the 1970s, resulted in a serious labour surplus and underemployment in rural China.

We would like to thank colleagues at Shanghai Academy of Social Sciences who participated in the surveys from which we draw our data, and the Ford Foundation for partial funding of the 1995 Shanghai Floating Population Survey. We would also like to thank Antonella Pinnelli and other reviewers of this paper for their helpful suggestions.

This is not the case for the last two decades. The share of the labour force participating in what the Chinese call the first industry—agriculture—declined steadily, from 70.5 per cent in 1978, to 60.1 per cent in 1990, and to 49.8 per cent in 1998 (SSB 1999: 34). Correspondingly, the official statistics report a rapid increase in non-agricultural employment in the Chinese countryside: those working in rural township and village enterprises (TVEs) and self-employed rose from 28.3 million in 1978 to 173.7 million in 1996, an over six-fold explosion in less than 20 years (SSB 1999: 33).

Both transformations have particularly profound impacts on Chinese women, especially those residing in the countryside. Whereas achieving gender equality was an important political agenda under socialism, a transition away from socialism has been accompanied by the state's weakening of its earlier commitment. Ideological preferences have given way to the needs of attracting foreign capital and to the profitability and efficiency of these and other capital. Unlike in a socialist planned economy where both capital and labour are under the same public ownership, a capitalist economy means that capital and labour are now pitted against each other. As a result of the state's ideological withdrawal, whether women should stay in the labour force or return to home as housewives became a publicly hotly debated subject in the 1980s. Factory managers also began to express openly their unwillingness to hire female workers.[1] Female labour migrants, whose employment is mostly in non-state controlled firms, are especially vulnerable to the powers of capital owners (Tan 1998: 128).

At the same time, while moving away from agriculture and moving into industries have opened up unprecedented opportunities for rural women, their migration into cities present them another set of challenges. Their fate would have been comparable to female migrants in other developing countries, had there not been the legacy of the Chinese socialism. This legacy is the deepened divide between urban and rural areas under socialism. Though not as an intended outcome, China's achieved its rapid industrialization goals at the expense of its rural population. Differential treatment of urban and rural labour force and a strict migration control policy between rural and urban areas resulted in effectively two different types of citizenship within a single national population (Chan 1994: Solinger 1999). The system of two types of citizenship within China was in part maintained by a household registration (*hukou*) system installed in the late 1950s that assigned residents 'agricultural' and 'non-agricultural' registration status separately. Urban residents, most of them belonged to the 'non-agricultural' category, received preferential social, political, and economic benefits. Not only did they

[1] The top two main reasons given by factory managers, according to a survey of 100 firms conducted by sociologist Xu Anqi, were 'women have too much household work, and ask for leave too often', and 'women's childbearing and maternity leave are too long' (Lu 1995: 31–2). A survey conducted by the Women's Department of China's National Labour Union in 1997 report among 423 leaders of surveyed enterprises, 71.6 per cent admit to prefer hiring male over female workers. Also, 36.6 per cent of these leaders and 40.6 per cent of surveyed women believe women's special needs as cited in Xu's study above contribute to female workers' laying off and their difficulty in re-employment. To the question of whether females are discriminated against in employment after being laid-off, 51.8 per cent of female workers and 77.1 per cent of male workers believe this is indeed the case (WDCNLU 1998: 110–11). The survey collected information from 6,413 laid off female workers and 669 male workers in 14 different provinces and municipalities of China.

have preferred access to urban infrastructure, they also enjoyed guaranteed employment. Along with employment in urban-based, state or collectively owned, institutions, urban employees received guaranteed income, their families virtually free public housing, and free public education and medical care (Cheng and Selden 1994). For those with 'agricultural' household registration status, there were no such state-rendered benefits. Instead, they relied on themselves for their livelihood, in the rural agricultural collectives. Moreover, with very few exceptions, changing one's 'agricultural' household registration status to 'non-agricultural' status was literally impossible under the socialist planned economy system. Although economic and social reforms in the past two decades have opened up new opportunities for rural labourers to migrate and to work in cities, rural labour migrants, whose number has reached as many as 60 million, are still treated in urban areas like secondary citizens. From legal residential status, labour market entrance and placement, income and benefits, to medical care and housing, rural migrants and local urban residents have so far co-existed but have not integrated. Female Chinese rural labourers, in other words, not only need to move into a non-agricultural labour market to compete with men, but also into the emerging labour markets in Chinese cities, to compete with *urban* Chinese *men and women.*

Female rural migrant labourers therefore represent a most interesting population group to examine the multi-faceted impacts of economic and political transitions on the lives of women. On the one hand, female migrants' move away from the countryside provides them with new employment and life style opportunities. On the other hand, in their new destination, they are subject to not only a deep-rooted system of gender discrimination in the society, but also system of urban bias with socialist characteristics against rural migrants. Female migrant labourers, therefore, may well face what we call a 'double jeopardy' in urban China.

In this chapter, we examine the fate of female rural migrant labourers in two overlapping labour markets: an emerging market-oriented labour market, overlaid on top of a remnant urban labour market influenced by socialist arrangements and legacies. We use Shanghai as our study location, not only because it is China's largest metropolis with 16 million people and 3 million migrants among them, but also because it has an abundance of rich data collected over the past decade. Between 1984 and 1997, the Shanghai municipal government implemented six large-scale surveys of migrants (floating population). In 1995, the Shanghai Academy of Social Sciences carried a more in-depth survey on demographic, migration, and labour market experiences of migrants in Shanghai. In the same year, the Academy also conducted a survey of local residents. Our analyses shall utilize some of these data and shall focus on two sets of comparisons: *female* migrant labourers compared with *male* migrant labourers, and female *migrant* labourers compared with female urban *resident* labourers.[2] Areas of comparisons include demographic and social background, as well as labour market experiences, such as industrial and occupational

[2] We leave out male residents in our comparisons to highlight the comparisons between gender (comparing female and male migrants only), and residential status (comparing migrant and non-migrant females only). See footnote 7 for more discussion of male labourers of residential status.

distributions and income and benefits. Moreover, by using micro-level data from the 1995 survey, we shall model explicitly the extent to which female migrant labourers are experiencing what we call a 'double jeopardy' in China's transitional economy: a simultaneous encounter with both a capitalistic and a socialist labour market.

FEMALE MIGRANTS AND FEMALE MIGRANT LABOURERS IN SHANGHAI

Chinese women have made up a major part of the recent massive labour flows from rural to urban China. Contrary to the belief that men go out to make a living and women stay home to raise children, Chinese women have seized the opportunity of upward social and economic mobility via the route of migration as much as men. A longitudinal survey of 222 villages conducted by the Institute of Rural Development of the Chinese Academy of Social Sciences, for instance, found that in 1986, only 21.8 per cent of out-migrants were females. In 1994, women's share rose to 37.6 per cent (Tan 1998: 118). In addition, they have also distinguished themselves from their male counterparts in several important ways (Wang 2000). First, females are more likely than males to show up in the unofficial migration streams, namely those who move without changing their official household registration status (Goldstein and Liang 2000; Yang 2000). Males, in other words, have continued to enjoy an advantage in obtaining official sanctions for their moves. Second, female migrants in some ways are less attached to their origins and are freer migrants than their male counterparts. This is shown by their younger age, a higher proportion in the never-married status than male migrants, and more of them intending to stay in cities. They are, in other words, more mobile and more ready to settle down in their new destinations (Tan 1998).[3] Third, female migrant workers are highly segregated into special trades. They have not only found a niche in industries such as textiles, tailoring, and electronics, they have also filled the vacuum of domestic services and sales in urban areas which are left unfilled by men. Such an occupational segregation has resulted in demographic imbalances in some locales, such as in Shenzhen Special Economic Zone in South China, where the 2.4 million temporary migrants heavily dominate the city's rapidly growing population (accounting for 72 per cent of all residents). In the early 1990s, for instance, females outnumbered males by 2.5–1 among 15–19 years old, and 1.25–1 among 20–24 years old (Liang 1996). Another study estimates that in the Pearl River Delta region, where foreign capital created a large number of labour-intensive processing factories, over 60 per cent of the 6 million migrant workers were females (Tan 1998: 119).

[3] The 1997 Shanghai Floating Population Survey report 9.3 per cent female migrants versus only 1.9 per cent who married local Shanghai residents (Zhang 1998: 238). There are also more female than male migrants who indicated their intention to stay in Shanghai. The overall percentage reporting an intention to stay is 24.9 per cent whereas the per cent among female migrants of reproductive age is 28.4 (Zhang 1998: 245, 482).

These and other special characteristics have far reaching implications for Chinese migrating women. Increased labour force participation in the extra-familial context has empowered a large number of rural women with both increased economic resources and expanded social horizons. At the same time, such a pattern of industrial and occupational concentration and segregation also leads to either aggravated collective exploitation (in the case of female-dominated processing factories) or heightened individual control (in the case of household servants). Unorganized and unprotected, female migrants are much more likely to be preys of all sorts of predators, and objects of all kinds of exploitation and manipulation (Tan 1998). In the Special Economic Zone of Shenzhen, for example, single female migrants, who staff over 80 per cent of many processing plants controlled by foreign capital, are socially constructed as 'maiden workers', emphasizing their 'single status, immaturity, imminent marriage, consequent short-term commitment to factory work in Shenzhen, low job aspirations, and low motivation to learn skills' (Lee 1995). In the absence of state intervention in providing welfare and regulating industrial relations, single migrant workers, who rely on waged employment for their livelihood and whose wages are tied to performance, are highly vulnerable and are subject to what Ching Kwan Lee terms a rule of 'localistic despotism' (Lee 1995).

Female migrants in Shanghai share some of the characteristics of Chinese female migrants observed elsewhere. In Shanghai, China's largest metropolis, there has not only been a rapid increase in the number of migrants in recent years, but also an increasingly larger number of female migrants. During the decade of 1983 and 1993, the number of migrants to Shanghai increased almost five-fold, from 0.5 million to 2.81 million. The percentage of migrants compared with resident population also rose correspondingly, from 4.2 per cent in 1983 to 22 per cent by 1993 (Sun 1997; Wang 1995: 31). In other words, by 1993, one out every five persons in Shanghai was an in-migrant. Women are representing an increasingly larger proportion of all migrants to Shanghai. As shown in Table 8.1, in 1988, when the fourth survey of migrants was conducted, 29.6 of all migrants accounted in Shanghai's migrant survey were females. Female migrants' share in all migrants rose to 33.5 per cent by 1993 and to 41 per cent by 1997.

Moreover, more female migrants are moving for economically related reasons, other than moving for attending schools or family reunification purposes (Shen 1995). Compared with 1988 when only less than half of all female migrants reported economic reasons as their purpose of migration, 60 per cent in 1993 and more than 70 per cent in 1997 reported so. Many of these economic migrants, or female migrant labourers, work in factory assembly lines in textile, toy making, garment, and food-processing industries. Among the 11,088 female migrant labourers surveyed in a 1993 survey, the majority, 75.4 per cent, engaged in production-related activities, whereas only 20 per cent in sales and services (Shen 1995). Among the 8,299 female economic migrants surveyed in 1997, the largest share was found in processing plants, 24.4 per cent. The next largest was in sales, 15 per cent. Female migrants also work in restaurant services and as household maids, accounting for 11.1 and 4.1 per cent of female economic migrants respectively (Zhang 1998: 241–2).

Table 8.1. *Changing Characteristics of Female Migrants in Shanghai*

Characteristics	Year		
	1988	**1993**	**1997**
% of female among all migrants	29.6	33.5	41.1
Age composition (%)			
Below 15	15.5	13.0	12.1
15–59	74.9	82.3	83.3
Among them 20–24	21.3	23.9	20.5
60 and above	9.6	4.7	4.6
Education (%)			
College and higher	1.4	3.0	2.8
Senior high school	10.0	9.6	8.3
Junior high school	41.1	43.3	47.4
Primary school	27.4	29.9	30.7
Illiterate or semi-illiterate	19.7	14.2	10.8
Marital status (%)			
Never-married	42.0[a]	35.6	30.1
Currently married	57.0	61.7	67.8
Widowed	0.4	2.3	1.7
Divorced	0.6	0.3	0.5
Reason for migration (%)			
Economic related	46.0	60.9	72.1
Education/training	1.5	2.0	1.4
Visiting relatives and friends/ medical treatment/sightseeing	52.5	37.1	26.5

[a] Among women aged 15 to 49 only.

Sources: Wu, F. (1989) for 1988; Wang, W. (1995) for 1993; Zhang, S. (1998) for 1997.

Over the past decade there have been noticeable changes in the demographic characteristics of female migrants in Shanghai, as shown in Table 8.1. Migrants are increasingly concentrated in working ages. The percentage of female migrants aged below 15 and above 59 both declined, and those aged 15–59 increased, from 75 per cent to 83 per cent between 1988 and 1997. Female migrants' educational composition has also improved somewhat, as seen in the clear reduction in the percentage of illiterate or semi-illiterate female migrants, from close to 20 to 11 per cent. As migration is turning into a permanent feature of Chinese society, more married migrants are moving together as a family. In Shanghai, this is seen in the increase in the proportion of married women among all female migrants, from 57 per cent in 1988 to 67.8 per cent in 1997.

Female migrant labourers also differ from both male migrant labourers and urban female labourers.[4] We present in Table 8.2 comparisons among these three groups based on an in-depth migrant survey and a survey of local Shanghai residents, both conducted in 1995 by the Shanghai Academy of Social Sciences.[5] Compared with male labour migrants, there are more younger females, as shown by the lower mean age. More female labour migrants are also never-married, 42 per cent versus only 33 per cent of males. The educational attainment of female migrants is generally lower than that of male migrants, with a higher percentage of females in the primary school and less schooling category, and a lower percentage in the senior high school category. Females also make substantially less income than males: their average monthly income was only about 70 per cent of male labour migrants'.

Both female and male labour migrants share some common characteristics when compared with female urban labour residents. Migrants have lower levels of educational attainment, lower occupational status, longer work hours, and lower pay. Over 9 per cent of female Shanghai local workers have college or above college education, whereas the percentage among labour migrants is negligible. A much higher percentage of local female labourers are employed in professional or white collar jobs, accounting for nearly 30 per cent of all, whereas the percentages among female and male migrants are only 2 and 4. Although both female and male labour migrants report an average of over 55 working hours per week, which is more than 25 per cent longer than local female workers, they both have lower reported incomes than local female workers. The income disparity is especially pronounced between female labour migrants and female local residents. Labour migrants' mean monthly income was only two thirds of local female labourers'. The economic advantage enjoyed by local residents actually far exceed what is reflected in these wage differences, because urban residents also receive a wide range of in-kind welfare not available to migrants, such as heavily subsidized housing, medical care, education of children, and pensions (Wang *et al.* 2002; Zhang 1998: 311–3).

[4] A labour migrant in our analyses is defined as a migrant who reported working for 5 hours or more at the time when the survey was conducted (see below for description of the survey).

[5] The migrant survey was designed as a stratified, multi-stage, cluster sample survey. Six out of the 12 Shanghai city districts were first selected to represent different areas of Shanghai city. Out of the six selected districts, one was from the urban centre, three from the Central Ring (*zhonghuan*) and two from city–suburb junction areas. Within each chosen district, two street districts (*jiedao*) were selected, and within each chosen street district, two neighbourhood resident committees (*juweihui*) were selected. These selection procedures resulted in the selection of 24 neighbourhood resident committees across Shanghai. At the last stage of sample selection, for each selected neighbourhood, every migrant residing in that area was interviewed, resulting in a sample of 6,609 migrants. Three criteria were used to differentiate a migrant from a non-migrant in this survey. First, neither the respondent nor the spouse of the respondent had an official household registration in Shanghai. Second, the respondent was 15 years or older. Third, the respondent was not in Shanghai for a short business trip, sightseeing, or seeking medical care, and the respondent had either been in Shanghai for a month or longer, or intended to stay for more than a month. These migrants are therefore what the Chinese call 'temporary migrants', namely those who moved without changing their place of household registration. The local population survey followed the above sampling design but only surveyed residents with Shanghai urban household registration status. The sample size for this survey is 3,000.

Table 8.2. *Female Migrant Labourers Compared with Male Migrant Labourers and Urban Female Non-Migrant Labourers*

Item	Female migrant labourers	Male migrant labourers	Female non-migrant labourers
Age (Mean)	26.6	29.3	37.1
(SD)	8.5	9.3	9.6
Marital status (%)			
Never married	41.9	33.3	8.6
Currently married	57.5	66.1	89.3
Remarried	0.3	0.2	1.1
Divorced	0.1	0.1	0.7
Widowed	0.4	0.3	0.3
Education (%)			
Primary and below	42.2	26.7	9.1
Junior high school	53.2	63.1	52.4
Senior high school	4.5	10.8	29.2
College and above	0.05	0.4	9.3
Occupation (%)			
Professional/leader	1.5	2.8	18.8
Office/clerk	0.4	0.9	10.3
Commerce/service	50.7	37.9	25.0
Worker			
Production worker	47.4	58.4	45.9
Hours worked per week (mean)	55.6	55.4	43.1
(SD)	15.4	14.9	10.5
Monthly income (Mean)	437.3	618.9	658.7
(SD)	282.5	446.8	328.3
Number of cases	1,968	3,527	1,295

Sources: 1995 Shanghai Migrant Survey and Shanghai Population and Housing Survey.

GENDER DIFFERENCE: FEMALE AND MALE MIGRANT COMPARISONS

Migration from rural to urban areas has clearly improved Chinese women's economic position, as seen in the income increases following migration, reported in Table 8.3. Overall, as shown in the last column of this table, female migrants witnessed at least a doubling of their monthly income. The most noticeable change is found among the least educated women, whose income increased by over three times. Such a drastic improvement, however, perhaps reflects more the fact of an urban income floor level received by even the least educated labourers than how well these migrant labourers are compensated for their labour. But the attraction to these least educated female migrants is certainly the greatest. At the high end of the educational ladder, we see the smallest relative change in income improvement, only

Table 8.3. *Improvement in Income Among Female Migrants, Shanghai, 1995*

Education	Monthly income (Yuan)				Income increase due to migration
	Before migration		After migration		
	Female	% Male	Female	% Male	
Illiterate	91.7	57	388.5	82	324
Semi-illiterate	112.4	64	303.8	59	170
Primary school	114.6	60	413.9	70	261
Junior high school	150.2	63	451.9	74	201
Senior high school	246.9	69	555.5	75	125
Number of cases	1,408		1,550		

Source and note: Data are from 1995 Shanghai Floating population survey. Income is the mean of reported income at place of origin, before migration, and mean income reported at the time of the survey in Shanghai. Both incomes are measured in Chinese currency Yuan, which by the official exchange rate equals 0.12 US dollars (1 USD = 8.2 Yuan). Some migrants did not report an income at home. Migrants with an educational level of college or higher are excluded from this table due to too few cases.

slightly more than doubling. Income improvement is clearly not proportional for all categories. Whereas these overall marked improvements in income do not necessarily mean an equivalent increase in disposable income, due to a much higher cost of living in cities, they nevertheless demonstrate clearly the positive impact of migration on women's lives.

Moreover, as also shown in Table 8.3, migration benefits women more than men if measured by income only. Whereas reported income before migration among migrating women was no more than 70 per cent of the income reported by migrating men, this is no longer the case after migration. With the exception of one educational category (semi-illiterate, which has a small sample size), female migrants earn at least 70 per cent of male migrants' income in their migrating destinations. Female migrants, in other words, experience a greater increase in their income than male migrants.

The remaining questions are: to what extent is the observed lower income among female migrant labourers (about 30 per cent compared to male migrants) due to their different characteristics such as younger age, lower education, and lower occupational status? To what extent is it due to a market discrimination simply because they are female migrants? To answer questions like these, we resort to analyses that take into considerations simultaneously these and other factors that could affect a migrant's income. We shall first make such comparisons between female and male labour migrants, and then in the next section, compare female migrants and local female urban residents.

The statistical tool we utilize is Ordinary Least Square (OLS) regression. We use the log of monthly income as the dependent variable, and model it as the function of the following sets of factors: seniority, labour input, human capital, and occupation status. A logarithm transformation of monthly income not only removes some of the non-linearity problem in the relationship between dependent and independent variables, but also makes interpretation of regression coefficients more readily understandable. In most cases the regression coefficients can be read as percentage change in income with one unit change in the associated independent variable. All the independent variables included are shown to have important effects on wages in the Chinese labour markets, just as in most other economies. Income is generally positively related to age, labour input, human capital endowment, and occupational status (Walder 1990). To make our comparisons, we introduce variables highlighting migrant status. In the case of the comparison between male and female migrants, we introduce a variable representing female migrants, to contrast them with male migrants. In the case of migrant and local labour comparison, we introduce a variable representing migrant status, to compare migrants with local residents. We use age (in years) and the squared form of age to represent seniority, with the latter used to capture the nonlinear effect. We use hours worked per week as an indicator of labour input, use levels of educational attainment as indicators of human capital, and use reported occupational category to represent occupational status.

The comparisons between female and male migrants are presented in Table 8.4. Here we have three different models. In Model 1, we include only age, age squared, hours worked, and female migrant status. Together these variables explain 12 per cent of the variations in monthly income among all migrants. As expected, age and age squared have positive and negative effects, respectively, and hours worked is positively related to income level. Most relevant to our interest, however, is the effect of female migrant status. The regression coefficient (−0.275) indicates that compared with male migrants, female migrants earn 27.5 per cent less, controlling for age and hours worked.

In Model 2 of Table 8.4, we further control two important income determining factors: education and occupation. Since female migrants have lower educational attainment and lower occupational status than male migrants, we expect by controlling these variables, much of the difference between female and male migrants can be explained away. The results in Table 8.4 show that indeed both educational and occupational attainments have important effects on income. Compared with migrants with primary school or less education, those with a junior high school education make 12.8 per cent more income and those with senior high school and college education make 26.1 and 35.4 per cent more income, respectively. At the same time, migrants whose job can be classified as professional or in a leader position (only a very small percentage falls into this category) make 40.6 per cent compared with manual labourers. Even after controlling for all these other factors, however, being a female migrant labourer still suffers a major economic disadvantage. Female migrants make 23 per cent less compared with male migrants, even when all other independent variables are controlled for.

To examine further the position of female labour migrants in the urban labour market, we introduce a set of interaction terms between female migrant status and educational, occupational, and age variables. The purpose of having these interaction terms is to examine whether the effect of education, occupation, and age also *vary*

Table 8.4. *Determinants of Income, Comparison between Female and Male Migrants, Shanghai, 1995 (Regression of Log Monthly Income)*

Variable	Model 1 B (SE B)	Beta	Model 2 B (SE B)	Beta	Model 3 B (SE B)	Beta
Age (year)	0.0537**	0.922	0.0508**	0.868	0.0535**	0.912
	0.004		0.004		0.005	
Age squared	−0.0007**	−0.838	−0.0006**	−0.758	−0.0007**	−0.780
	0.000		0.000		0.000	
Gender (female = 1)	−0.275**	—	−0.233**	—	−0.105**	—
	0.170		0.017		0.013	
Hours worked per week	0.0019**	0.061	0.0026**	0.084	0.0023**	0.073
	0.000		0.000		0.000	
Education (ref. = primary)						
Junior high school		—	0.128**	—	0.130**	—
			0.018		0.018	
Senior high school		—	0.261**	—	0.261**	
			0.031		0.031	
College or above			0.354**		0.326**	
			0.15		0.151	
Occupation (ref. = manual labour)						
Prof./leader			0.406**	—	0.469**	—
			0.050		0.059	
Office/clerk			0.1160	—	0.132	—
			0.085		0.093	
Commerce/service			−0.095	—	−0.0142	—
			0.017		0.022	
Interactions						
Female migrant × Prof.					−0.266**	—
					0.115	
Female migrant × Office					−0.115	—
					0.237	
Female migrant × Commerce/service					0.0115	—
					0.035	
Female migrant × Age					−0.0051**	−0.127
					0.002	
Constant	5.349		5.214		5.172	
Adjusted R^2	0.120		0.158		0.160	
N	4,025		4,011		4,011	

** Significant at 5% or higher level.

according to female migrant status. We report the regression results with these added variables in Model 3 of Table 8.4. Only occupational and age interaction terms are reported, as none of the educational interaction effects is found to be statistically significant. The results in Model 3 reveal a number of further disadvantages experienced by female migrant labourers. Although being in the professional and leadership category is associated with a significantly higher income, it is much more so for males than for females. For male migrants, the difference is a whopping 47 per cent. For female migrants, such an advantage is reduced to only 20 per cent, a more than 50 per cent cut. Another interesting result is the age effect on female labour migrants' income. Whereas age in general is positively related to income, for female migrant labourers, this advantage is less than that for males. The coefficient for female and age interaction terms is negative and slightly attenuates the positive age effect. Such an effect is not due to differences in education or occupation between older and younger female migrants, as these variables are all controlled for. Older female migrant labourers, in other words, are subject to further market discriminations.

In sum, we observe a clear pattern of gender disadvantage for female migrant labourers in Shanghai. In spite of a more marked improvement in income for females (Table 8.3), male migrants are nevertheless, not surprisingly, clearly favoured over female migrants in the urban labour market. Although female migrant labourers work as hard as males, as shown by the same length of working hours per week, females received much lower pay than males, on average about 30 per cent less. This gap in income, however, cannot be explained away by the differences between female and male migrants in educational and occupational backgrounds. Even after controlling for these and other factors, female migrant labourers are still paid about 25 per cent less than males. Moreover, such a gender penalty is more pronounced in the highest occupational category and it increases with age for female labour migrants. This is the first type of jeopardy experienced by female migrant workers in the Chinese urban labour market: a penalty for being females.

INSTITUTIONAL BARRIERS: FEMALE MIGRANTS VERSUS FEMALE URBAN LABOUR

In the Chinese urban labour market, migrants in general also experience a second kind of discrimination, due to their outsider status. Without legal residential status, and with less schooling and lack of access to the urban social networks, migrants not only end up in jobs eschewed by urban residents, they also receive much lower pay and fewer benefits (Chan 1997; Solinger 1999; Wang and Zuo 1999; Yang and Guo 1996). Although comparisons between urban residents and migrant workers are available, no explicit comparison between female migrants and female urban residents is present. In this section, we continue our examination of the position of female migrant labourers in the urban labour market by comparing their status with that of local, resident, female labourers.

We use the same methodology and largely the same variables used in the previous section for such an examination. Instead of comparing female migrants with male migrants, we compare female migrants with female urban residents. Female urban residents all have legal household registration status in Shanghai and most of them are life-long residents there as well. We restrict our sample to those who are actively employed and use their monthly income at the time of the survey in 1995 as the dependent variable (again we use the log form of monthly income). The results of the multivariate regression analyses are presented in Table 8.5.

Table 8.5. *Determinants of Income, Comparison between Female Migrants and Female Local Workers, Shanghai, 1995 (Regression of Log Monthly Income)*

Variable	Model 1 B (SE B)	Beta	Model 2 B (SE B)	Beta	Model 3 B (SE B)	Beta
Age (year)	0.0590**	1.304	0.0627**	1.131	0.0630**	1.316
	0.005		0.005		0.005	
Age squared	−0.0008**	−1.335	−0.0009**	−1.281	−0.0009**	−1.284
	0.000		0.000		0.000	
Migrant status (migrant = 1)	−0.311**	—	−0.179**	—	−0.168**	—
	0.025		0.027		0.032	
Hours worked per week	0.0043**	0.152	0.0018**	0.049	0.0018**	0.049
	0.001		0.001		0.001	
Education (ref. = primary)						
Junior high school		—	0.124**	—	0.125**	—
			0.023		0.023	
Senior high school		—	0.233**	—	0.235**	—
			0.033		0.033	
College or above			0.362**		0.370**	
			0.055		0.056	
Occupation (ref. = manual labour)						
Prof./leader			0.127**	—	0.122**	—
			0.037		0.041	
Office/clerk			0.0942**	—	0.101**	—
			0.044		0.046	
Commerce/service			0.0207	—	−0.0410	—
			0.021		0.035	
Interactions						
Female migrant × Prof.					−0.0669	—
					0.102	
Female Migrant × Office					−0.107	—
					0.213	
Female Migrant × Commerce/service					0.0309	—
					0.043	
Constant	5.204		5.058		5.045	
Adjusted R^2	0.147		0.200		0.199	
N	2,847		2,661		2,661	

** Significant at 5% or higher level.

In Model 1 of Table 8.5, we include only age, hours worked, and migrant status variables. With age and length of work controlled for, female migrant workers make about 30 per cent less than urban female workers ($b = -0.311$). Together these variables explain about 15 per cent of total income variation among female labourers, migrant, and non-migrant combined, in Shanghai in 1995. Similar to the simple calculations presented in Table 8.2, female migrant labourers make about 30 per cent less than female urban labourers.

A substantial proportion of the migrant disadvantage is indeed due to migrants' educational and occupational disadvantage compared with urban female labourers.

As education and occupation are controlled for in Model 2, the migrant disadvantage is reduced significantly, from 31 to 18 per cent. Additional controls of interaction terms between migrant status and occupation and age, as reported in Model 3 of Table 8.5, do not reveal any further significant results and modify very little the migrant disadvantage: this decreases from 18 to 17 per cent.

Chinese female labour migrants, therefore, do pay a price for their outsider status. Such a price, about 18 per cent less in income, persists after migrants' educational and occupational disadvantages are taken into consideration (Table 8.5, Model 2). Given migrants are also more likely to end up in lower occupational categories, partly because of their outsider status, the income difference may well be larger. Moreover, migrants also are denied welfare benefits such as housing, medical care, education, and pension available only to urban residents. This is the second type of jeopardy experienced by female migrant workers in the Chinese urban labour market: a penalty for being migrants.

Several institutional barriers contribute to migrants' disadvantages in Chinese cities. First and foremost is migrants' lack of urban residential status. The Chinese dual household registration (*hukou*) system, which differentiates agricultural and non-agricultural registration status, has marked rural migrants with a permanent stamp of secondary citizenship (Cheng and Selden 1994; Solinger 1999; Yang 1993). Although the system has undergone some major changes in the past decade, it has not lost its importance in the Chinese social and political configurations. Non-agricultural *hukou* was made available for certain rural populations, but it was mostly only applicable in small towns, not cities (Chan and Zhang 1999; Malle 1995; Wang 1997). In more desirable places such as medium and large cities, *hukou* was generally not allowed for open sale. Under a few circumstances where it is possible to obtain an urban *hukou* in a large city, the price is often exorbitantly high. In Shanghai, for instance, the 'blue sealed' *hukou* (official Shanghai household registration status for migrants) initially carried a price tag of 200,000 US dollars if one comes as a foreign investor, or 1 million Yuan for a domestic investor. Such a number is well beyond the reach of most, if not all, rural migrants, as this price is equivalent to150 times an ordinary rural migrant's annual income.[6] Commercial housing prices have declined recently due to oversupply and lack of demand, but even these reduced prices are still well above the reach of most migrants. Moreover, with no chance in sharing the existing free public housing and employment benefits, those who obtained, and in many cases purchased, urban *hukou* soon realized that what they had paid for was largely a piece of useless paper. Having an urban *hukou* alone is not going to be of much use. In order to live and work in cities and to have all the urban benefits of the current residents, one needs other resources as well.

On top of residential control is direct labour market intervention by urban governments that favour urban residents over migrants. Urban governments in various parts of China have formulated and implemented explicit regulations to exclude migrants from certain jobs. These measures are implemented partly to give preference to

[6] Wang (1995) contains the regulation of the Blue Seal registration booklet in Shanghai. Note that the mean annual income for rural migrants in Shanghai in 1995 is only about 6,600 Yuan.

laid-off urban workers due to reforms of the state-owned enterprises. In Shanghai, jobs are classified into three categories, A, B, and C. Whereas migrants can be recruited in category A jobs, and in category B jobs under certain circumstances, jobs under category C are closed to migrant labourers. Over two dozen industries or jobs are off limits to migrants under this category. Some examples include: finance and insurance industries, front desk clerks of star-rated hotels, taxi drivers, telephone exchange operators, kindergarten teachers, warehouse guards, and door security guards (Wang 1995: 175). Although urban employers can save money by hiring cheap migrant labourers, they are required to pay a 50 Yuan fee per month for each migrant labourer, but not local resident, they hire. Moreover, half of all the collected fees, which eventually come out of migrant labourers' labour cost, are used as an unemployment fund which is only available to urban workers (Zhang 1998: 435). Urban employers also receive certain tax breaks for hiring local laid-off workers. Similar policies are also formulated elsewhere, such as in the capital city of Beijing. According to a report from Beijing Daily (April 10, 1997), at the same time when certain professions have been permitted to open to migrants, the Labour Bureau of one of its city districts also slipsided at least 35 types of jobs in which migrants should not be used.

In additional to these explicit policies, there are also other, less direct, forms of barriers. A significant proportion of urban residents still get some assistance from government institutions to enter the labour market (in Shanghai about 40 per cent of those who found jobs during the last ten years did so). These jobs are no doubt generally in better occupations with higher pay and better benefits. Even for the increasingly larger number of urban residents who rely on friends, relatives, or self to find a job (account for over a third in Shanghai now), their advantage over rural migrants in getting better jobs shall not diminish. This is so not only because urban job seekers are better educated, but also because they are better 'situated' within the urban social and cultural contexts. Urban youth do not look like 'country pumpkins' and more importantly, the social networks they rely on to get jobs are distinctively different from those of rural migrants.

CONCLUSION

China's dual transformations of the past two decades, from a planned to a market economy and from an agrarian to an industrial economy, have resulted in an unprecedented number of female labour migrants in Chinese cities. Increased employment opportunities in urban areas, and the gradual relaxation of the government's migration control policy, have enabled tens of millions of Chinese women from the countryside to move into cities to work and to live. At the same time as such increased migration has narrowed the economic gap between male and female labourers, it has also opened up unprecedented opportunities of social mobility for Chinese women in the countryside.

At the same time as these female labour migrants improve their economic well-being and increase their social mobility, they also find themselves entrapped not in one emerging market, but two overlapping markets: one dominated by the capitalistic free-market spirit and principles, and the other by socialist arrangements that still favour and protect the old urban establishment. The hierarchy of the Chinese urban labour market, therefore, consists of four layers: male urban workers, male migrant workers, female urban workers, and female migrant workers, in that order.[7] Female migrant labourers are at the bottom of this stratification order. These female migrant labourers from the Chinese countryside, known as *dagongmei* (the little sisters who came to work), live at the very margins of the Chinese society (Tan 1998). Large influx of global capital, a result of these transformations, has found its ideal human agents among female Chinese migrant labourers. These labourers are not only the cheapest, but also the easiest to control and to exploit (Tan 1998: 121–6). In this chapter, by using Shanghai as a case, we are able to identify partly how low Chinese female migrant labourers are located in this stratification ladder. If we rely on nominal income alone, which by no means is a complete measure of one's status, we find female migrant labourers earn only 70 per cent of male migrants, and only 66 per cent of urban female workers.

Moreover, most of these observed differences are not due to female migrants' disadvantaged background. Even after controlling for factors such as age, length of work per week, educational and occupational background, female labour migrants still earn about 18 per cent less than female urban labourers (Table 8. 5 model 2), and 23 per cent less than male migrant labourers (Table 8. 4 model 2). Differences in educational and occupational background explain some of the differences in income, especially the differences between female urban residents and female migrant labourers, but a substantial unexplained part remains. These remaining net disadvantages experienced by female migrant labourers are what we call the 'double jeopardy' faced by female migrant labourers in urban Chinese labour markets.

Such double disadvantages faced by female migrant labourers reveal to some extent the very nature of overlapping markets in a transitional economy. Whereas female migrants in other economies also face dual discriminations, it is more likely to be on an international scene, involving international, rather than internal migration (Roberts 1997). In the Chinese case, its dual transformations have resulted in such double discriminations against migrant women in the urban labour market. Female labourers' entry into the emerging labour market has positioned them to face the familiar gender discrimination, as shown here between female and male migrant labourers. At the same time, these female migrant labourers are not just any female labourers, because they are also subject to a second kind of discrimination, a discrimination due to their outsider status. While it is almost certain that the first kind of discrimination, namely discrimination by gender, shall persist and may well expand in the urban Chinese labour market, it is also unclear how soon will the second kind of discrimination disappear or even lessen.

[7] In a separate analysis, we show that compared with urban male workers, male migrant labourers suffer an income disadvantage of 21 per cent, female urban labourers 30 per cent, and female migrant labourers 43 per cent. These results are estimated by multivariate analysis, controlling for demographic and other social characteristics of the individuals included in the analysis (Wang *et al.* 2001).

References

Chan, K. W. (1994), *Cities with Invisible Walls: Reinterpreting Urbanization in Post-1949 China*, Hong Kong: Oxford University Press.

—— (1997), 'Post-Mao China: A Two-class Urban Society in the Making', *International Journal of Urban and Regional Research*, 20: 134–50.

—— and Zhang, L. (1999), 'The Hukou System and Rural–Urban Migration in China: Processes and Changes', *The China Quarterly*, 160: 818–55.

Cheng, T. and Selden, M. (1994), 'The Origins and Social Consequences of China's Hukou System', *The China Quarterly*, 139: 644–68.

Goldstein and Liang, Z. (2000), 'Migration, Gender, and Labour Force in Hubei Province, 1985–1990', in B. Entwisle and G. Henderson (eds.), *Re-drawing Boundaries: Work, Household, and Gender in China*, Berkeley, CA: University of California Press, 214–30.

Lee, C. K. (1995), 'Engendering the Worlds of Labour: Women Workers, Labour Markets, and Production Politics in the South China Economic Miracle', *American Sociological Review*, 60: 378–97.

Liang, Z. (1996), 'Market Transition, Foreign Investment, and Temporary Migration: The Case of Shenzhen Special Economic Zone, China, 1979–1994', Research manuscript.

Lu, Z. (1995), 'Redian zhengmin: funu jiuye wenti yanjiu' (heated debate over women's employment issues) in Shanghai funuxuehui and Shanghai shi hunyi jiating yanjiuhui (eds.) *Funu yanjiu zai Shanghai* (Women Research in Shanghai), Shanghai: Shanghai kexuepuji chubanshe, 17–49.

Mallee, H. (1995), 'China's Household Registration System under Reform', *Development and Change*, 26: 1–29.

Naughton, B. (1995), *Growing Out of the Plan: Chinese Economic Reform 1978–1993*, Cambridge: Cambridge University Press.

Roberts, K. D. (1997), 'China's "Tidal Wave" of Migrant Labor: What Can We Learn from Mexican Undocumented Migration to the United States?' *International Migration Review*, 31: 249–93.

SSB (State Statistical Bureau of China). (1984), *China Statistical Yearbook 1984*, Beijing: China Statistical Publishing House.

—— (1995), *China Statistical Yearbook (1995)*, Beijing: China Statistical Publishing House.

—— (1999), *A Statistical Survey of China*, Beijing: Zhongguo tongji chubanshe.

Shen, A. (1995), 'Shanghai nuxing liudong renkou de tezheng yu cunzai de wenti', (Characteristics and Existing Problems of Shanghai Female Migrant Population). *Renkou* 4: 47–53.

Solinger, D. J. (1999*), Contesting Citizenship: Peasants Migrants, the State, and the Logic of the Market in Urban China*, Berkeley and Los Angeles: University of California Press.

Sun, C. (1997), 'Floating population in Shanghai: A perspective of Social Transformation in China', in T. Scharping (ed.), *Floating Population and Migration in China: The Impact of Economic Reforms*, Hamburg: Institute of Asian Studies, 201–15.

Tan, S. (1998), 'Zhujiang sanjiaozhou wailai dagongmei de xianzhuang yu fazhan' (current Status and Development of In-migrating Female Labourers in the Pearl River Delta region), in Y. Jin and B. H. Liu (eds), *Shiji zhijiao de zhongguo funu yu fa zhan* (Chinese Women and Development at the Turn of the Century), Nanjing: Nanjing daxue chubanshe, 117–31.

Walder, A. G. (1990), 'Economic Reform and Income Distribution in Tianjin, 1976–1986', in D. Davis and E. Vogel (eds), *Chinese Society on the Eve of Tiananmen: The Impact of Reform*, Cambridge, MA: Harvard University Press, 135–56.

Wang, F. (1997), 'The Breakdown of a Great Wall: Recent Changes in Household Registration System in China', in T. Scharping (ed.), *Floating Population and Migration in China: The Impact of Economic Reforms*, Hamburg: Institute of Asian Studies, 149–65.

—— (2000), 'Gendered Migration and the Migration of Genders in Contemporary China', in B. Entwisle and G. Henderson (eds), *Re-drawing Boundaries: Work, Household, and Gender in China*, Berkeley, CA: University of California Press, 231–42.

—— and Zuo, X. (1999), 'Inside China's Cities: Institutional Barriers and Opportunities for Urban Migrants', *American Economic Review*, 89(2): 276–80.

—— Ruan, D., and Zuo, X. (2001), 'Invisible Walls within China: Migration and the Emergence of a Dual Society in Urban China', paper presented at the American Sociological Association Annual meeting, Anaheim, CA.

—— Zuo, X., and Ruan, D. (2002), 'Rural Migrants in Shanghai: Living Under the Shadows of Socialism', *International Migration Review*, 36(2): 520–45.

Wang W. (ed.) (1995), *Jiushi niandai shanghai liudong renkou* (Floating Population in Shanghai in the 1990s), Shanghai: Huadong daxue chubanshe.

WDCNLU (Women's Department of China's National Labor Union) (1998), 'Guanyu xiagang nuzhigong zai jiuye nandian de diaocha baogao' (a Report of Survey of Difficulties Faced by Laid-off Female Workers), in Y. Jin and B. H. Liu (eds), *Shiji zhijiao de zhongguo funu yu fa zhan* (Chinese Women and Development at the Turn of the Century), Nanjing: Nanjing daxue chubanshe, Nanjing, 103–16.

Wu, F. (1989), 'Problems in China's Rural Education Reform', *Chinese Education*, 22(4): 49–58.

Yang, Xiushi. (1993), 'Household registration, Economic Reform, and Migration', *International Migration Review*, 27: 796–18.

—— (2000), 'Interconnections among Gender, Work, and Migration: Evidence from Zhejiang Province', in B. Entwisle and G. Henderson (eds), *Re-drawing Boundaries: Work, Household, and Gender in China*, Berkeley, CA: University of California Press, 197–13.

Yang, Q. and Guo, F. (1996), 'Occupational Attainment of Rural to Urban Temporary Economic Migrants in China, 1985–1990', *International Migration Review*, 30: 771–87.

Zhang, S. (ed.) (1998), *Shanghai liudong renkou de xianzhuang yu zhanwang* (Current Status and Prospect of Migrant Population in Shanghai), Shanghai: Huadong daxue chubanshe.

9

Migration, Gender, and Returns to Education in Shenzhen, China

ZAI LIANG AND YIU POR CHEN

During the past two decades, major social and economic transformations have occurred in China. One of the demographic consequences of these changes is the large increase in the migrant population. In the pre-reform era, the Chinese government strictly controlled and regulated migration through the household registration system (*hukou*) and other mechanisms. Since the late 1970s, however, the role of household registration has weakened so much that one does not need to obtain local *hukou* to migrate. Migration, especially temporary migration, is clearly on the rise.[1]

The increase of migration has also given rise to booming research on migration in China. Social scientists are quick to take the opportunity to study different aspects of migration, for example, measuring trends and distribution of migration (Chan 1994; Liang and White 1996); the evolution and major reform of China's household registration system (Chan 1994; Chan and Zhang 1999; Wang 1997; Wong and Huen 1998); case studies of specific cities or provinces (Scharping and Huaiyang 1997); and detailed analysis of causes and consequences of migration (Solinger 1999; Yang and Guo 1996). Not surprisingly, most studies of migration focus on migrant men even though women constitute a high proportion of the migrant population. According to the 1990 Chinese Census, migrant women account for 46 per cent of intraprovincial migrants and 42 per cent of interprovincial migrants in China. Thus, we know that women participate in the migration process in substantial numbers. The question is to what extent do women benefit from the migration process? An even more important question is to what extent migration improves or erodes women's position vis-à-vis men? In recent years, several scholars have begun to examine the interplay between migration and gender in the context of migration in China; some benchmarks for further empirical evaluation have been recently published or are forthcoming (Fan and Huang 1998; Fan forthcoming; Goldstein *et al.* 2000).

This research is supported by grants form the National Institute of Child Health and Human Development (1R55HD/OD3487801A1 and 1R29HD3487801A2) and the Queens College Presidential Research Award. We gratefully acknowledge their support. We are grateful to Wang Feng for a conversation that stimulated the idea for this paper. We also thank the volume editors for their helpful comments on previous versions of the paper.

[1] We define temporary migrants as migrants who do not have *hukou* at their place of destination and permanent migrants as migrants who have *hukou* at their place of destination.

Using data from the Shenzhen Special Economic Zone in China, we endeavour to contribute to the emerging literature on migration and gender in China. Our research is motivated by three research questions. First, it has been well documented that traditionally women always migrated, but often for reasons such as marriage and joining other family members. With the transition to a market economy in China and the large increase of joint venture enterprises in Shenzhen, has this traditional pattern of female migration been challenged and shifted toward more economically-motivated and independent migration?

Second, given the continuing advantages associated with having *hukou* at the place of destination, the important research question is whether migrant women have the same chance of getting *hukou* at their place of destination, when controlling for socio-demographic characteristics? This question is important because it indicates who faces the fewest barriers in getting *hukou* among migrants; and thus, who assimilate easily into the mainstream society.

Third, what are the labour market consequences of migration for female migrants? We approach this research question through several steps. We compare the occupational attainment of female migrants with that of male migrants. We also compare the occupational attainment of female migrants with that of local women (non-migrants) in Shenzhen. Finally, going beyond the existing studies of gender and migration in China, we compare the occupational attainment of migrants with non-migrants at the place of origin by gender.

MARKET AND THE FLOW AND FORTUNES OF MIGRANT WOMEN IN SHENZHEN

In this section, we begin with a description of Shenzhen's recent history as it is related to the issue of migration and gender. The Shenzhen Special Economic Zone is located in the Southern part of Guangdong province and adjacent to Hong Kong. In 1979, Shenzhen was designated as a Special Economic Zone along with three other cities in the Southeast coast of China (Zhuhai and Shantou in Guangdong Province and Xiamen in Fujian Province; Vogel 1989). The rationale of establishing a SEZ is similar to export processing zones found in other developing countries in that it uses foreign capital to stimulate export and national development (Sassen 1988; Woon 1994). As Crane (1990) summarized, the major objectives of SEZs are: 'technology transfer and capital investment, regional development and employment, foreign exchange earnings and export promotion, and management upgrading and training' (p. 31). These objectives coincided with a trend of internationalization of production in the world economy and China's transition to a market-oriented economy (Nee 1989; Sassen 1988); large multinational companies look increasingly to China and Shenzhen, in particular, for labour-intensive manufacturing. Areas along China's 'golden coast' and the Pearl River Delta Region have been the front runners in taking advantage of the opportunities for export-oriented production (Lee 1995; Woon 1994; Yang 1990). Entrepreneurs from Hong Kong and other countries quickly opened plants in Southern China, Shenzhen in particular. The increase of foreign investment in Shenzhen is striking. In 1979 when Shenzhen first became SEZ, only \$15 million of foreign capital was invested; by 1994, foreign investment capital had soared to \$1.7 billion (SZSB 1995).

Along with the increase in foreign investment in Shenzhen, the number of migrants, especially temporary migrants (migrants without *hukou*), has increased dramatically since 1979. The percentage of Shenzhen's temporary migrant population rose from less than one per cent in 1979 to 72 per cent in 1994 (SZSB 1995). Several features of Shenzhen's migrant population set it apart from other cities in China. First, Shenzhen is the only city in China where the number of temporary migrants is larger than that of local residents. This reflects the nature of Shenzhen's economy which has a large number of joint venture enterprises and a heavy reliance on temporary migrants for labour. Shenzhen is also unique because of the large concentration of female migrants in the age group of 15–29. This reflects a strong preference among employers for young female workers because they are easy to manage and complain less than men about working conditions (Lee 1995).

The Shenzhen case is important because, in many ways, Shenzhen is a showcase of the so-called 'socialist market economy with Chinese characteristics'. For one thing, Shenzhen indeed has a vital economic market: a vibrant stock market, booming foreign investment, an unusually large number of joint venture enterprises, and the emergence of a labour market. One could argue that a market could provide a fair playing field where both men and women can compete equally (Bian *et al.* 2000). Thus there is a sense in which perhaps the market will help to reduce, if not eliminate, gender inequality. At the same time, we also need to note that for a long time, as part of the Communist propaganda, it was always claimed that women should hold half of the sky (Whyte and Parish 1984). There was also a Chinese version of affirmative action whereby women would receive equal pay for equal work. The increasing influence of the market indicates a declining influence of the remaining Communist ideology. This change suggests that gender inequality will increase with the waning of the Communist ideology. In sum, the case of Shenzhen allows us to explore a series of issues related to gender and migration in the age of market transition.

GENDER AND CONSEQUENCES OF MIGRATION: THEORETICAL AND METHODOLOGICAL ISSUES

The issue of gender and consequences of migration has attracted increasing attention from scholars in recent years, perhaps due to the fact that women participate heavily in the migration process throughout the world (Hagan 1998; Pedraza 1991; Pessar 1999; Tienda and Booth 1991).[2] A central issue is whether or not migration improves

[2] It should be noted that there is a literature on migration and gender that deals with gender differences in determinants of migration (see Cerrutti and Massey 2001; Grasmuck and Pessar 1991; Pessar 1999; Riley and Gardner 1993). Due to the focus of our paper, our discussion is limited to issues related to gender and consequences of migration only.

the position of women. Although the question initially seems simple, it becomes more complicated once we begin to address it. The current literature covers both studies on internal and international migrations. Pessar's (1999) review suggests that immigrant women in the United States 'generally gain greater personal autonomy and independence, while men lose ground' (p. 63). This gain can be found in two areas. Women's participation in paid labour gives them more power in household decision-making and at the same time migrant men are more likely to help in domestic work (Pessar 1999). In contrast, Hagan's (1998) recent study of immigrants in Houston's Maya community shows that women suffer as a result of unequal access to 'weak ties'.

Turning to the issue of gender and consequences of internal migration, the consensus seems to be that migrant women's wages are generally higher than what they would have been in rural areas (Rodenburg 1993; also see Davin 1997, in the case of China). However, Rodenburg is quick to add that 'female migrants often [are] at a disadvantage when compared with male migrants' (p. 286). In addition, the women's position has dimensions beyond wages. Accordingly, Tienda and Booth (1991) cautioned us to be aware that women's position changes following migration depend on several factors. These factors include productive roles both in origin and destination, reasons for migration, family and marital obligations, and the nature of the move (temporary versus permanent migration) (Tienda and Booth 1991).

Aside from these various aspects of women's position before and after migration, an assessment of the consequences of migration by gender is further complicated by data limitations and methodological difficulties (Bilsborrow 1993). Migration surveys are usually conducted at places of destination. This type of data usually allows researchers to make comparison among migrant women, men and local residents on measures of research interests, such as wages and occupations. Migration surveys conducted at places of origin allow us to examine the determinants of migration by gender, but miss households in which all members have left. A comprehensive assessment of the consequences of migration requires data that can link individuals at both the places of origin and destination (Singley and Landale 1998). A major advantage of origin–destination linked data sets is that they can be used not only to evaluate migration consequences by gender at the place of destination, but also to enable researchers to assess how migrants fare, compared to non-migrants at their places of origin. Several studies cited in this section also advocate the use of such data sets (Bilsborrow and UN Secretariat 1993; Tienda and Booth 1991). Unfortunately, such data sets are usually not available.

In the absence of a genuine origin-destination linked data set, we will use data from China's 1990 Census to create a data set that will allow us to conduct this comparison. The basic idea is to select a city (i.e. Shenzhen) within a province that has a large number of migrants. Then, we will construct another data set that consists of (1) migrants in this city, but coming from other parts of this province; and (2) non-migrants in this province. Because of features (1) and (2), we are able to make comparisons between migrants at their places of destination and non-migrants at the origins. As we will demonstrate in this paper, such a strategy will yield interesting and important findings, regarding gender and the consequences of migration in China.

GENDER AND CONSEQUENCES OF MIGRATION: RECENT STUDIES ON CHINA

Although there is an increasingly large body of literature on migration in China, the study of migration and gender is still in its early stage. Using the Hubei portion of the 1990 China Population Census and a 1988 Survey of Migration in Hubei Province, Goldstein *et al.* (2000) examined the interplay between migration and gender. Their analysis found that men were more likely to be unofficial migrants (temporary migrants) and women are more likely to be permanent migrants. In addition, women tended to move shorter distances. Despite the constraints facing women, the general conclusion of the study suggested that migration has enabled women to benefit from economic opportunities and provided them with a degree of freedom that was not possible at their places of origin. In contrast, Wang and Shen (see Chapter 8 of this book) were not so optimistic. Based on the 1995 Survey of Floating Population in Shanghai, these authors showed that migrant women are at an earnings disadvantage when compared to migrant men and local women. Therefore, Wang and Shen (Chapter 8 of this book) characterized the status of migrant women as suffering a 'double jeopardy'.

To study gender and migration in Zhejiang Province, Yang (2000) took advantage of unique data for Zhejiang Province. Researchers in Zhejiang Province attached a special questionnaire to the 1990 Chinese Census to gather additional information on *de facto* permanent out-migrants (individuals who left their place of origin for more than a year). This data collection procedure is important because it allows analysts to compare migrants with non-migrants at their places of origin. The results again reinforced some of the prevailing ideas about migration and gender. Yang (2000) found that women had a lower rate of *de facto* permanent migration than men, particularly in interprovincial migration. The study also found that a higher proportion of women than men migrated for non-economic reasons; nearly two-thirds of migrant women migrated in search of economic opportunities. Although Yang's study sheds significant light in terms of migrant/non-migrant differentials, there is no systematic comparison of occupations of migrants with non-migrants at their places of destination or origin.

Among scholars who study migration and gender, geographer Cindy Fan has conducted perhaps the most systematic empirical analyses, covering such issues as gender differences in reasons for migration; marriage migration as a strategy of economic advancement; and the geography of female migration (Fan and Huang 1998; Fan forthcoming). Challenging the traditional view of female marriage migration, which sees female migration as a consequence of marriage, Fan and Huang (1998) argued that rural women from less developed regions in China, actually used marriage to achieve social and economic advancement. This new type of marriage migration also shows interesting findings about the men who are involved in these types of marriages. As Fan and Huang (1998) wrote, 'as for the men who married female migrants,...they were also socially and economically disadvantaged. But their favourable position in the spatial hierarchy seem to have compensated for what may be less desirable personal attributes, and allow them to draw peasant women from poorer regions...' (p. 246). Thus, migration allows women from less developed regions to achieve socio-economic mobility and it also offers opportunities for local men to choose more desirable women as their spouses.

In another paper on gender differences in Chinese migration, Fan (forthcoming) shows that marriage is still the leading reason of migration for female migrants during 1985–90, accounting for 28 per cent among female migrants. The corresponding percentage for male migrants is only 2.4 per cent. Fan (forthcoming) further underscores the gender differences in several aspects: male migrants are more likely to move to urban areas than female migrants; male migrants are also more likely to transfer from agricultural jobs to non-agricultural jobs; and male migrants are more likely to work in prestigious occupations. Based on the above findings, Fan (forthcoming) concludes that migration has widened the gender gap in occupational distribution. However, Fan did not control for demographic and socio-economic characteristics between male and female migrants without which important alternative hypotheses cannot be eliminated. Moreover, Fan (forthcoming) makes no distinction between temporary and permanent migration in her study. This could pose potential problems since permanent and temporary migrants may exhibit different patterns of occupational attainment at their places of destination.

Building on previous work on migration and gender in China, we explore gender differences in migration outcomes in several ways. *Hukou* was and continues to be an important institution that is associated with entitlements, such as housing, medical care, certain jobs and schooling of children; therefore, who gets local *hukou* has important implications for socio-economic advancement in Shenzhen. Thus, we begin our analyses with the examination of the question who gets *hukou* among migrants in Shenzhen, focusing on gender differences. We then carefully examine occupational attainment for migrants in Shenzhen. In assessing occupational attainment, we make a distinction between temporary migrants and permanent migrants. Given the fact that permanent migrants enjoy the same privileges as the local residents, we do not expect their chances of being in elite occupations to be different from that of local residents. Specifically, we compare occupational attainment of migrant women with that of migrant men and local women, controlling for all socio-demographic characteristics. Given the salience of *hukou*, we make a distinction between temporary migration and permanent migration in our comparison exercise. In addition, because of the importance of education in occupational attainment and social stratification in China (Deng and Treimen 1997), we pay particular attention to returns to education on occupational attainment by gender. Finally, given the suggestion of recent researchers (Bilsborrow and UN Secretariat 1993; Yang 2000), we also compare the occupational attainment of migrants with that of non-migrants at the place of origin, using, as mentioned before, a specially constructed data set from the 1990 China Population Census.

DATA AND METHODS

The major data set for this paper is the 1 per cent Sample of the 1990 China Population Census (PCOSC and SSB 1991). We extracted data for Shenzhen Special

Economic Zone and Guangdong Province. The 1990 Chinese Census was the first Chinese census to contain information on migration. Similar to migration questions from censuses in other countries, the 1990 China Population Census asked respondents whether or not they had migrated in the five years prior to the date of the census (i.e. during 1985–90). If they migrated, their provinces of origin, as well as their rural or urban status, were identified.

There are several advantages in using the 1990 Chinese Census data for migration research. The 1990 Chinese Census asked about migration information during 1985–90. The late 1980s and early 1990s were a time of accelerating migration and the 1990 Census captures this important period. The 1990 Chinese Census also includes information on major demographic and socio-economic variables, which allows us to compare permanent migrants, temporary migrants and non-migrants on these important characteristics. We will pay particular attention to the occupational attainment of migrants.

Despite the richness of the data, the census data are not without limitations. For example, the Chinese census data do not have information on wages, one of the standard ways to measure gender inequality. Because of this limitation, we focus instead on occupational attainment and realize that different conclusions may be drawn if we were to use wages. It should be noted that the 1990 Chinese Census missed temporary migrants who had resided at their destinations for less than a year and who had left their places of household registration for less than a year. Thus, our measure of temporary migration clearly underestimates the magnitude of temporary migration in China.

Our empirical exercise starts by selecting individuals, ages 15–59, who are in Shenzhen. The focus on ages 15–59 mainly reflects our interest in examining the labour market consequence of migration by gender. Again, we define temporary migrants as migrants in Shenzhen who do not have permanent Shenzhen household registration. Similarly, permanent migrants are migrants who have permanent Shenzhen household registration.

Aside from providing descriptive statistics on the migrant population in Shenzhen, we will estimate a series of statistical models. Our first statistical model is to predict who gets *hukou* in Shenzhen among migrants, paying particular attention to whether or not migrant women are advantaged or disadvantaged in obtaining *hukou* compared to migrant men. Since the dependent variable is a dummy variable (1 = a migrant has *hukou*, 0-otherwise), we will employ a standard logistic regression technique.

We have three sets of statistical models to estimate gender differences in occupational attainment. We collapse the detailed census occupational classifications into three large categories for the convenience of our analyses: (1) professional and managerial; (2) sales and service; (3) agricultural work, manufacturing, and transportation.[3]

[3] Initially, we intended to use seven occupational categories for our analysis of occupational attainment. However, due to the small number of cases in the permanent migrant population for both men and women, statistical models cannot be successfully estimated. Therefore, we decided to further collapse occupations into three main groups.

Because we have three categories for dependent variables, we will estimate multinomial logit models. The first model of occupational attainment is to compare occupational attainment of migrants with that of local residents in Shenzhen. We focus on the extent to which gender matters in terms of obtaining good occupations. The second model of occupational attainment compares occupational attainment of migrants in Shenzhen who are from other parts of Guangdong with corresponding non-migrants in Guangdong (not including local residents in Shenzhen). Results from the latter model will give us insights about the extent to which male and female migrants benefit from the migration process through occupational attainment.

For the second model, we need to construct a separate data set. Because we have data for both Shenzhen and Guangdong Province as a whole, we are able to conduct some innovative comparisons of migration consequences by gender. The idea is that not only can we compare migrant women with migrant men at their places of destination, but also we can compare migrant women with women from places of origin within Guangdong Province. This analysis will involve first selecting migrants in Shenzhen who are from other parts of Guangdong Province. We will then construct another data set that contains individuals who reside in Guangdong (not including Shenzhen) and who do not have migration experience during the period of 1985–90. We then merge these two data sets for an estimation of a model of occupational attainment.

For all statistical models (either for a model that estimates the probability of obtaining *hukou* or occupational attainment), we include other independent variables: education, age, rural/urban origin, Guangdong origin and marital status. We expect individuals from rural areas to continue to suffer disadvantages when they move to Shenzhen. Therefore, their probability of obtaining *hukou* or obtaining prestigious occupations is lower than individuals who are from urban areas because rural people are located at the lower level of rural-urban hierarchy. We also expect that individuals who are from other parts of Guangdong Province to also enjoy advantages in getting Shenzhen *hukou* and occupational attainment. Although the official policy of preference for local Guangdong people is only in the area of employment, in reality, individuals from Guangdong may enjoy advantages in both getting Shenzhen *hukou* and obtaining prestigious occupations. For example, migrants from other parts of Guangdong speak Cantonese and most of the joint-venture companies are owned or partially owned by people from Hong Kong. This language homogeneity may give Guangdong origin people living in Shenzhen some leverage in getting ahead.

RESULTS

Statistical description of migrants in Shenzhen

Table 9.1 compares basic socio-demographic characteristics across categories of temporary migrants, permanent migrants, and local Shenzhen residents. Our description begins with some broad strokes. Comparing migrants with local residents confirms some of the common features of migrant versus non-migrant differentials. The general picture is that migrants (especially female temporary migrants) are much

Table 9.1. *Socio-demographic Characteristics by Migration Status and Gender, Shenzhen 1990*

	Permanent migrants		Temporary migrants		Local resident	
	Male	Female	Male	Female	Male	Female
Age (%)	10.91	7.46	10.57	31.32	12.93	12.45
15–19	40.61	43.65	56.98	53.07	35.33	37.55
20–29	31.52	33.70	19.23	9.41	24.82	22.94
30–39	12.12	11.05	8.57	3.28	12.67	11.93
40–49	4.85	4.14	4.65	2.92	14.25	15.14
50+	30.70	30.90	28.36	23.96	33.00	33.16
Mean age (years)						
Education (%)						
Illiterate & elementary school	0.91	5.25	16.28	27.70	16.55	31.13
Junior high school	16.97	26.52	59.88	61.42	35.13	39.12
Senior high school	49.70	41.44	19.05	9.07	32.57	23.00
Technical high school	7.27	12.71	1.60	0.72	6.70	3.54
Technical college & university	25.15	14.09	3.18	1.09	9.06	3.21
Original residence (%)						
City	63.94	64.36	15.26	8.53	64.54	52.69
Town	29.09	26.52	11.74	8.60	0.33	0.00
Rural	6.97	9.12	73.00	82.87	35.13	47.31
Marital status (%)						
Currently married	62.12	75.97	43.44	27.00	66.58	71.95
Top three migrants origins (%)						
1. Both = Guangdong	74.85	74.59	71.34	66.18	—	—
2. Permanent migrant: Both = Hubei	5.15	4.42	—	—	—	—
Temporary migrant: Both = Guangxi	—	—	7.33	11.14	—	—
3. Permanent migrant: Male = Guangxi Female = Sichuan	2.73	4.42	—	—	—	—
Temporary migrant:Both = Sichuan	—	—	6.13	6.18	—	—
Other province origin	17.27	76.57	15.20	16.51	—	—
Interprovincial migration (%)	25.20	25.40	28.66	33.82	—	—
Reason for migration (%)					—	—
Relocation on job	62.42	60.22	10.61	2.22	—	—
Job assignment	5.15	3.87	0.06	0.03	—	—
Business or factory work	16.06	10.22	87.78	87.36	—	—
School or training	1.21	0.55	0.10	0.13	—	—
Move in with relatives	0.61	0.83	0.44	2.02	—	—
Retirement	0.00	0.83	0.20	0.34	—	—
Move with spouse	12.12	13.54	0.14	1.96	—	—
Marriage	0.00	4.42	0.02	0.23	—	—
Others	2.42	5.52	0.64	5.71	—	—
Total number	330	362	4,993	3,870	1,523	1,526

Source: 1990 Chinese Census.

younger than local residents. For instance, the mean age for local women is 33, whereas the mean age for temporary migrant women is 24. This difference in age distribution between migrants and local residents is also reflected in marital status with a much higher proportion of local residents currently married as compared to either migrant men or migrant women. What is also clear in the case of Shenzhen is that temporary migrants overwhelmingly dominate the migrant population. This is true for both permanent and temporary migrants. Migrants in Shenzhen predominantly come from counties or cities in Guangdong Province. Among interprovincial temporary migrants, Guangxi, being the neighbouring province, topped the list in sending migrants to Shenzhen. Somewhat surprisingly, the proportion of interprovincial migrants among female migrants is slightly higher than for male migrants.

Further comparisons between temporary and permanent migrants show other interesting patterns. First, we consider the difference between temporary migrants and permanent migrants. For both male and female migrants, temporary migrants are overwhelmingly from rural areas (73 per cent for men and 83 per cent for women). In contrast, less than 10 per cent of permanent migrants are from rural areas. This difference suggests that urbanites not only enjoy advantages when they do not migrate, but also when they do; it is easier for them to get *hukou* in Shenzhen. Another major difference between temporary and permanent migrants is that more than 60 per cent of permanent migrant men reported the relocation of work as their reason for migration. For temporary migrants, nearly 90 per cent reported seeking business or factory work as their reason for migration. We note also that contrary to findings for China as a whole (see Fan forthcoming), the proportion of those reporting marriage as their reason for migration is negligible, for both temporary and permanent female migrants in Shenzhen.

Gender differences exist within temporary migrant and permanent migrant groups. Male and female permanent migrants share an almost identical distribution on almost all variables, with the exception of marital status: 76 per cent of permanent migrant women are currently married, as compared to 62 per cent of permanent migrant men. In contrast, higher proportion of temporary migrant men reported currently married compared to temporary migrant women, this reflects the much younger age distribution of temporary migrant women. Temporary migrant women (83 per cent) are more likely to come from rural areas than male migrants (73 per cent). Female temporary migrants have a much younger age distribution than that of male temporary migrants. Almost a third of female temporary migrants range in age group of 15–19 years. Nearly 85 per cent of them are in the age group of 15–29. This is consistent with the image of maiden workers, portrayed in TV series and popular literature. The high concentration in the younger age group also explains the lower proportion of female temporary migrants who are currently married. Migrant women have a higher proportion of interprovincial migrants than migrant men. This does not necessarily mean that women are more likely to participate in interprovincial migration than intraprovincial migration, because the data we have are for migrants who are already in Shenzhen. It may be that Shenzhen is particularly attractive to women from other provinces.

Who gets Shenzhen hukou?

Shenzhen is a unique city in several ways. As indicated, it is the only city in China where the migrant population is much larger than the local resident population. Data from the 1990 Census show that the number of migrants is more than three times greater than that of the local resident population. Despite the large size of the migrant population, Shenzhen has been reluctant to issue *hukou* to its migrant population; thus a large temporary migrant population has resulted. It is reported that the quota for Shenzhen *hukou* for 1991, which was set by Shenzhen city government, was only 2,200 (Liao *et al.* 1992: 79). Knowing the difficulties and benefits of obtaining Shenzhen *hukou*, who gets Shenzhen *hukou* reflects a migrant's position in the social stratification system. Because migrants from urban areas represent an advantaged position in the rural-urban hierarchy, it is easier for them to obtain *hukou* in Shenzhen. We expect highly educated individuals to be more likely to get *hukou* because they are more likely to work in the white-collar occupations that often ensure *hukou*. The central variable of our concern is gender, do migrant women have equal chance of getting *hukou* than migrant men? Using data from the China 1990 Census, Goldstein *et al.* (2000) showed that women are less likely to become temporary migrants and more likely to become permanent migrants (with *hukou*). They attributed this tendency largely to the fact that women migrated for marriage. In Shenzhen, however, it is not the case; there, marriage migration accounts for only a tiny proportion (0.6 per cent) of migrant women. Therefore, we expect little significant difference between male and female migrants as far as their probability of obtaining *hukou*.

To examine who gets *hukou* among migrants, we selected all migrants in Shenzhen and estimated a logistic regression model predicting the probability of obtaining Shenzhen *hukou*. We coded education into five categories: illiterate and elementary school, junior high school, senior high school, technical high school, technical college and above. Ideally, we want to separate individuals who are illiterate from those who have some level of education. As Table 9.1 shows, most male migrants have at least some elementary school education (i.e. few migrant men (less than 1 per cent) are illiterate). We have combined illiterate with elementary school education because otherwise statistical estimations would be impossible. We know education is important in getting Shenzhen *hukou*, but the extent to which it differs by gender is a question that interests us. Thus, we include several interaction terms between education and gender. We control for marital status and age. The results are presented in Table 9.2. Consistent with our expectation, education is clearly important in obtaining *hukou* in Shenzhen. The higher a migrant's level of education, the more likely a migrant is to obtain *hukou*. The coefficients are particularly sizeable for migrants who have an education level of technical high school and technical college and above. Issuing *hukou* to highly educated migrants seems to be a constant priority among policy makers, as manifested in the recent efforts to reform Shenzhen's household registration system. Other factors being equal, migrants from Guangdong Province are more likely to have *hukou*. This is actually a form of nepotism that is officially sanctioned by the Shenzhen government, that is, giving preference to people from Guangdong Province.

Table 9.2. *Logistic Regression Model Predicting* Hukou *Status in Shenzhen*

Variable name	Coefficient	Standard error
Constant	−9.54**	0.67
Age 15–19	−0.65	0.48
Age 20–29	0.45	0.29
Age 30–39	0.85**	0.28
Age 40–49	0.66	0.30
(ref. = 50+)		
Junior high school	1.44*	0.61
Senior high school	3.03**	0.60
Tech. high school	3.12**	0.65
Tech. college or above	4.012**	0.61
(ref. = illiterate and elementary school)		
Junior high school × female	0.02	0.74
Senior high school × female	−0.46	0.72
Tech. high school × female	0.81	0.81
Tech. college or above × female	−0.17	0.76
Urban origin	3.11**	0.18
Guangdong origin	1.60**	0.14
Female	1.34	0.71
Currently married	0.96**	0.14
Number of observations	—	8,980
$chi^2(16)$	—	1990.52
Prob > chi^2	—	0
Pseudo R^2	—	0.459

* $p < 0.05$.
** $p < 0.01$.

Source: 1990 Chinese Census.

Somewhat surprisingly, migrant men are less likely than migrant women to have *hukou*. However, the result is not statistically significant. It is also interesting that there is no detectable difference between male and female migrants in the effect of education on having Shenzhen *hukou* (see the interaction terms between education and gender). All interaction terms are not statistically significant. Overall, the results from Table 9.2 suggest that there is no evidence that female migrants are being discriminated against—nor advantaged—as far as obtaining Shenzhen *hukou* is concerned.

Occupational attainment: the first comparison

In the next few tables, we carefully scrutinise patterns of occupational attainment for migrants by gender. Before we introduce results from regression models, let us look at the basic occupational distribution for migrants by gender in Table 9.3. We reclassified detailed census occupations into seven major occupational categories. Clearly, permanent migrants, both men and women, are more likely to concentrate in white-collar

Table 9.3. *Occupational Distribution of Migrants by Gender*

Occuptional classification (%)	Male migrant		Female migrant	
	Temporary	Permanent	Temporary	Permanent
Professional & technical workers	3.06	19.51	2.98	50.33
Managers & administrators	2.53	15.33	0.23	2.67
Office workers	1.60	11.50	1.19	14.00
Sales workers	8.45	23.00	3.41	12.00
Agricultural workers	13.39	0.35	8.71	1.00
Manufacturing & transportation	65.94	28.57	76.28	8.33
Number of working population	4,936	287	3,457	300

Source: 1990 Chinese Census.

occupations. The gender difference among permanent migrants is even more striking. Over half of the permanent migrant women are employed in professional and technical occupations. In contrast, only less than 20 per cent of permanent migrant men are in professional and technical occupations. We use the term 'permanent migrant women advantage' to refer to this phenomenon; this advantage in occupational attainment is somewhat surprising given our early results showing that female permanent migrants are not better educated than male permanent migrants. In fact, compared with permanent migrant men, a higher proportion of permanent migrant women were in low education categories (e.g. illiterate, elementary school, and junior high school).

It should be noted, however, that the picture is not so rosy once we examine the actual jobs held by permanent migrant women. Among the permanent migrant women who reported professional and technical occupations, about 65 per cent were in accounting. As we discussed earlier, a majority of Shenzhen's large number of joint venture enterprises hires migrant women. It is very possible that most of these permanent migrant women work in these joint venture firms as accountants. Although accountants are regarded as working in professional occupations, they usually have little authority and few subordinates, unlike real elite occupations (Walder 1994). The fact that more than 15 per cent of permanent migrant men were managers or administrators (as compared to less than 3 per cent for permanent migrant women) suggests that permanent migrant men still hold more powerful jobs than women. Among temporary migrants, however, no significant difference exists in occupational distribution between male and female migrants except for the fact that temporary migrant men still have an advantage in managerial and administrator jobs. The largest concentration of temporary migrants—over 65 per cent—is in manufacturing and transportation for both male and female temporary migrants.

To estimate the model of occupational attainment, we rearranged seven occupational categories into an even smaller number of categories. We use the sample of migrants and local residents in Shenzhen. Again, we are forced to collapse agriculture, manufacturing and transportation into a single category because no single male permanent migrant was employed in an agricultural occupation in 1990. For ease of interpretation, we also collapsed the following occupations: professional, technical, and managerial occupations into a category—professional; sales workers and service workers into sales and service. We estimated a multinomial logit model with a dependent variable that has three categories: (1) professional and managerial, (2) sales and service workers; and (3) agriculture, manufacturing, transportation and other manual workers. We use agricultural, manufacturing, and transportation as the reference category.

The first important finding from Table 9.4 is that permanent migrants have a higher probability of working in sales and service jobs compared to local residents.

Table 9.4. *Occupational Attainment of Migrants Compared with Non-migrants in Shenzhen*

Variable name	Professional & managerial		Sales & service	
	Coefficient	Standard error	Coefficient	Standard error
Constant	−1.37**	0.23	−2.29**	0.19
Permanent migrant	−0.10	0.19	0.49**	0.19
Permanent migrant × female	1.10**	0.31	0.40	0.31
Temporary migrant	−1.61**	0.12	−0.16	0.10
Temporary migrant × female	−0.44**	0.17	−0.61**	0.14
Age 15–19	−2.37**	0.25	−0.99**	0.18
Age 20–29	−2.23**	0.17	−0.66**	0.15
Age 30–39	−1.78**	0.17	−0.38**	0.15
Age 40–49	−1.10**	0.18	−0.37*	0.16
(ref. = 50+)				
Junior high school	1.27**	0.19	0.13	0.11
Senior high school	2.33**	0.20	0.58**	0.13
Tech. high school	3.85**	0.27	1.10**	0.27
Tech. college or above	4.99**	0.27	1.61**	0.25
(ref. = illiterate and elementary school)				
Junior high school × female	0.82*	0.34	0.11	0.16
Senior high school × female	1.74**	0.34	0.44*	0.19
Tech. high school × female	1.89**	0.55	0.23	0.56
Tech. college or above × female	1.46**	0.57	−0.23	0.62
Urban residence	0.68**	0.10	0.76**	0.07
Guangdong origin	−0.02	0.11	0.72**	0.08
Female	−0.39	0.32	0.62**	0.17
Currently married	0.56**	0.10	0.48**	0.08
Number of observation	—	11,183		
chi^2 (40)	—	5,152.97		
Prob > chi^2	—	0		
Pseudo R^2	—	0.2839		

Outcome Agricultural, Manufacturing, and Transportation is the comparison group.

* $p < 0.05$.

** $p < 0.01$.

Source: 1990 Chinese Census.

A consistent finding throughout the world is the typical story that migrants are not doing as well as local residents. However, in Shenzhen, the story is somewhat different. We argue that two factors contribute to this 'anomaly'. One is that Shenzhen is a relatively young city that consists of mostly migrants. Even among Shenzhen local residents, some of them may simply be migrants themselves, who came a few years earlier.[4] Thus, it is likely that we are actually comparing the occupational attainment of a recent cohort of migrants with earlier arrivals. Another possibility is that in the late 1980s, as Shenzhen's economy further prospered, it attracted a highly selective group of individuals. Turning to temporary migrants, it is not surprising to find that temporary migrants have a lower probability of obtaining prestigious jobs, again compared to local residents. So the hierarchy of occupational attainment is the following: permanent migrants, local Shenzhen residents, and temporary migrants.

Not surprisingly, one's level of education is very important in obtaining prestigious jobs. Migrants from urban areas still enjoy an advantage in getting prestigious professional, managerial jobs, as well as positions in sales and service. Migrants from other parts of Guangdong are only advantaged in getting sales or service jobs. Our major research question—gender effects in occupational attainment among migrants—presents mixed, but very interesting findings. On the one hand, permanent migrant women are more likely to be in professional and managerial positions than their male counterparts and the results also are statistically significant (see the interaction term between permanent migration and gender). In contrast, for temporary migrants (who dominate the migrant flow), the pattern is just the opposite: migrant men are doing better than migrant women. Returns to education on occupation differ by gender. With the same level of education, women have a higher probability of obtaining professional and managerial jobs than men (for both migrants and local residents). Women seem to benefit the most from an education at the technical high school level (see the largest coefficient among education and gender interactions). This underscores the importance of education in reducing gender inequality in occupational attainment.[5]

Once we control basic socio-demographic variables as well as unequal returns to education, women in Shenzhen still are less likely to be in sales and services, the coefficient for professional and managerial occupations is not significant. To understand whether gender inequality worsened in Shenzhen than at the place of migrant origin, we also estimated a similar model using non-migrants in Guangdong Province (not including Shenzhen). The results (not shown here) show that even when we control all the variables as we did in Table 9.4, the gender variable is still statistically significant. This gives us one message, that is, to the extent that discrimination against women persists, it is much less so in Shenzhen than in the place of migrant origin.

[4] Since the time dimension of migration in the 1990 China Census covers only the period of 1985–90, individuals who came to Shenzhen in the early 1980s and the late 1970s with local *hukou* will be counted as local residents.

[5] Other scholars such Bian *et al.* (2000) and Xie and Hunnum (1996) found that women receive higher return to education on earnings. They attribute this largely to the significantly low earnings of women at low levels of education. However, it is not the case for occupational attainment in Shenzhen.

Occupational attainment: the second comparison

As we discussed earlier, very often the standard procedure of assessing the consequences of migration is to compare migrants with local residents. Though this strategy is important from our theoretical perspective in terms of adaptation and assimilation into the local society, a natural comparison from the perspective of migrants themselves is often with the people at their places of origin. Here we adopt such a research strategy. We selected those migrants in Shenzhen who are from other counties or cities in Guangdong Province and then we compared the characteristics of those migrants with people who currently live in other cities or counties in Guangdong Province (place of origin).

We first compare the labour force participation rates of migrants from Guangdong with local Shenzhen residents and the results are reported in Table 9.5. The first major finding is that, with the exception of male permanent migrants, the labour force participation rates for migrants are much higher than that of local Shenzhen residents. Migrants came to look for economic opportunities and are more likely to be working than local residents. The second finding is that temporary migrants have a higher level of labour force participation than permanent migrants. The largest difference is found in labour force participation rates of male temporary migrants (nearly 100 per cent) and male permanent migrants (86 per cent). The third finding is that male migrants have a higher labour force participation rate than that of female migrants. The gender difference in occupational attainment favours females in that nearly 47 per cent of female permanent migrants are in professional and technical occupations, compared to 17 per cent of male permanent migrants.

We turn next to a comparison of labour force participation and occupation between those migrants who are from Guangdong and non-migrants in Guangdong Province (again not including Shenzhen). Some interesting patterns emerge. On labour force participation, again, temporary migrants have a higher rate of labour force participation than people who remain in the places of origin in Guangdong Province.[6] While for both men and women, more than half of the local Guangdong population are still engaged in agricultural production, a very small proportion of migrants are doing agricultural work. Instead, the occupational distribution for migrants is quite diverse with a large concentration in manufacturing and transportation.

For male and female migrants, a pattern of transfer from agricultural work to manufacturing and transportation type occupations is clearly evident. For example, 65 per cent of local male Guangdong residents are in agricultural work, while 63 per cent of male temporary migrants work in manufacturing and transportation occupations. The same can be said about female temporary migrants. The general conclusion that can be drawn from this comparison is that temporary migration really represents the transformation process from agricultural to non-agriculture work.

[6] Part of this reasons for the high level of labour force participation for temporary migrants may reflect the fact that temporary migrants who failed to get jobs returned home because of the lack of social service (such as unemployment benefits) for them. We thank one reviewer for pointing out this to us.

Table 9.5. *Occupational Distribution by Gender and Migration Status*

	Male				Female			
	Guangdong resident	Shenzhen resident	Temporary migrant	Permanent migrant	Guangdong resident	Shenzhen resident	Temporary migrant	Permanent migrant
Occupational classification (%)								
Professional & technical workers	4.87	15.62	1.64	17.45	4.03	24.13	1.99	46.55
Managers & administrators	2.27	10.10	1.39	13.21	0.37	1.53	0.05	2.30
Office workers	1.96	11.34	1.14	9.90	0.86	10.26	0.90	14.28
Sales workers	4.47	15.07	10.15	23.58	3.11	15.28	4.43	12.44
Service workers	2.01	3.57	5.38	2.35	2.61	11.03	7.73	12.90
Agricultural workers	65.14	10.33	17.36	0.00	73.36	15.61	13.10	1.38
Manufacturing & transportation	19.28	33.95	62.94	33.48	15.66	22.16	71.76	10.14
Number of working population	160,318	1,287	3,509	212	134,722	916	2,212	217
Labour force participation rate (%)	85.84	85.50	98.51	85.82	77.95	60.03	86.38	80.37
Total number	186,764	1,523	3,562	247	172,831	1,526	2,561	270

Note: Guangdong Resident = the person resides in Guangdong (but exluding Shenzhen) and has Guangdong *hukou*. Shenzhen Resident = the person resides in Shenzhen and has Shenzhen *hukou*. Temporary Migrant = the person is Guangdong origin and temporary migrant in Shenzhen. Permanent Migrant = the person is Guangdong origin and permanent migrant in Shenzhen.

Source: 1990 Chinese Census.

Table 9.6. *Occupational Attainment of Shenzhen Temporary Migrants from Guangdong Compared with Guangdong Local Residents (Males Only)*

Variable name	Professional & managerial		Sales & service	
	Coefficient	Standard error	Coefficient	Standard error
Constant	−3.38**	0.04	−3.21**	0.04
Temporary migrant	0.66*	0.26	1.39**	0.12
Age 15–19	−2.72**	0.10	−0.56**	0.06
Age 20–29	−1.86**	0.03	−0.22**	0.04
Age 30–39	−1.80**	0.03	−0.29**	0.03
Age 40–49	−0.56**	0.03	−0.14**	0.04
(ref. = 50+)				
Junior high school	1.62**	0.03	0.54**	0.03
Senior high school or above	3.48**	0.03	0.85**	0.03
(ref. = illiterate and elementary school)				
Junior high school × temporary migrant	−0.76**	0.28	−0.67**	0.13
Senior high school or above × temp. mig.	−1.17**	0.28	−0.62**	0.15
Urban residence	1.22**	0.02	1.46**	0.02
Currently married	0.46**	0.03	0.26**	0.03
Number of observations	—	164,373	—	—
$chi^2(22)$	—	33,245.33	—	—
Prob > chi^2	—	0	—	—
Pseudo R^2	—	0.1848	—	—

Outcome Agricultural, Manufacturing, and Transportation is the comparison group.
* $p < 0.05$.
** $p < 0.01$.
Source: 1990 Chinese Census.

Next, we estimate a multinomial logit model of occupational attainment. The objective here is to compare migrants from Guangdong (who were residing in Shenzhen at the time of census) with non-migrants of Guangdong Province. Since we selected only Shenzhen migrants who are from Guangdong Province, the sample sizes for both temporary and permanent migrants are reduced.[7] To make the statistical models estimable, we decided to eliminate permanent migrants from this part of our analysis. This adjustment is unlikely to alter our major conclusions since temporary migrants constitute the overwhelming majority of the migrant population. We do this for men and women separately. We enter interaction terms between education and migrant status because we expect that at each level of education, migrants will receive fewer returns compared to non-migrants at their places of origin. Table 9.6 reports the results from the multinomial logit model of occupational attainment for

[7] This reduction in sample size creates some difficulties in statistical estimation. For example, only 212 permanent migrant men are from Guangdong Province. To make the statistical models estimable, we eliminated permanent migrants and we also collapsed education classifications into three categories: (1) illiterate and elementary school; (2) junior high school; (3) senior high school and above.

Table 9.7. *Occupational Attainment of Shenzhen Temporary Migrants from Guangdong Compared with Guangdong Local Residents (Females Only)*

Variable name	Professional & managerial		Sales & service	
	Coefficient	Standard error	Coefficient	Standard error
Constant	−4.20**	0.07	−3.69**	0.06
Temporary migrant	−0.62	1.00	1.74**	0.13
Age 15–19	−2.28**	0.10	−0.48**	0.07
Age 20–29	−1.68**	0.07	−0.17**	0.05
Age 30–39	−1.49**	0.07	−0.05	0.05
Age 40–49	−0.25**	0.07	0.33**	0.05
(ref. = 50+)				
Junior high school	2.48**	0.06	0.92**	0.03
Senior high school or above	4.66**	0.06	1.31**	0.04
(ref. = illiterate and elementary school)				
Junior high school × temporary migrant	0.13	1.02	−1.28**	0.16
Senior high school or above × temp. mig.	−0.15	1.02	−1.69**	0.24
Urban residence	1.87**	0.03	2.37**	0.03
Currently married	−0.27**	0.04	−0.03	0.04
Number of observations	—	136,969	—	—
$chi^2(22)$	—	35,455.48	—	—
Prob $> chi^2$	—	0	—	—
Pseudo R^2	—	0.3049	—	—

Outcome Agricultural, Manufacturing, and Transportation is the comparison group.
* $p < 0.05$.
** $p < 0.01$.
Source: 1990 Chinese Census.

migrant men and non-migrant men in Guangdong. Correspondingly, Table 9.7 is for women. For comparison purposes, we discuss results from Tables 9.6 and 9.7 together. Three major findings emerge from our analysis. The first one is that, temporary migrant men are more likely to be in professional and managerial jobs than non-migrant men at their places of origin, when controlling for socio-demographic variables and differential returns to education by migration status. However, no similar results emerge for women, i.e. temporary migration does not improve women's chance of obtaining professional and managerial jobs. Therefore, if we use working in professional and managerial occupations as an indication of occupational mobility, temporary migrant men benefit more from migration than temporary migrant women.

The second important finding is that the impact of marital status differs by gender. For men, being married increases the likelihood of obtaining professional, managerial, and sales and service jobs; for women, however, marriage is a constraint that decreases the likelihood of obtaining professional or managerial jobs. It should be noted that the above two findings cannot be revealed if we only look at migrants at the place of destination. Another finding from Tables 9.6 and 9.7 is that, for both men and women, migration increases the probability of working in sales and service occupations, as compared to agricultural and manufacturing positions. The transition to a market-oriented economy in Shenzhen has brought about prosperity in service industries. As in other places in the world, migrants are usually highly represented in service industry jobs.

CONCLUSION AND DISCUSSION

China's transition to a market-oriented economy since the late 1970s has been accompanied by a major increase in migration, a magnitude rarely seen in the last 50-year history of the People's Republic. In this paper, we have tried to explore the consequences of migration for women, using the Shenzhen Special Economic Zone as a case study.

It is well established that Chinese women have always migrated, but primarily as associational migrants, migrating to their husbands' homes or with families. This clearly changed in the late 1980s and 1990s. In Shenzhen both male and female migrants are motivated by economic reasons. Consequently, the percentage of migrant women reporting marriage or joining family members as reasons for migration is almost negligible (less than 4 per cent).

Our findings regarding the consequences of migration for women offer a message of limited optimism because migration process benefits women in two major aspects. First, permanent migrant women are more likely than permanent migrant men to be engaged in professional jobs; Second, to the extent there is discrimination against women in occupational attainment, it is less so in Shenzhen than at the place of migrant origin. We suggest that this relatively equalized gender relationship in occupational distribution in Shenzhen is due in large part to Shenzhen's economic structure. As we know, the majority of Shenzhen's migrants work in manufacturing occupations, very likely for joint venture companies. In addition, Shenzhen is relatively a new society and consists mainly of migrants; it is a city that perhaps has the least traditional constraints of gender hierarchies, thus allowing female migrants opportunities to work in relatively prestigious occupations. Having said that, let us quickly add that this 'female permanent migrant advantage' is only in comparison with male migrants; temporary female migrants are not doing as well as local residents in Shenzhen.

Although descriptive statistics reveal that migrant women are less educated than migrant men, at each level of education migrant women receive a higher return on education than migrant men (see Table 9.4). In addition, once a differential return to education is taken into account, the gender variable is no longer statistically significant. This indicates that migrant women's lesser representation in prestigious occupations in Shenzhen is due largely to their low level of education. Thus, one of the ways to reduce gender inequality in occupational attainment is to promote women's education. In addition, given the fact that permanent migrant women are more likely than permanent migrant men to be in professional occupations, easing control on *hukou* can also help migrant women to get ahead in Shenzhen.

Given the several pieces of good news we reported regarding migrant women, it may be tempting to identify migration as a process tending to reduce gender inequality. This is true only for a small portion of migrant women. In fact at the place of destination in Shenzhen, temporary migrant women are not doing as well as temporary migrant men in obtaining professional and managerial jobs. Moreover, compared to migrants at their places of origin, temporary migrant men, but not temporary migrant women, are more likely to obtain professional and managerial jobs, after we control for socio-demographic characteristics and differential returns to education by migration status. Lastly, migrant women in Shenzhen are much more constrained by family obligations than men, as shown by the model of comparison between temporary migrants in Shenzhen and at their places of origin. The disturbing news is even more troubling when we realize that the temporary migrant population is the majority of the Shenzhen's migrant population. There is still a long way to go before migrant women can achieve equal status with migrant men.

Methodologically, we want to stress our innovation of comparing characteristics of migrants both at their places of destination and places of origin. In fact, as we demonstrate in this paper, significant insights can be gained by conducting a comparison both at the places of origin and destination. Moreover, the implementation of this procedure is perhaps particularly relevant for developing countries where data collection is usually less than ideal and where data collection budgets do not allow researchers to conduct surveys both at places of origin and destination.

References

Bian, Yanjie, John R. Logan, and Xiaoling Su. (2000), 'Wage and Job Inequalities in Working Lives of Men and Women in Tianjin', in Barbara Entwisle and Gail E. Henderson (eds), *Re-Drawing Boundaries: Work, Households, and Gender in China*. Berkeley, CA: University of California Press, 111–33.

Bilsborrow, Richard E. and the United Nations Secretariat. (1993), 'Internal Female Migration and Development: An Overview', in *Internal Migration of Women in Developing Countries*. New York: United Nations Publications, 1–20.

Chan, Kam Wing. (1994), *Cities with Invisible Walls: Reinterpreting Urbanization in Post-1949 China*. Hong Kong: Oxford University Press.

Chan, Kam Wing and Li Zhang. (1999), 'Hukou and Migration in China', *The China Quarterly* 160: 818–55.

Cerrutti, Marcela and Douglas S. Massey. (2001), 'On the Auspices of Female Migration from Mexico to the United States', *Demography* 38: 187–200.

Crane, George T. (1990), 'The political Economy of China's Special Economic Zones', Armonk, NY: M.E. Sharpe, INC.

Davin, Delia. (1999), *Internal Migration in Contemporary China*. New York, NY: St Martin's Press.

—— (1997), 'Migration, Women, and Gender Issues in Contemporary China', in Thomas Scharping (ed.), *Floating Population and Migration in China, the Impact of Economic Reforms*. Hamburg, Institute of Asian Studies, 297–314.

Deng, Zhong and Donald Treiman, J. (1997), 'The Impact of the Cultural Revolution on Trends in Educational Attainment in the People's Republic of China', *American Journal of Sociology* 103: 391–428.

Fan, C. Cindy and Youqin Huang. (1998), 'Waves of Rural Brides: Female Marriage Migration in China', *The Annals of the Association of American Geographers* 88: 227–51.

—— 'Gender Difference in Chinese Migration', Forthcoming in Chiao-min Hsieh and Max Lu (eds), *The Changing China: A Geographical Appraisal*, Boulder: Westview Press.

Goldstein, Sidney, Zai Liang, and Alice Goldstein. (2000), 'Migration, Gender, and Labor Force in Hubei Province, 1985–1990', in Barbara Entwisle and Gail E. Henderson (eds), *Re-Drawing Boundaries: Work, Households, and Gender in China*. Berkeley, CA: University of California Press, 214–30.

Gramuch, Sherri and Patricia R. Pessar. (1991), *Between Two Islands: Dominican International Migration*. Berkeley, CA: University of California Press.

Hagan, Jacqueline Maria. (1998), 'Social Networks, Gender, and Immigrant Incorporation', *American Sociological Review*. 63: 55–67.

Lee, Ching Kwang. (1995), 'Engendering the Worlds of Labour: Women Workers, Labour Markets, and Production Politics in the South China Economic Miracle', *American Sociological Review* 60: 378–97.

Liang, Zai and Michael J. White. (1996), 'Internal Migration in China: 1950–1988', *Demography* 33: 375–84.

Liao, Bowei, Wang Yujian, Song Enrong, and Liu Peiqong. (1992), *China's Economic Reform and Economic Development in Zhujiang River Delta Region*. Hong Kong: Nanyang Commercial Bank.

Nee, Victor. (1989), 'A Theory of Market Transition: From Redistribution to Markets in State Socialism', *American Sociological Review* 54: 663–81.

PCOSC and SSB (Population Census Office under State Council and State Statistical Bureau). (1991), *10 Per cent Sampling Tabulation on the 1990 Population Census of the People Republic of China (Computer Tabulation)*. Beijing, China: China State Statistical Publishing House.

Pedraza, Silvia. (1991), 'Women and Migration: The Social Consequences of Gender', *Annual Review of Sociology* 17: 303–25.

Pessara, Patricia R. (1999), 'The Role of Gender, Household and Social Networks in the Migration Process: A Review and Appraisal', in Charles Hirshman, Philip Kasinitz, and Josh DeWind (eds), *The Handbook of International Migration: The American Experience*. New York: Russell Sage Foundation, 54–70.

Riley, Nancy E. and Robert Gardner. (1993), 'Migration Decision: The Role of Gender', in *Internal Migration of Women in Developing Countries*. Proceedings of the United Nations Expert meeting on the Feminisation of Internal Migration, Aguacalientes, Mexico, 22–25 October 1991, 195–206.

Rodenburg, Janet (1993), "Emancipation or Subordination? Consequences of Female Migration for Migrants and Their Families", in *Internal Migration of Women in Developing Countries*. New York, United Nations Publications, pp. 273–289.

Sassen, Saskia. (1988), *Mobility of Labour and Capital: A Study in International Investment and Labour Flow*. New York, NY: Cambridge University Press.

Scharping, Thomas and Sun Huaiyang (eds) (1997), *Migration in China's Guangdong Province: Major Results of a 1993 Sample Survey on Migrants and Floating Population in Shenzhen and Foshan*. Hamburg, Germany: Institute fur Asienkunde.

Shenzhen Statistical Bureau (SZSB), (1995), *Handbook of Shenzhen Statistics, 1979–1994*. Shenzhen, Shenzhen Statistical Bureau.

Singley, Susan G. and Nancy Landale. (1998), 'Incorporating Origin and Process in Migration-Fertility Framework: the Case of Puerto Rican Women', *Social Forces* 76: 1437–60.

Solinger, Dorothy. (1999), *Contesting Citizenship: Peasant Migrants, the State and the Logic of the Market*. Berkeley, CA: University of California Press.

Tienda, Marta and Karen Booth. (1991), 'Gender, Migration, and Social Change', *International Sociology* 61: 51–72.

Vogel, Ezra. (1989), 'One Step ahead in China: Guandong under Reform', Cambridge, MA: Harvard University Press.

Walder, Andrew. (1994), 'Career Mobility and the Communist Political Order', *American Sociological Review* 60: 309–28.

Wang, Feng. (1997), 'The Breakdown of a Great Wall: Recent Changes in Household Registration System in China', in Thomas Scharping (ed.), *The Floating Population and Migration in China: The Impact of Economic Reforms*. Hamburg: Institute for Asian Studies, 149–65.

Whyte, Martin and William Parish. (1984), *Urban Life in Contemporary China*. Chicago, IL.: The University of Chicago Press.

Wong, Linda and Wai-Po Huen. (1998), 'Reforming the Household Registration System: A Preliminary Glimpse of the Blue Chop Household Registration System in Shanghai and Shenzhen', *International Migration Review*. 32: 974–94.

Woon, Yuen-fong. (1994), 'Circular Mobility in Post-Mao China: Temporary Migrants in Kaipin County, Pearl River Delta Region', *International Migration Review* 27: 578–604.

Xie, Yu and Emily Hunnum. (1996), 'Regional Variation on Earnings Inequality in Urban China', *American Journal of Sociology* 101: 950–92.

Yang, Dali. (1990), 'Patterns of China's Regional Development Strategy', *China Quarterly* 122: 230–57.

Yang, Quanhe and Fei Guo. (1996), 'Occupational Attainment of Rural to Urban Temporary Economic Migrants in China, 1985–1990', *International Migration Review* 30: 771–87.

Yang, Xiushi. (2000), 'Interconnections among Gender, Work, and Migration: Evidence from Zhejiang Province', Barbara Entwisle and Gail E. Henderson (eds), *Re-Drawing Boundaries: Work, Households, and Gender in China*. Berkeley, CA: University of California Press, 197–213.

PART IV

INCREASING FEMINIZATION OF THE LABOUR FORCE: BALANCING WORK AND FAMILY

10

Women and Part-time Employment: Workers' 'Choices' and Wage Penalties in Five Industrialized Countries

ELENA BARDASI AND JANET C. GORNICK

INTRODUCTION

A large literature on part-time work concludes that it is most useful to conceptualize part-time work as a trade-off, or series of trade-offs. For many women, part-time work offers flexibility at the cost of some lost remuneration; an hourly wage gap between part-time and full-time workers has been well-documented (Bassi 1995; Gornick and Jacobs 1996; OECD 1994; Rubery 1992; EBRI 1993; Simpson 1986). For others, it constitutes a compromise state between full-time homemaking and full-time employment, when either of those might be optimal but neither is feasible. Some scholars, especially feminist scholars, have framed the trade-off for women as one of short-term gains versus long-term losses. While part-time work offers limited labour market attachment to women who might otherwise have none, women's disproportionate participation in part-time work in the short run cements sexual divisions of labour in both paid and unpaid work in the long term.

This conceptualization of part-time work as a trade-off makes explicit that any comprehensive analysis of part-time work requires incorporating both demand-side and supply-side factors. From the complex and multidisciplinary literature on part-time work, we conclude—as does Addabbo (1997)—that '[d]emand-side constraints seem to be the overriding determinants of the level of part-time work'. At the same time, supply-side factors probably dominate in determining *which* women fill the available part-time jobs—especially with respect to household-related factors, our main interest.

Furthermore, a combination of demand-side and supply-side factors would contribute to the pay gap between full-time and part-time workers. Some portion of the pay gap is likely explained by measurable differences between full-time and part-time workers (which combines demand- and supply-side factors), while some portion will be due to differing occupational and industrial distributions between the full-time and part-time labour forces, and to differing *returns* to both worker- and job-related factors (primarily, driven by demand-side factors).

In this chapter, we use data from the Luxembourg Income Study (LIS) to analyse patterns of part-time work, and its consequences for women, in five industrialized countries—Canada, Germany, Italy, the United Kingdom, and the United States—as of the middle 1990s.[1] First, we investigate women's employment choices, specifically the three-option decision between non-employment, part-time employment, and full-time employment, with a focus on the household variables that shape those choices. Second, we analyse the direct economic consequences of part-time work for women, in the form of hourly pay penalties. In the next section, we present four research questions that structure our investigation and we summarize our prior expectations; we then turn to our empirical analyses.

WORKERS' CHOICES AND WAGE PENALTIES: RESEARCH QUESTIONS AND EXPECTATIONS

The conceptualization of part-time work as a trade-off—and our understanding of the interplay of demand and supply factors—motivated us to frame a series of research questions about the factors underlying women's decision to work part-time, and the rewards and penalties associated with that decision.

On the one hand, part-time work is understood to offer women the advantage of providing more time away from employment, primarily for family-related activities. As implied in Hakim's (1997) claim that women have heterogeneous sex role preferences, work orientations, and behaviours, many women may choose part-time over full-time employment because they have dependent care responsibilities at home *and* because they can well afford it economically. Thus, our first three questions concern the effects of household factors—that is, children in the home, 'dependent adults', and the level of other income in the household—on women's employment decisions, especially on the choice of part-time work.

On the other hand, engaging in part-time work may imply losses in remuneration, in particular, in the hourly wage rate. In response to this claim, our fourth question concerns the direct economic consequences, for women, of the decision to engage in part-time versus full-time work. We are particularly interested in the extent to which the hourly earnings of part-time workers lag those of full-time workers. Furthermore, if we find that there are substantial differences in the pay of part-time and full-time workers, we need to understand what underlies those differences. Are the differences attributable to measurable differences between the two groups of workers—for example, in their qualifications? Or does the explanation lie elsewhere?

Below, we pose these four research questions, and we follow each question with a brief summary of our prior expectations about patterns of cross-national commonality, as well as our expectations about variation across these five countries.

Question #1. How do the presence, and age, of children affect women's employment choices (i.e. between full-time, part-time, and non-employment)? And how do these child-related effects vary across these countries?

[1] Although this chapter is about women's engagement in part-time work, and the associated costs, we include men when we report rates of part-time work across countries (Table 10.1) so that we can assess the extent to which part-time work is female-dominated.

The classic female labour supply model predicts that the presence of children in the home will have an impact on women's employment decisions in at least two ways. First, children are expected to increase women's reservation wage by raising the value that they place on their time at home. Second, the out-of-pocket costs of alternative childcare arrangements will also lower women's effective market wages, that is, their wages net of child care costs. A large empirical literature—most of it from the English-speaking countries—confirms that the more a woman's childrearing responsibilities increase, the less likely it is that she will choose to participate in paid work; and, for women who are labour force participants, greater childrearing responsibilities (e.g. the presence of very young children) will reduce hours in paid work (Connelly 1991; Leibowitz *et al.* 1992).

At the same time, cross-national empirical research has concluded that the magnitude of the (negative) effects of children on various measures of women's labour market attachment vary across countries (Gornick *et al.* 1998; Knudsen and Peters 1994; Phipps 1993). Gornick *et al.* (1998) found that, in half of fourteen countries studied, mothers of preschool-aged children were no less likely to be in paid work than were mothers of children over age 12, *ceteris paribus*. They concluded that this cross-national variation in the effect of children is largely due to variation in the generosity of public policies that support maternal employment, especially short-term maternity leave and publicly-supported childcare. In some countries, these policies contribute to reducing the negative effects of children on women's labour supply to low levels and, in others, to eliminating the young child effects entirely. Across the five countries in this study, public supports for maternal employment are fairly limited in cross-national terms, with the exception of Italy, the only one of the five to have adopted a policy of universal preschool enrollment for children starting at age three (Kamerman and Kahn 1999).

Although we have argued that supply-side factors dominate in determining *which* women fill existing part-time jobs, it may be that some demand-side forces shape the cross-national pattern of child-related effects. In countries with very small part-time labour markets, women's preferences for choosing part-time work (e.g. when they have young children) may be more constrained, in effect, forcing them to remain in either full-time work or non-work. In other words, in countries with small part-time labour markets (such as Italy), the association between child-related factors, *ceteris paribus*, and participation in part-time work may be weakened.[2]

What do we expect to see across these countries? Overall, we expect to see a general pattern in which the presence of children lowers the likelihood that women choose full-time work, and raises the likelihood that they choose non-work.

[2] This interpretation is consistent with OECD (1999) findings indicating that, across countries, as the size of the female part-time labour market increases, the share of part-time employment that is voluntary (according to the traditional definition) also increases. That relationship holds, for the most part, across these five countries. In Germany and the United Kingdom, where female part-time work is most common, the share of part-time workers who are voluntary is very high (85–90 per cent), whereas in Italy, where part-time work among employed women is much less common, the voluntary share is just over 50 per cent, which is way below the European average (OECD 1999).

Similarly, we expect that, among mothers, the presence of very young children will do the same—decrease full-time work and increase non-work—with the size of the effect decreasing as children get older. Note that the direct effect of the presence, or age, of children on the likelihood of working part-time is ambiguous, because children, especially young children, are expected to 'pull' mothers into part-time work (from full-time work) and 'push' them out as well (into non-work).

At the same time, we expect that the magnitude of the child-related effects (i.e. the direct effect on full-time and non-work) will vary across countries. Considering these two sets of factors together—the extent to which national public policies support maternal employment and the size of the part-time labour force—we expect to see strong child effects in Germany and the United Kingdom (where policies that support maternal employment are weak and part-time work is widely available), negative but smaller child effects in the United States and Canada (where support for maternal employment is also weak but where part-time work is more limited), and weak or no child effects in Italy (where substitute care for children is more widely available, especially for children over age three, and where part-time jobs are much less available).

Question #2. How does the presence of other non-earning adults in the home shape women's employment choices? And how do these 'dependent adult' effects vary across countries?

The effects of household composition on women's employment choices are not limited to child-related factors. Many working-age women have complex combinations of adults in their homes—including spouses, grown children or siblings, and elderly relatives. Furthermore, many of these household members are non-wage-earning, and their presence may affect the employment outcomes of working-age women, all else equal. Some of these non-earning adults in the home may be unemployed (i.e. able and willing to work), whereas others may be out of the labour force, perhaps because they are disabled and/or elderly (and in need of care). In either case, we expect the presence of a variety of non-earning adults, overall, to affect women's labour market attachment.

The case of the unemployed spouse has received considerable attention in economic theory and prior empirical research. Despite some expectation to the contrary—that is, the 'added worker' effect—empirical evidence from various countries concludes that in general women married to unemployed men are less likely to be employed, all else equal (Elias 1997; Ercolani and Jenkins 1999; Giannelli and Micklewright 1995). Several factors may explain this association. First, spouses generally face similar demand-side conditions. Second, they may share unobserved characteristics that are associated with unemployment. Third, psychological factors may play a role and some women may choose non-work when their husbands lose their 'breadwinner role' so as not to upset the balance in the marriage. Finally, and most importantly, the design of benefit schemes may play a role; if an unemployed husband's benefits are income-tested at the household level, that may constitute a disincentive for his wife to work for pay. While there is little research on the effect of husbands who are out of the labour force (rather than unemployed), we would expect that many of the same factors would apply, thus lessening their wives' labour force attachment. That could mean a reduction in wives' full-time employment, with some shifting into part-time employment, and others out of employment overall.

What do we expect to see across these countries? Our expectation is that in all five countries, the presence of a non-earning spouse in the home will reduce full-time work and increase non-work; the net effect on part-time work will depend on the balance of these two effects. We also expect that the effects of a non-earning spouse will be stronger in the 'liberal' welfare states (Canada, the United Kingdom, and the United States) than they will be in the two 'conservative' countries (Germany and Italy), because in the former countries, a larger share of the overall social benefit package is income-tested (Esping-Andersen 1990). In addition, as with the child-related effects, the size of the part-time labour market may play some role. The magnitude of these effects may be further diminished in countries, such as Italy, where the part-time labour market is very small.

In addition to non-earning spouses, some non-earning adults in the home will be in need of care. Much research has established that—like childcare-giving work at home—unpaid care for disabled and elderly household members is largely provided by working-age women. Thus, we expect that the presence of other non-earners in the home—especially *elderly* non-earners—will have the same effect as young children, overall. These 'dependent adults' will reduce women's likelihood of working full-time, and increase their likelihood of non-work. Again, as with children, the effect on women's part-time work is ambiguous.

One possibility is that the magnitude of these dependent-adult effects—especially for the elderly—will be smaller in countries with more extensive public home help services for older people to alleviate the burden on women family members. In actuality, all five of these countries have comparatively low levels of home help for older people (Rostgaard and Fridberg 1998; Sainsbury 1999), so our expectation is that these effects will be fairly uniform across these countries. Once again, we may see diminished effects in Italy, in that many women who would prefer part-time work may be constrained to either full-time work or non-work.

Question #3. How does the level of 'other income' in the home affect women's employment choices? And how does the effect of household income vary across countries?

The 'other income' in a woman's home (i.e. her household's income, excluding her labour market earnings) is traditionally understood as constituting her 'endowed', or non-earned, income. Classic labour supply theory predicts that, all else equal, the higher a woman's endowed income, the lower will be her labour supply, vis-à-vis both participation and hours. Once again, the effect of 'other income' on women's part-time work is ambiguous, as higher income will push some women from full-time into part-time work, and others from part-time to non-work.

For married women—the majority of working-age women—a large portion of their 'other income' is their husband's income (assuming shared resources within the home). Recent research suggests that the expected negative correlation between husbands' income and wives' employment has fallen in recent years. One reason is that, increasingly, highly-educated men, who have high earnings, marry highly-educated women. Those highly-educated women are likely to have high labour supply; this education association between spouses would counteract the negative correlation between husbands' earnings and wives' labour market attachment. Furthermore, married women's labour supply has become more elastic, over time, to their own potential wage rates, which in turn reduces their sensitivity to their husbands' income (Blau *et al.* 1998). In fact, a body of empirical research suggests that the direction, and magnitude, of the effect of household income on women's participation and hours varies across countries (Cancian and Schoeni 1992; Stichter 1990).

Recent work by Hakim (1997) has re-awakened interest in the question of the relationship between household income and women's engagement in part-time work. Her claim that women part-time workers, for the most part, are primarily committed to their domestic roles and rely (happily) on their 'breadwinner husbands' for income, suggests that higher household income would be associated with more engagement in part-time work. Thus, women who choose part-time work, for the most part, do not 'need' the income that full-time work would bring.

What do we expect to find across countries? Despite Hakim's argument—which suggests that women part-time workers disproportionately come from high income homes—the recent empirical findings that question the association between other household income and women's labour supply lead us to expect that the effect of 'other income' on women's employment levels will be small or non-existent across these five countries. In other words, higher 'other income' will decrease full-time work, and increase non-work, slightly, or not at all. Taken together, we expect to find little relationship between other income and women's likelihood of working part-time. Once again, however, we would expect that the size of the part-time labour market might play a role in shaping these 'other income' effects, with larger effects seen in the countries with larger part-time labour markets (such as Germany and the United Kingdom), and smaller effects seen where the option to choose part-time work is more limited (e.g. in Italy).

Question #4. Do full-time hourly wages exceed part-time hourly wages in all of these countries? Do these pay differentials remain after we control for full-time/part-time differences in worker- and job-related characteristics? How do these pay differentials—'unadjusted' and 'adjusted'—vary across countries?

We expect full-time hourly wages to exceed part-time hourly wages—both with and without worker- and job-related controls—in all countries, for several reasons. The first reason is linked to the assumption that, overall, full-time workers have higher levels of *human capital* than do part-time workers. The classic human capital framework indicates that as individuals' human capital increases, their potential wage increases; in turn, as their wage increases, they will raise their desired number of hours in the labour market. Therefore, workers with higher human capital will be more likely to enter full-time work, and we would expect to find a general pattern of higher wages among them, at least before human capital controls are introduced. It is also true, however, that because 'leisure' (time out of paid work) is typically a normal good—as are the fruits of household labour—it is possible that high wage earners might also choose shorter (part-time) hours. In practicality, this is an empirical question and a positive association between current wage and hours worked is found for wages that do not exceed a given threshold, above which the relationship becomes negative.[3]

A second reason given for the existence of a full-time/part-time pay gap is that full-time and part-time workers differ on *unmeasurable characteristics*. According to Hakim (1997) and others, women workers are very heterogeneous, and a substantial number whose priority is their non-market activity choose undemanding part-time employment. That suggests that women full-time and part-time workers may differ on a host of unobservable traits; presumably, women with the 'part-time' traits are less productive (and would command lower wages) than those whose orientation is toward full-time employment and toward labour market attachment more generally. Any wage gap due to differences in unmeasurable traits would remain, even after controlling for measurable traits, including human capital variables.

A third reason to expect a wage gap between full-time and part-time workers results directly from the existence of *discrimination* operating inside the enterprise. As Maier (1994) notes, 'the differentials between female part-timers and full-timers have to be explained in part as a result of more or less direct wage discrimination against part-timers by excluding them from relevant parts of the overall effective remuneration (like shift-work premium, premiums for work in the late evenings or weekend, overtime premiums, and employer-provided benefits...)' (p. 168–9). This would mean that part-time and full-time workers with similar characteristics are paid differently. Employers might be especially likely to 'discriminate' against part-time workers (relative to comparable full-time workers), and pay them a lower effective hourly wage, when they face high fixed labour costs (e.g. forms of social insurance contributions that are assessed per employee); the employer may lower the part-time hourly wage to compensate for the higher per-hour fixed costs, including costs associated with interviewing and hiring. Regulations aimed at pay equity between full-time and part-time workers would be expected to reduce this type of differential.

A fourth reason underlying the expected pay gap—the existence of *dual and segmented labour markets*—comes from the non-neoclassical framework. This perspective stresses the existence of two tiers in the labour market. The upper tier comprises good jobs offering higher wages, more security, and more extensive benefits, while the lower tier comprises bad jobs, characterized by lower wages, high job insecurity, and little chance of promotion. For several reasons—for example, lower levels of unionization—we can expect there to be a correlation between part-time jobs and 'bad jobs'. This association is likely to be the strongest in countries where the size of the part-time labour market is small, that is, where part-time work is more likely to be in a 'marginalized' fringe of the labour market. Regulations aimed at combating the unequal treatment of part-time workers are likely to be ineffective in alleviating this source of the pay gap.

[3] Note that the expected human capital differential between full-time and part-time workers, related to education, is likely to be reinforced by human capital differences associated with on-the-job training and learning-by-doing. Employers are likely to invest more in training for full-time workers, and workers who generally work full-time may accumulate more work experience.

What are our expectations about size and cross-country variation of wage differentials? Overall, we expect the adjusted wage gap—that is, adjusted for observable worker- and job-related controls—to be smaller than the unadjusted wage gap in all countries. Furthermore, we expect that wage differentials (both unadjusted and adjusted) will be higher in countries with higher fixed labour costs and/or weaker part-time regulations, because there are stronger incentives for employers to discriminate directly (in the form of lower returns). Finally, we expect that wage differentials will be higher in countries with smaller part-time sectors, given the likelihood of a stronger association of part-time jobs and 'bad jobs'. Because many elements of 'bad jobs' cannot be captured in standard occupational and industrial controls, we expect that this association (smaller sector, larger pay differential) will be seen with respect to both unadjusted and adjusted wage gaps.

The above forces may work in opposite directions within countries. Germany and Italy, for example, are understood to be the countries, among these five, with the strongest regulations that protect part-time workers (as of the middle 1990s), but at the same time they have quite rigid labour markets with relatively higher labour costs, and presumably higher fixed labour costs (the former would reduce direct discrimination, while the latter might exacerbate it). At the same time, Italy, Canada, and the United States have smaller part-time labour markets; in these countries, we expect part-time work to be more concentrated 'in the fringes' of the labour market and, for this reason, we expect to find larger full-time/part-time wage gaps.

DATA, METHODS, AND ANALYSIS PLAN

Our empirical analysis is conducted in two stages. In the first stage, we investigate the choice made by working-age women among three options: non-employment versus part-time employment versus full-time employment. In the second stage, we estimate the wage gap—among women—between part-time and full-time workers, using regression techniques and the Oaxaca decomposition of the wage differential. The analysis is carried out on five industrialized countries, using micro-data from the Luxembourg Income Study (LIS).[4]

Data

The Luxembourg Income Study is an archive of micro-datasets from a large number of industrialized countries.[5] Individual- and household-level data on income, employment and demographic variables are included in the datasets. The variables

[4] The five LIS datasets used in our analysis are Canada 1994, the United States 1994, Germany 1994, the United Kingdom 1995, and Italy 1995. Our Italian results were calculated directly from the Banca d'Italia dataset, rather than from the reduced version of the same dataset that is included in LIS. We used the original database because some key variables are missing in the LIS version.

[5] At present, over 70 datasets covering the period 1968–95 are included in the database. For details on the Luxembourg Income Study, and on the datasets, see the LIS web site (http://lis.ceps.lu).

in the datasets have been standardized by the LIS staff, so that cross-country comparisons are possible.

We selected five countries for this study, based on the availability across the LIS datasets of the necessary dependent and independent variables. We also sought to include countries with varied welfare state and regulatory designs (see Esping-Andersen 1990). Our five selected countries include three 'liberal' welfare states (the United States, the United Kingdom, and Canada) and two 'conservative' welfare states (Italy and Germany). Unfortunately, no 'social democratic' welfare states—primarily, the Nordic countries—could be included, because of data limitations. The period under consideration is the mid-1990s, corresponding to the last available 'wave' of the LIS data.

Variable definitions and sample selection

In the first stage of our analysis, we seek to explain how working-age women choose their 'labour market status'—meaning here, the choice among non-employment versus part-time employment versus full-time employment. This stage involved constructing, or adjusting, a series of variables. Our first task was to identify 'employed' versus 'non-employed' women. Ideally, the 'non-employed' should be further divided between 'out of the labour force' (inactive) and 'unemployed' (not employed but seeking employment). However, the LIS data, in general, do not reliably report unemployment status, so we pool the inactive and the unemployed, and treat that as an undifferentiated group. Fortunately, the costs of this decision are limited, given that our main interest is in comparing the behaviour and the wages of part-time versus full-time workers. In that sense, the 'non-employed' group is treated as a residual category.[6]

In the second stage of our analysis, we estimate the wage differential between part-time and full-time workers. Our dependent variable is the (logarithm of the) hourly wage rate. Hourly wages are not directly available in these LIS datasets, so we built an hourly wage variable using annual gross earnings of the individual, average weekly hours worked, and the number of weeks worked during the year.

A key decision, that affects both stages, involves the definition of 'part-time' work. The definition of 'part-time' in comparative research is always problematic because no statutory definition exists in most countries and, when definitions are adopted—for example, in national labour force surveys—they vary widely cross-nationally (EIRR 1990; Eurostat 1984;[7] OECD 1994; Van Bastelaer *et al.* 1997). For example, in Italy and Germany, part-time is generally defined by a 'number of hours lower than

[6] Moreover, the distinction between unemployed and out-of-the labour force is less clear cut for women than for men, because many women do not seek employment—although they would prefer it—due to supply-side constraints, such as the lack of appropriate child care.

[7] Eurostat (1984) reported that, in the 1980s, at least six different definitions of part-time work were in use in the European Community alone. This resulted from a variety of definitions in use across employer and household surveys, collective agreements, and administrative records.

the standard hours', whereas in the United Kingdom and Canada, despite the absence of any statutory definition, a threshold of 30 hours is adopted in most surveys. In the US, the Current Population Survey classifies a job as a part-time one if it is for fewer than 35 hours a week. Moreover, given that 'standard' working time itself is likely to vary across sectors, the definition of part-time may vary within countries as well. Finally, given that in many surveys, the individual worker is asked to define herself as part-time versus full-time, this subjective element is likely to introduce a further variability in the definition.

In the present study, we adopt the *self-definition* of part-time work. The self-definition offers the advantage of not imposing a uniform line across countries, allowing instead the adoption of the country-specific concept of part-time and, inside each country, the sector- or industry-specific definition. We tested an alternative definition, which uses a fixed threshold of 30 hours/week, but this did not allow us to reliably distinguish between full-time and 'proper' part-time workers.[8]

In defining part-time employment, a second problem arises in that some workers report working fewer than 10 hours per week. Following Hakim (1997), we defined this employment status as 'marginal part-time', and in our multivariate analyses we combine these workers with the inactive and unemployed. One reason to exclude them is that many of these marginal part-time workers hold so-called 'junk' jobs—often occasional and temporary jobs—and we expect these workers to have idiosyncratic characteristics. Moreover, inaccurate reporting of weekly hours and/or annual earnings will produce, among such short-hour workers, large errors in the estimated hourly wage rate. Given that marginal part-time workers are relatively few everywhere, excluding them from the group of part-time workers does not cause meaningful selection bias.

Finally, we have excluded from our sample all agricultural and self-employed workers, due to well-known difficulties in measuring the earnings of these two categories of workers. Moreover, we have restricted the sample to the population aged 25–59, in order to exclude most students and retired people. Excluding these two groups helps us to identify and analyse cross-national variation in employment patterns and wages net of the effects of educational and retirement institutions and policies, which vary substantially across countries.

The model

The choice model

As noted earlier, the model that we estimate in the first stage of our empirical analysis is a model of the allocation of workers across three employment statuses, that is, distinguishing between part-time, full-time, and non-employment. We model this 'choice' using a multinomial logit regression.[9] The model we have adopted, in fact, is

[8] The difference is evident when we consider the case, for example, of Italian teachers. A large percentage of Italian teachers (66.7 per cent) report working fewer than 30 hours per week on average, because the official teaching time is normally 18 hours per week. However, these workers are, according to both their contract and to their self-definition, full-time workers. Furthermore, Van Bastelaer *et al.* (1997) note that using a 30-hour cut-off, rather than self-definition, would double the estimated rate of part-time work in Italy.

a reduced form, in which the estimated coefficients of the selection equation are the combined result of supply- *and* demand-side decisions. In this sense it is not exact to refer to it as a 'choice model', but as a 'selection model'.

The multinomial logit model assumes that individual i allocates herself/is allocated in state j depending on the value of her underlying 'propensity index':

$$I_{ij}^{*} = Z_i\gamma_j + \varepsilon_{ij} \tag{1}$$

If the error terms are independently and identically distributed as a type-I extreme value distribution, the underlying probability of being in state m is given by:

$$P_{im} = F(\eta_{im}) = \frac{\exp(Z_i\gamma_m)}{\sum_{k=1,2,3}\exp(Z_i\gamma_k)} \tag{2}$$

This model has been estimated for the sample of women, in each country. The effect of the explanatory variables is assessed by computing the change in the predicted probabilities for an hypothetical woman designed as our 'reference' case. These simulations, which will help in interpreting the results of the multinomial logit, are presented in the third Section.

The wage model

In the second stage of our analysis, we estimate the wage gap between part-time and full-time workers. We estimate two human capital equations, one for part-time and the other for full-time workers:

$$\ln Y_1 = X'B_1 + u_1 \tag{3}$$

$$\ln Y_2 = X'B_2 + u_2 \tag{4}$$

where X is the vector of independent variables, B_1 and B_2 are the two sets of coefficients to be estimated and the subscripts 1 and 2 indicate the part-time and the full-time status.

Estimation of the two regressions (3) and (4) above may produce biased coefficients, if the two groups of part-time and full-time workers are not random samples of individuals. And we believe that this is the case, given that it is exactly this process that we have modelled at step one above.

The problem of non-random selection may be handled by adopting an extension to the three-outcome selection model of the well-known two-stage Heckman procedure:[10]

$$\begin{aligned}\ln Y_j &= X'B_j + \sigma_j\rho_j\frac{\phi[J(\eta_j)]}{F(\eta_j)} + \nu_j = X'B_j + \mathrm{cov}(u_j\eta_j)\lambda_j + \nu_j \\ &= X'B_j + \delta_j\lambda_j + \nu_j \end{aligned} \tag{5}$$

[9] Note that our 'choice equation' fulfils two roles. First, it allows us to analyse, substantively, the effects of a range of variables on women's employment choices. Second, it is functionally used to correct the wage regressions in order to obtain unbiased estimates.

[10] For a detailed explanation of the selection problem and the two-step Heckman procedure see Maddala (1983), Mansky (1989), and Lee (1982, 1983).

where:

$$J(\eta_j) = \Phi^{-1}[F(\eta_j)]$$

Φ^{-1} being the inverse distribution function of the standard normal. In eqn (5) σ_j is the standard error of u_j, ρ_j is the correlation between u_j and η_j, λ_j is the 'correction factor' computed from the multinomial logit ($\lambda = \varphi\ [J(Z'\gamma)]/F(Z'\gamma)$), δ_j is the lambda coefficient to be estimated ($\delta_j = \sigma_j \rho_j$) and v_j is a zero mean error. Note that if δ_j is found to be significantly different from zero, this will mean that correlation between u_j and η_j actually exists.

After having estimated the two human capital equations, we measure and decompose the part-time/full-time wage differential, using the Oaxaca procedure (Oaxaca 1973):

$$\overline{\ln w^{PT}} - \overline{\ln w^{FT}} = \sum_z \hat{\beta}_z^{PT}(\overline{X}_z^{PT} - \overline{X}_z^{FT}) + [(\hat{\beta}_0^{PT} - \hat{\beta}_0^{FT}) + \sum_z \overline{X}_z^{FT}(\hat{\beta}_z^{PT} - \hat{\beta}_z^{FT})] + (\delta^{PT}\overline{\lambda^{PT}} - \delta^{FT}\overline{\lambda^{FT}}) \tag{6}$$

where $\hat{\beta}_z^{PT,FT}$ are the estimated coefficients in the two wage of the variable z, and $\overline{X}_z^{PT,FT}$ are the average values of the variable Xz in the two groups.[11]

The first term on the right-hand side picks up the portion of the differential attributable to differences in observable characteristics (the 'fair part' of the differential). The second term, in square brackets, captures the portion attributable to differences in the estimated coefficients—and therefore the part of the differential that cannot be explained by differences in *observed* background characteristics of the worker, but that is due, instead, to the employer, or to the 'economic system'. This component is generally referred to as the 'unexplained part' or—in the literature on discrimination—as the 'discrimination component'. Note that the difference between the constants is also included in this 'unexplained' part (as discussed in Jones and Kelley 1984 and Oaxaca and Ransom 1999). The last term is the part attributable to the sample selection effect.

The independent variables

The choice analysis

In our 'choice analysis', the dependent variable is the 'employment status' of the working-age woman, that is the choice among non-employment versus part-time employment versus full-time employment. It is widely known that this 'choice' is

[11] In the specification above, the average wage differential is decomposed under the assumption that full-time workers are paid according to the part-time wage coefficients. Different results for each single component of the decomposition would be obtained if the opposite assumption were made (part-time workers being paid as full-time workers), even though the total differential will be the same. We thought that it is more reasonable to imagine that full-time workers can be paid as part-time workers, because not all part-time jobs have a full-time counterpart.

influenced by a series of individual and household variables. In section 1 we examined in detail the expected effects on a woman's labour supply of the factors that we are most interested in, that is, a range of household factors.

First, the (potential) wage rate is a fundamental explanatory variable in any labour supply equation. To proxy the wage rate, we have included among the explanatory variables the age of the woman, and her education level. In a comparative context, it is quite difficult to include detailed education categories, partly due to data limitations and partly due to fundamental differences in educational institutions across countries. Thus, we were only able to construct three education categories: 'low', 'medium', and 'high'. Despite the importance of including age and education in the selection equation, these two variables are not the focus of our analysis, and we treat them as controls.[12]

Second, the presence and the age of children in the household are crucial variables in our analyses.[13] We first coded women as 'mothers' or not (unfortunately, in our datasets it is not possible to determine parental status for individuals who are not heads of household or spouses of heads of households. However, we believe that the vast majority of mothers in these countries are either heads or spouses). We further assume that every child living in the household influences the labour market behaviour of these women. In addition, parental and marital status are likely to interact, so we included an interaction term ('married *and* parent'). Children's ages have been captured by a set of dummy variables that indicate whether or not the household contains children in a specific age range. We have identified four age intervals that correspond generally to children's involvement in different categories of childcare and after-school programmes: 0–2, 3–5, 6–11, and 12–17 years old.

A third independent variable—one that is less often included in labour market analyses—captures the presence of 'adult dependents' in the household. By 'adult dependent', we mean an adult in the household who reports no earnings in the reference year. We have singled out four categories of adult dependents, first a 'dependent spouse aged 18–64' (for example, a retired or disabled or long-term unemployed husband[14]); second, 'other adult dependent aged 18–64', including children, parent(s), and other household members who are unemployed or out-of-the-labour-force; third, 'persons aged 65–74' and, fourth, 'persons aged 75 and older',

[12] Note that the occupation and industrial sector, included among the regressors in the wage equation, are not included in the choice equation because they cannot be observed for the non-employed group.

[13] This model disregards the possibility of endogeneity between women's employment outcomes and child-related (fertility) variables. Lehrer (1992) notes that the consensus in the labour supply literature is that no adequate empirical solution to the problem exists; instrumenting fertility is virtually impossible due to incomplete theoretical specifications and data limitations. Lehrer summarizes: 'In light of these difficulties, many recent analysis of short-run female labor supply (hours, weeks, or some other dimension of current employment status) have treated the number and ages of children as predetermined variables' (p. 425). We also assume, for the sake of these estimations, the exogeneity of the adult dependent variables.

[14] Throughout this study, 'spouse' is coded in such a way as to include cohabitors as well as legal marriage partners. The United States is an exception; 'spouses' are limited to partners in legal marriages and, unfortunately, cohabitors cannot be identified.

these two last categories including mainly retired household members. As in the case of the child variables, the dummies indicate the presence in the household of an individual in the specified category.[15]

Finally, we included among the regressors in the selection equation, 'other household income'. This variable has been constructed as the total earnings of other adult household members (other than the woman in question) plus the cash property income of the household as a whole. In economic terms, this captures the woman's 'endowment'.[16]

The wage analysis

In the second stage of our empirical analysis—the estimation of the wage equations—we employ the classical human capital model. The dependent variable is the employed woman's estimated (logarithm of) hourly wage, and the independent variables include age, education (coded, again, as 'low', 'medium', and 'high'), as well as dummy variables indicating both her occupation and industrial sector. Age both exerts an independent effect and acts as a proxy for total work experience.[17] As with education, only three categories have been created for the occupational classification: 'professionals', 'sales and clerical', and 'blue-collar'. Industrial sector dummies are included as well, to capture demand-side effects on the differentials. Unfortunately, information on the industrial sector is not available for the United Kingdom.

For detailed information on the coding of these variables, see Bardasi and Gornick (2000).

RESULTS

Patterns of part-time employment in the 1990s

Cross-national variation in part-time employment

An overall portrait of women's and men's labour market activity in these five countries is presented in Table 10.1. In the top panel, we present activity breakdowns first for all working-age adults, and then for workers only (i.e. excluding the marginally- employed and the non-employed).

[15] Note that including the household variables in the selection equation—in addition to having substantive meaning in explaining the allocation of workers—also serves the econometric function of allowing identification of the selection equation coefficients.

[16] This specification assumes, for simplicity, that the level of 'other household income' is exogenous to a women's own employment decisions. Clearly, among married couples, this can be problematic, in that husbands' earnings may be shaped by their wives' labour market status. Nevertheless, most labour economists consider this to be a reasonable assumption in the industrialized countries, even into the 1990s, because, for the most part, very high rates of labour force participation and of full-time work are the norm among married men.

[17] Labour economists often measure 'total work experience' as age minus years of education minus age of compulsory school entry; we rejected that formulation because our education variables are generally categorical rather than continuous and, furthermore, because this estimation method is poorly suited to women.

Table 10.1. *Activity Rates in Five Countries, Women and Men (Percentages)*

	Canada		United States		United Kingdom		Germany		Italy	
	Total	Employed	Total	Employed	Total	Employed	Total	Employed	Total	Employed
Women										
Full-time	50.6	81.1	54.6	81.2	41.4	71.9	36.8	68.2	34.4	88.0
Part-time	11.8	18.9	12.7	18.8	16.2	28.1	17.1	31.8	4.7	12.0
Marginal part-time	1.6	—	1.4	—	3.4	—	0.9	—	0.3	—
Non-employed	36.0	—	31.3	—	39.1	—	45.2	—	60.7	—
Total	100.0	100.0	100.0	100.0	100.0	100.0	100.0	100.0	100.0	100.0
Men										
Full-time	72.7	96.7	79.9	95.4	70.0	98.5	76.4	98.6	71.1	98.6
Part-time	2.5	3.3	3.9	4.6	1.1	1.5	1.1	1.4	1.0	1.4
Marginal part-time	0.4	—	0.3	—	0.4	—	0.1	—	0.0	—
Non-employed	24.4	—	15.9	—	28.5	—	22.4	—	27.8	—
Total	100.0	100.0	100.0	100.0	100.0	100.0	100.0	100.0	100.0	100.0
Part-time rate, ratio: women/men	4.8	5.8	3.3	4.1	15.2	18.8	15.4	22.2	4.5	8.3
Female share										
Full-time labour market	42.5		44.0		41.8		34.1		36.8	
Part-time labour market	83.7		79.1		94.9		94.3		84.5	
Marginal part-time	80.3		82.5		91.6		91.4		93.6	
Non-employed	61.1		69.4		62.4		68.4		72.5	

Notes: Agricultural, military, and self-employed workers are excluded; The sample is restricted to persons aged 25–59; Part-time status is self-defined.

Source: Own calculations based on the Luxembourg Income Study.

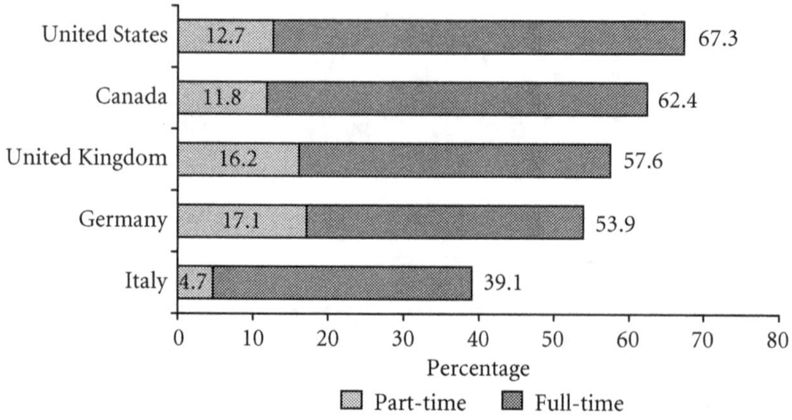

Figure 10.1. *Full-time and Part-time Employment in Five Countries, Women*

Notes: See Table 10.1; The numbers to the right of the bars indicate total employment rates (part-time and full-time combined).

Source: Own calculations based on the Luxembourg Income Study.

Table 10.1 reveals a set of inter-related findings. First of all, there is substantial variation in women's rates of part-time work across these five countries. Among working-age women as whole, the percentage working part-time (excluding marginal part-time work) ranges from a low of 4.7 per cent in Italy, to a much higher 17.1 per cent in Germany. Figure 10.1 summarizes the distribution of women between full-time and part-time work, as well as the overall employment rates in the five countries. Among *employed* women, part-time work rates vary from 12.0 per cent, again in Italy, to a high of 31.8 per cent in Germany. Part-time work among women in the UK is nearly as common as in Germany. In the two North American countries, the United States and Canada, part-time employment is much less common than in the United Kingdom and Germany, but much more so than in Italy.

Second, men's rates of part-time work vary as well, but much less. Among employed men, for example, rates of part-time work—which are far lower than women's—range from approximately 1.5 per cent in Italy, Germany, and the United Kingdom, to 3.3 per cent in Canada, to a high of 4.6 per cent in the United States.

Third, there is no clear relationship between rates of female part-time work and overall women's employment rates, as Fig. 10.1 clearly reveals. The two countries with the lowest women's employment rates, Germany and Italy, also have both the least and most part-time work. The two with the highest women's employment rates—the United States and Canada—both have moderate rates of part-time employment.[18]

[18] Others have reported little or no relationship between employment rates and rates of part-time work, over time or across countries (Gornick 1999; OECD 1994; Rosenfeld and Birkelund 1995).

Finally, marginal part-time work is clearly a limited phenomenon—with the highest rate (among working-age women) reported in the United Kingdom (3.4 per cent). This supports our decision to include the marginal part-time workers in the group of non-working population.

The gendered nature of part-time employment

It is often noted in the literature that '*part-time work is women's work*' and that is clearly confirmed throughout these countries (see the lower panel of Table 10.1). Here, we see, that among working-age adults, women's probability of being employed part-time is three to five times greater than men's in Italy, Canada, and the United States—and over fifteen times greater in Germany and the United Kingdom. Among the employed, the gender differentials are even greater because smaller percentages of women than men are employed.

The highly gendered nature of part-time employment can be seen as clearly when we look at women's share in part-time work. Even in the United States—the country with the least gender differentiation in part-time work—the part-time labour force is nearly 80 per cent female. In the United Kingdom and Germany, part-time workers are nearly 95 per cent female.

Workers' choices

Simulation

The results from the estimation of the multinomial logit models are reported in Table 10.2. Here, we estimate a three-way decision structure, where the dependent variable is: not employed versus part-time employed versus full-time. The non-employed are designated as the base category. In the table we have reported the relative risk-ratios, which are more easily interpretable than the coefficients themselves.

However, to facilitate the assessment of the effects of the explanatory variables on the probabilities of working full-time, part-time, or not at all, we carried out a simulation exercise to produce a story that is more easily interpreted. We computed the independent, or marginal, effect of each explanatory variable as the change in the 'base' probability of being in each of the three outcome states, given a change in the independent variable under consideration, *ceteris paribus*. The 'base' probabilities were computed for a hypothetical woman, with a set of fixed individual and household characteristics: she is 35-years old, has a medium level of education, is married, has one child in the age range 12–17, has no dependent adults in the household, and has other household income at the country mean.[19]

[19] Throughout our empirical analyses on 'choice', we focus on the effects of our household variables on *married* women's employment choices. The labour supply of single mothers is very complex, largely due to the effects of income transfers. A full analysis of single mothers' employment choices is beyond the scope of this paper.

Table 10.2. *Multinomial Logit Results in Five Countries, Women*

	RR ratio				
	Canada	United States	United Kingdom	Germany	Italy
Full-time					
Married	0.993	0.816**	1.462**	1.025	0.480**
Parent	0.552**	0.788**	0.167**	0.475**	1.475
Married* parent	1.378**	1.109*	2.062**	1.206	0.747
Children 0–2	0.583**	0.511**	0.346**	0.056**	0.753**
Children 3–5	0.547**	0.502**	0.358**	0.287**	0.783*
Children 6–11	0.567**	0.606**	0.473**	0.477**	0.656**
Children 12–17	0.987	0.940*	1.386**	1.003	0.642**
Spouse dependent 18–64	0.504**	0.562**	0.270**	0.573**	0.928
Adult dependent 18–64 (no spouse)	0.592**	0.753**	0.575**	0.884	0.636**
Adult dependent 65–74	0.637**	0.623**	0.505**	0.607*	0.686**
Adult dependent 75+	0.722**	0.806**	0.549*	0.622	1.042
Adult dependent 65–74*child 0–5	3.072**	1.619**	10.484**	2.099	0.542
Other household income	1.002**	0.997**	0.995	0.994**	1.050*
Other household income squared	1.000**	1.000**	1.000	1.000	0.996**
Age	1.306**	1.179**	1.280**	1.179**	1.697**
Age squared	0.996**	0.998**	0.996**	0.997**	0.993**
Education level: high	4.551**	4.281**	3.048**	3.412**	5.517**
Education level: medium	2.819**	2.503**	2.285**	1.496**	3.836**
Part-time					
Married	1.171*	1.032	2.440**	2.133**	0.669*
Parent	0.625**	0.873*	0.921	2.359**	3.000**
Married*parent	1.689**	1.484**	1.664*	0.582*	0.520
Children 0–2	0.690**	0.628**	0.409**	0.140**	0.860
Children 3–5	0.835**	0.686**	0.609**	0.418**	0.827
Children 6–11	0.937	0.932	0.688**	0.703**	0.524**
Children 12–17	1.130*	1.147**	0.876	0.870	0.597**
Spouse dependent 18–64	0.481**	0.521**	0.381**	0.697*	0.749
Adult dependent 18–64 (no spouse)	0.717**	0.752**	0.605**	0.954	0.611**
Adult dependent 65–74	0.871	0.765**	0.360**	0.822	0.880
Adult dependent 75+	0.625**	0.764**	1.025	1.164	1.205
Adult dependent 65–74*child 0–5	1.211	1.203	dropped	2.042	0.491
Other household income	1.008**	1.003**	1.002	1.002	1.011
Other household income squared	1.000**	1.000**	1.000	1.000	0.998
Age	1.110**	1.091**	1.128**	1.193**	1.733**
Age squared	0.999**	0.999**	0.999**	0.998**	0.993**
Education level: high	3.314**	2.796**	1.236	2.535**	1.629**
Education level: medium	2.138**	1.991**	1.404**	1.607**	2.506**
Observations—total	22,607	37,084	3,856	3,806	5,248
Observations—part-time	2,543	4,247	568	587	219

Table 10.2. *Continued*

	RR ratio				
	Canada	United States	United Kingdom	Germany	Italy
Observations—full-time	9,843	18,113	1,415	1,360	1,574
Observations—non-worker	10,221	14,724	1,873	1,859	3,455
Log-likelihood	−20,241.11	−32,971.42	−3,418.14	−3,446.87	−3,645.01
Pseudo R2	0.084	0.073	0.135	0.118	0.147

Note: The comparison group is the outcome 'non-worker'; Relative risk ratios (rather than coefficients) are reported in this table; the relative risk ratio associated with a one unit change in the explanatory variable is measured as exp(b*i*) where b*i* is the estimated coefficient of variable *i*.

** Indicates significance at the 5% level.

* Indicates significance at the 10% level.

Source: Own calculations based on the Luxembourg Income Study.

This hypothetical woman has the following predicted employment probabilities:

	Full-time	Part-time	Non-work
Canada	0.596	0.142	0.263
United States	0.585	0.171	0.244
United Kingdom	0.685	0.176	0.139
Germany	0.515	0.233	0.252
Italy	0.502	0.129	0.368

The marginal effects of each of our categorical variables of interest (i.e. children and adult dependents) are then shown in Fig. 10.2. The effect of 'other household income', a continuous variable, is depicted in Fig. 10.3.[20] Note that these graphs are read as follows. The hypothetical woman in the UK, for example, has a 68 per cent probability of working full-time, an 18 per cent probability of working part-time, and a 14 per cent probability of not working at all. If we 'take away' her 12–17 year-old child and 'replace' that child with one aged 3–5 (holding all other individual and household characteristics constant), her probability of working full-time would fall by 28 percentage points; concomitantly, her probability of working part-time would rise by 10 percentage points and her probability of non-work would rise by 18 percentage points. The sum of the three changes is always equal to zero.

Child-related effects

Our first research question concerned the effects of the presence and age of children in the household. We first assess the effect of *parenting status per se*. The effect of being a parent can be seen (in reverse) in Fig. 10.2 when this hypothetical woman is

[20] Note that the marginal effects of the explanatory variables in logit models can be computed only after setting values for the regressors; they are not independent of these chosen values.

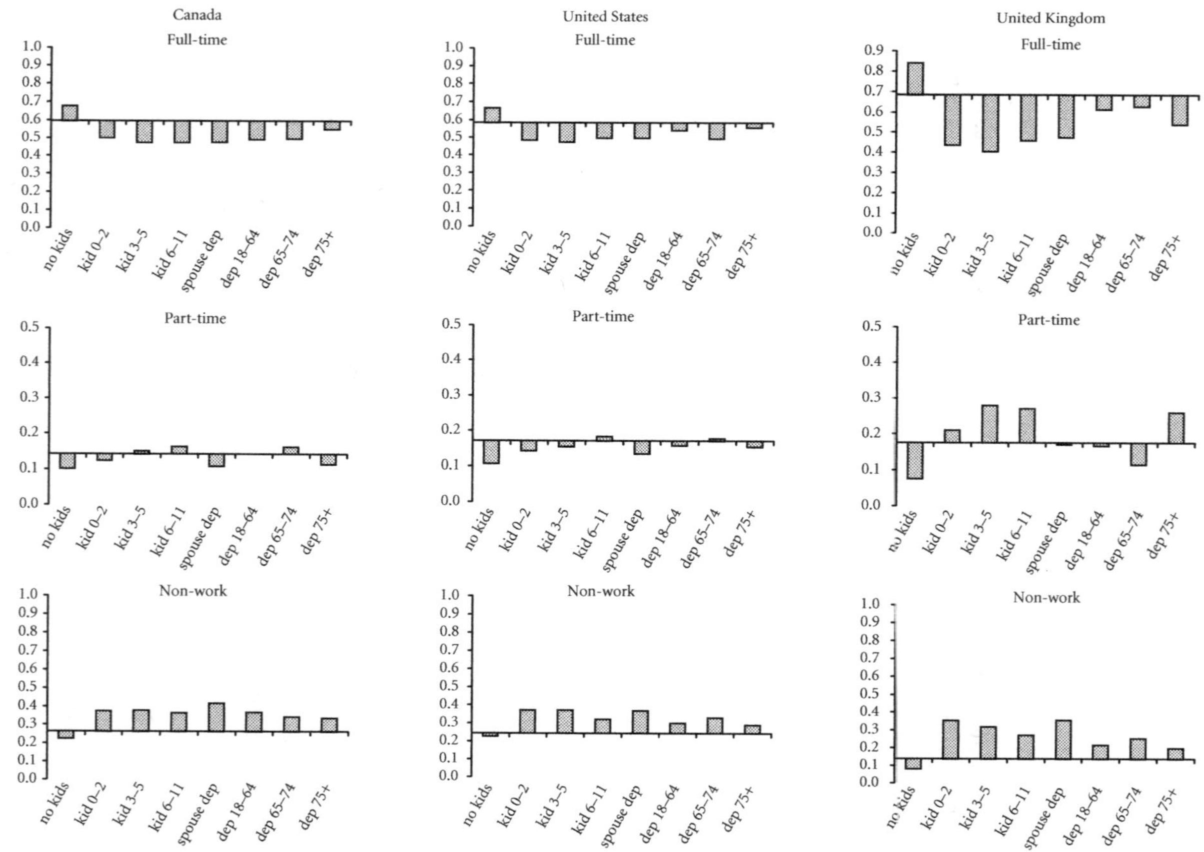

Figure 10.2. *Effects of Children and Adult Dependents on Three Employment Outcomes in Five Countries, Women*

Note: The three bar graphs drawn for each country represent the estimated effects on women's probability of working full-time, part-time, or not at all, produced by a change in one explanatory variable at a time. The horizontal line in each panel corresponds to the base probability of each employment outcome (see the text of the paper), and the length of each bar represents the magnitude of the predicted **change** (positive or negative) in the probability of each outcome that is associated with a change in that one explanatory variable.

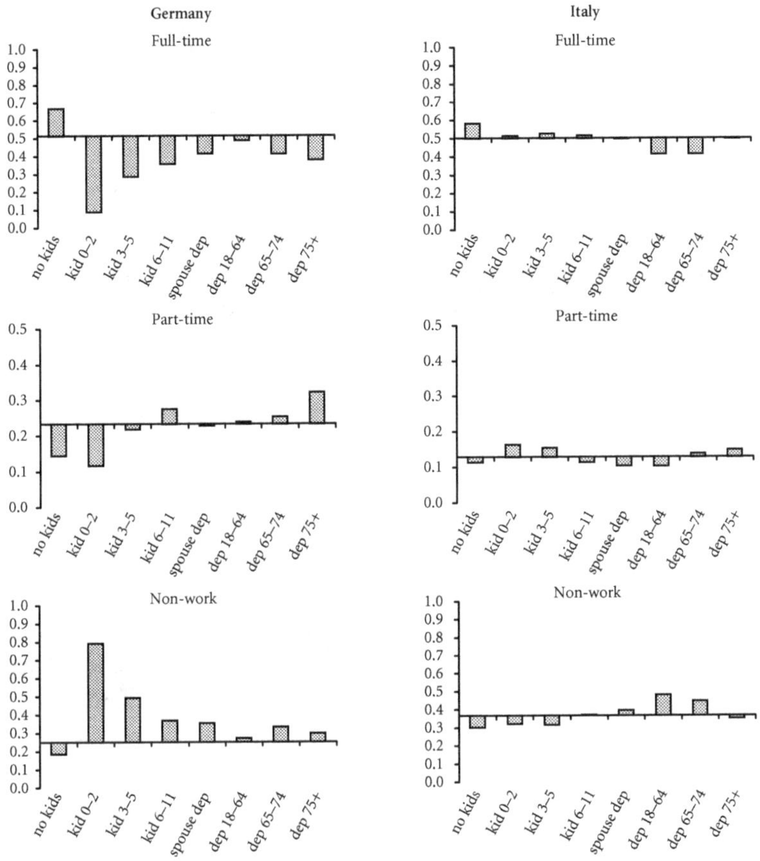

Figure 10.2. *Continued*

'changed' from being a parent to being childless (in other words, when her one child, aged 12–17, is 'taken away'). The effect is uniform across countries: a decrease in the probability of working part-time. Moreover, in all countries, the decrease in part-time work is more than compensated for by the increase in the probability of working full-time; thus we see a net decrease in the probability of non-working. In other words, as we expected, for married women, the presence of children, overall, decreases the probability that a woman chooses to participate in full-time work and increases the probabilities of both non-working and—our empirical results show—of working part-time.

In order to assess the effects, among mothers, of the *age of children*, we 'take away' the 12–17 year-old child from our hypothetical woman, and replace that child with a younger one. Figure 10.2 shows a strong common pattern of those changes; in all of our countries—except Italy—the probability of working full-time decreases, sometimes substantially, and the probability of non-working increases. The age-of-children effects are particularly strong for children below school age (i.e. age 6, in most cases),

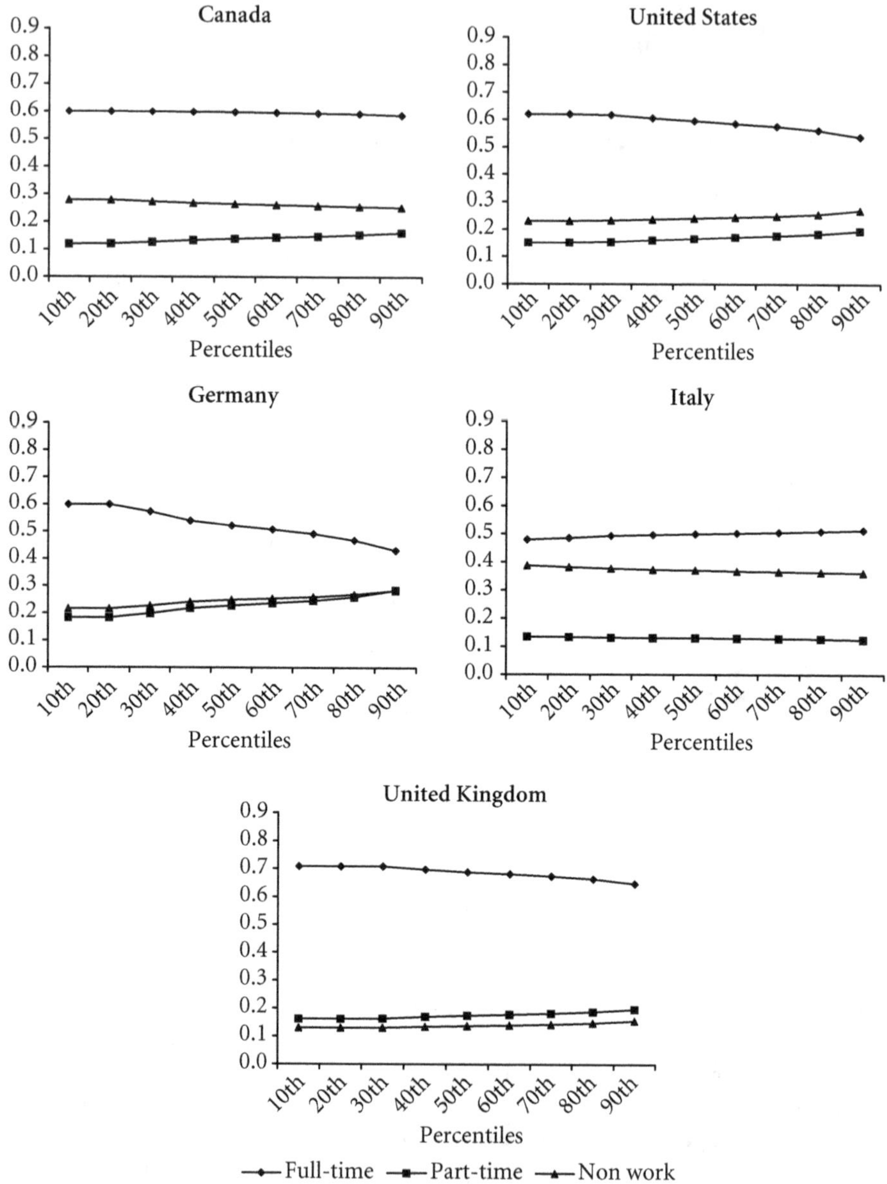

Figure 10.3. *Effect of Household Income on Three Employment Outcomes in Five Countries, Women*

Note: The graphs show predicted changes in the probabilities of each outcome state, as women's 'other family income' varies across income deciles. All other explanatory variable are fixed at the level designated for the hypothetical woman (see the text of the paper for her characteristics).

especially in Germany, the United Kingdom, and—to a lesser extent—the United States. This confirms our expectation that, overall, the presence of young children decreases their mothers' probability of full-time work and increases the likelihood of non-work. At the same time, the magnitude of the effects varies considerably across countries, and in accord with our expectations. We find larger age-of-children effects in Germany and in the United Kingdom, and smaller—although still substantial—effects in Canada and in the United States. Finally, in Italy, the employment status of the mother is virtually unaffected by the age of her children.[21] The larger effects in Germany and the United Kingdom are likely driven by the widespread availability of part-time jobs—in accord with our expectations—and the minimal child effects in Italy may be attributed to a combination of limited part-time work and the availability of nearly universal preschool for children starting at the third birthday.

The empirical effect on part-time work—the direction of which is theoretically ambiguous—varies depending on the age of the child. The presence of a very young child, aged 0–2, decreases the probability of working part-time in three countries, namely Canada, the United States, and Germany, and increases it in Italy and the United Kingdom. When we 'give' the mother a child aged 3–5—again, in comparison to a child aged 12–17—the effect on the probability of the mother's working part-time is very small. An important exception is the United Kingdom, where the probability of working part-time increases substantially when the child is in this age range. The presence of a child aged 6–11 has a positive effect everywhere, except Italy, on the probability of working part-time, and always at the expense of working full-time. To summarize, when the child is very young (age 0–2), non-work is more likely to be the preferred solution adopted by mothers needing to balance employment and dependent care responsibilities. As their children leave infancy (0–2), and enter the preschool age (3–5), and then eventually reach the young school-age years (6–11), part-time—instead of non-work—becomes the more common alternative to full-time work.

Can other household members mitigate the age-of-children effects? These results show that, as we expected, the presence of very young children (under age 6) generally lower mothers' likelihood of full-time work and raise their probability of non-work. However, one possibility is that the presence in the household of an older person—especially one aged 65–74—might mitigate these 'child-penalties'; these (relatively young) elderly household members may assume some 'babysitting' responsibilities for young children in the household. To assess this possibility, we included an interaction term among the regressors ('non-earning adult aged 65–74 *and* child aged 0–5'). The results in Table 10.2 allow us to begin to disentangle the positive effect of this (potentially) 'babysitting' elderly household member from the negative effect of the presence of a young child. Unfortunately, there are a small number of cases—especially in Germany, Italy, and the United Kingdom—in which a woman works part-time and lives in a household where both an adult dependent aged 64–74 and a child aged 0–5 are present, so we are limited, for the most part, to

[21] The surprising absence of child-related effects in Italy has been reported, previously, by Colombino and Del Boca (1990) and by Gornick *et al.* (1998).

assessing the effects of these 'babysitters' on women's likelihood of working full-time. Table 10.2 reveals that in three countries—Canada, the United States, and the UK—the coefficient on the 'babysitter' is significantly positive with respect to full-time work, meaning that having these adults in the home raises the likelihood that mothers work full-time instead of not at all. Note that this 'babysitter effect' is strong enough in Canada and the United Kingdom (although not in the US) to reverse the negative effect of the presence of a young child (both 0–2 and 3–5).[22] The effect on part-time work is much less clear, mainly because of the limited number of cases. Nevertheless, in the four countries in which we could estimate the 'babysitter' effect on part-time employment (versus non-employment), the coefficient is positive (though non-significant) in three; the exception is in Italy, where the effect on part-time work is negative (also non-significant). These results suggest that the 'babysitter' effect on women's employment choices—both full-time and part-time—might be greater in those countries where out-of-home childcare alternatives are fewer.

Dependent adults

We suggested, in our second research question, that the presence of various non-wage-earning adults in the household might exert separate, independent, effects on women's employment choices. First, we consider non-earning, or 'dependent', spouses. Figure 10.2 shows that, in all five countries, the effect on full-time work and on non-working has the sign that we expected—negative in the first case, positive in the second. Moreover, as we expected, these estimated effects are stronger in Canada and in the United Kingdom, weaker in Germany, and almost non-existent in Italy—an outcome that we attribute to the larger share of means-tested income in the social benefit packages in the former countries (these effects in the United States however, are weaker than those in the other 'liberal' welfare states, and the explanation for that is not evident). The estimated effect on part-time work, which again was theoretically indeterminate, varies across countries. In two countries—Germany and the UK—the presence of a non-earning spouse has no effect on the probability of working part-time; in the other three countries—Canada, the United States, and Italy—the estimated effect is negative.

If the 'dependent adult' in our hypothetical woman's home is not her spouse, but instead another household member aged 18–64 (e.g. a non-working child older than age 17, parents or siblings who are unemployed, retired, or out of the labour force), the effects are very similar (as we expected). That is, the probability of working full-time decreases and the probability of non-working increases, while the probability of the woman working part-time decreases—or varies very little.

When the 'dependent adult' is an elderly individual—aged 65–74 or older than 75—the effects on women's employment choices are again very similar as in the previous

[22] The total effect of a variable that is included both alone and in interaction with another variable among the regressors is computed by multiplying the two RR-ratios.

cases, although not as strong. The probability of working full-time decreases everywhere, and the probability of non-working increases; we attribute these effects to the fact that many of these household members are in need of care, and much of that care is provided by working-age women in the home. The estimated signs on the probability of working part-time, again, vary by country. In general, the probability of working part-time increases, except in Canada and in the United States in the case of an elderly individual aged 75 or more, and in the United Kingdom in the case of an individual aged 65–74.

To summarize, when the non-earning adult is aged 18–64 (either the spouse or another household member), the probability of being employed both full-time and part-time decreases everywhere. In the case of elderly household members, there is instead some shift to part-time from full-time (even if the most substantial shift is again from full-time to non-employment).

Other household income

Finally, our third research question concerned the effect of *other household income* on women's employment choices. These results can be seen in Fig. 10.3, where the 'base' income of our hypothetical woman—which has been set at the country mean for all the prior simulated employment patterns—varies across the 'other household income' distribution. Interestingly, the effect of other household income, when controlling for all other variables, is almost non-existent on any of the three employment probabilities. Only in Germany does the part-time rate increase substantially when the other earnings in the household increase (and this at the expenses of full-time employment). Therefore, the hypothesis that part-time work is heavily concentrated among women in relatively high-income families does not seem to be confirmed in our empirical findings. The exception, in Germany, may be partially explained by the large part-time labour market operating there, that is, if there is an income effect, it will likely be most evident where women have the greatest options to choose part-time work.

Wage differentials

The results in the top row of Table 10.3 indicate that, among employed women, part-time workers suffer unadjusted wage penalties, relative to full-time workers in all five countries; these wage differentials are unadjusted in the sense that no controls are included.[23] The results in this table reveal that the largest unadjusted gaps between part-time and full-time wages (approximately 22 per cent) are found in Italy and the United States The United Kingdom ranks in an intermediate position with a full-time/part-time wage gap of 15 per cent. Finally, in Canada and Germany, the wage differentials are lower: 12 and 8 per cent, respectively. These results are, to some extent, in line with our

[23] These unadjusted part-time/full-time wage gaps are calculated as the exponential of the difference between mean *logged* part-time wage and mean *logged* full-time wage.

Table 10.3. *Decomposition Results, Part-time/Full-time Differentials in Five Countries, Women*

	Canada		United States		United Kingdom		Germany		Italy	
Total (unadjusted) differential	−11.7%	1.000	−21.7%	1.000	−15.1%	1.000	−8.4%	1.000	−22.1%	1.000
Component attributable to:										
Characteristics		0.205		0.213		0.928		0.089		0.350
Returns (includes the constant)		−0.684		−0.520		−0.333		1.681		−0.524
Selection		1.479		1.307		0.405		−0.770		1.174
Adjusted differential	−9.3%		−17.1%		−1.1%		−7.7%		−14.4%	

Notes: Agricultural, military, and self-employed workers are excluded; The sample is restricted to persons aged 25–59; Marginal part-time workers (fewer than 10 hours) have been excluded; The distribution of wages have been 'cleaned' of outliers by dropping the top and the bottom 5th percentile groups; The total differential indicates the gap between part-time and full-time workers in percentage terms (−11.7% means that part-time workers are earning 11.7% less than full-time workers); The decomposition reported in the second column of each country section is expressed in percentage points out of the total differential; Given that the total differential has been rescaled to 1, a positive number indicate that component explains a portion of the adjusted wage differential, while a negative number indicates that component actually reduces the unadjusted wage differential; The adjusted differential has been computed as the total (unadjusted) differential reduced by the percentage attributable to observable characteristics.

Source: Own calculations based on the Luxembourg Income Study.

expectations. The large full-time/part-time differential in Italy may be explained by the fact that the part-time sector is especially small (and perhaps disproportionately comprising 'bad jobs'); the US gap is likely due, in part, to the lack of regulations that affect the pay of part-time workers. The decomposition analysis that follows allows us to begin to investigate the sources of these unadjusted pay differentials.

In the subsequent rows of Table 10.3, we present the results of the Oaxaca decomposition of the full-time/part-time wage differential, computed according to eqn (6). Here, we report the contribution to the wage gap of the various components—differences in observable characteristics, in returns (and the constant), and in unobservables (the selection component).[24] The complete OLS results that underlie the decomposition are presented in Appendix Table 10.A1.

Table 10.3 reveals that the composition of the gap varies remarkably across countries. First of all, in the United Kingdom, differences in *observable characteristics* between full-time and part-time workers explain almost the entire unadjusted wage gap (93 per cent). In this case, the wage differential is interpreted primarily as a 'fair'

[24] These are expressed as ratios to the total differential—the three components indicated on the right hand side of eqn (6).

one, in the sense that measured full-time/part-time differences in age, education, and occupation explain a large portion of the unadjusted wage gap. That the wage differential is largely 'explained' in the United Kingdom is not surprising because, in recent decades, the United Kingdom—unlike the other four countries—had an explicit policy aimed at fostering the growth of part-time jobs for women. As a result of organized state intervention, many less-educated and low-skilled women were pulled into part-time work in low-paid occupations with little prospect of advancement.[25]

In contrast, in Germany, the *returns* component, combined with the *constant* component, is the dominant one. In this case, the largest share of the differential is due to differences in the 'base' pay of part-time versus full-time workers, combined with differences in returns to observable characteristics between the two labour forces. In other words, in this case, part-time workers are 'discriminated against' in that a broadly similar full-time worker is paid more per hour. This may be due to the very high fixed labour costs in Germany; these could lead employers to discriminate against part-time workers to keep their hourly costs in line with full-time workers, despite protective legislation.

Finally, in Canada, the United States, and Italy, the *selection effect* component—that is the role of the 'unobservable' characteristics—explains the largest share of the differential. In these countries, the gap is primarily explained by differences between the two groups of workers in unobservable factors that we are not able to control for in our model. These could be supply- and/or demand-driven differences, including, for example, differences in aptitude, motivation, tenure, or other worker-and job-related factors.[26] Interestingly, these countries are again the ones with the smallest part-time labour markets, that is, the countries where part-time work is more likely to be confined to 'marginal areas' of the labour market. Therefore, although this component cannot be 'technically' defined as 'discrimination', it is possible that it is nevertheless related to some sort of discrimination mechanism that operates through the selection of workers into the two labour markets.

Finally, how do the unadjusted wage gaps compare to the adjusted ones? That is, what is the direction and magnitude of the wage differential, across these countries, *after* we remove the component attributable to differences in observable characteristics between the two groups of workers? The second row in Table 10.3 reports, for each country, the direction and magnitude of the component attributed to observable characteristics. As we expected, that number is positive everywhere, which means that controlling for differences in observables reduces the part-time/full-time wage gap in all countries. However, the portion of the unadjusted gap explained by

[25] Burchell *et al.* (1997) note that in response to labour shortages in the 1960s, an active UK state policy began recruiting women into part-time work. 'Jobs were set up in a context in which married women were seen as "a necessary expedient to tide over a period of labour shortage"... and on the assumption that their primary responsibilities lay at home. Thus, part-time work was explicitly designed to be undemanding and lacking in promotion prospects and responsibility. The ramifications of this are still being experienced by women today' (p. 211).

[26] Note that some of these factors are theoretically unobservable (e.g. aspects of motivation), while others are unobservable due to lack of information in the dataset (e.g. tenure).

observables varies dramatically—from only 9 per cent in Germany, to 20–35 per cent in Canada, the United States, and Italy, to nearly 93 per cent in the United Kingdom.

The last row of Table 10.3 presents the adjusted wage gaps. Clearly, the ranking of the countries is considerably different than the ordering with respect to the unadjusted gaps. The largest gaps—when measured worker- and job-related differences are accounted for—are still found in the United States (17 per cent) and in Italy (14 per cent). However, the ranking of the United Kingdom shifts markedly; if part-time and full-time workers had the same observable characteristics the wage gap would have been only slightly more than 1 per cent. Germany and Canada rank in an intermediate position (8 per cent and 9 per cent).

CONCLUSIONS

Summary of findings

In this study, we used cross-nationally comparable micro-data to analyse the patterns and consequences of part-time employment among women in Canada, Germany, Italy, the United Kingdom, and the United States, as of the middle 1990s. Our results indicate that there is marked variation across these countries, but they reveal a number of uniformities as well.

First, we explored overall *patterns of part-time employment* in these countries, and found that, as expected, the percentage of working-age women who work part-time (versus full-time or not at all) varies substantially across countries—from 5 per cent in Italy to 17 per cent in Germany. We also found, again as expected, that men's rates of part-time work are much lower everywhere, and vary less. These results, taken together, are clearly consistent with the widely-reported claim that, in all of the industrialized countries, 'part-time work is women's work'. We found that women's share in part-time work ranges from about 80 per cent in the United States to 95 per cent in the United Kingdom. Clearly, part-time work is deeply 'gendered' in all of these countries. Any analysis of its roots and consequences must be based in an understanding that part-time work is extremely female-dominated.

Second, we turned our attention to *women's employment 'choices'*, specifically to the three-option decision between non-employment, part-time employment, and full-time employment. Our results reveal that, as expected, *child-related factors*—both the presence and age of children—are crucial to women's employment outcomes in nearly all cases. In all countries, being a mother (compared to being childless), *ceteris paribus*, decreases the probability that a woman selects full-time work, and increases the probabilities of both non-working and of working part-time. *Among* mothers, the effects of having young children vary across countries, with the largest effects—decreases in full-time work, increases in non-work—seen in Germany and in the United Kingdom, and smaller effects seen in Canada and the United States. Part-time work, as a substitute for full-time work, typically becomes a more common option as women's young children leave infancy and enter their preschool, then their school-age, years. The cross-national pattern is consistent with our expectations; the effects of young children are smaller, overall, where part-time work is less widely available and (in the case of Italy) where the state provides more preschool slots. It is interesting that the effects of young children are mitigated, to some extent, by the presence of non-earning elderly household members, especially in the English-speaking countries where out-of-home childcare options are fewer.

One of our most interesting findings is the strong and consistent effect of the presence of a *non-wage-earning adult* in the home on working-age women's labour market attachment. These adults may be unemployed or out of the labour market for a variety of reasons; many 'adult dependents', especially those who are elderly, will be in need of care. As expected, the presence of 'adult dependents'—spouses and non-spouses—exerts substantial downward pressure on women's probability of working full-time, and in several cases on the probability of working part-time as well. The effects of 'adult dependents' are more widespread in the English-speaking countries, possibly because a larger share of the overall social benefit package is means-tested in these countries, which may introduce some work disincentives for wives whose husbands (or other relatives) collect benefits. In general, we find weaker effects in Italy, where the part-time labour market is smaller and women's options to choose part-time work are more limited.

Finally, we were somewhat surprised to find that the effect of the level of *market income earned by other household members* is not particularly influential, at least not once control variables are introduced. Actually, only in Germany does the part-time rate increase substantially when the other earnings in the household increase. This means that, despite some claims to the contrary, we find that women from relatively high-income homes are not disproportionately likely to work part-time. Further research on the relationship between women's engagement in part-time work and household economic well-being is clearly needed. We need to better understand both the impact on women's decision-making of her family's economic status, as well as the consequences of her choices.

Third, we turned our attention to the direct economic consequences for women workers of engaging in part-time rather than full-time employment—that is, to the question of *wage penalties* associated with part-time employment. We find *unadjusted* penalties (based on mean logged wages) everywhere, ranging from 8–12 per cent in Canada and Germany, to 15 per cent in the UK, to as high as 22 per cent in the US and Italy; meaning that part-time workers earn that much less than full-time workers in each of these countries. Although controlling for measurable worker- and job-related characteristics fails to fully explain the gap in any country, our controls reduce the observed gap in all countries; the reduction due to measured characteristics ranges from 9 per cent in Germany to over 90 per cent in the United Kingdom. After controlling for measurable characteristics, the largest wage gaps are still found in the US (17 per cent) and in Italy (14 per cent). Wage gaps—adjusted and unadjusted—may be larger in these countries (the United States and Italy) due in part to their smaller part-time labour markets (where part-time work is more marginalized); the very low level of regulation in the United States may also drive the gap upwards.

While the unadjusted wage differential in the United Kingdom is mainly due to differences in observable characteristics, in three countries—Canada, the United States, and Italy—the wage gap is mostly due to the 'selection effect'. This means that women are selected into the two labour forces in a way that increases the gap between their earnings, although we are not able to explain what is different about the two groups of workers. Finally, in Germany the wage gap is mostly due to differences in returns, combined with the differences in the constants. In this sense, only in Germany there is evidence of pay 'discrimination' directed at part-time workers, relative to their full-time counterparts.

Directions for future research: comparative policy analysis

Our results reveal that there is considerable uniformity across these countries; in all five, part-time work is women's work, household variables 'matter', and women part-time workers earn substantially less than their full-time counterparts. However, there is also marked variation across these countries. One obvious and important place to look for explanation is at policy and institutional variation. In this Chapter, our comments about the roles that policy and institutions play in shaping women's employment choices, and the consequences of those choices, are necessarily speculative and *ad hoc*. In order to test—and quantify—policy impacts, more countries and (in several arenas) more policy variation is needed. Three important questions stand out as the basis for future research on the interplay between policy and part-time work across countries.

First, how—and to what extent—does cross-national policy variation help to explain variation in women's employment statuses (part-time versus full-time versus non-work) as well as variation in the factors that influence women's choices? In this Chapter, we have argued that some of the cross-national variability in employment patterns appears to be shaped by cross-country variation in a range of social and family policies, for example, in services that support mothers' employment, and in policies that provide assistance to persons caring for elderly family members. A large literature has established that all of these policies vary dramatically across the industrialized countries; provisions are particularly limited in the English-speaking countries (e.g. Gornick *et al.* 1997; Rostgaard and Fridberg 1998; Sainsbury 1999). One important line of research entails assessing—and quantifying—the extent to which variation in the effects of dependent care responsibilities is explained by cross-country variation in policies that potentially offset the downward pressure that caregiving demands exert on women's labour market attachment. Other policies, as well, shape the interaction between family-related variables and employment choices—including income transfer policies (especially the structure of means testing), income taxation rules, and various elements of family law—and the potential effects of these, too, demand further study.

Second, does cross-national policy variation help to explain the variation that we find in the size and source of the part-time/full-time wage differentials? There has been substantial policy development in recent years, at both the supra-national and national

Appendix

Table 10.A1. *Wage Estimation Results in Five Countries, Women*

	Canada		United States		United Kingdom		Germany		Italy	
	Coeff.	*t*-stat.	Coeff.	*t*-stat.	Coeff.	*t*-stat.	Coeff.	*t*-stat.	Coeff.	*t*-stat.
Part-time										
Lambda	−0.147	*−1.918*	−0.207	*−4.643*	−0.040	*−0.499*	−0.043	*−0.509*	−0.137	*−1.067*
Age	0.025	*2.196*	−0.001	*−0.181*	−0.029	*−1.592*	0.026	*1.398*	0.040	*1.778*
Age squared	0.000	*−1.712*	0.000	*0.186*	0.000	*1.308*	0.000	*−1.212*	0.000	*−1.457*
Education level: high	0.054	*1.286*	0.267	*10.294*	0.389	*6.062*	0.128	*1.720*	0.060	*1.245*
Education level: medium	−0.017	*−0.406*	0.113	*4.401*	0.154	*3.508*	−0.001	*−0.017*	−0.032	*−0.497*
Professional	0.234	*8.457*	0.253	*13.392*	0.371	*7.345*	0.176	*3.816*	0.174	*2.267*
Blue-collar	−0.083	*−1.517*	0.010	*0.339*	−0.073	*−1.684*	−0.160	*−3.668*	−0.124	*−2.908*
Trade	−0.140	*−4.437*	−0.138	*−7.761*			−0.173	*−3.995*	0.029	*0.691*
Transport	0.125	*1.983*	0.089	*2.238*			0.095	*1.287*	0.085	*0.504*
Finance	0.021	*0.595*	0.010	*0.366*			0.288	*3.021*	−0.032	*−0.291*
Manufacturing	−0.051	*−0.907*	0.019	*0.606*			−0.140	*−2.965*	0.048	*1.169*
Public administration	−0.094	*−1.580*	−0.055	*−1.149*			0.066	*1.214*	0.000	*−0.004*
Constant	1.994	*6.712*	2.255	*11.761*	2.326	*5.542*	2.360	*5.128*	1.662	*2.780*
Observations	2543		4247		568		587		219	
Adj. R^2	0.087		0.159		0.267		0.170		0.143	
Full-time										
Lambda	−0.070	*−3.402*	−0.017	*−1.137*	0.013	*0.499*	−0.154	*−5.166*	0.024	*0.620*
Age	0.024	*5.958*	0.029	*10.705*	0.022	*2.688*	0.022	*2.792*	0.028	*3.400*
Age squared	0.000	*−4.508*	0.000	*−9.197*	0.000	*−2.715*	0.000	*−2.277*	0.000	*−2.539*

Table 10.A1. *Continued*

	Canada		United States		United Kingdom		Germany		Italy	
	Coeff.	*t*-stat.	Coeff.	*t*-stat.	Coeff.	*t*-stat.	Coeff.	*t*-stat.	Coeff.	*t*-stat.
Education level: high	0.184	*10.122*	0.355	*25.707*	0.255	*9.735*	−0.004	*−0.112*	0.145	*4.408*
Education level: medium	0.094	*5.641*	0.187	*15.022*	0.112	*5.054*	−0.070	*−2.922*	0.070	*2.140*
Professional	0.211	*25.442*	0.261	*39.794*	0.263	*13.625*	0.169	*7.302*	0.214	*13.732*
Blue-collar	−0.003	*−0.179*	−0.054	*−4.998*	−0.121	*−4.827*	−0.140	*−5.480*	−0.102	*−5.274*
Trade	−0.118	*−9.523*	−0.092	*−10.618*			−0.143	*−5.041*	0.043	*1.372*
Transport	0.200	*11.689*	0.189	*14.779*			0.027	*0.575*	0.105	*1.738*
Finance	0.022	*2.022*	0.053	*6.111*			0.232	*6.188*	0.171	*4.315*
Manufacturing	0.032	*2.209*	0.092	*9.741*			0.068	*2.927*	0.046	*1.733*
Public administration	0.160	*12.576*	0.108	*9.267*			0.041	*1.535*	0.126	*4.925*
Constant	1.777	*19.610*	1.343	*22.821*	1.260	*7.710*	2.604	*17.035*	1.558	*7.868*
Observations	9843		18113		1415		1360		1574	
Adj. R^2	0.186		0.251		0.312		0.169		0.438	

Source: Own calculations based on the Luxembourg Income Study.

levels, aimed at insuring equity in remuneration between part-time and full-time workers. For example, both the 1994 adoption of the ILO's *Part-Time Work Convention* (175) & *Recommendation* (182) and the 1997 passage of the Council of the European Union's *Directive on Part-Time Work* were directed at assuring equal treatment of part-time workers relative to full-time workers (Bolle 1997). It is interesting that as of the middle 1990s, we find the strongest evidence for wage 'discrimination' aimed at part-time workers in Germany, one of the two countries (along with Italy) that had the most formal protections in place at that time (EIRR 1990). The development, implementation, and effectiveness of these part-time equity policies constitute an important line of future research.

And finally, do public policies operating in these countries tend to re-enforce or counteract the wage penalties? We find clear evidence that part-time workers in all of the countries earn less in cash wages than do full-time workers, both before and after controls. But we know little about how other factors operate—including policies and legislation—that either exacerbate or offset the wage penalties. Social security and labour market regulations, which vary across countries, affect the degree to which part-time workers have access to public and occupational benefits, as well as the extent to which they are awarded job-related protections, including the right to overtime, holiday and vacation days, and training and career-enhancement opportunities (ILO 1989; Maier 1991, 1992). Understanding the ways in which policies that affect part-time workers overall interact with the part-time/full-time wage structure constitutes a third crucial area for future research.

References

Addabbo, Tindara (1997), 'Part-Time Work in Italy', in Hans-Peter Blossfeld and Catherine Hakim (eds), *In Between Equalization and Marginalization: Women Working Part-Time in Europe and The United States of America*. Oxford: Oxford University Press, 113–32.

Bardasi, Elena and Janet C. Gornick. (2000), 'Women and Part-Time Employment: Workers' "Choices" and Wage Penalties in Five Industrialized Countries'. Luxembourg Income Study Working Paper No. 223. Differdange: Luxembourg Income Study.

Bassi, Laurie (1995), 'Policy Implications of Part-Time Employment', part of a Symposium on Part-Time Employment and Employees, *Journal of Labor Research*, 16(3): 315–18.

Blau, Francine, Marianne Ferber, and Anne Winkler (1998). The *Economics of Women, Men, and Work*. Upper Saddle River, New Jersey: Prentice Hall.

Bolle, Patrick (1997) 'Part-Time Work: Solution or Trap?', *International Labour Review*, 136(4): 557–79.

Burchell, Brendan, Angela Dale, and Heather Joshi (1997), 'Part-Time Work Among British Women', in Hans-Peter Blossfeld and Catherine Hakim (eds), *In Between Equalization and Marginalization: Women Working Part-Time in Europe and The United States of America*, Oxford: Oxford University Press, 210–46.

Cancian, Maria and Robert F. Schoeni (1992), 'Female Earnings and the Level and Distribution of Household Income in Developed Countries', Luxembourg Income Study Working Paper No. 84. Differdange: Luxembourg Income Study.

Colombino, Ugo and Daniela del Boca (1990), 'The Effect of Taxes on Labor Supply in Italy', Journal of Human Resources, 25(3): 390–414.

Connelly, Rachel (1991), 'The Importance of Child Care Costs to Women's Decision Making', in David M. Blau (ed.), *The Economics of Child Care*. New York: Russell Sage Foundation, 87–117.

Elias, Peter (1997), 'The Effect of Unemployment Benefits on the Labour Force Participation of Partners', Working Paper of the Institute for Employment Research. Warwick: The University of Warwick.

EBRI (Employee Benefits Research Institute) (1993), 'Part-Time Work: Characteristics of the Part-Time Work Force: Analysis of the March 1992 Current Population Survey'. Working Paper P-55.

EIRR (European Industrial Relations Review) (1990), 'Non-Standard Forms of Employment in Europe: Part-Time Work, Fixed Term Contracts, and Temporary Work Contracts'. EIRR Report No. 3.

Ercolani, Marco G. and Stephen Jenkins, P. (1999), 'The Labour Force Participation of Women Married to Unemployed Men: Is There an Added Worker Effect?'. Paper presented at the XIII Meeting of the European Society for Population Economics, Turin, June 1999.

Esping-Andersen, Gosta (1990), *The Three Worlds of Welfare Capitalism*, New Jersey: Princeton University Press.

Eurostat (1984), *Working Time Statistics: Methods and Measurement in the European Community*, Luxembourg: Eurostat, Statistical Office of the European Communities.

Giannelli, Gianna C. and John Micklewright (1995), 'Why Do Women Married to Unemployed Men Have Low Participation Rates?'. *Oxford Bulletin of Economics and Statistics*, 57(4) 471–86.

Gornick, Janet C. (1999), 'Gender Equality in the Labour Market', in Diane Sainsbury (ed.), *Gender Policy Regimes and Welfare States*, Oxford: Oxford University Press, 117–46.

—— and Jerry Jacobs, A. (1996), 'A Cross-national Analysis of the Wages of Part-time Workers: Evidence from the United States, the United Kingdom, Canada, and Australia', *Work, Employment and Society*, 10(1): 1–27.

——, Marcia Meyers, K., and Katherin Ross, E. (1997), 'Supporting the Employment of Mothers: Policy Variation Across Fourteen Welfare States', *Journal of European Social Policy*, 7(1): 45–70.

——. (1998), 'Public Policies and the Employment of Mothers: A Cross-national Study', *Social Science Quarterly*, 79(1): 35–54.

Hakim, Catherine (1997), 'A Sociological Perspective on Part-time Work', in Hans-Peter Blossfeld, and Catherine Hakim (eds), *In Between Equalization and Marginalization: Women Working Part-Time in Europe and The United States of America*, Oxford: Oxford University Press, 22–70.

ILO (International Labour Office). (1989), 'Part-time Work', *Conditions of Work Digest*, 8/1. Geneva: International Labour Office.

Jones, F. L. and Jonathan Kelley (1984), 'Decomposing Differences Between Groups: A Cautionary Note on Measuring Discrimination', *Sociological Methods & Research*, 12(3): 323–43.

Kamerman, Sheila and Alfred Kahn (1999), 'Child and Family Policy in an Era of Social Policy Retrenchment and Restructuring', paper presented at the Luxembourg Income Study Conference on 'Child Well-Being in Rich and Transition Countries', Luxembourg, September 30–October 2, 1999.

Knudsen, Christen and H. Elizabeth Peters (1994), 'An International Comparison of Married Women's Labor Supply', Luxembourg Income Study Working Paper No. 106. Differdange: Luxembourg Income Study.

Lee, Lung-Fei. (1982), 'Some Approaches to the Correction of Selectivity Bias', *Review of Economic Studies*, 49: 355–72.

——. (1983), 'Generalized Econometric Models with Selectivity', *Econometrica*, 51: 507–12.

Lehrer, Evelyn L. (1992), 'The Impact of Children on Married Women's Labor Supply: Black–White Differentials Revisited', *Journal of Human Resources*, 27(3): 422–44.

Leibowitz, Arleen, Jacob Alex Klerman, and Linda Waite (1992), 'Employment of New Mothers and Child Care Choice: Difference by Children's Age', *Journal of Human Resources*, 22(1): 223–133.

Maddala, G. S. (1983), *Limited-dependent and Qualitative Variables in Econometrics*, Cambridge: Cambridge University Press.

Mansky, Charles F. (1989), 'Anatomy of the Selection Problem', *Journal of Human Resources*, 24: 343–60.

Maier, Frederike. (1991), 'Part-Time Work, Social Security Protections, and Labour Law: An International Comparison', *Policy and Politics*, 19(1): 1–11.

——. (1992), 'The Regulation of Part-time Work: A Comparative Study of Six EC Countries', Report prepared for the Commission of the EC, April 1992.

——. (1994), 'Institutional Regimes of Part-time Working', in Gunther Schmidt (ed.), *Labor Market Institutions in Europe: A Socioeconomic Evaluation of Performance*, London: M. E. Sharpe.

Oaxaca, Ronald L. (1973), 'Male-Female Wage Differentials in Urban Labor Markets', *International Economic Review*, 14(3): 693–709.

—— and Michael Ransom, R. (1999), 'Identification in Detailed Wage Decompositions', *The Review of Economics and Statistics*, 81(1): 154–57.

OECD (Organization for Economic Co-operation and Development) (1994), *Woman And Structural Change: New Perspectives*, Paris: Organization for Economic Co-operation and Development.

——. (1999), *Employment Outlook*. Paris: Organization for Economic Co-operation and Development.

Phipps, Shelley A. (1993), 'Determinants of Women's Labor Force Participation: An Econometric Analysis for Five Countries', Luxembourg Income Study Working Paper No. 99. Differdange: Luxembourg Income Study.

Rostgaard, Tine and Torben Fridberg (1998), 'Caring for Children and Older People: A Comparison of European Policies and Practices', Copenhagen: The Danish Institute of Social Research.

Rosenfeld, Rachel A. and Gunn Birkelund, E. (1995), 'Women's Part-Time Work: A Cross-National Comparison', *European Sociological Review*, 11(2): 111–34.

Rubery, Jill (1992), 'Pay, Gender and the Social Dimension to Europe', *British Journal of Industrial Relations*, 30(4):

Sainsbury, Diane (1999), 'Gender, Policy Regimes, and Politics', in Diane Sainsbury (ed.), *Gender and Welfare State Regimes. Oxford: Oxford University Press*, 245–75.

Simpson, Wayne (1986), 'Analysis of Part-Time Pay in Canada', *Canadian Journal of Economics*, 19(4): 798–807.

Stichter, Sharon (1990), 'Women, Employment, and the Family: Current Debates', in Sharon Stichter and Jane Parpart (eds), *Women, Employment and the Family in the International Division of Labour*, Philadelphia: Temple University Press, 11–71.

Van Bastelaer, Alois, George Lemaitre, and Marianna Pascal (1997), 'The Definition of Part-Time Work for the Purpose of International Comparisons', Labour Market and Social Policy Occasional Papers No. 22. Paris: OECD.

11

Economic Opportunities and the Transition to Marriage among Young Women in the United States

AMY G. COX, JOAN M. HERMSEN, AND JACOB ALEX KLERMAN

INTRODUCTION

During the last few decades, women's participation in the paid labour force has increased, and their position in the labour market, relative to men's, has risen as well. These trends are unlikely to reverse as the female-dominated service sector continues to grow. The dramatic changes have occurred within systems of gender that, although varied, tend to emphasize family caregiving as women's responsibility and income generation as men's responsibility. In this context, the growing presence of women in the marketplace suggests important consequences for marriage, childbearing, and other demographic processes associated with women. Indeed, one of the most pronounced demographic changes over the past few decades has been substantial delays and declines in marriage rates in many developed countries (Cherlin 1992; Espenshade 1985).

The economic changes that have increased women's labour market presence in the United States have given them greater economic opportunities that allow for economic independence, and we explore the degree to which the decline in marriage among young women in the United States is due to these greater economic opportunities. This question is important for at least two reasons. First, for the study of demography, current analyses of family formation need to account for the major economic changes that have lowered the gains to marriage for many women. Second, for the study of gender, we suggest that the delay (or rejection) of marriage by a larger number of young women represents a change in women's collective status in a manner similar to increases in women's labour force participation, declines in fertility, and other such phenomena. Unlike previous literature, we analyse women's marriage choices in the context of general theories of women's status. This approach is consistent with scholars such as Blumberg (1991), Chafetz (1984), and Mason (1986), who examine the factors influencing women's status on other dimensions. We expect that the factors contributing to women's entry into marriage are similar to factors influencing women's status on other dimensions because these scholars argue that the factors promoting women's status are interdependent. However, this is not the conceptual framework behind most of the research on US women's marriage patterns.

We argue that economic opportunities for women may lead women to delay marriage, or avoid it altogether, by making alternate sources of income available.

Conversely, women without such alternatives to fulfilling family roles likely marry at younger ages. In this paper, we focus on delayed marriage and evaluate the impact of variations in economic opportunity on the likelihood that a young woman in the United States will remain unmarried. The specific question we ask is: Are women who live in areas with high levels of economic opportunity for women more likely to delay marriage than women who live in areas with low levels of such opportunity?

PRIOR LITERATURE

There is a tradition of interest in young women's marriage patterns and the factors contributing to marriage that stems from more general interests in marriage and in women's changing economic position. Studies that examine marriage timing address individual determinants of marriage most often and sometimes address structural determinants. Typical individual-level characteristics include age, educational attainment, whether the young woman had a premarital birth, religion, and race/ethnicity. Structural explanations for marriage timing address the particular social context in which the transition to marriage occurs (Cooney and Hogan 1991). These explanations focus on the marriage market, often defined as the quantity and quality of available men. The boundaries of the marriage market are defined by time period or by place, and by like groups (e.g. race/ethnicity). A limited number of studies of women's marriage patterns have extended structural arguments to include those that focus on *women's* economic status and their opportunities for economic independence outside of a marriage.

These different theoretical orientations require different research designs. Studies focusing on individual level determinants of the transition to marriage (e.g. see Becker 1981; Clarkberg 1999; Oppenheimer 1988; Oppenheimer *et al.* 1995) use data that are limited to individuals. In contrast, studies that focus on structural determinants of marriage use either macro-level data (e.g. see Butz and Ward 1979; Cherlin 1992; Easterlin 1978; Espenshade 1985; McLanahan and Casper 1995; South and Lloyd 1992) or integrate individual and macro-level data (e.g. see McLaughlin *et al.* 1993; Landale 1989; Lichter *et al.* 1995; South and Crowder 1999). Such studies exploit the idea that the transition to marriage is influenced by social and historical factors that transcend the characteristics of the individuals themselves. The present study follows the latter strategy as our interest is in assessing the influence of structural factors at the state level, namely women's and men's economic opportunities, on individual chances of delayed marriage.

In selecting this approach, we concur with Lichter *et al.* (1991) that there is a spatial dimension to mate selection and the propensity to marry. For example, in a study of marital partner preferences, South (1991) finds that women residing in counties with higher poverty rates report a greater preference not to marry someone earning less than themselves than do women living in less poor counties. McLaughlin *et al.* (1993) conclude that women residing in the south and women living in nonmetropolitan areas have a greater likelihood of transitioning to first marriage between ages 18–28 than do their northern and urban counterparts.

THEORETICAL BACKGROUND

As noted above, our central interest is how structural economic factors influence marriage timing among young women. Structural approaches to explaining women's entry into marriage generally fall into two categories: (1) those examining the effect of women's economic opportunities and (2) those focusing on the effect of an availability and quality of marriageable men. In simplified form, the theoretical discussion follows two strands, a focus on the labour market and a focus on the marriage market. Most scholars recognize, however, that the forces influencing young women's marriage are indeed more complex and complementary than any one perspective suggests.

The economic opportunity hypothesis centres on women's economic independence and incentives to marry, essentially arguing that where women's labour market opportunities are good (i.e. high pay, availability of clerical jobs), the rate of marriages will be lower. For a more detailed review of this perspective, see Lichter *et al.* (1991). By economic independence, we mean the financial ability to live on one's own. Economic independence gives women the choice to remain unmarried by reducing the economic penalties of nonmarriage (Oppenheimer 1988). Economic resources also give women the option to take more time in the search for a suitable partner. In area level studies, economic opportunities are generally operationalized as the median women's earnings for the aggregate area under study. There is empirical support for this perspective, with higher earnings being associated with a lower proportion of women ever married (Lichter *et al.* 1991; McLanahan and Casper 1995; Preston and Richards 1975; South and Lloyd 1992).

The concept of economic opportunity has expanded beyond labour market opportunities in the last decade to include public assistance as another measure of opportunity. Studies have found that the higher the level of public assistance, the lower young women's marriage rates. However, whether this is because public assistance allows women to choose to remain unmarried by providing an economic alternative to marriage, or requires them to remain unmarried when they would rather marry by restricting eligibility to nonmarried persons is not clear (Lichter *et al.* 1991; South and Lloyd 1992).

In contrast to the studies of marriage rates, however, few contextual analyses of marriage timing incorporate measures of women's economic opportunity. More commonly, analyses of women's marriage omit specific indicators of women's macro economic opportunity in favour of measures of the marriage market (see e.g. Lichter *et al.* 1992, 1995). We find it intriguing that while macro studies of women's marriage rates generally account for women's economic opportunities, at least indirectly, micro–macro studies rarely do. We believe this omission is due to the prevailing interest in the marriageable men hypothesis and the assumption (often unstated) that women's entry into marriage is conditioned foremost by the quantity and quality of men and not by the quantity and quality of their own opportunities for economic independence.

The marriageable men hypothesis takes two distinct forms (Lichter *et al.* 1992). The first form recognizes that women's marriage requires a quantity of available men

(Gutentag and Secord 1983). This perspective argues that where the pool of available men is small, women's rates of marriage will be low as there are fewer people from whom to select partners. The quantity of available men is most often conceptualized as the male–female sex ratio (Fossett and Kiecolt 1991). The evidence on sex-ratios is mixed; some research finds that the quantity of available men has no effect on marriage rates (Lichter *et al.* 1991), while other work concludes that a greater availability of men does increase the marriage rates of women (South and Lloyd 1992).

The second form of the marriageable men hypothesis draws on the work of Oppenheimer (1988) and Wilson (1987) and argues that not only is the quantity of marriageable men important, but the quality of those men, in particular, their economic fortunes, is also important. Declining fortunes for men reduce the gains to marriage for women and therefore, the demand for marriage declines. Wilson (1987) has applied this argument to low income urban Blacks and argues that the decline in marriage among them is due to the lack of 'quality' marriageable men. Male average earnings and nonemployment rates are the standard measures of 'quality' employed in studies of marriageable men. In a recent paper, South and Crowder (1999) examine family formation using an index of neighbourhood disadvantage, which includes male joblessness as a component but no measure of women's economic opportunity (or lack thereof). Research indicates that male nonemployment decreases marriage rates while higher male earnings lead to higher marriage rates (Lichter *et al.* 1991; South and Lloyd 1992).

While some support is found in the macro and contextual research for both labour market and marriage market explanations of women's marriage rates, we see some weaknesses in the existing literature. First, there is a de-emphasis on women's labour market opportunities through inadequate operationalization of the major concept, economic opportunity. Some studies measure economic opportunity only at the micro level, while others use macro-level indicators that are problematic.

Micro-level measures alone, for example, education, employment experience, earnings, do not adequately capture the conditions and opportunities, including the demand for their labour and the price of their labour, that help structure individuals' lives. Moreover, using only a general indicator that operates at the individual level, such as a woman's earnings, conflates the two levels of opportunity. For those interested in distinguishing the influence of macro-level opportunity, this poses a problem.

Even when included at the macro level, economic opportunity is often measured with women's median earnings, as noted above. However, such a gross measure fails to account for the variation in labour market opportunities available to women of different racial/ethnic groups, of different educational levels, and of different age intervals. Because women's labour market positions are stratified (Amott and Matthei 1991; Browne 1999), we believe that the measure of women's economic opportunity should reflect these basic differences in access to valued resources.

Related to this point, we suggest that women's economic opportunities can be better modelled by returning to the theme of earlier work, labour market measures, than by relying on welfare payment levels. Welfare payments, namely Aid to Families with

Dependent Children (AFDC), are applicable to a limited share of the adult female population and are an appropriate explanatory variable in a model exploring factors contributing to marriage among young *mothers*, as opposed to among all women. More importantly, though, we suggest that the typically low level of AFDC payments means that government assistance represents economic survival or a *lack* of opportunity rather than a range of economic opportunities.

Thus, we argue that macro-level economic opportunity varies among women, and that it cannot be adequately assessed and may not be wholly captured with micro-level measures or with welfare benefits. The path through which it might influence individual marriage choices is likely complex, as local opportunity likely operates through several individual economic and family factors. Our present interest is in evaluating whether macro-level economic opportunity has an effect on marriage, and we take a two-tiered approach to examine this. We operationalize contextual opportunity with exogenous measures, and we also include individual level factors that are related to opportunity and affect marriage as well, including education and employment experience.

METHODOLOGY

In this analysis, we examine the influence of economic opportunity and selected individual and family characteristics on the likelihood that a woman will delay (or forgo) marriage.[1] Using discrete time event history methods with logistic regression, we model the log odds of remaining unmarried among US women.

Data

The individual level data for this study come from the 1979–94 waves of the National Longitudinal Survey of Youth (NLSY). The NLSY is a nationally representative survey of young adults aged 14–21 in 1979. We restrict the sample to White, African American, and Hispanic women. Our sample includes the oversamples of African American and Hispanic women, but not the oversample of poor White women. We exclude the oversample of poor Whites because, unlike the oversamples of African Americans and Latinas, the precise characteristics specifying the poor White oversample, and more importantly, how those characteristics change over time, are not clear. Interpreting event history analyses with such data is difficult at best and is likely to be biased. Our sample of women with data on all variables consists of 3,190 respondents. The unit of analysis is individual women, and this is further divided in the regression model into person–years; there are 36,367 person–years of data in the

[1] We focus on marriage in this chapter, and do not include the related state of cohabitation, for two reasons. First, marriage remains a bigger commitment, socially, economically, and legally, than cohabitation in the United States. Legal marriage remains the widespread norm in the United States, and cohabitation is usually a transitory state, leading either to marriage or to dissolution. In addition, the social significance of cohabitation—what it means as a union—changes over the time period that our data covers.

sample. Although the NLSY has a high response rate (94 per cent; NLSY 1997), data are sometimes missing from individual years. For each woman in the sample, we include each year of data from 1979 until she marries or until she is not interviewed (is right censored), whichever comes first. Right censored cases occur when a respondent was lost from follow-up interviews before she first married.

We attach contextual indicators of economic opportunity and marriage market conditions to each record in the sample. These are measured at the state level (including Washington, DC) for each year in the analysis. We use US Census Public Use Microdata (PUMS) and the Current Population Survey (CPS) to construct our contextual measures. We use PUMS data for 1970, 1980, and 1990 to make state level demand for labour and average earnings measures. We linearly interpolate for the years between each census and extrapolate for 1991–94. The indicators of labour supply and the sex ratio come from CPS data and are also interpolated for missing years. Further details on the contextual measures are described below.

Dependent variable

The dependent variable is a binary variable indicating whether the respondent remained unmarried or entered her first marriage during the period of observation. Although we have the date of first marriage for all women, we are missing some independent variables (e.g. education level) for women who married at very young ages and before the survey began. We minimized the amount of this left censoring in the data by imputing independent variables for most women who married before the survey began. However, we made such imputations only as far back as age 16 at the youngest, to remain conservative. As a result, we excluded from the study 60 women who were less than 16 when they first married (1.3 per cent of the sample) . In this analysis, we are particularly interested in the determinants of delayed/foregone marriage, and for this reason, we code the dependent variable 1 if the respondent remained unmarried during the observation period. The variable is coded 0 if the respondent did marry. Thus, factors promoting delayed marriage will have a positive coefficient and those promoting early marriage will have a negative coefficient.

Economic opportunity measures

The main explanatory variables are the measures of women's and men's economic opportunity. We capture opportunity by using predictions of a model of women's and men's earnings as determined by local labour market characteristics. The opportunity variables can be thought of as the amount that women with a particular set of characteristics (gender, race/ethnicity, age, and education) can expect to earn in a given labour market, not necessarily what they currently earn. Unlike actual earnings, which conflate labour market determinants with individual determinants, the measures of potential earnings capture economic *opportunity*; they reflect the portion of earnings that is due to labour market variation, rather than to individual variation. We estimate earnings for each state–year–gender–race–age–education cell (e.g. in Alabama in 1984, for

White women age 21–25 with a high school degree) and then merge these predicted earnings to the record of each woman in the NLSY based on her state, race, age, and education characteristics each year.

These earnings are estimated as a function of the demand for and supply of labour, broken down by gender and skill level (e.g. the demand for low-skilled women's labour), and the sex ratio. We used a measure of the industrial demand for labour as a proxy for labour market opportunities. The industrial demand for labour is measured as the expected number of jobs in each state–year by gender and education level. We calculate the demand separately by gender because of the gender stratification known to exist in the US labour market, and we assign different values of labour demand to men and women of three different education levels—low, medium, and high. We use these education distinctions as proxies for skill level. The number of expected jobs is derived by taking the proportion of each gender–education cell in each industry in the national labour market and multiplying this proportion by the number of people in each industry in the state–year. This gives the expected number workers in each gender–education category given that state's industrial structure. We also include measures of the supply of labour, which we calculate with a similar standardizing technique. We multiplied the national labour force participation rates of each gender–race/ethnicity–age–education group for each state–year by the total number of persons in each group in each state–year. This gives us the expected supply of workers in each group. Finally, we include racial/ethnic–specific sex ratios, which we define as a ratio of the number of women age 21–30 to the number of men age 21–30 in each state–year cell. The predicted wages that we calculate for the various groups are thus determined by industrial composition, the relative supply of labour, and the sex ratio. Further estimation details are provided in Appendix 11.1.

In the logistic regression model, we include women's predicted earnings to capture the effect of economic opportunity on women's propensity to marry. As stated above, we hypothesize that when women have greater economic opportunities they will delay (or forgo) entry into marriage. In our main model, each woman is also given the predicted earnings of her male counterpart as a measure of the 'quality' of men in her marriage market. Based on previous studies, we expect that the higher these male earnings, the higher the probability women will be married, as women have more attractive marriage partners. Because earnings vary along a number of dimensions besides gender, we tested the possibility that the two predicted wage variables were collinear. As expected, they correlate highly, but after running our models, we rejected the null hypothesis that the effects of the two variables are equal. We therefore include both in the regression model. For clarity, we also report a model with only women's predicted wages and a model with only men's predicted wages.

The marriage and labour market boundaries are state boundaries. Although we realize that these may be rather gross market delineations, we believe for this initial study of economic opportunity such boundaries are within reason. Smaller labour market areas are appealing, but two problems arise when using smaller units. First, labour market area boundaries are often defined by commuting patterns and these boundaries are subject to change over time. County boundaries do not change, but we believe they represent areas that are too small to capture the true opportunity structure and in addition, the sample sizes for estimating demand, supply, and earnings for women of colour may be so small as to be problematic. In addition, the census data we use for the labour market variables combine women in rural areas into county groups, which also have boundaries that change over time.

Independent variables

We include as controls several additional variables that may affect women's probability of first marriage: welfare benefit levels, education level and current school enrollment, immigrant status, pre-marital birth, employment experience, religious denomination, employment aspirations, mother's education, mother's employment, and whether raised in a single mother family. Previous studies indicate that some of these characteristics correlate with delayed marriage, including higher welfare benefits, current school enrollment, non-marital births, employment aspirations, a Roman Catholic upbringing, being African American or Latina versus being White, mother's greater education and employment, and whether raised in a single mother family (Bennett *et al.* 1989, 1995; Cooney and Hogan 1991; Goldscheider and Waite 1986; Hammond *et al.* 1993; Landale 1994; Landale and Tolnay 1991; Lichter *et al.* 1991; Michael and Tuma 1985; Sander 1993; South and Lloyd 1992; Thornton *et al.* 1995). As a result, we expect these characteristics will contribute to more delayed marriage among women. Research related to the remaining variables is either sparse or shows less consistent relationships between them and marriage timing (Blossfeld 1995; Clarkberg 1999; Thornton *et al.* 1995; Dobson and Houseknect 1998; Ferguson 1995; Landale 1994; Lichter *et al.* 1992, 1995; Marini 1985; Sander 1993). We therefore make no predictions about the impact of education level, employment experience, immigrant status, and recession year on the likelihood that women will remain unmarried. Definitions for all of the control variables are in Appendix 11.2.

Some of the independent variables are fixed, while others may vary over time. Time-independent covariates (e.g. immigrant status and mother's employment status) represent variation among respondents, and time-dependent covariates (such as years of schooling or employment experience) represent variation both among and within respondents (i.e. over time). We model time with a quadratic function, using respondents' age and squared age. This function assumes that the likelihood of marriage decreases exponentially as a woman gets older. We also include a year variable to account for secular increases in age at marriage. See Table 11.1 for the mean and standard deviation of each control variable. We report these for the last year that the respondent was in the sample.

Analytic strategy

Our analytic strategy is to estimate a logistic regression model of the likelihood of remaining unmarried that includes the measures of women's and men's economic

Table 11.1. *Means and Standard Deviations of Covariates for Women in Sample, Weighted*

	Mean	Standard deviation
Predicted female earnings (ln)	7.970	0.560
Predicted male earnings (ln)	8.412	0.543
Welfare benefits ($ hundreds)	6.883	1.346
Completed Education		
Less than high school	0.157	0.366
12 years	0.404	0.493
13–15 years	0.244	0.432
16 or more years	0.195	0.398
School enrollment	0.344	0.477
Cumulative weeks employed (10's)	23.674	18.504
Nonmarital birth	0.115	0.320
Immigrant status	0.031	0.175
Work aspirations	0.671	0.472
Roman Catholic affiliation	0.325	0.471
Race/ethnicity		
White	0.884	0.322
African American	0.099	0.301
Latina	0.017	0.129
Mother's education	11.848	2.444
Mother's employment	0.543	0.501
Single mother family background	0.095	0.294
Year	84.308	4.402
Recession year	0.215	0.413
Age	22.917	4.138
Age squared	542.149	204.760
Number of women	3190	

Source: Authors' calculations based on the 1979–94 waves of the National Longitudinal Survey of Youth (NLSY), US Census Public Use Micro data (PUMS), and the Current Population Survey (CPS).

opportunity in addition to the numerous individual-level control variables. We present three models: one that includes only economic opportunity for women, one that includes only economic opportunity for men, and one that includes economic opportunity for women and men. Although we estimated additional models that controlled for the quantity of men in the marriage market, using racial/ethnic specific sex ratios, the sex ratio coefficients were never significant and did not affect the coefficients for women's and men's economic opportunities. Therefore, for ease of exposition and to keep the focus on economic opportunities, we report only those models that omit the sex ratios.

RESULTS

Descriptive statistics

We also generated descriptive statistics for the dependent variable. These statistics control for the overrepresentation of African American and Latina women in our sample. Approximately 23.9 per cent of women in the sample remained unmarried during our years of observation. Of those in the sample who did marry, the average age at marriage is 22.5. Figure 11.1 illustrates the relationship graphically. The figure is a survival curve, an estimate of the likelihood of remaining unmarried at different ages. The figure also controls for the African American and Hispanic oversamples. The chance of remaining unmarried for another year is quite high for very young women, dropping as women enter their thirties.

In this chapter, our central interest is the relationship between the likelihood of nonmarriage and economic opportunity, as indexed by predicted log earnings.

Figure 11.2 plots the bivariate relationship between the age at marriage, for the 71 per cent of the women in the sample who married during our years of data, and their predicted log earnings. As shown, there is a clear positive relationship between these two measures. The two measures have a zero-order correlation of +0.66. Greater economic opportunity in a given market, as indexed by macro-level predicted earnings, is associated with an older age at marriage. Thus, the bivariate relationship suggests that women's marriage chances are indeed related to the degree of economic opportunity available.

Logistic regression results

In Table 11.2 we present the results for the logistic regression analyses predicting the logged odds that a woman will remain never married. We begin our discussion of the

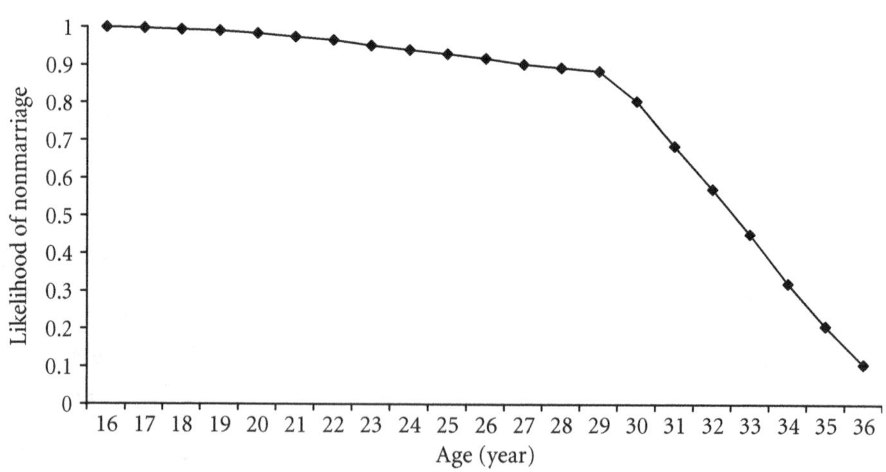

Figure 11.1. *Survival Function for Remaining Unmarried, by Age*

Source: National Longitudinal Survey of Youth.

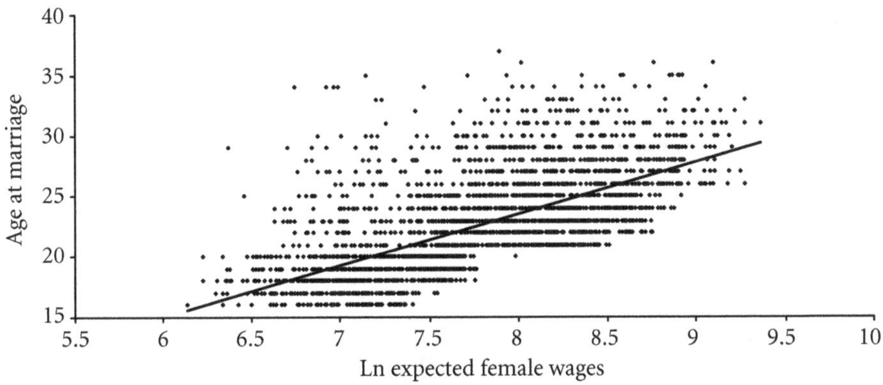

Figure 11.2. *Bivariate Relationship Between the Age at Marriage and Predicted Log Earnings*
Note: Predicted wages are for the year that women marry, and are in 1970 constant dollars.
Sources: National Longitudinal Survey of Youth; US Census PUMS.

results by highlighting the effect of economic opportunity on the likelihood of remaining unmarried. We then move to a discussion of the other predictors of nonmarriage.

We hypothesized that the greater women's economic opportunity, the more likely they would be to delay marriage. Our findings confirm this, such that the higher women's predicted wages are, the greater are the log odds that they will delay marriage. This relationship is evident in Model 1, where we include only women's predicted wages, and it is even stronger in Model 3, where we also control for men's predicted wages.[2] For the average woman (i.e. using the means of all variables to calculate predicted odds), the odds of delaying marriage versus of marrying are 0.376, or a woman is 62 per cent less likely, on average, to remain unmarried as she is to marry in a given year. However, women whose expected wages are higher and lower than average have different likelihoods of delaying marriage. Compared to the average expected wage of $2893, a woman whose expected wages are $4000 is 49 per cent less likely to remain unmarried (an odds ratio of 0.511), while a woman whose expected wages are only $2000 is 74 per cent less likely to remain unmarried (an odds ratio of 0.264). The results thus indicate that the economic opportunity available to women does affect their marriage choices, by giving women with more opportunity the option of delaying marriage.

While we expected that greater economic opportunities for women act to delay marriage and increase the chances of remaining never married, we hypothesized that greater economic opportunities for men make men more attractive marriage partners and lead women into marriage. The results confirm this hypothesis; greater economic opportunity for men significantly lowers women's likelihood of delaying marriage. That is, women living in marriage markets where men's opportunities are

[2] In Model 3, the equivalent absolute values of the coefficient for female and male economic opportunities are coincidence and do not imply any other relationship.

Table 11.2. *Logistic Regression Coefficients Predicting Never Married Status by Type of Economic Opportunity*

	Female	Male	Both
Predicted female earnings (ln)	0.193**	—	0.957***
Predicted male earnings (ln)	—	−0.204**	−0.957***
Welfare benefits ($ hundreds)	0.039***	0.055**	0.018***
Completed education			
Less than HS	0.144**	−0.041	0.196**
12 years	—	—	—
13–15 years	−0.344***	−0.266***	−0.371***
16 or more years	−0.578***	−0.325***	−0.549***
School enrollment	0.078*	0.072*	0.084*
Cum. weeks employed (tens)	−0.008***	0.007***	−0.007***
Nonmarital birth	0.454***	0.450***	0.463***
Immigrant status	0.095	0.092	0.090
Work aspirations	0.147***	0.148***	0.149***
Roman Catholic affiliation	−0.294***	−0.289***	−0.297***
Race/ethnicity			
White	—	—	—
African American	0.873***	0.709***	0.662***
Latina	0.578***	−0.450***	0.448***
Mother's education	0.021***	0.022***	0.022***
Mother's employment	−0.047	−0.048	−0.047
Single mother family background	0.239***	0.234***	0.237***
Year	0.076***	0.067***	0.062***
Recession year	0.057	0.066*	0.099**
Age	−0.200***	−0.120**	−0.187***
Age-square	0.007***	0.006***	0.007***
Intercept	−8.378***	−5.747***	−5.501***
N	32,323	32,323	32,323
Chi-square	6960.6***	6961.9***	7040.6***

* $p < 0.05$; ** $p < 0.01$; *** $p < 0.001$.

Source: Authors' calculations based on the 1979–1994 waves of the National Longitudinal Survey of Youth (NLSY), US Census Public Use Micro data (PUMS), and the Current Population Survey (CPS).

greater tend to marry more quickly than women living where men's opportunities are smaller do.

Although the focus of this analysis is the impact of economic opportunity, several other interesting factors promote or impede marriage as well. We address the other findings below. We focus here on Model 3, since results are quite similar across the three models.

There is limited evidence in our analysis of the effect of welfare levels on marriage. The size of state welfare benefits shows a weak impact on the likelihood of remaining unmarried, such that an additional $100 in monthly benefits increases the chance of remaining unmarried by 1.8 per cent, compared to the chance of marrying.

The existing literature on education and the timing of marriage is inconclusive. On the one hand, increased schooling can delay or prevent marriage by shortening the time when a woman is actively searching in the marriage market. However, increased education may also lead to earlier marriage by increasing a woman's cultural capital and making her a more attractive marriage partner. We find support for the latter hypothesis: higher levels of education significantly lower the chance that a woman will remain never married. Compared to having a high school education, women with less than 12 years of school are more likely to delay marriage, and those with more than 12 years of school are less likely to delay marriage. An exception to this relationship is in the second model, which includes only male economic opportunity. Here, women with less than a high school education are not significantly different from those with a high school education. As noted earlier, current school enrollment has been found to inhibit marriage. We found that women who were enrolled in school at some point during the previous year are slightly more likely to remain unmarried, consistent with previous research.

As with education level, the literature on marriage timing offers no conclusive evidence on the relationship between women's employment experience and marriage. We find that women with more extensive employment experience are slightly less likely to delay marriage than those with less experience. These women may be viewed as more attractive marriage partners because of their labour market experience and the economic resources they may bring to the relationship.

Non-marital births are also associated with delayed marriage, consistent with previous studies. It is unclear, however, if the birth itself deems these women unsuitable marriage partners or if the birth, by making women eligible for welfare, prevents them from marrying and lowers their need to marry for economic support.

With regard to time-invariant characteristics, we find that immigrant status is not significantly related to the odds of delaying marriage. However, women who planned to be employed at age 35 are more likely to delay marriage. This suggests that women may view employment goals as incompatible with marriage.

The limited research on religion and the transition to marriage indicates that White Catholics delay marriage relative to Protestants. Our findings fail to support this relationship. In general, we find that women raised as Roman Catholics are significantly less likely to delay marriage than their peers who were raised as Protestant, another religion, or with no religious affiliation.

Consistent with marriage patterns in general, we find significant differences in marriage timing by race/ethnicity. Compared to White women, African American and Latina women are more likely to delay getting married. This supports findings reported elsewhere (Landale 1994; Landale and Tolnay 1991; Lichter *et al.* 1991, 1992; Raley 1996).

We hypothesized that a woman's mother's characteristics might also influence marital timing, and we find that having a mother with a higher level of education contributes to delayed marriage. However, mother's education has no significant effect on women's marriage timing. Being raised in a single mother family also contributes to delayed marriage patterns, as women raised in single mother families are more likely to remain unmarried than women raised in other family structures.

Finally, we included the time variables of calendar year and women's age. Given the significant public concern over the diminishing importance of marriage in US society, as well as the trend of an increasing age at marriage, we expected to find the probability of remaining never married would be positively related to calendar year. That is, we predicted that the chances of marriage would be lower in the 1990s than in the early 1980s. Our results are consistent with data published elsewhere, with the probability of remaining unmarried growing over time. In addition, women are slightly more likely to postpone marriage during recession years, compared to their likelihood when the economy is strong. This relationship is statistically significant, however, only in Models 2 and 3, which include male opportunity and female and male opportunity, respectively. Consistent with the descriptive results, women are significantly more likely to delay marriage as the get older.

DISCUSSION AND CONCLUSION

In this chapter we explore the relationship between women's economic opportunities and their chance of remaining unmarried. We find support for the hypothesis that women delay marriage when they live where they can expect to earn more money. The bivariate association between labour markets and the timing of marriage is strong; where women's opportunity is estimated to be higher, the age at marriage is also higher. This positive relationship between macroeconomic opportunity and individual marriage timing is confirmed in the multivariate analyses. Greater labour market opportunities lead women to delay marriage. Thus, labour markets that offer the potential for higher earnings do contribute to delayed, and possibly forgone, marriage. Finally, because we measured economic opportunity with general units, at the state level, the relationship may be even stronger when examined at a less aggregated level. We hope that future research will explore this possibility.

The relationship exists even after controlling for individual women's education and work experience, both of which may be considered proxies for individual level economic opportunity. Indeed, the individual and macroeconomic measures are in direct contrast. An analysis of only the individual level proxies for economic resources, namely education and work experience, would suggest that more resources lead to early marriage. The inclusion of macroeconomic characteristics in our analysis, however, indicates how economic opportunity actually contributes to delayed marriage. These individual and macroeconomic processes appear distinct. Research that continues to model women's economic resources simply with their own individual characteristics misses an important and independent factor influencing marriage timing.

We also included a measure of men's economic opportunity in our models, and we find substantial support for the 'marriageable men' hypothesis. The availability of high quality spouses promotes early marriage among all three groups of women. However, in models not reported here, we find no support that the quantity of men matters, once one accounts for the quality of men's economic opportunity.

We argued at the beginning of the paper that early marriage is one indicator of the status of women as a group. We find that where women's economic opportunity is higher, they marry later, and we interpret this to mean that where women have more opportunity to be financially self-sufficient, their opportunity to remain unmarried is also greater. In this way, we consider the postponement of marriage to be an outcome that indicates increasing economic power and social independence for women. It is important to note, however, that postponement may also reflect changing social norms about women that are due to changing expectations without a notable change in status. At the least, our findings indicate that greater structural opportunities for women appear essential for enhancing women's ability to postpone or forgo marriage.

In short, this analysis suggests that the potential for economic independence provides an important alternative to marriage, particularly early marriage, for young women. In an era when women's employment is rising globally, these results indicate that such labour market changes may result in continued declines in young women's marriage. This study shows the importance of incorporating measures of women's economic opportunity with the more familiar men's opportunity measures when seeking to understand recent declines in marriage in more industrialized countries. Finally, when combined with other research (Cotter *et al.* 1998, 1999; Cox 1999) on the impact of economic opportunity on aspects of women's status, these findings point to the importance that increasing women's labour market opportunities has for increasing gender equality. Earlier studies have demonstrated that greater employment opportunity for women is associated with women's upward mobility, greater female share of the paid labour force, greater occupational integration, and higher women's earnings relative to men's. Similarly, the relationship observed here, between female economic opportunity and another aspect of the status of women—the delay of early and universal marriage, reinforces the relevance of labour market opportunities for gender equality.

Appendix 11.1: Estimation of predicted earnings

We estimated predicted log annual earnings at the aggregate level for each NLSY respondent. To do so, we first calculated mean natural log of earnings for 22,032 state–year–sex–race–age–education cells using 1970, 1980, and 1990 US Census PUMS data. For example, we calculated average log earnings of white men in 1970 in Alabama who were between the ages 26–30 and had 16+ years of education. Mutually exclusive combinations of the following variables defined the cells:

State: 50 states plus the District of Columbia
Year: 1970, 1980, 1990
Sex: Male, Female

Race: African American, Hispanic, White
Age: Categories 16–20, 21–25, 26–30, 31–35, 36–40, and 41–64
Education: Categories less than 12 years, 12 years, 13–15 years, and 16+ years

The average earnings for 1980 and 1990 dollars were adjusted by the Consumer Price Index (130.5 for 1980; 275.1 for 1990) to make them comparable to 1970 dollars. If any cells had missing earnings because there was no person of that group in the Census data (e.g. black man less than age 20 with a college degree in Wyoming in 1970), we imputed the national mean for the group. Next, we interpolated (and extrapolated for 1991–94) the earnings between census years for each cell to obtain the mean log annual earnings in each state in each year for each sex–race–age–education group.

The next step in estimating macroearnings was to estimate OLS regression equations using the state–year–sex–race–age–education cells as the unit of analysis. We calculated predicted earnings by race and gender for each state–year–age–education cell as a function of state, age, and education, as well as of the demand for female and male labour, the supply of female and male labour, and racial/ethnic specific sex ratios. We merged these predicted earnings to each NLSY respondent so that each respondent received the predicted earnings that corresponded to her race, age, education, state, and year in the person–year file.

Appendix 11.2: Definitions of control variables

Variable	Definition
Welfare benefit levels	This variable is the combined AFDC, Medicaid, and food stamp monthly 'guarantee' for a family of four in the state where a respondent lives each year. The measure was compiled by Robert Moffitt with Current Population Survey data (Moffitt 1994).
Education	
Completed	We use four dummy variables that reflect years of completed schooling: 12 years of school (the omitted category), less than 12 years, 13–15 years, and sixteen or more years.
Current enrollment	This is a binary variable measuring whether a woman was enrolled in school during the previous year.
Employment experience	The measure reflects the cumulative number of weeks employed to date, grouped into 10-week units.
Non-marital birth	This is a dummy variable coded 1 if the respondent had a non-marital birth, 0 if no non-marital birth.
Employment aspirations	Also a binary variable, this is coded 1 if the respondent intended to be employed at age 35. We use a question asked when respondents were age 20 (or their age in 1979 for those who older than 20 at the start of the survey).
Religion	This is a dummy variable representing Roman Catholic affiliation. We use the religious denomination designated by respondents at the first interview, as Mosher *et al.* (1992) argue that religious upbringing is more

	important to family formation than current religion.
Immigrant status	We measure this with a dummy variable coded 1 if the respondent is an immigrant and 0 if she is not.
Race-ethnicity	We use three binary variables for race-ethnicity: Anglo-White (the omitted category), Non-Hispanic African American, and Latina.
Family background	
Mother's employment	This binary variable reflects whether the adult female in a respondent's household (e.g. mother, step-mother) worked for pay when the respondent was 14.
Mother's education level	This variable represents the years of schooling completed by a respondent's mother as of 1979.
Single mother family	Also a dummy variable, this measure is coded 1 if a respondent lived in a single mother family at age 14.
Recession year	We measure recession years with a binary variable coded 1 if the United States was in a recession during that year. Recession years during our years of data are 1974, 1975, 1980, 1981, 1982, and 1991.

References

Amott, T. L. and Matthei, J. A. (1991), *Race, Gender, and Work: A Multicultural Economic History of Women in the United States*. Boston: South End Press.

Becker, G. S. (1981), *A Treatise on the Family*. Cambridge, MA: Harvard University Press.

Bennett, N., Bloom, D., and Craig, P. (1989), 'The Divergence of Black and White Marriage Patterns'. *American Journal of Sociology*, 95: 692–722.

—— and Miller, C. (1995), 'The Influence of Nonmarital Childbearing on the Formation of First Marriages', *Demography*, 32(1): 47–62.

Blossfeld, H. P. (1995), *The New Role of Women: Family Formation in Modern Societies*. Boulder, CO: Westview Press.

Blumberg, R. L. (1991), 'Introduction: The Triple Overlap of Gender Stratification, Economy, and the Family', in R.L. Blumberg (ed.), *Gender, Family and Economy*. Newbury Park, CA: Sage.

Browne, I. (ed.) (1999), *Latinas and African American Women at Work: Race, Gender, and Economic Inequality*. New York: Russell Sage Foundation.

Butz, W. and Ward, M. (1979), 'The Emergence of Countercyclical United States Fertility', *American Economic Review*, 69: 318–28.

Chafetz, J. S. (1984), *Sex and Advantage: A Comparative Macro-Structural Theory of Stratification*. Totowa, NJ: Rowman and Allenfeld.

Cherlin, A. (1992), *Marriage, Divorce, Remarriage*. Cambridge, MA: Harvard University Press.

Clarkberg, M. 'The Price of Partnering: The Role of Economic Well-being in Young Adults' First Union Experiences, *Social Forces*, 77(3): 945–68.

Cooney, T. M. and Hogan, D. P. (1991), 'Marriage in An Institutionalized Life Course: First Marriage among American Men in the Twentieth Century', *Journal of Marriage and the Family*, 53: 178–90.

Cotter, D. A., DeFiore, J., Hermsen, J. M., Kowalewski, B. M., and Vanneman, R. (1998), 'The Demand for Female Labor', *American Journal of Sociology*, 103(6): 1673–712.

—— Hermsen, J. M., and Vanneman, R. (1999), 'Women's Work and Working Women: The Demand for Female Labor', Working Paper, Department of Sociology, University of Missouri.

Cox, A. (1999), 'The Demand for Female Labor and Upward Mobility Among Low Income Women', paper presented at the Annual Meetings of the American Sociological Association, August 1999, Chicago.

—— and Hermsen, J. (1995), 'Women's, Employment Opportunities and Marriage Rates: A Labor Market Analysis', paper presented to the Eastern Sociological Society, March 1995, Philadelphia.

Dobson, C. D. and Houseknect, S. K. (1998), 'Black and White Differences in the Effect of Women's Educational Attainment on Age at First Marriage', *Journal of Family Issues*, 19(2): 204–23.

Easterlin, R. (1978), 'What Will 1984 Be Like? Socioeconomic Implications of Recent Twists in Age Structure', *Demography*, 15(4): 397–432.

Espenshade, T. (1985), 'Marriage Trends in America: Estimates, Implications, and Underlying Causes', *Population and Development Review*, 11: 193–245.

Ferguson, S. J. (1995), 'Marriage Timing of Chinese American and Japanese American Women', *Journal of Family Issues*, 16(3): 314–43.

Fosset, M. A. and Kiecolt, K. J. (1991), 'A Methodological Review of the Sex Ratio: Alternatives for Comparative Research', *Journal of Marriage and the Family*, 53: 941–57.

Goldscheider, F. K. and Waite, L. J. (1986), 'Sex Differences in the Entry into Marriage', *American Journal of Sociology*, 92: 91–109.

Gutentag, M. and Secord, P. F. (1983), *Too Many Women? The Sex Ratio Question*. Beverly Hills, CA: Sage.

Hammond, J. A., Cole, B. S., and Beck, S. H. (1993), 'Religious Heritage and Teenage Marriage', *Review of Religious Research*, 35(2): 117–33.

Landale, N. S. (1989), 'Agricultural Opportunity and Marriage: The United States at the Turn of the Century', *Demography*, 26: 203–18.

—— (1994), 'Migration and the Latino family: The Union Formation Behavior of Puerto Rican Women', *Demography*, 31(1): 133–57.

—— and Tolnay, S. E. (1991), 'Group Differences in Economic Opportunity and the Timing of Marriage: Blacks and Whites in the Rural South, 1910', *American Sociological Review*, 56: 33–45.

Lichter, D. T., LeClere, F. B., and McLaughlin, D. K. (1991), 'Local Marriage Markets and the Marital Behavior of Black and White Women', *American Journal of Sociology*, 96: 843–67.

—— McLaughlin, D. K., Kephart, G., and Landry, D. J. (1992), 'Race and the Retreat from Marriage: A Shortage of Marriageable Men?', *American Sociological Review*, 57: 781–99.

—— Anderson, R. N., and Hayward, M. D. (1995), 'Marriage Markets and Marital Choice', *Journal of Family Issues*, 16(4): 412–31.

Marini, M. M. (1985), 'Determinants of the Timing of Adult Role Entry', *Social Science Research*, 14: 309–50.

Mason, K. O. (1986) 'The Status of Women: Conceptual and Methodological Issues in Demographic Studies', *Sociological Forum*, 1: 284–300.

McLanahan, S. and Casper, L. (1995), 'Growing Diversity and Inequality in the American Family', in R. Farley (ed.), *State of the Union: America in the 1990s*. New York: Russell Sage Foundation, 1–45.

McLaughlin, D. K., Lichter, D. T., and Johnston, G. M. (1993), 'Some Women Marry Young: Transitions to First Marriage in Metropolitan and Nonmetropolitan Areas', *Journal of Marriage and the Family*, 55: 827–38.

Michael, R. T. and Tuma, N. B. (1985), 'Entry into Marriage and Parenthood by Young Men and Women: The Influence of Family Background', *Demography*, 22: 515–44.

Mosher, W. D., Williams, L. B., and Johnson, D. P. (1992), 'Religion and Fertility in the United States', *Demography*, 29(2): 199–214.

Oppenheimer, V. K. (1988), 'A Theory of Marriage Timing', *American Journal of Sociology*, 94: 563–91.

—— Blossfeld, H. P., and Wackerow, A. (1995), in Blossfeld (ed.), *The New Role of Women: Family Formation in Modern Societies*, 150–73. Boulder. CO: Westview Press, Chapter 7.

Preston, S. H. and Richards, A. T. (1975), 'The Influence of Women's Work Opportunities on Marriage Rates', *Demography*, 12: 209–22.

Raley, R. K. (1996), 'A shortage of marriageable men? A note on the role of cohabitation in black-white differences in marriage rates', *American Sociological Review*, 61: 973–83.

Sander, W. (1993), 'Catholicism and Marriage in the United States', *Demography* 30(3): 373–84.

South, S. J. (1991), 'Sociodemographic differentials in mate selection preferences', *Journal of Marriage and the Family*, 53: 928–40.

—— and Lloyd, M. K. (1992), 'Marriage Opportunities and Family Formation: Further Implications of Imbalanced Sex Ratios', *Journal of Marriage and the Family*, 54: 440–51.

—— and Crowder, K. D. (1999), 'Neighborhood Concentration Effects on Family Formation', *American Sociological Review*, 64(February): 113–32.

Thornton, A., Axinn, W. G., and Teachman, J. D. (1995), 'The Influence of School Enrollment and Accumulation on Cohabitation and Marriage in Early Childhood', *American Sociological Review*, 60: 762–44.

Wilson, W. J. (1987), *The Truly Disadvantaged*. Chicago: University of Chicago Press.

12

Education, Career Opportunities, and Changing Patterns of Fertility: A Study of Women in the Labour Market in Twentieth-Century Sweden

MARIA STANFORS AND LARS SVENSSON

INTRODUCTION

Two distinct features of societal change in twentieth century Sweden are the changing socio-economic roles of women and the changing patterns of fertility. As the Swedish economy has changed, from being a predominantly agrarian economy at the turn of the century, to an industrial and further to a post-industrial economy, Swedish women have increased their level of education and made more use of it through increased labour force participation. They have also moved into new sectors and occupations and the earnings gap between men and women has been reduced. Together with these changes, period fertility rates have fluctuated dramatically and at some points in time, as for instance the late 1980s and early 1990s, Sweden showed a combination of one of the highest birth rates in Western Europe and a very high female labour force participation rate. Cohort fertility has, however, been remarkably stable at about two children per woman, during more than half of the twentieth century.

This Chapter will not explain fertility variations but will aim at analysing and explaining the interactions between women's education, career opportunities, labour force participation, policy measures, and fertility from an economic-historical perspective. We thus stress the importance of a long-term time perspective. The time series used, show that the long-term development has not been even and continuous. Change has rather been concentrated to certain distinguishable periods. The female relative wage in manufacturing increased during the periods 1919–22, 1944–49, and 1961–80. Also, female labour force participation increased during these periods, especially during the 1920s, and the 1960s and 1970s. New jobs opened up for women through reform in 1923 and the number of female jobs expanded in the emerging clerical and commercial sectors during the 1920s and in the public sector during the 1960s and 1970s. Educational reforms, of significance especially for girls and women, were also concentrated to the selfsame periods of expansion. Thus, we see the 1920s, the post-war 1940s and the 1960s and 1970s as important periods of change when it comes to gender equality in education and the labour market. The 1990s also appear to have been a distinct period of change. All periods, however, hold special characteristics. When changing patterns of fertility are brought into the picture, we see that not only economic structural change but also policy changes have influenced women's lives. Gradually, the compatibility between women's double roles has changed. We thus see, against the background of structural change in the Swedish economy and the fundamental transformation of Swedish society during the twentieth century, how women over time have chosen different strategies, meaning different combinations of education, career, and fertility.

We start by describing the long-term trends with respect to women in education, female wages, female labour force participation, and occupational segregation as well as fertility trends by age and educational and occupational status. Departing from the aggregate long-term trends, we investigate in what way the changes in women's education relate to changing career opportunities of Swedish women, and in what way fertility changes reflect changes in educational patterns, female labour force participation and career orientation. As the education and work components of Swedish women's lives have increased, the age pattern of fertility has shifted toward older ages. We hypothesize that the general trend toward later childbearing is most pronounced among better-educated and more career-oriented women. This is based on theoretically assumed relationships between education and fertility as well as among career orientation, labour force participation, and fertility.

The data material partly consists of aggregate time series and is partly derived from the *Swedish Family Survey*, which is a retrospective survey conducted in 1992/1993.[1]

LONG-TERM TRENDS IN WOMEN'S EDUCATION, WAGES, AND LABOUR FORCE PARTICIPATION

Education

One of the most remarkable developments in twentieth century Sweden has been the expansion of mass education of young people, especially young women. The long-term trend in education has been towards a higher level of female involvement, yet it has fluctuated in accordance with economic cycles and periods of educational reform. Today, the number of women exceeds that of men in secondary as well as in higher education. The difference between young men and women is not a matter of the extent of educational participation but rather a matter of the education's relevance for future labour force participation.

In industrial and post-industrial societies, schools play a major role in preparing young people for adult and working life. However, educational aspirations differed for a long time according to class as well as gender. Despite the introduction of compulsory publicly provided education as early as in 1842, schooling was, well into the post-war period, segregated with private as well as public schools and single-sex schools as well as co-educational schools and for a long time, the educational

[1] We also refer to some results from register data that has been provided by Britta Hoem, Statistics Sweden. We are most grateful for her kind assistance and sharing with us.

opportunities for boys and girls were different. In the late 1920s, a four-year universal elementary school was established with a choice of devoting another two years in either elementary school or grammar school, which led young students onto either a vocational path towards blue-collar work or a theoretical path towards higher education and intellectual work. A goal was clearly that different people were to fill different positions in society. Academic education was mainly for the few and privileged and male dominated.[2] Girls were concentrated in girls' schools and were mainly educated and prepared for their roles as wives and mothers. The reform of 1927 meant that the state took equal responsibility for the education of boys and girls. For young girls this was important as they could thenceforth attend more public schools, benefit from state-subsidized education and enjoy the same curriculum as boys, which was a prerequisite for further studies. Their transition rate to secondary schooling thus increased during the 1940s. During the 1940s, two government commissions also worked on a plan for further expansion of the school system. The issue of separate education for boys and girls was debated but was not a major issue. Between 1962 and 1973, single-sex schools disappeared as the differentiated school system was replaced by a comprehensive school system. What used to be a separated school system has thus, in the twentieth century, gradually been integrated into one school system with a goal of equal educational opportunities for all irrespective of gender, class, or geographical location.

The period of life devoted to formal education has gradually been extended and thus the educational level of the Swedish population has increased. Compulsory schooling has been extended but compulsion is not the full answer to why more people stay in school longer because, today, compulsion ends after nine years at the age of 16. However, almost all young men and women stay in upper secondary school for another three years. In 1998, the transition rate from compulsory to secondary education was 97.1 per cent for boys and 97.3 per cent for girls. Education is obviously regarded as a worthwhile investment and an entrance ticket to the labour market and the different career segments thereof.

Since the 1960s, most students continue in upper-secondary school, either in vocational or theoretical programmes, and the number that continues to higher education has increased. The transition rate to higher education, within three years from graduation from secondary school, increased from 21 to 35 per cent between 1986 and 1995. In general, the transition rate is about 8 percentage points higher among women. In the same period, degrees of at least 120 credits[3] have doubled from 13, 000 to 26,000 and are achieved by more women than men.

The gradual increase of the educational level has made education more a question of age and gender than of gender *per se*. There are still differences between men's and women's education and they are most pronounced when it comes to the point where

[2] Women were admitted to Swedish universities in 1873. However, not all faculties were open to women and technical schools did not open their doors for women until the early 1920s. Even though women were given the formal right to higher education in 1873, they were in reality cut off from the opportunity to make use of their education and get a qualified position until reform in 1923 (1925).

[3] 120 credits are equivalent to 3 years of full time studies.

education becomes relevant for labour market preparation (see also Hoem 1995). Gender differences are most pronounced in vocational training as girls are concentrated in health care and administration whereas boys are concentrated in industry-related subjects. There has been relatively little change over time when it comes to gender-specific choices and specialization in vocational training. Gender-specific choices in the theoretical programmes in upper-secondary school have changed more, but gender differences in educational choice are persistent, especially when it comes to the dominance of boys in technology and girls in arts. The different destinies of young men and women in the labour market seem to have served as warrants for traditional gender-specific educational choice. However, as in the labour market, girls have been more inclined to move into traditionally male-dominated programmes than boys have been to move into traditionally female-dominated programmes. And what is more, government intervention has been more directed towards bringing girls into male-dominated subjects such as science and technology than bringing boys into female-dominated areas of study.

Since the late 1970s, more women than men are in higher education. The strong increase of women in Swedish universities is largely brought about by the incorporation of female-dominated programmes such as teaching and nursing, due to the reform of higher education in 1977. Men and women still end up in gender-segregated majors and the differences between men and women in higher education are similar to those between boys and girls in upper-secondary school. The gender differences in higher education are rooted at earlier stages of the educational career and even though women seem more interested in and dependent on higher education, the programmes offered in higher education appear to be better adapted to men's demands. Relatively more male applicants are admitted mainly because men and women apply for different programmes. Women dominate shorter programmes such as teaching and nursing while men dominate longer prestigious programmes mainly because they dominate science and technology. In the 1970s, there was a tendency towards more gender equality as more men moved into women-dominated programmes, but this seems to have been a temporary phenomenon. However, there has been and still is a tendency towards an increasingly larger proportion of women in male-dominated programmes such as engineering, and longer study programmes such as dentistry, medicine, and law that lead to traditionally high status jobs are, today, gender equal. Today, we see that more women are changing their educational and occupational orientation in a more non-traditional and less gender-specific way.

Long-term relative wage developments

In 1913, the average hourly wage of female blue-collar workers amounted to 58 per cent of the corresponding male wage. By 1995, it had reached 90 per cent. Figure 12.1 demonstrates that the long-term process of wage equalization includes the alternation of periods of rapid rise in the female relative wage with periods of stability or even decline. The relative wage increase did in fact occur within three clearly distinguishable periods: 1919–22, 1944–49, and 1961–80. A similar pattern of change can

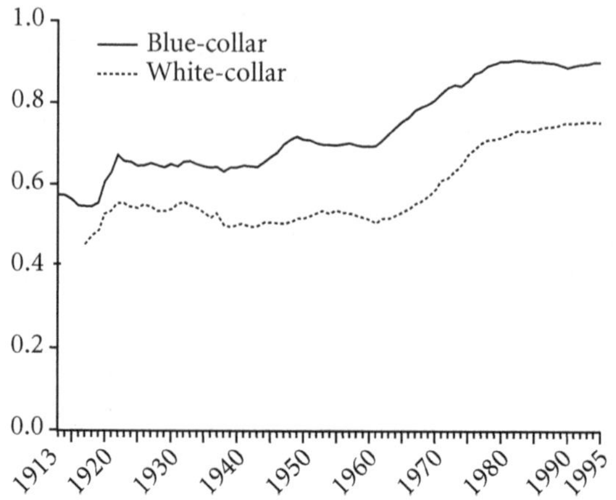

Figure 12.1. *Ratio of Female-to-male Hourly Wages of Blue-collar Workers in Manufacturing 1913–95, and Female-to-male Monthly Wages of White-collar Workers in Manufacturing 1917–95*

Sources: Own computations from Social Reports (Sociala meddelanden) 1913–27, Socialstyrelsen, Stockholm, Statistical Yearbook of Wages (Lönestatistisk Årsbok) 1928–51, Socialstyrelsen, Stockholm, Official Statistics of Sweden, Wages (SOS Löner) 1952–60, Socialstyrelsen, Stockholm 1952–60, Statistiska Centralbyrån, Stockholm 1961–95.

be found in the development of white-collar female relative wages that rose from 45 to 75 per cent of the male wage between 1917 and 1995. Thus, the increase was of the same magnitude and show the same temporal pattern as for blue-collar workers but at a lower level.

Manufacturing has, however, only constituted a minor part of the labour market of Swedish women. Barely 30 per cent worked in industry until the mid-1960s, a share that shrank to 10 per cent in the mid-1990s. Unfortunately, the empirical basis for the construction of time series on relative wages covering other parts of the labour market is fragile. Svensson (1997) computed aggregate female relative wages for a few benchmark years starting in 1920. The scattered evidence suggests that there was a common temporal pattern of change in the female-to-male wage ratio across the labour market. The most rapid change in the aggregate wage gap obviously occurred during the 1960s and the 1970s. However, one third of the total reduction between 1920 and 1995 occurred in the period 1920–40.

With respect to the average annual change in relative wages, there is obviously no big difference between the pre-1960 and post-1960 periods. The determinants of the process, however, were different. Before 1960, the changes were almost entirely due to changes in the distribution of women and men over sectors. One could state that women left low-paid domestic service to enter the better-paid sectors of public service and trade and commerce. This was partly related to the expansion of secondary education for girls, but also to the opening-up of parts of the public sector for women. In contrast, the lion's share of the post-1960 rise in the female relative wage was due to the effect of changes in the wage structure since there was a general compression of the wage structure through the 1960s and 1970s. This was favourable to women who were and still tend to be crowded in the lower tail of the wage distribution (Svensson 1997). From around 1980 and onwards, notably in the 1990s, wage differentials increased within occupational groups, however this was balanced by a favourable redistribution of women to higher positions within the employment structure. In the public sector, this generally brought a net effect of relative wage stability, while in the private sector the net effect was positive.

The general wage equalization of the 1960s and 1970s, and more specifically the narrowing of the gender wage gap, has attracted much interest. Some authors have suggested that ideological and political factors as the solidaristic wage policies and equal opportunity legislation, were the dominant forces behind the narrowing of the gender wage gap but an alternative explanation has been proposed by Svensson (1995), where the long-term relative wage movement has been interpreted within a simple model of price determination in the labour market. In this framework, the rapid and continuous rise in relative wages was triggered by a dynamic shortage of female labour in the period of extensive rationalization of production processes and the expansion of the public service sector in the 1960s and 1970s. The structural crisis of the mid-1970s and the following transformation of industrial production, which included extensive technical change and renewal (see Schön 1998), brought about a decrease in demand for female labour, and so did the simultaneous deceleration of public sector growth. Furthermore, during the 1970s a number of institutional shifts, for example in tax system and family policy, eventually served to eliminate the shortage of female labour by increasing the supply at fixed relative wages (Svensson 1995: 126–7).

Female labour force participation

The first Swedish Labour Force Survey (Arbetskraftsundersökningen, AKU) was carried out in 1963. For information on employment before that date, we have to rely on censuses, where definitions generally have been less strict and thus the data derived from the different sources are not fully comparable. In the 1920 census, 28 per cent of the women of active age were recorded as gainfully employed. In spite of persistently high unemployment during the 1920s, the female employment intensity increased to 33 per cent in 1930. The increase was particularly strong among young urban women. In the non-agrarian population, there was an increase in the employment intensity for women aged 15–19 from 47 to 55 per cent and for women aged 20–29 from 55 to 63 per cent. The 1920s also brought an increase in paid work of married women, notably those under 30. The ratio between female and male employment rose from 30 to 35 per cent, since men's employment fell slightly, during the 1920s. This ratio remained stationary until the 1950s, when the difference began to narrow, at first more because men's employment intensity fell rather than that of women rose. In 1963, 54 per cent of the women between 20 and 64 years of age were in the labour force, that is, had or were seeking a job. In the following

10 years, this increased by 10 percentage points. In 1988, 85 per cent of the female population aged 20–64 belonged to the labour force. The slump of the early 1990s brought a change of trend, and by 1997 the female participation rate had decreased to 78 per cent. The ratio between the female and male participation rates increased from 59 to 81 per cent during the 15-year period 1963–78. The change was somewhat slower over the following 15 years, but by 1993, women's labour force participation had reached 93 per cent of men's. By 1997, it had fallen to 92 per cent.

However, changes in relative labour force participation do not tell the whole truth about the gainful employment of women. There are observable differences between women with different levels of education. Women with higher education have, according to AKU, higher labour force participation and a higher propensity to work full-time than women with primary or secondary education. If we study the number of hours worked, we find that women's contribution differs according to educational level, as mentioned above. In 1997, women's contribution to hours worked amounted to 72 per cent of men's. While the number of women in the labour force increased by 45 per cent between 1963 and 1997, the number of hours worked by women only rose by 22 per cent. More women came on to the labour market, but the average time they spent there fell perceptibly. There are two main components of this change: part-time work and temporary absence, that is, absence extending over more than the measured week due to sickness, vacation, or leave for study purposes or the care of children. The distinction made by the Labour Force Surveys between different grades of commitment to the labour force makes it possible to study the changes in the relative importance of both components.

In 1963, a bare 9 per cent of *employed* women were absent. For the remaining 91 per cent *at work*, the average working time was 35.6 hours per week. By 1978, the absence frequency had doubled and the average working time had fallen to 30.8 hours per week. On average, shorter working time per week reduced women's total number of hours worked by 23 per cent between 1963 and 1978. Women's average working time increased again during the 1980s and by 1997 it had risen to 35.6 hours per week. The significance of absence in the AKU sense, that is, mainly sickness, vacation or leave of absence for studies and care of children, was modest during the 1960s. There was a sharp increase between 1973 and 1983, and in 1983 the number of hours worked would have been 19 per cent higher if the absence frequency had remained at the 1963 level. The absence frequency has then diminished somewhat from the mid-1980s. Obviously, a new pattern of labour force participation emerged during the 1960s and 1970s. This had a connection with the fact that the addition to the labour force, to a large extent, originated from women with children of pre-school age (i.e. under seven). Between 1963 and 1990, the employment intensity of women with children aged 0–6 rose from 40 to 86 per cent. By 1997 it had, however, decreased to 80 per cent. Mothers of young children apparently had a crucial role in the development of labour supply, a role that was determined to a large extent by the special design of the Swedish welfare state. These are facts that justify a more detailed treatment both of the labour market history of this group and of some significant features of the Swedish welfare state.

Table 12.1. *Labour Force Participation Rates, At-work Rates, and Working Hours Per Week 1963–97*

Year	Women (20–64)			Women with children (0–6 years old)		
	Participation rate	At-work rate	Hours per week	Participation rate	At-work rate	Hours per week
1963	54	47	35.6	38	32	28.2
1968	57	48	33.2	42	33	27.0
1973	64	53	31.6	54	39	27.1
1978	74	59	30.8	69	49	27.0
1983	81	63	31.2	82	54	27.8
1988	85	64	32.7	86	55	29.2
1993	82	73	33.5	84	52	30.0
1997	78	64	33.1	80	56	30.6

Source: Statistics Sweden, Labour Force Surveys.

Table 12.1 demonstrates that, although there was a significant increase in both the participation rate and at-work rate of mothers of young children, there was also a growing disparity between these two indicators until the mid-1980s. The difference, which amounted to 6 per cent in 1963, stabilized around 30 per cent in the mid-1980s. This means that a large number of mothers entered the labour force, but tended to spend fewer days at work on average. The average weekly working time of those at work was, however, quite stable at around 27 hours. Of course, the whole difference between participation rates and at-work rates was not due to childcare responsibilities. However, while the ratio of mothers (with children 0–6)-to-male participation rates amounted to 95 per cent in the late 1980s, the corresponding figure for at-work rates was 72 per cent. Looked at from a different angle, there was a significant difference between men's and mothers' absence frequency which increased substantially from the late 1970s.

The 1960s and the 1970s brought a significant expansion of the female labour market together with an increase in the relative wage. In the early 1980s, several indicators of this expansion stabilized at a high level. The performance of mothers with pre-school children had been crucial to the development. As we shall see from the examples below, there is a clear link between the temporal pattern in this process and the design of the Swedish welfare state.

Example 1: Tax system and tax reform

Between 1947 and 1971, the Swedish tax system became increasingly unfavourable to gainfully employed married women. The combination of strong progressivity of tax scales and joint taxation of married couples, imposed a high marginal rate of tax on married women's work. When separate taxation was introduced in 1971, it fell considerably. For a normal working family, the wife's marginal tax on part-time (50 per cent) work was 55 per cent immediately prior to the tax reform. The switch to separate taxation reduced it to 32 per cent, a level maintained for the rest of the decade (Sundström 1987: 119). Thus, it became economically rational for the wife to enter the labour market if only on a part-time basis.

Example 2: Local authority childcare

Increased government responsibility for welfare, education, and care for the young and the elderly signified a transfer of the production of services from unpaid work in the home to paid work in central and local government. This increased the households', that is, the women's, labour supply in otherwise unchanged conditions. The care of small children is generally an obstacle to mothers' market work and also the element of domestic work for which it is most difficult to substitute services produced elsewhere, however, in Sweden this obstacle was not impossible to overcome.

Since 1943, there has been government-subsidized childcare even though very small-scale in the beginning and mainly a complement to crèches run by charity organizations. The government subsidy from 1943 onwards should, however, be seen as a statement and a policy orientation towards publicly provided care, available to all women even though it took time to live up to this aspiration. The expansion of publicly provided day nursery and family day-care capacity did not start until the 1960s and accelerated in the 1970s. Not until then, publicly provided childcare became an important prerequisite of the increased employment intensity of women with children of pre-school age and the establishment of the two-earner family. In the early 1960s, employers, especially in the engineering industry where rationalization had been carried furthest and the demand for female labour was high, pushed eagerly for the local authorities to solve the childcare problem. Later on, in the 1970s, representatives of the central government and local authorities played an active part in extending the much-needed childcare facilities and local authority childcare services came in for heavy subsidies as well so by the middle of the 1970s, charges covered only 15 per cent of the costs. This of course contributed to the favourable effect of childcare on female labour supply (Table 12.2).

Alongside the physical expansion of capacity, a process was going on which might be called an ideological offensive, the importance of which, if not also its deliberate intention, was to reduce any possible emotional resistance existing against leaving children in local authority care. Attitudes to this question changed greatly between the early 1950s and late 1980s (Moqvist and Kallos 1994: 17). The shift of reproductive responsibility from family to public childcare also received legitimacy through faith in the ability of institutions to provide children with the social skills that were regarded as necessary in an increasingly complex and demanding society.

Example 3: Design of public parental leave

As far as the 1960s and 1970s are concerned, most of the discrepancy between the proportion of women employed and the proportion of women at work is explained by the increased incidence of part-time work. From the middle of the 1970s onwards, absenteeism becomes of greater significance. This shift coincides with changes in family policy.

Table 12.2. *Children in Publicly Provided Day Care, 1950–70 and 1972–97, Per cent*

Year	Day care	Day care (others)	Nursery schools (pre-schoolers)
1950	9,700	2,000	19,000
1960	10,300	2,400	38,400
1965	11,900	3,000	52,100
1966	12,800	3,900	56,400
1967	15,600	4,100	60,000
1968	20,200	5,000	71,200
1969	26,900	5,200	75,500
1970	33,000	6,500	86,000

Age of child	1972	1980	1990	1997
1–6	12	36	57	73
7–9	6	22	50	58
10–12	1	3	7	6

Sources: Kyle, G. 1979: p. 303; SOU 1972: 34, p. 70; Statistics Sweden.

Swedish family policy, in its present form, started to develop in the late 1960s. Earlier, childbearing and family were mainly a woman's concern. She could actually lose her job when pregnant (until 1939), was not allowed to work immediately after childbirth and thus got no pay. In 1937, Swedish women could benefit from maternity insurance and in 1948 they were also given a small child allowance. Over time, the maternity leave was extended. In 1974, however, a number of benefits linked to childbirth and family were combined to form a system of 'parental insurance' run by the state. The parental leave entitlement was given jointly to the mother and father and extended from 6–7 months but more important, the cash benefit was improved, income-based and established at the same level as the sickness benefit, which for most people meant 90 per cent of gross pay. From 1978 onwards, the leave was further extended to 12 months, though with the last three at a lower flat rate benefit. Wider freedom of choice was introduced in the way leave could be taken—either full-time or part-time—and parents with children under eight also became legally entitled to reduce their working time to 75 per cent (Olsson 1990: 136). In addition, parents are entitled to compensation for temporary childcare, for example when a child gets sick.

One consequence of family policy expansion was a pronounced increase in the absenteeism of gainfully employed women, particularly for those with pre-school children, from the middle of the 1970s. In 1973, 73 per cent of the women, with children aged 0–6, who were in the labour force were also at work. Ten years later it was 65 per cent. The change was most pronounced during the second part of the period,

Table 12.3. *Compensated Days for Childcare within the Framework of Parental Leave, 1974–97. Number of Days ('00) and Share (%) of Days of Parental Leave for Women and Men, Respectively*

Years	Parental leave			Temporary parental leave		
	Number of days	Used by (%)		Number of days	Used by (%)	
		Mothers	Fathers		Mothers	Fathers
1974	19,017	100	0	689	60	40
1980	27,020	95	5	3,042	63	37
1985	33,193	94	6	4,156	67	33
1990	48,292	93	7	5,731	65	35
1995	47,026	90	10	4,890	68	32
1997	39,073	90	10	4,489	69	31

Source: National Board of Insurance.

that is, after the more extensive reform of parental insurance in 1978. This may be interpreted as fewer women felt themselves forced to choose between children and a job as childbearing and a career were made more compatible through the generous parental leave. Labour market legislation and social insurance in concert with family policy created the possibility of combining the two roles under conditions that more and more people considered reasonable (cf. Lewis and Åström 1992: 76).

However, the major part of parental leave days have been used by mothers (see Table 12.3). The fathers' share has increased slowly and since the late 1980s has remained at about 10 per cent. The fathers' share mainly increased as the entitlement period was extended. However, after the introduction in 1995 of a special month for 'daddy only',[4] the number of parental leave days used by fathers decreased, and it seems as if one month, more or less, is regarded as being enough (cf. Sundström and Duvander 1999: 3).[5] Despite the dramatic change in women's labour force participation and emergence of the two-earner family, the division of unpaid work in the home has changed modestly. The care of young children and family is still very much a woman's concern and it is mainly women who take parental leave and work part-time in order to combine children and a career. It is also mainly women who take temporary parental leave in order to look after a sick child. This unequal division of labour is often attributed to rational choice as the husband has a more career-oriented job and higher wages than the woman who thus has to be the flexible one. A study by Näsman (1992) found that many fathers experienced obstacles to taking parental leave and thus did not go on leave. These fathers were to a high degree white-collar

[4] As the Swedish parental leave system is gender neutral, the mother and father are supposed to share and take 6 months each. However, the sharing is up to the parents to decide; the reform of 1995 made it compulsory for each to take at least one month leave or the benefit of that month will be lost.

[5] After 1995 the number of leave days also decreases for women.

workers in high positions in the private sector. The fathers took more parental leave if the mother of their child was highly educated and a professional (Haas 1992; Näsman 1992: 14–15). However, fathers who took at least 1 month were more educated and more often employed in female-dominated occupations in the public sector than those who did not take any leave.

Is there a new pattern developing in the 1990s?

Several indicators of female labour force participation stabilized at a high level in the early 1980s. Some of them show signs pointing to a change from the early 1990s. The labour force participation rate fell for women with pre-school children from 84.3 per cent in 1992 to 80.4 per cent in 1997, while the at-work rate increased from 52.4 to 55.5 per cent and the absence frequency fell from 34.8 to 27.1 per cent. The fall in participation rate is certainly associated with the rise in unemployment in the period. Male labour force participation also fell, although to a lesser degree. The rise in at-work rate and the fall in absence frequency may have been related to the downswing in fertility, because fewer women had children under one year of age in 1997 than in 1992. However, there was also a simultaneous 4 per cent decrease in the absence frequency of mothers with children under one. Furthermore, the fall in fertility may not have been entirely exogenous.

Economic crisis with rising unemployment and cutbacks in welfare state provision, together with new organization at the workplace, that is, less job and income security, seem to have made women more cautious and work-oriented when combining work and family in the 1990s, with low fertility, less absenteeism, and less part-time work as a result. However, men have also changed their behaviour during the 1990s and the number of days of parental leave used by fathers has decreased, and so has their share of temporary parental leave.

Occupational segregation in the Swedish labour market

Women have always worked, but the distinction between women's work for pay and work for family is different from men's, as women more often have combined the two. Well into the twentieth century, the recorded labour force participation of Swedish women was low, both in absolute numbers and in relation to men. At the turn of the century, employed women were most likely young and single, whereas today women work all their lives and employed women are very likely to be married or cohabiting mothers. At the turn of the century, more than half of the female workforce outside agriculture was employed in domestic work and in textile and clothing industry. Since then, women have entered new areas in the labour market. Despite the fact that female labour force participation rates and patterns have changed, the Swedish labour market is still to a high degree gender-segregated, and women are still concentrated in a limited number of occupations in relation to men. The ten most common occupations for women attract around half of the working women, whereas men are less concentrated. Only one out of five private sector industrial workers is a woman, while four out of five workers in the local government sector are women. Around half of all employed women work for central or local authorities. The public sector is thus the most female-dominated sector in the Swedish economy but also the sector with the largest share of employees with higher education. Over time, there is a pattern of women entering male-dominated jobs, and in some cases even feminization, in times of economic expansion and excess demand for labour (Florin 1987; Jonung 1993; Reskin 1984). Thus, during the 1920s, and the 1960s and 1970s, when demand for labour, notably female labour, was high, segregation by gender diminished.

During the early decades of the twentieth century, and especially after the First World War, women moved into the new jobs that were created in the commercial, educational, and health sectors. The expansion of new sectors demanded both unskilled and skilled female labour. In the commercial sector, large stores and offices replaced small family businesses and employed shop assistants and clerks, and the expanding welfare state and the public provision of health and education increased the demand for nurses, white-collar staff and teachers, yet the absolute figures remained low until after the Second World War. For women with middle-level and higher education, the reform of 1923, which opened up public administration and professional positions for women, was important. The immediate results of the enforcement of this law in 1925 were meagre when it came to promotion of gender equality in the labour market but the reform was an important statement of at least formally equal opportunities in high status occupations. As more women benefited from the educational reforms of the 1920s and increased the supply of middle-level and higher educated women, there was more of a change. This change was further reinforced by the post-war expansion of the welfare state, which created new and relatively attractive opportunities to work (cf. Oppenheimer 1970). The expansion of female-intensive activities in the public sector was particularly rapid in the 1960s and the 1970s. To enter the labour force and work in occupations representing caring and household activities in the public sector seemed favourable to many women through so called woman-friendly working conditions. The formal opportunity of part-time work enabled many women to combine work and family without being severely punished in terms of a slower wage development as in the private sector (Nordli Hansen 1997; OECD 1985). The expansion of female-intensive activities in the public sector was also important in supporting working women to combine work and family responsibilities. The sphere of the public sector increased rapidly and employment in education, health and medical care together with other social services, which to a high degree has been monopolized by government, amounted to 8.5 per cent of total employment in 1950 and 10 per cent in 1960. It then increased to 16 per cent in 1970 and eventually stabilized at a level just below 30 per cent in 1980 onwards. Education as well as health and medical care demanded, to a large extent, young and educated female labour that came out of the upper segments of the reformed educational system, while social services, for example, care for children and the elderly, demanded labour that came from the vocational segments. Social services could, however, also absorb large groups of older less-educated women entering the labour force.

Structural change and changing demand for female labour has thus had a significant impact on female labour force participation rates, leading to different patterns of employment varying from one cohort to another, and also to different patterns of employment growth varying from one sector to another. The trend toward desegregation is persistent but remarkably slow and mainly caused by women moving into new sectors and new occupations. The degree of segregation differs between educational and occupational categories and decreases with higher education as men and women choose occupations in a more similar way than women and men with lower education. However, men and women are still, as a whole, concentrated in different sectors and in different jobs and what is more, when working in the same sector men and women still have different jobs and positions.

Paradoxically, a high degree of horizontal as well as vertical occupational segregation by gender persists in Sweden, despite low wage differentials and extensive female participation in education and the labour force, and despite an emphasis on gender equality in society and the labour market. The fact that men and women more or less have two separate labour markets with different wage levels and career opportunities, and work side by side in occupations with different status helps explain this paradox. Public sector occupations, where many women work, are more female-dominated than private sector occupations, where most men are concentrated. Men are also relatively more concentrated in higher status occupations and in higher positions whereas women in Sweden, as elsewhere, seem to face a 'glass ceiling' and are less likely than men to advance to top positions (cf. Melkas and Anker 1998). It should be noted, however, that the tendency for women to be concentrated in low status occupations has decreased since 1970, as better-educated and more career-oriented women have moved into traditionally male-dominated areas of study and work. The gradual feminization of traditionally male-dominated high status occupations is reflected in the increasing representation of young women in these occupations. For example, between 1970 and 1990 Swedish women increased their share in the traditionally male field of engineering by 5–11 percentage points, depending on alignment. There are more women in architecture (34 per cent in 1996) and chemistry (29 per cent in 1996) than in other alignments (e.g. 7 per cent women in electrical engineering and computer science). All women engineers (except for those in mining) have had an increase in real income during the selfsame period. Women have also increased their share in law and administration. The feminization of the medical profession has gone further than that of engineering and, today, women make up almost half the number of doctors (37 per cent in 1996) and dentists (43 per cent in 1996). The share of women increased between 1970 and 1990 by 16 and 13 percentage points, respectively, and has continued to increase further. However, the income development has not been as favourable as for engineering, and has actually deteriorated for women as well as for men. When it comes to traditionally female-dominated occupations such as teaching and nursing, where women make up a large majority (80 per cent in compulsory school teaching and 92 per cent in nursing, in 1996), we observe that more men have entered nursery schools and nursing whereas women have increased their share in teaching even more. At the same time, they enjoyed a stable but lower level income than men and women in the above mentioned high status occupations.

Women and men not only work in different jobs and positions, they also allocate their time differently and most likely this is an explanation of the observed differences in their career orientation, and work. Women are still, in the 1990s, more likely to devote fewer hours to market work and to take time off from work to care than are men (Flood and Gråsjö 1997). In particular, married or cohabiting women and women with children still put in more hours of housework[6] and assume more responsibility for the caring of children. The difference between men and women in housework has decreased mainly because women devote fewer hours to housework. When it comes to childcare in the home, the difference between men and women is more or less the same, but the division of childcare evened out somewhat between 1984 and 1993 (Flood and Gråsjö 1997: 163–8). When it comes to childcare in the form of parental leave, women in 1997 still took the lion's share, 90 per cent, of parental leave (see Table 12.3). Even though one may say that, in Sweden, there has been a joint revolution in female as well as in male labour market involvement with men moving time out of and women moving time into the labour market, the changes in female labour force participation have been faster than the changes in men's share of household responsibilities (Blau and Ferber 1992; Jonung and Persson 1993).

The fact that women work in a limited number of 'female' occupations and work fewer hours affects their total earnings and their chances for a career through on-the-job training and promotion. The female strategy of combination and time out for childcare makes it hard for women to compete. Childbearing and the rearing of children usually occur at the time when workers need to prove themselves on the job in order to start a career and advance. In Sweden, woman-friendly working conditions, parental leave, and the opportunity to work part-time are important factors that influence the allocation of labour and time use and, as seen above, these factors influence women more than men. A more equal distribution of housework and childcare would probably have a positive effect on women's earnings and occupational attainment, and probably also on occupational segregation through new patterns of behaviour among younger cohorts of men and women when it comes to educational and occupational choice and time use. As the educational system is to prepare young men and women for labour market entry, the different occupational destinies and future earnings probably affect the choices and educational lives of young men and women. Paradoxically, the long-standing tradition of occupational segregation has had repercussions down the educational system. Thus, gender differences in educational choice are reflected in the occupational structure. There are signs of change as especially highly educated women are entering male-dominated professions on a bigger scale than less educated women. However, regardless of educational level, men have higher salaries than women. In 1997, women with postgraduate education had on average 84 per cent of the monthly salary (full-time equivalent) of men with the same educational background whereas women with higher education longer than 3 years had only 75 per cent of the salary of men. There were also substantial

[6] About two thirds of the unpaid non-market work is done by women. The time devoted to housework does not only vary between men and women but also between the different phases of the individual's life cycle.

differences between sectors with regard to female relative wages for these groups. In the government sector relative wages were 0.89 and 0.86 and for those employed by local authority 0.90 and 0.91 while in the private sector relative wages were down to 0.80 and 0.74, respectively. This is to a large extent a reflection not only of occupational segregation but also of internal labour market segmentation, and the fact that men and women hold different positions due to promotion (Petersen *et al.* 1996). Studies have shown that due to wage differentials and the occupational career ladder, working in the public sector seems like a rational choice for many women, which in turn makes permanent the pattern of occupational segregation (Mincer and Ofek 1982; Nordli Hansen 1997; Polachek 1976, 1979). However, the public sector does not attract all women. During the 1990s, we have seen a pattern of polarization emerge as one, increasingly larger, group of women chooses to enter traditionally male-dominated fields of study, for example engineering, and to pursue a traditionally male-dominated career, whereas another group of women chooses a traditionally female-dominated education, such as nursing or teaching, that leads to a typically female career. The development of the 1990s is difficult to evaluate, being not only a recent but also a rather short period. There are, however, indications that the mainly quantitative change of the previous period has transformed into qualitative progress. One of the features of this development is the pronounced difference in labour market behaviour and outcome between women of different educational status. This also seems to be closely related to the change in fertility patterns.

Change has been more pronounced in some periods than in others. The periods of change bear common traits, as they are all periods of economic expansion and renewal of social and cultural life. Another common trait is that it is women who have changed their behaviour rather than men. In short, we see women gradually changing roles in a changing economy and a changing society. Different cohorts of women have faced different contemporaneous factors and responded to them in their own special way. The equalization of men's and women's wages, the increase in female labour force participation and the slow desegregation of educational and occupational structures are all macro-level indicators of economic and social change that vary with time, and have bearing on the micro-level incentive and utility structure of individuals, and influence their choice of education and occupation, and time allocation between work and family. We will therefore look closer into how fertility changes reflect changes in education as well as female labour force participation and career orientation.

FERTILITY TRENDS AND FERTILITY VARIATIONS

The development of Swedish fertility is, by international comparison, interesting. Fertility has varied considerably over time, both secularly and cyclically. Although the long-term fertility trend shows the same pattern in many countries, levels differ, and waves and fluctuations are more dramatic in the Swedish case.

The Swedish fertility decline started in the 1880s (Bengtsson and Ohlsson 1994). The total fertility rate (see Fig. 12.2) continued to decline in the first few decades of

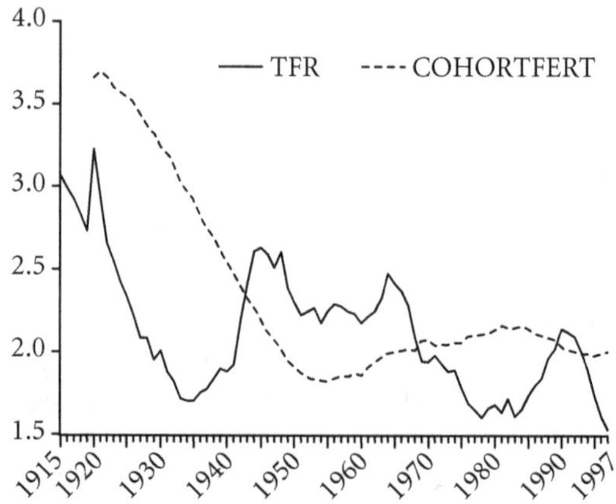

Figure 12.2. *Total Fertility Rate 1915–97 and Accumulated Fertility up to 50 Years of Age for Cohorts of Women Born 1870–1947*

Source: Statistics Sweden, Population Statistics.

the twentieth century and, although the precise timing is unclear, fertility decline turned into cyclical variation in the 1920s or early 1930s. After an all time low in the mid-1930s, fertility rates increased and culminated in the baby boom of the 1940s. After 1945, fertility rates declined but stabilized and remained rather high throughout the 1950s. In the early 1960s, the total fertility rate increased, that is the baby boom of the 1960s, which was less extensive than the boom of the 1940s. In the mid-1960s, the total fertility rate declined and reached a very low level in 1978. Fertility stayed low in the late 1970s and early 1980s, but from 1983 to 1990, the total fertility rate increased again, to a level above replacement level, matching the 1960s and making Sweden one of the highest fertility countries in Western Europe (Hoem 1990). After 1990, the fertility rate declined and in the late 1990s Swedish fertility reached a low matching and even surpassing the years of the so called population crisis in the 1930s and the low of the 1970s.

The distinction between cohort and period fertility is of importance when studying the development of twentieth century fertility in Sweden. The period fertility rates, total as well as age-specific, have fluctuated dramatically over time while cohort fertility has been remarkably stable around two children. The long-term fertility trend until the 1930s shows a change in cohort fertility towards a stable, smaller completed family size whereas the medium-term fluctuations, since the 1930s, primarily show a change in period fertility. Since the 1930s, as can be seen in Fig. 12.2, there have been dramatic waves as period fertility has fluctuated. The fluctuations are the results of aggregate timing and spacing effects which ensue when women of different cohorts, in a synchronized way, respond to contemporaneous factors and alter their reproductive behaviour by, for example, postponing childbearing and then compensating for this later on by shortening birth intervals. The fluctuations of the period total fertility rate thus mask the constancy of the cohort fertility pattern. For more

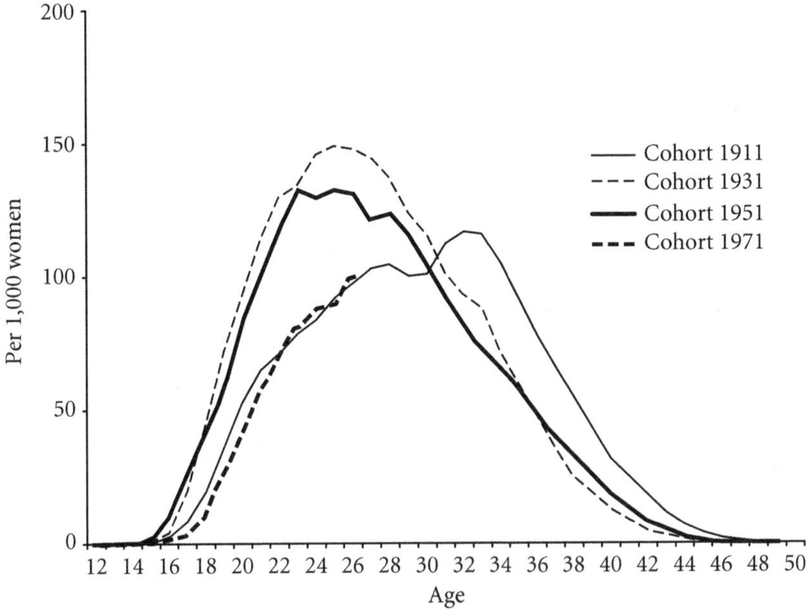

Figure 12.3. *Age-specific Fertility for Four Different Cohorts of Women*

Source: Statistics Sweden 1999.

than half a century, the two-child norm has reigned as cohort fertility has only varied between 1.8 and 2.2 children per woman.[7] The cohort born in 1905 had the lowest level of completed fertility and, as a whole, cohorts of women born in the early decade of the twentieth century had low levels of completed fertility (see Figs 12.2 and 12.3). These cohorts did not differ very much from their predecessors with respect to schooling, but were increasingly urban and employed in the emerging commercial and clerical sectors when young. They were severely hit by the Great Depression and the recession of the 1930s. The experience of economic crisis and insecurity during their twenties made many women respond to the contemporaneous factors and postpone fertility into their thirties. The experiences of women born in the 1930s through 1950s were completely different. Cohorts of women born around 1930 had a high level of completed fertility, and, even though these women experienced advances in schooling, they had their children relatively early, often around 25. These cohorts also married relatively young and thus experienced less increase in labour force participation when young, compared to the cohorts born around 1910. Obviously, the experience of post-war prosperity in the 1950s and new opportunities during the golden years of the 1960s made many women respond to contemporaneous beneficial economic and social factors, which resulted in high total fertility.

[7] This is accumulated fertility at age 50 for cohorts of women born 1895–1948.

However, women born around 1930 increased their labour force participation when older and they found to a high degree, employment in the expanding public sector.

The fertility pattern of cohorts of women born around 1950 shows a striking resemblance to that of the cohorts born around 1930. However, one should bear in mind that the cohorts of women born in the 1930s and 1940s are somewhat special as they manifest a turning point in the changing fertility patterns of Swedish women by seemingly having their children relatively early in life in comparison with other birth cohorts. Nonetheless, with educational expansion and changing labour market conditions, women born in the 1930s, and even more so women born in the 1940s, showed increasingly differentiated fertility patterns according to age and education. Thus, also the fertility pattern of women born around 1950 conceals a more complex underlying pattern with differentiated fertility according to level of education, which shows that women with higher education start childbearing later, tend to have fewer children and work more than women with lower levels of education. Women born around 1950 are the youngest for which completed cohort fertility can be studied. They experienced significant advances in education, not only secondary but also higher education, and therefore had somewhat lower labour force participation when young. However, they increased their labour force participation in their late twenties and early thirties and were among the first cohorts to work throughout the life course by responding not only to economic but also to political contemporaneous factors in the 1970s. The cohorts of women born around 1970 are now reaching 30 and have thus not yet completed their fertility. Still, they show a striking resemblance to the fertility pattern of the cohorts born around 1910. Economic crisis and recession have struck both cohorts and they have responded to this by postponing fertility. We are but to speculate whether women born around 1970 will postpone childbearing like their predecessors or remain childless to a larger extent. However, the stability of cohort fertility seems to persist, as the estimated completed fertility of recent cohorts is nearly identical to the completed fertility levels of earlier cohorts. This is, of course, particularly true for birth cohorts, which are near the end of their reproductive period.

The period total fertility rates also mask interesting age-specific patterns. In brief, the secular fertility decline is most notable among older women (i.e. age groups 35–49) whereas the cyclical variations are most notable among younger women (age 20–29). However, a shift in childbearing to later age, from 1955 and onwards, is obvious. This change is due as much to a rapid decline of fertility rates among the younger age groups, as to an increase of fertility rates among the older age groups. For younger age groups (15–24), fertility rates fell sharply, whereas fertility rates of the older age groups have shown an upwards trend since the late 1970s with the exception of the downturn in the early 1990s.

The most important explanation of the shift of fertility toward older age is the increased involvement of women in education and the increased opportunities for women to pursue a career. According to Statistics Sweden (1998), the dramatic drop in fertility during the 1990s can to a large extent be explained by the fact that more women stay longer in education. As the education and work components of the lives of Swedish women over time have increased, together with a higher degree of commitment to education and career orientation, the age pattern of fertility has shifted toward older ages. It is, however, not so much the quantity of fertility, but rather the timing of fertility, and how this timing varies with the level of education, career orientation, and occupational status that is of interest.

We hypothesize that the general trend toward later childbearing is most pronounced among the better-educated and most career-oriented women, who are women in the upper segments of the educational and occupational distributions. This hypothesis is based on theoretically assumed relationships between education and fertility as well as the interrelationship of career orientation and labour force participation, and fertility (see Becker 1960, 1981, 1985; Goldin 1995). Becker and other proponents of the new home economics hold that fertility can be analysed within a neo-classical framework in which the decision to have another child is based on a cost–benefit analysis. Fertility decline can thus be seen as a response to the net effect of increasing costs and decreasing benefits of begetting another child. There is a direct cost of a child, but the major cost of a child is the indirect opportunity cost of the mother's time. With an increase in women's investment in education and labour force participation, added to increasing women's wages compared to men's, the cost of children increases and thus economically rational couples are induced to have fewer children. Economic incentives as well as institutional and social arrangements of relevance for the cost–benefit analysis, such as compulsory education, day care availability, and social and tax policy, vary greatly with time. Thus, couples are induced to change their childbearing behaviour, for example, by advancing or postponing childbirth and/or by shortening or lengthening birth intervals as a response to changing contemporaneous factors. According to the new home economics, the key to fertility decision-making is mainly to be found in educational investments of women and the relative labour market situation of women, that is in their prospects of finding a job, their relative wages, and their entitlement to social benefits (Becker 1981: 245–7). Hence, we anticipate that higher education is associated with low fertility and fertility at older ages, and that low education is associated with higher fertility and childbearing at younger ages. In a similar way, we anticipate that career orientation as well as high or non-traditional occupational statuses are associated with lower fertility and later childbearing. It could also be anticipated that a favourable labour market situation for women is an important contemporaneous factor associated with periods of declining fertility, and that a less favourable labour market for women is associated with periods of increasing fertility, if institutional factors do not affect and complicate the cost–benefit analysis. However, in Sweden there has been since the early 1970s, an extensive framework of institutional factors that do seem to affect the cost–benefit analysis as well as the decisions about fertility and labour force participation among couples.

As indicated above, Swedish women have changed their productive as well as reproductive behaviour and, with increasing involvement in education and the labour market, postponed childbearing, and reduced the intervals between births.

They have also responded to changing economic conditions and public policy initiatives (Hoem and Hoem 1997; Olàh 1998; Sundström and Stafford 1992; Walker 1995). In the late 1960s, the Swedish government adopted a policy line with the aim of giving women and men equal places in economic and social life by emphasizing equality in the labour market as well as in the household and all gender differences in public aid and benefits were removed. The parental leave scheme of 1974 had benefits allotted in proportion to foregone earnings. Thus, in line with the rest of the social insurance system, there were strong incentives for women to work before the birth of her first child. The expansion of good quality highly subsidized childcare and the introduction of an extensive institutional framework and a comprehensive family policy has made it possible to combine work and family. However, as the focus of policy and public programmes has mainly been on facilitating women's double roles, gender differences still remain when it comes to behaviour and decisions.

We now go on to see how Swedish fertility relates to general economic and institutional conditions for women and, in order to test our hypothesis, how fertility differs according to age as well as educational and occupational status.

Differential fertility

There has only been minor variation in completed fertility since the 1930s whereas period fertility has fluctuated. Although women of different cohorts give birth to about the same number of children, there are differences in the timing and spacing patterns of fertility. Even though the inverse relation between economic factors like education, female labour force participation, and the female relative wage, as suggested by the new home economics, and fertility has been recognized for long, the causal relationship has been debated. As the cohort pattern of fertility shows stability over time, despite dramatic changes in economic conditions and determinants, the effect of economic conditions is on the timing and spacing patterns of period fertility. In Sweden, particularly low total fertility rates were recorded in the early 1930s, in the early 1980s and in the 1990s. In these cases, one could say that economic depression, a troubled labour market situation and educational expansion caused women to postpone childbearing, which was a major force behind the declines and lows. The postponement of births, especially that of first births, in turn resulted in a rapid catching-up during the years of economic prosperity in the 1940s and late 1980s. The increase in fertility during the late 1980s was attributable to shorter intervals between births. In Fig. 12.3, we see that this is clearly manifested not only in total and age-specific period fertility rates but also in the fertility pattern of four different cohorts of women. Whether history will repeat itself or there is a new pattern developing in the 1990s is yet to be seen.

Age

In 1997, 70 per cent of all 25-year-old women were still childless. From the *Swedish Family Survey 1992/93*, we see that, among women born in 1949, almost 75 per cent had at least one child at age 28, and it was not unusual for them to have had more than one child. Among women born in 1959 and 1964, almost 40 per cent were still childless at 28. At older age, the cohorts are more similar, but of course, women born in 1959 had younger children at older age than women born in 1949 as a result of the increasing age at first birth.

Fertility decline among women under 30 has thus been especially pronounced. From the turn of the century until the 1970s, the mean age of women giving birth decreased. From then on, it has increased, notably for women giving birth to their first child. The late twenties remain the primary childbearing years for Swedish women, but an increasing share of mothers have children in their thirties. Except for a difference in level, the time series patterns of period fertility rates for women in their mature childbearing years (25–39) have been nearly identical. However, in the late 1990s a new pattern has emerged with a more pronounced increase in childlessness and age at first birth, and a tendency to falling fertility among older women. Our hypothesis is that the general trend toward later childbearing is most pronounced among the better-educated women. Data from the *Swedish Family Survey 1992/93* show that education is an important determinant of age at first birth and thus support our hypothesis. Among women born in 1949, about 60 per cent with only primary education had had at least one child at age 23, compared with only 13 per cent of the women with higher education. Whereas an increasing share of the women with primary education had had two or even three children at age 28, almost 50 per cent of the women with higher education were still childless. With increasing age, childlessness and the number of children born become increasingly similar and by 43, the differences between women with different levels of education even out.

Education

Swedish women seem to want children irrespective of education. However, among women born in 1949, we distinguish groups of women with differential educational behaviour with consequences for their fertility pattern. One group, that is women with only primary education, is more oriented toward a traditional female role as a mother than others. In accordance with the new home economics, low education is associated with higher fertility at younger ages as these women specialize early in home production and the rearing of a family. Higher education is associated with low fertility at increasingly older ages as these women are more career-oriented, have better job prospects and thus specialize in market work. Hence, the delay in childbearing among women with higher education is also in line with our hypothesis. There are, however, other reasons that should be added to the human capital approach. For one, as educational investments take time, education affects the ability to live an 'adult' life and have a child. In Sweden, a student is not so dependent on parents but highly dependent on government student loans and indebted. Higher education is also challenging and demanding. Thus, finishing higher education and starting a career may be a prerequisite for childbearing (cf. Statistics Sweden 1998). With more women participating in higher education in the 1970s, first births were delayed and period fertility depressed as a whole. In the 1990s, the delay in first births are probably, to a high degree, again caused by a combination of unfavourable economic conditions, for example, increased unemployment and insecurity, and an increase in the share of women in education.[8]

Higher education seems to result in later childbearing but not necessarily lower fertility. This generalization, however, masks a more complex pattern among women with higher education since there are two groups with different fertility, that is those who have children and those who do not. A closer look at differential fertility according to educational attainment reveals that it is the *kind* of education rather than the *level* of education that matters for Swedish women. A reason for this is that different kinds of education have very different career orientation and status, so women with different kinds of education face different labour market situations.

Teaching and nursing

Since the reform of higher education in 1977, a number of traditionally female-dominated higher education programmes have been incorporated into Swedish universities. These programmes lead to occupations, such as teacher and nurse, which are traditionally less career-oriented and more compatible in the combination of the worker and mother roles than other traditional university programmes.

Data derived from the Swedish Fertility Register and the Swedish Educational Register, presented by Britta Hoem, show that women born in 1940–49 with higher education such as teaching (at pre-school or primary school level) and nursing have about as high fertility as women with primary and secondary education, and the degree of childlessness is about the same. Women with higher education, such as teaching and nursing, are also just about as likely to have not only a first but also a second child as women with lower education. Another demographic distinction is that these women are as likely to be or to have been married as women with lower education. Both teaching and nursing are major professional areas for women in Sweden and both occupations are highly gender-segregated. In teaching, there is a gap between lower and higher status teaching occupations, that is, the lower the level in the school system and the younger students that are to be taught, the larger share of female teachers. In medical occupations, there was a gap between nurses and doctors, that is, female nurses and male doctors. This gap has narrowed as some men have become nurses and more young women have become doctors. Being a teacher or a nurse warrants a fairly good income together with work schedules that permit time to spend with one's children and maybe to do some work at home. This kind of public sector job also permits part-time work and absence without any severe 'punishment' with respect to career development or salary. Thus, thanks to the compatibility between worker and mother

[8] Between 1989 and 1996, women's income deteriorated and the share of women dependent on some kind of unemployment insurance or student loans increased from 2.2 to 17.5 and from 13.3 to 31.8, respectively (age 21–24); corresponding figures for age 25–28 are 2.2–15.6 and 8.2–12.9 (Statistics Sweden 1998).

roles, women in the primary teaching and nursing professions are among the most fertile groups of women, born in 1940–49, with higher education, with total fertility rates of 2.11 and 2.05, respectively, for all women, and 2.33 and 2.30, respectively, for mothers.

Dentists and doctors

There are also other groups with surprisingly high fertility. Women with higher education such as dentistry and medicine are also among the most fertile groups of women, born in 1940–49, with higher education, with total fertility rates of 2.05 and 1.96, respectively for all women and 2.32 and 2.39, respectively for mothers. It is somewhat surprising to find that women with time-demanding higher education and a high degree of career orientation have such high total fertility rates. However, dentists and doctors are, to a higher degree than teachers and nurses, childless, and they are less likely to be or to have been married. Data from the Swedish Fertility Register confirm the complex relation between educational attainment and actual fertility behaviour. The inverse relation between education and fertility is empirically documented, but the existence of deviant cases has called the existence of a general rule into question. Westoff and Potvin (1967) studied educational attainment and fertility values in the United States and found that, among Catholics, women with higher education had higher fertility values than those with less education. This was especially the case for women who attended Catholic colleges. The question was whether the higher fertility was due to selection, religious beliefs, or indoctrination. Westoff and Potvin suggest that the anomaly is explained by selection and the result of the study does not twist the finding of a reverse relation between higher education and fertility. The selection reasoning may also be applicable to the study of Swedish women, their educational attainment and fertility values. Some women with higher education may have higher fertility values than those with the same and even less education. Thus, they are selected into higher education with a high degree of career orientation which, later on through labour force participation, is made compatible for a combination of career and family. Those women who combine dentistry and medicine with a family are just as likely to have one, two or three children as are teachers and nurses, and even more than women with lower education. Women, who combine dentistry and medicine with a family, probably work in the public sector thereby making their worker role more compatible with their mother role. For dentists and doctors in the private sector (who, by the way, most often are men), part-time work and absence is more severely 'punished' with respect to career development or salary. The most career-oriented women probably work in private practice or specialize in rewarding fields, and to a higher degree therefore forgo a family.

Engineering, administration, and arts

Women born in 1940–49 with higher education in engineering, administration, and arts as well as women with postgraduate education, have somewhat lower total fertility rates than the above mentioned groups. Lawyers, economists, and artists are childless to a higher degree than the other groups and they are also less likely to be or to have been married. Women with higher education such as engineering, administration, arts majors and women with postgraduate education are less likely to have a second or a third child than other women. Following the selection reasoning, these women have lower fertility values than others and have chosen an education that is highly career-oriented and/or leads to a non-traditional career. Engineering is still very much a male occupation and the 'glass ceiling' in business as well as in public administration is obvious. Thus, the labour market for women with higher education, such as engineering and administration, may be less compatible with a combination of a career and family than more traditional female jobs in the public sector.

Women born in 1940–49 are, as noted above, somewhat special as they manifest a turning point in changing fertility patterns. The average fertility pattern masks that among women with higher education there are two groups, one group with children (very likely two or even three) and another group without children. However, women born in the 1940s were in a sense pioneers in that they, almost regardless of level of education, chose the so called 'mommy track' and that women with higher education, to a large extent, combined this with high labour force participation rates and a family. However, the 'mommy track' seems to result in a setback for women in their child-bearing years as women's income as a percentage of men's is more depressed than women's work hours as a percentage of men's. Since women are more inclined to take time off to care for children, their income, irrespective of educational attainment, becomes lower than men's. Clearly, the presence of children stir up gender differences and the combination of work and family is still an obstacle to equality in the labour market, even in the 1990s. Thus, it is rational for women who want to combine work and family to choose an education and an occupation where the 'punishment' of taking time off to care is low. It is also rational for women who want more of a career to make it compatible with a family, which is increasingly seen today as women with higher education marry or cohabit with men that are the most inclined to take parental leave and to share household responsibilities. Some women, however, forgo marriage and a family. According to our hypothesis, these women are supposed to be the most career-oriented and non-traditional. Whether this is the case, we cannot but speculate. However, we do know that children have been and still are an important part of the lives of Swedish women and that the two-child norm has been persistent over time, though a recent study undertaken by Statistics Sweden in 1998 and 2000, notes somewhat lower fertility values among young women (aged 22–30 years old) today compared to the findings from the *Swedish Family Survey 1992/93*.

CHANGING COMPATIBILITY OVER A CENTURY—CONCLUDING REMARKS

The long-term historical perspective applied in this paper shows that Swedish women's roles have altered as the economy and society have changed. This change has not been even and continuous but rather concentrated in certain periods. We see the 1920s, the post-war 1940s and the 1960s and 1970s as important periods of change when it comes to increasing gender equality in education, wages, and labour force participation. The periods of change bear common traits, as they are all periods of expansion and renewal, not only of the economy but of society as a whole. Another common trait is that it is women who have changed their behaviour during these periods. Different cohorts of women have faced different realities and contemporaneous conditions and responded to them in their own special way: by increasing their education and labour force participation, by moving into new sectors and occupations and breaking male-dominance and by postponing or bringing forward fertility. Thus, period fertility has varied, during the twentieth century, as the fluctuations of the period fertility rate are the results of aggregate timing and spacing effects, which occur when different cohorts of women respond, in a synchronized way, to contemporaneous conditions and change their reproductive as well as productive behaviour. However, the fluctuations of period fertility mask the constancy of cohort fertility around two children per woman, and also the fact that Swedish women, for more than half a century, have chosen different strategies, meaning different combinations of education, career, and fertility.

As women's economic status has changed and the education and work components of women's lives have increased, the age pattern of fertility has shifted towards older ages. This is most pronounced among better-educated women. Higher education does not, however, necessarily result in lower fertility, as differential fertility according to educational attainment reveals a complex underlying pattern. Whereas one group of women with higher education chooses to postpone fertility and have few if any children, another group chooses to have a larger family with two or more children. A reason for this is that different kinds of higher education have very different career orientation and status, so women with different education face different labour market situations and thus different opportunities to combine family and work. This pattern was definitely established with cohorts of women born in the late 1940s and early 1950s, whose changed productive as well as reproductive behaviour mark a turning point. They experienced significant advances in secondary as well as higher education and had somewhat lower labour force participation when young but they were among the first to keep up work and have a career going throughout the life course. They responded to contemporaneous economic factors but also to political factors and institutional change, which in the early 1970s increased the compatibility between women's double roles—between work and family—through tax reform, extended parental leave, and the expansion of publicly provided child care. These reforms were formally gender-neutral but worked mainly through women who changed their behaviour within existing labour market structures, and confirmed a traditional gender division of labour in the labour market as well as in the home that even today is manifested through a high degree of occupational segregation in the labour market.

References

Becker, G. S. (1960), 'An Economic Analysis of Fertility', in NBER, *Demographic and Economic Change in Developed Countries*, Princeton, NJ: NBER, 209–30.

—— (1981), *A Treatise on the Family*, Cambridge, MA: Harvard University Press.

—— (1985), 'Human Capital, Effort and the Sexual Division of Labour', *Journal of Labor Economics*, 3: S33–58.

Bengtsson, T. and Ohlsson, R. (1994), 'The Demographic Transition Revised', in T. Bengtsson (ed.), *Population, Economy, and Welfare in Sweden*, Berlin-Heidelberg: Springer-Verlag, 13–36.

Blau, F. D. and Ferber, M. A. (1992), *The Economics of Men, Women and Work*, Englewood Cliffs, NJ: Prentice-Hall.

Flood, L. and Gråsjö, U. (1997), 'Tid för barn, tid för arbete', in G. Ahrne and I. Persson (eds), *Familj, makt och jämställdhet (SOU 1997: 138)*, Stockholm: Fritzes, 159–88.

Florin, C. (1987), *Kampen om katedern. Feminiserings- och professionaliseringsprocessen inom den svenska folkskolans lärarkår 1860–1906*, Umeå: Umeå universitet.

Goldin, C. D. (1995), 'Career and Family: College Women Look to the Past', NBER Working Paper, No 5188, Cambridge, MA: NBER.

Haas, L. (1992). *Equal Parenthood and Social Policy*, Albany, NY: State University of New York.

Hoem, B. (1995). 'The Way to the Gender-segregated Swedish Labour Market', in K. Oppenheim Mason and A.-M. Jensen (eds), *Gender and Family Change in Industrialized Countries*, Oxford: Clarendon Press: 279–96.

Hoem, J. M. (1990), 'Social Policy and Recent Fertility Changes in Sweden', *Population and Development Review*, 16: S735–48.

—— and Hoem, B. (1997), 'Sweden's Family Policies and Roller-Coaster Fertility'. Stockholm Research Reports in Demography, No 115, Stockholm: Department of Demography.

Jonung, C. (1993), 'Yrkessegregeringen på arbetsmarknaden', in *Kvinnors arbetsmarknad. 1990-talet—Åertågets Årtionde? (Ds 1993: 8)*, Stockholm: Allmänna Förlaget, 56–91.

Jonung, C. and Persson, I. (1993), 'Women and Market Work. The Misleading Tale of Participation Rates in International Comparisons', *Work, Employment & Society*, 7: S259–74.

Lewis, J. and Åström, G. (1992), 'Equality, Difference and State Welfare: Labour Market and Family Policies in Sweden', *Feminist Studies*, 1: S59–87.

Kyle, G. (1979). Gästarbeterska i manssamhället. Studier om industriarbetande kvinnors villkor i Sverige. Stockholm: Liber Förlag.

Melkas, H. and Anker, R. (1998), *Gender equality and occupational segregation in Nordic labour markets*, Geneva: International Labour Office.

Mincer, J. and Ofek, H. (1982), 'Interrupted Work Careers: Depreciation and Restoration of Human Capital', *Journal of Human Resources*, 17: 3–24.

Moqvist, I. and Kallos, D. (1994), 'Mammor då och nu', *Social Forskning*, 2: S17–19.

Näsman, E. (1992), 'Parental leave in Sweden—a workplace issue?'. Stockholm Research Reports in Demography, No 73, Stockholm: Department of Demography.

Nordli Hansen, M. (1997), 'The Scandinavian Welfare State Model: The Impact of the Public Sector on Segregation and Gender Equality', *Work, Employment & Society*, 11: 83–99.

OECD, (1985), *The Integration of Women into the Economy*, Paris: OECD.

Olàh, L. S. (1998), 'Do Public Policies Influence Fertility? Evidence from Sweden and Hungary from a Gender Perspective', Stockholm Research Reports in Demography, No 130. Stockholm: Department of Demography.

Olsson, S. E. (1990), *Social Policy and Welfare State in Sweden*, Lund: Arkiv.

Oppenheimer, V. K. (1970), *The Female Labor Force in the United States: Demographic and Economic Factors Governing its Growth and Changing Composition*, Westport, CT: Greenwood Press.

Petersen, T. *et al.* (1996), 'The Within-job Gender Wage Gap, The Case of Sweden', IUI Working Paper. Stockholm: IUI.

Polachek, S. W. (1976), 'Occupational Segregation: An Alternative Hypothesis', *Journal of Contemporary Business*, 5: 1–12.

——(1979), 'Occupational Segregation among Women: Theory, Evidence and a Prognosis', in C. B. Lloyd, E. S. Andrews, and C. L. Gilroy (eds), *Women in the labour market*, New York, NY: Columbia University Press, 137–57.

Reskin, B. F. (ed.) (1984), *Sex Segregation in the Workplace*, Washington DC: National Academy Press.

Schön, L. (1998), 'Industrial Crises in a Model of Long Cycles: Sweden in an International Perspective', in T. Myllintaus (ed.), *Crisis and Restructuring in Small Countries*, Berlin: Scripta Meracaturae.

Statistics Sweden, (1998), 'Barnafödande och sysselsättning. Upp- och nedgången i fruktsamheten 1985–1997', (Demografiska rapporter 1998: 1), Stockholm, Statistics Sweden.

——(1999), 'Befolkningsutvecklingen under 250 år. Historisk statistik för Sverige'. (Demografiska rapporter 1992: 2), Stockholm, Statistics Sweden.

Sundström, M. (1987), 'Det svenska arbetskraftsutbudet—förändringar och framtidsutsikter', in *Arbetsmarknadspolitik under debatt. 10 forskares syn på arbetsmarknadsproblem*, Stockholm: EFA / Liber.

——and Duvander, A-Z. (1999), 'Family Division of Childcare: Why Do—or Don't—Swedish Fathers Take Parental Leave?', Stockholm Research Reports in Demography, No 139, Stockholm: Department of Demography.

——and Stafford, F. (1992), 'Female Labor Force Participation, Fertility and Public Policy', *European Journal of Population*, 8: S199–215.

Svensson, L. (1995*a*), *Closing the Gender Gap. Determinants of Change in the Female-to-Male Blue Collar Wage Ratio in Swedish Manufacturing 1913–1990*, Lund: Ekonomisk-historiska föreningen.

——(1995*b*), 'Arbete, löner och kön. En studie av befattningsstruktur och relativa löner i kontorsyrken vid mitten av 1930-talet', *Historisk Tidskrift*, nr 3: S277–303.

——(1997), 'En historia om löneutjämning—kvinnors och mäns löner i ett långsiktigt perspektiv', in I. Persson and E. Wadensjö (eds), *Kvinnors och mäns löner—varför så olika? (SOU 1997: 136)*, Stockholm: Fritzes, 14–44.

SOU (1972), Familjestöd. Betänkande avgivet av Familjepolitiska kommittén.

Walker, J. R. (1995), 'The Effect of Public Policies on Recent Swedish Fertility Behavior', *Population Economics*, 8: S223–252.

Westoff, C. and Potvin, R. H. (1967), *College Women and Fertility Values*, Princeton, NJ: Princeton University Press.

13

Family, Quality of Jobs, and Female Labour Force Patterns in Buenos Aires, Argentina

MARCELA CERRUTTI

INTRODUCTION[1]

Female labour force participation rates have been recently increasing in Argentina.[2] The growing participation of women in the labour market has coincided with the adoption of structural adjustment and economic reform policies (Sautu 2000; Wainerman 2000). These policies—including a reduction in social expenditures, privatization of public services, deregulation of labour markets, and trade liberalization—had negative repercussions on labour conditions and employment generation (Cerrutti 2000*a*; Marshall 1998). Thus, the rising presence of women in the labour market has taken place at the same time labour instability increased and employment opportunities, particularly in the formal sector, decreased.

In this context, a concern with women's welfare leads one to examine the conditions under which they are incorporated in the labour market. In Argentina, as in many developing countries, women's economic activities for the market have traditionally been subordinated to their roles in childbearing and taking care of the household. Women's work, particularly the work of women in poor families headed by males, has often been seen as purely supplementary to household needs. Therefore, by choice, and often as a necessity, women have flexible participation in the labour market in terms of hours worked, time schedule, and proximity to home.

More recently, with a general deterioration of employment conditions, women's economic contribution to the households has been growing.[3] Still, in Buenos Aires' labour market, women are far from equal to males. They are highly concentrated in a few 'female' type occupations, over-represented as part-time workers and subjected

[1] This chapter is based on materials from my doctoral dissertation 'Coping with Opposing Pressures: A Comparative Analysis of Women's Intermittent Participation in the Labour Force in Buenos Aires and Mexico City', University of Texas at Austin 1997, and on extensions of that work.

[2] In the metropolitan area of Buenos Aires, with one a third of the country's population, women's labour force participation (LFP) rates grew sharply from 38 per cent in 1991 to 46 per cent in 1995. In just four years the rate went up 20 per cent and in the last 15 years almost 40 per cent (Cerrutti, 2000*a*).

[3] Rosa Geldstein (1994) shows that in Buenos Aires, the proportion of women who are main economic providers in the households grew from 19 per cent of total households in 1980 to 25 per cent in 1993.

to lower incomes than men with similar levels of education. Furthermore, women are more likely than men to frequently enter and leave the labour force, even during very short periods of time, just for a few months. For example, among women who participated in the labour force in any given moment during an 18-month period, 31 per cent changed status at least once and another 24 per cent at least twice. Only 45 per cent have continuously participated in the labour force.

Even though a significant number of Argentine women enter and leave the labour force frequently, little is known about this particular trait of women's employment and its consequences on their welfare. In contrast to the developed world,[4] studies based on representative longitudinal data of female labour force behaviour are rare in Latin America.[5] This paper seeks to contribute to the study of this aspect of women's employment by focusing on determinants and repercussions of female labour force mobility.

To study labour force behaviour over time is particularly important because it can serve as a mechanism for the perpetuation of gender inequalities in labour markets and in other areas of social life. The inquiry into the determinants and consequences of intermittent employment will provide insights about the conflictive nature of women's work in developing countries. Entering and leaving the labour force frequently is often the primary means of income generation for women with competing responsibilities who cannot work full-time. Formal contractual part-time jobs are rare in Argentina, and so working women with domestic responsibilities are likely to procure an informal type of job; these jobs generally are more unstable and precarious than full-time jobs in the formal sector. In addition, working intermittently in any kind of job has potentially negative effects in women's careers since it prevents the accumulation of work experience and social capital, undermines promotions—internal labour markets—and decreases the likelihood of obtaining other benefits acquired from a stable job, especially social security and health insurance.

[4] In the developed world, longitudinal studies on labour force behaviour have a long-standing tradition. They have focused on the relationship between the female life cycle and changes in both labour force status and jobs (Rosenfeld 1992; Felmlee 1984; Tuma and Hannan 1984). They show that women's employment status is affected by transitions to adulthood (Phang 1994), births (Shapiro and Mott 1994; Desai and Waite 1991; Nakamura and Nakamura, 1994) and gender differentials in job mobility (Hachen 1988; Felmlee 1982). These studies have shown that women are more likely to exit the labour force than men are, and that the rate of employment exit is higher among women with young children and lower among those with higher wages. Furthermore, women's employment duration is positively related to prior work experience (Hill 1990; Hill and O'Neill 1992) and employment behaviour early in life (Shapiro and Mott 1994). Though these studies rarely paid attention to the relationship between types of jobs and labour force instability, they clearly show how women's labour force attachment is associated with returns to human capital as well as their demographic characteristics.

[5] To my knowledge, there are just a few empirical studies on women's labour force mobility in Latin America. Cruz (1995) found that in the cities of the Mexican northern border region, young, married, and poorly educated women were more likely to enter or exit the labour force during short-term periods. Pacheco Gomez and Parker (1997), in their study of female labour market mobility during periods of economic crisis in Mexico, showed that women experience longer spells of unemployment and are more likely than men to leave the labour force after an unemployment spell. Differences in the mean duration of complete spells of unemployment for men and women were also found in the case of Brazil (Barata Bivar 1993).

Also, the existence of large numbers of women who work intermittently introduces conceptual and technical challenges to the study of female labour supply in developing countries (Dixon-Mueller and Anker 1988; Donohoe 1998; Standing 1978; Wainerman and Giusti 1994). It calls into question the idea that working and non-working women, especially those from low socio-economic backgrounds, can be neatly distinguished.

The purpose of this chapter is three-fold: first, to analyse how individual and family circumstances affect women's labour force patterns; second, to establish how those patterns are connected to the quality of jobs to which they have access; and third, to understand from women's own experiences and perceptions the reasons and rationale for having an intermittent participation in the labour force. The study is carried out in Buenos Aires, Argentina's largest metropolitan area at the beginning of the 1990s, and employs panel data and retrospective life histories.

The chapter is organized as follows. First, I present working hypotheses on expected relationships between women's individual, family and job-related characteristics, and their labour force behaviour over time. Second, I describe the data employed for the analysis. Third, I present the empirical results in three subsections. Based on short-term representative panel data, I empirically assess the way in which individual, family and household characteristics affect women's short-term labour force patterns. I show how women's intermittent participation in the labour force appears to be an income-generating strategy for married women with children and those with low levels of education. Also using panel data, I examine the relationship between types and quality of jobs and labour force instability. I determine whether women who have a stable participation in the labour force tend to work full time on a regular basis, whereas those who enter and leave the labour force frequently are more likely to work without labour contracts, as self-employed, and/or for a limited number of hours a week. I also analyse the synergetic effect of family and individual circumstances, and job-related characteristics on women's probabilities of working intermittently. Finally, based on ethnographic materials from in-depth interviews I provide interpretative evidence on the rationale for labour force patterns of different groups of women. In this last part of the chapter, I explore facets of women's employment that are not easily analysed through labour force surveys, namely life histories, family and labour market contexts, attitudes, and perceptions. The contrast between groups of women in different family and socio-economic contexts helps to understand why intermittent employment takes place and why it is a more common behaviour among specific groups.

DETERMINANTS OF LABOUR FORCE MOBILITY

Individual characteristics and family circumstances

Several working hypotheses about the influence of individual as well as family characteristics on women's labour force behaviour over a short period are proposed in this study. Regarding the effect of age, I expect intermittent employment to be more frequent among very young women and among those close to retirement ages. Studies have shown in other societies that labour force and job mobility is higher among youth (Rosenfeld 1992). This is because when they enter the labour force, younger women tend to be less committed with their jobs either because they have other priorities, such as studying, or because they are experimenting with jobs. People close to retirement ages may also be more likely to change labour force statuses. In contexts where social security coverage is not universal—due to the high incidence of informal employment—and pensions are very low, as is the case of Argentina, it is expected that the older worker without social security or with meagre pensions will need to keep working in order to make a living. However, for these workers, in particular for women, occupational opportunities are very restricted and generally more casual and unstable than for younger workers.

As for the effect of family roles on labour force patterns, I expect that married women with children under schooling age, particularly those from economically disadvantaged households, will not only participate less in the labour force but also they will enter and leave the labour force more frequently than childless women or those with older children. This is mainly due to the difficulty in obtaining satisfactory and affordable childcare. The effect of the difficulties in getting childcare on women's patterns of participation was apparent in a previous study that focused only on married women (Cerrutti 2000*b*) which shows that mothers have more stable participation when they can rely on the support of other female family members who are out of the labour force. These results suggest that having another woman in the household who can take care of domestic chores facilitates a more stable labour force participation.

Regarding human capital, I expect that independent of other characteristics, women with high levels of education will be more likely not only to work but also to stay in the labour force for longer periods than women with less education. The positive relationship between education and labour force attachment can be understood in terms of women's greater opportunity costs of staying at home, as educated women have access to better jobs and higher wages (Psacharopoulos and Tzannatos 1992). However, it can also be argued that higher education also influences women's perceptions concerning their roles and expectations (Garcia and Oliveira 1994; Wainerman 1995). Women with higher education tend to be more career oriented, less likely to rely on traditional gender stereotypes and more likely to have stronger bargaining positions in their families. Those with higher education are also more likely to live in middle- or high-income households and, therefore, are able to pay others to take care of domestic chores as well as childcare. Thus, the socio-economic level of the household mediates the influence of family composition on women's labour careers.

Types of jobs and labour conditions

Recurrent changes in labour force status among Buenos Aires women are thus proposed to be associated with household constraints that arise from a persistent traditional division of labour within the family and a lack of institutional support for working mothers. If this is the case, then economically disadvantaged women, particularly those with children, will tend to look for flexible jobs, generally unstable and part-time jobs, since they make it possible to combine paid work with childcare and housework.

It is expected that women with limitations on constant participation in the labour force will have access to only specific types of jobs different from those available for women without those limitations. However, it may also be the case that women's likelihood of entering and leaving the labour force is also affected by the nature and characteristics of jobs (i.e. casual jobs in the informal sector, temporary or seasonal jobs, jobs in restructuring sectors of the economy). Thus, the causal relationship between types and quality of jobs on the one hand and intermittent employment on the other is not easy to assess. Furthermore, it could be expected that these two attributes will reinforce each other by feedback relationships.

We can anticipate, thus, that intermittent employment will be more common among women with informal types of jobs.[6] These types of jobs often offer flexible or part-time schedules. Faced with the necessity of generating income, poor women also encounter the opposing pressures of taking care of household chores and their children. Consequently, they often end up working in the informal sector, whether through self-employment in commerce, domestic or other personal services, or as wage workers in small workshops. In many informal activities, which generally provide low income and no fringe benefits, women are able to control the number of hours worked and also, if they are wage workers, they may have more personal relationships with employers. Greater instability of informal type activities is related to their vulnerability to business cycles—changes in demand—and competition, and their difficulties in reaching broader markets and consumers. Another source of instability stems from the fact that informal activities are used as a way to diminish economic uncertainty by passing it to the weakest parts of a subcontracting chain (informal workshops or women working in their homes as 'self-employed').

A second labour demand factor that is expected to affect labour force mobility is the lack of regular part-time white-collar jobs in the Buenos Aires labour market. Job alternatives for women who either prefer to work part-time or are not able to work full time for different reasons are practically non-existent in Buenos Aires. For these women, the alternatives are either staying out of the labour force, or working only sporadically. This is because the vast majority of white-collar occupations in the formal sector demand long hours out of home, and the few existing part-time jobs are generally low paying without fringe benefits.[7] For example, in Buenos Aires, only

[6] Bear in mind that the informal sector consists of relatively easy entry activities that are not regulated, small in scale, and of low productivity (Portes 1993; Portes *et al.* 1989; Portes and Walton 1981; Roberts 1993).

[7] As Beechey and Perkins (1987) note: 'Part-time jobs are highly segregated from full-time jobs, especially from full-time men's jobs... In the main, part-time jobs are manual jobs in service industries and occupations, and they are usually located at the bottom of the occupational ladder. Even those women who work part-time in higher-level jobs... are also frequently excluded from benefits such as sick pay and maternity pay, paid holidays and occupational pensions schemes' (pp. 2–3).

3.5 per cent of women work as wage workers with labour benefits *and* work less than 20 hours a week.

Finally, a third factor that might affect women's intermittent employment is the recent process of precarization of labour conditions due to economic restructuring. Structural adjustment policies, liberalization of trade and deregulation of labour markets ought to have an obvious impact on women's labour force mobility. Rationalization of the public and private sectors, and the difficulties experienced by small and medium scale enterprises to compete in a more liberalized environment have increased job mobility and competition in the labour market as well as open unemployment (Cerrutti 2000*a*). These processes were accompanied by changes in labour regulation that exacerbate the use of temporary workers.

DATA

I employ a quantitative analysis based on representative household surveys and a qualitative analysis of in-depth interviews. The quantitative analysis is based on short-term panel data constructed from consecutive surveys of the *Encuesta Permanente de Hogares*, EPH, (Household Continuous Survey) collected between October 1991 and May 1994 in the metropolitan area of Buenos Aires. The EPH is a representative household survey, with a multistage and stratified sampling design, and contains information on the demographic, economic, and social characteristics of the population living in private households. This survey is collected twice a year, with one fourth of the respondents being replaced every six months. Panel databases were constructed by merging information collected in different waves for each individual throughout an 18-month period. Four partially overlapping 18-month panels from October 1991 to October 1994 were constructed and aggregated in one data set. This type of data allows the examination of the effects of individual, household, and job characteristics on women's short-term labour force behaviour.

I also employ a qualitative analysis of 39 in-depth interviews conducted in Buenos Aires. It provides interpretative evidence from retrospective life histories that allow us to understand differences in women's labour market behaviours.[8] Interviewees were selected accordingly to their stage of family formation (age and position in the household) and the socio-economic level of their household (low and middle class).[9]

[8] The interview protocol consisted of a semi-structured instrument with three parts. The first collected information on individual, current household, and household-of-origin basic characteristics. The second asked about women's life histories connecting three dimensions: family events, education, and employment. The third part consisted of sets of questions relating to current occupation, job satisfaction, labour prospects, husbands' jobs, income generation, control over resources and expenditure decisions, and, finally, access to public services.

[9] I selected cases through personal contacts and I also employed a 'snowball' method. I conducted interviews from October 1995 to December 1995. Due to the considerable heterogeneity in housing conditions, availability of public services and infrastructure of Buenos Aires I aimed to interview women living in very different socio-economic areas (Federal District, San Martin, Tigre, San Isidro, Berazategui, Hurlingam, Jose C. Paz, and Avellaneda).

These two criteria appeared to be of significant importance in survey results. Since the focus of the study was on intermittent employment, women from upper-middle and high socio-economic households and women who had completed college were excluded from the sample.

The purpose of these retrospective life histories was to understand women's labour trajectories[10] as the result of a series of decisions that were influenced by subjective, cultural, and material conditions. These data also allowed the examination of the relationship between short-term labour force participation patterns and long-term careers. To comprehend why 'unstable' and 'stable' labour careers take place, I paid particular attention to the decision-making priorities with respect to jobs and domestic activities. I also focused on conflicts resulting from working outside the home, the relationship between women's earning power, type of work, and women's perceptions of their employment opportunities.

RESULTS

Assessing the role of individual and family circumstances on labour force patterns

To examine the effects of individual and family circumstances on Buenos Aires women's labour force patterns, I used short-term panel data to estimate a multinomial logistic regression that predicts women's probabilities of having different labour force patterns during an 18-month period. I distinguish among five types of labour force patterns according to women's behaviours over an 18-month period. The first type is having continuously participated in the labour force during the 18-month; the second type is having continuously stayed out of the labour force; the third type is having entered the labour force (for those who initially were out of it); the fourth type is having left the labour force (for those who initially were in it); and finally, the fifth type is having participated in the labour force intermittently (i.e. changing status two times of more during the period). These five types of labour force patterns constitute the outcome variable of the estimated multinomial logistic model. The independent variables included in the model are age, education, family situation—a combination of position in the household, the presence and age of children—household income decile, and education of the household head.

Table 13.1 shows that women's short-term labour force behaviour is strongly associated with their individual and family characteristics. The effect of women's stage in the life-cycle, indicated by their age, on their labour patterns can be clearly established from the odds ratios. As expected, very young women (aged 15–25) and those closer to retirement ages (aged 55 and over) are at least three times more likely to

[10] A labour trajectory is defined as the sequence in time, duration and space of labour force events such as entering and leaving the labour force, changing jobs, or changing job positions. These events are analysed from a life course perspective, which emphasizes the connection between individual, family, and social processes.

Table 13.1. *Coefficients and Effects (Relative Odds) for the Multinomial Logistic Regression Model Predicting LF Participation During an 18-Month Period*

Independent variables	Never in the LF/ continuously in the LF		Intermitt/ continuously in the LF		Leave the LF/ continuously in the LF		Enter the LF/ always in the LF	
	Coeff.	Relative odds	Coeff.	Relative odds	Coeff.	Relative odds	Coeff.	Relative odds
Intercept	0.740[a]		−0.277		−0.973[a]		−0.571[c]	
Age groups								
From 15 to 24	1.483[a]	4.41	1.262[a]	3.53	0.307	1.36	1.432[a]	4.19
From 40 to 54	−0.131[a]	0.88	−0.194	0.82	−0.198	0.82	−0.510[b]	0.60
55 and over	3.053[a]	21.17	1.422[a]	4.14	1.477[a]	4.38	1.052[a]	2.86
(*From 25 to 39*)								
Formal education								
Secondary incomplete	−0.355[c]	0.70	−0.144	0.87	−0.109	0.90	−0.222	0.80
Secondary complete	−1.187[a]	0.31	−0.727[a]	0.48	−0.691[b]	0.50	−1.095[a]	0.33
College Inc. and complete	−0.237[a]	0.79	−1.088[a]	0.34	−1.525[a]	0.22	−0.958[a]	0.38
(*Up to primary complete*)								
Position in the household								
Head alone	−1.632[a]	0.20	−1.862[a]	0.16	−1.213[a]	0.30	−1.650[a]	0.19
Head with children	−2.069[a]	0.13	−1.027[a]	0.36	−0.884[a]	0.41	−0.763[a]	0.47
Couple alone	−0.807[a]	0.45	−0.579[b]	0.56	−0.486	0.61	−0.546	0.58
Couple and children under 6	0.853[a]	2.35	0.131	1.14	−0.083	0.92	0.230	1.26
Daughter w/younger siblings	−0.716[b]	0.49	−0.952[b]	0.39	−0.986[c]	0.37	−0.161	0.85
Daughter with older siblings	−1.242[a]	0.29	−1.387[a]	0.25	−0.795[a]	0.45	−0.748[a]	0.47
Other relative	−1.539[a]	0.21	−1.205[a]	0.30	−1.318[b]	0.27	−1.564[b]	0.21
(*Couple and children older than 6*)								
Head formal education								
Secondary incomp. and more	0.277[c]	1.32	0.168	1.18	0.651[a]	1.92	0.189	1.21
(*Up to primary school complete*)								
Per capita household income								
33% Inferior	−0.442[b]	0.64	−0.058	0.94	−0.188	0.83	−0.186	0.83
66%	0.013	1.01	0.312	1.37	0.256	1.29	0.244	1.28
(*Top 33%*)								
Zero income −2 log likelihood: 5848 $n = 2{,}409$	0.003	1.00	0.334	1.40	0.191	1.21	0.008	1.01

[a] $p < 0.001$, [b] $p. < 05$, [c] $p. < 01$.

Source: Panel data from Encuesta Permanente de Hogares.

work intermittently than their counterparts at adult central ages. Also women at younger ages are four times more likely to enter the labour force than middle age women, whereas those aged 55 and over are four times more likely to exit the labour force than the same reference group.

In addition to life-cycle effects, women's position in the household is also a significant factor affecting short-term labour force behaviours. Having a husband and children at home is a deterrent for a continuous participation in the labour force. As expected, married women who are mothers are considerable more likely to stay out of the labour force or to work intermittently than any other group of women—daughters, heads with or without children at home or other relatives. Mothers of very young children under schooling age are the least likely to be continuously employed.

Finally, regarding the effect of formal education in accordance with expectations, Table 13.1 shows that those with higher levels of education are significantly more likely not only to work but also to stay in the labour force for longer periods than their counterparts with less education. However, only those with at least secondary school attainment are significantly less likely to be intermittently employed.

The relationship between types of jobs and labour force mobility

In this section, I examine some of the proposed relationships between types of jobs and labour force mobility. Using short-term representative panel data I compare the job characteristics of women who have different patterns of participation in the labour force, and examine the relationship between those patterns and quality of jobs net of the influence of individual and household characteristics.

Table 13.2 shows that there is an association between women's labour force patterns and types of jobs. Women who have continuous participation in the labour force during an 18-month period are more frequently employed in large establishments, receiving fringe benefits and working full time. In contrast, one out of two women who have changed labour force status at least twice during the period were employed as non-wage workers or as informal employees in small-scale establishments or worked part-time. There are also differences in the sector of activity in which women are employed. Those who have continuously participated in the labour force are more likely to work in social services—which on average demand more skills and provide fringe benefits—whereas those who work intermittently are more concentrated in manufacturing.

The vast majority (71 per cent) of women working full time in the formal sector, that is as a wage-worker receiving labour benefits, have continuously participated in the labour force (see Table 13.3). In contrast, only a minority of part-time workers in the informal sector had that labour behaviour (24 per cent). These results suggest, and further empirical evidence supports it, that labour force instability and informal employment are tightly connected. The associations between informal conditions of employment and labour force instability take place mainly in manufacturing and social services (Table 13.3).

Table 13.2. *Female 15 and over Who were in the Labour Force at any Given Moment During a 18-Month Period Classified by Their Labour Force Pattern and Occupational Characteristics*

Employment characteristics	Labour force participation during 18 months								
	Distribution in each category (%)					Difference of each category in relation to always in the LF (%)			
(%)	Always in LF	Enter LF	Leave LF	Interm. Part.	Total	Always in LF	Enter LF	Leave LF	Interm. Part.
Position at work									
Domestic servant	18.6	21.6	25.4	22.2	21.0	100	116	137	119
Non-Wage worker	22.1	34.6	23.3	39.0	28.0	100	157	105	176
Wage worker[a]	6.5	11.8	10.4	10.9	8.9	100	182	160	168
Wage worker[b]	6.3	2.0	10.4	7.5	6.7	100	32	165	119
Wage worker[c]	5.1	7.8	10.4	3.4	6.0	100	153	204	67
Wage worker[d]	41.6	22.2	20.2	16.9	29.5	100	53	49	41
Total	100.0	100.0	100.0	100.0	100.0				
					1,124				
Hours worked									
Less than 30 hrs. a week	25.8	53.5	53.4	54.9	41.1	100	207	207	213
More than 29 hrs. a week	74.2	46.5	46.6	45.1	58.9	100	63	63	61
Total	100.0	100.0	100.0	100.0	100.0				
					1,124				
Industry									
Manufacturing	16.1	29.0	17.2	20.6	18.9	100	180	107	128
Commerce	21.4	22.6	19.8	23.9	21.8	100	106	93	112
Personal services	19.3	23.9	21.7	21.6	20.9	100	124	112	112
Social services	43.2	24.5	41.3	33.9	38.4	100	57	96	79
Total	100.0	100.0	100.0	100.0	100.0				
					1,311				

[a] Small establishment with no benefits.
[b] Small establishment with benefits.
[c] Medium and large establishments with no benefits.
[d] Medium and large establishments with benefits.

Source: See Table 13.1.

Table 13.3. *Female 15 and over Who were in the Labour Force at any Given Time During an 18-Month Period, Classified by Labour Force Pattern, Formal/Informal Job, Hours Worked, and Industry*

Employment characteristis	Always active	Change LF status once	Change LF status 2 times or +	Total
Formal	59.4	23.7	16.9	100.0
Manufacturing	53.6	25.8	20.6	100.0
Commerce	51.3	30.8	18.0	100.0
Personal services	41.9	29.0	29.0	100.0
Social services	66.4	20.6	13.0	100.0
Part-time	35.3	35.8	28.9	100.0
Full-time	71.4	17.8	10.8	100.0
Informal	34.7	36.6	28.7	100.0
Manufacturing	21.4	45.3	33.3	100.0
Commerce	41.3	30.7	28.0	100.0
Personal services	41.2	35.6	23.2	100.0
Social services	38.1	32.0	29.9	100.0
Part-time	24.1	42.4	33.5	100.0
Full-time	47.1	29.4	23.5	100.0

Source: See Table 13.1.

In order to examine if the effect of job characteristics[11] on labour force instability persists even after controlling for the effect of individual and family traits, I estimated a binomial logistic regression predicting women's probabilities of changing labour force status in a 6-month period as a function of combined characteristics.[12] Table 13.4 shows that significant job-related effects persist. Part-time workers are 2.2 times more likely to experience a change in their labour force status than those who work full time. Non-wage working women—the vast majority of whom are self-employed—and employers—who are predominately employers in very small businesses—are 3.6 and 2.0 times more likely to change status than their counterparts working as formal wage-workers, in firms with more than five employees. Moreover, those who work in any position other than a formal wage worker in a large firm are significantly more likely to experience a change in their labour status than any other women.

[11] The job related independent variables included in the model are position at work, which combines three employment characteristics that capture part of the heterogeneous conditions of the informal sector (i.e. employee or non-wage worker; size of establishment and labour benefits); hours worked per week; and industry.

[12] This regression is estimated for women who have been in the labour force at any given moment in time during the 18-month period. The estimation was carried out using GENMOD procedure in SAS.

Table 13.4. *Binomial Logistic Regression Estimates Predicting the Probability of Experiencing a Change in Labour Force Status. Women Who were in the Labour Force at any Given Moment During an 18-Month Period*

Independent variables	Coefficient	Relative odds
Intercept	−1.0988[a]	
Age groups		
Age < 25	−0.1017	0.90
25–34	−0.6443[a]	0.53
35–44	−0.6053[a]	0.55
45–54	−0.5221[a]	0.59
(55 and +)		
Education		
(No educ/prim. incomp)		
Primary complete	0.0564	1.06
Secondary incomplete	−0.0864	0.92
Secondary complete	−0.2312	0.79
College incomplete	−0.3834[a]	0.68
College complete	−0.8935[a]	0.41
Position in the household		
Head (alone)	−0.6153[a]	0.54
Head (and children)	−0.3338[a]	0.72
Married (w/husband)	−0.1798	0.84
Married (w/children < 6)	0.2039	1.23
Married w/children aged 6 and +		
Daughters	−0.3363[a]	0.71
Other relatives	−0.2404	0.79
Hours worked		
(30 hrs. a week and +)		
Less than 30 hrs a week	0.7948[a]	2.21
Industry		
Manufacturing	0.3210[a]	1.38
Commerce	0.0011	1.00
Personal Services	−0.3720[a]	0.69
(Social Services)		
Position at work		
Employer	1.2867[a]	3.62
Self-Employed and Family worker	0.6825[a]	1.98
Wage worker (WW)*	0.5453[a]	1.73
WW,**	0.5458[a]	1.73
WW,***	0.3900[a]	1.48
(WW)****		

[a] $p \leq 0.05$.

Source: See Table 13.1.

* Small firm with no benefits.

** Small firm with benefits.

*** Medium and large firm with no benefits.

**** Medium and large firm with benefits.

The lack of significant differences in the likelihood of experiencing a change in their labour status among formal and informal wage-workers in small establishments could be explained by the nature and recent performance of small scale enterprises in Argentina.[13]

As was mentioned before, the complex nature of the determinants of labour force patterns is once again manifested in the statistical results. Even when job characteristics are controlled, the effects of education, age, and position in the household remain strong.

Intermittent employment from women's own experiences

From the quantitative results, it can be suggested that intermittent participation in the labour force appears to be an income-generating strategy for married women with children and those with low levels of education. The fact that women with an intermittent participation are more likely to work in informal and flexible types of activities also supports this idea. It can also be suggested that both factors, that is family constraints and the types of jobs available for women who cannot work full time or who have low education, have a synergetic effect on women's labour force mobility.

Yet, findings from representative employment surveys are not sufficient to explain the rationale for women's labour force behaviours. They do not shed light on how women make labour force decisions in specific family and labour market contexts. In order to overcome these limitations and to understand differences in female labour market behaviour, I present a qualitative analysis of 39 in-depth interviews conducted in Buenos Aires. As was mentioned before, interviewees were selected based on criteria found to influence labour force patterns: socio-economic background—low and middle class—and position in the household—single parent heads, married spouse, and single daughters.

First, I briefly depict general differences on labour force trajectories of women from low and middle class backgrounds, and soon after I present a characterization of several types of labour trajectories and their main determinants. As will become apparent, the materials that will be presented in this section not only confirm the quantitative results but also qualify them. The analysis will introduce caveats to the general relationships established using survey data showing how individual, family and job-related factors intertwine and result in different labour force patterns.

Regarding general differences determined by their socio-economic backgrounds, most of the middle-class interviewees have spent a relatively large number of years in the labour force. Compared to their counterparts in households with low socio-economic rankings, they started to work later, generally when they graduated from

[13] Small-scale independent activities have traditionally played an important role in the Buenos Aires economy and labour market. However, more recently, with the adoption of trade liberalization and structural adjustment policies, many of them either went out of business or had to lay off employees. The relatively high LF mobility of women working as formal wage workers in the small business sector might be therefore due to the recent instability experienced by these businesses.

secondary school, and stayed longer in the labour force. They also obtained their jobs through more formal channels and show greater satisfaction with working outside home. All middle-class interviewees worked before getting married, and most kept working after marrying. Among them, the single most important event in explaining their first career interruption was the birth of a child. If they started working after having a child, however, they did so sooner than poor women. Also, they made a greater proportional income contribution to their family budget than lower class women, and several of them were households' main economic providers.

Married women

Survey data showed that on average middle-class women with complete secondary school have a relatively stable participation in the labour force and that married women with children were more likely to have an intermittent participation. Data from in-depth interviews suggest that women's labour trajectories are affected by a convergence of factors that were not so easy to establish a priori using panel data information. Family circumstances affect interviewees' labour force patterns through the lack of reliable and affordable childcare, but also through husband's employment instability, and consequently through husband's economic contribution to the household. Women's labour trajectories are also affected by labour market conditions, in particular the kind of job and the sector of activity in which the woman worked. The third factor is related to the particular economic moment—recession or expansion—when women were looking for work. A final factor is employers' prejudice against hiring married women with children.

Two main types of labour force trajectories can be distinguished among middle-class married women: *stable participation*—those who have been in the labour force almost continuously, with only a few job changes—and *intermittent employment*—those who enter and leave the labour force frequently.

Those with stable participation in the labour force were able to have such trajectories because, first, they made satisfactory domestic arrangements and could count on the support of other people to take care of domestic responsibilities (their mothers or trustful maids). Second, they were public employees or employees in a flourishing economic activity with possibilities for advancement. And third, they needed to have stable jobs in order to counterbalance their husbands' unstable labour careers as independent workers.

In a context of significant labour market changes, as was the case of the Buenos Aires labour market since the mid-1990's, it makes a considerable difference whether a person is working in a public sector job, in a job in an economically successful economic sector, or in a job in a declining economic sector. Middle-class women currently working in public administrative offices and one as health insurance broker, are those with the most stable labour force careers. They have been working without interruptions most of their lives. Furthermore, two have spent more than 10 years in the same job and one more than 15 years in the same occupation. They have spent more time in their current jobs than most other women. They work full-time, five days a week, between 6 and 9 hours a day, and they receive fringe benefits. Public employees value their jobs because they are stable, guarantee '*a pay cheque every month*', provide labour benefits, mainly health insurance, and allow certain flexibility in the schedule.

All the women with stable careers are currently the main economic providers in their households, since their husbands currently are and have lately been in very unstable labour situations.[14] These women felt that they had to be the stable workers in order to ensure a basic standard of living, while their male counterparts were the ones able to take chances in the business world.

A set of determinants of middle-class married women *intermittent trajectories* can be distinguished. These are: difficulties in getting affordable childcare, lack of any kind of support from their husbands in household reproduction activities, and labour demand factors—in particular open discrimination against married women with young children, lack of regular part-time jobs[15], and the recent proliferation of temporary jobs. The effect of all these factors could not be assessed by available survey information and they could only be identified by asking women about their own experiences and perceptions.

One common aspect found in this group that coincides with the quantitative results is that all these women with intermittent trajectories have small children at home. However, the lack of affordable childcare is not the only family-related constraint that these women face. All are also married to husbands who are employees with stable jobs but who spend long hours—sometimes even up to 14 hours!—out of their homes. So, these women cannot count on any kind of support for household chores or childcare from their partners. Because their husbands spend most of their time out of home, they expect their wives to be 'good mothers and housekeepers'.

These women were either out of the labour force or were currently working in temporary jobs or self-employed. The association between working in informal activities and labour force instability is thus again supported. Many of these women have often worked in commercial activities. Though more unstable, informal commercial activities, particularly as self-employed, are often 'preferred' by women who, as said before, are also mainly responsible for childcare and housework. They greatly value being able to control their own time and/or working close to home, because they can devote more attention to their children and household. They sell things by themselves and do not pay taxes. With only a few exceptions informal workers in commerce work part-time, and, in most of the cases, it has been difficult for them to estimate the number of hours worked per week.

Finally, another relevant factor that was clearly pointed out by women in this group who have been recently searching for work is the discrimination of prospective employers against mothers of young children. So much difficulty in getting a job

[14] In a recent study, Cerrutti and Zenteno (2000) found support for the association between husbands' and wives' labour force patterns in the case of urban Mexico. Women's labour force participation and their types of jobs appeared to be the result of joint decision-making processes by wives and husbands.

[15] Generally white collar jobs demand long hours out of home, thus if women are not able (or just do not want) to work so many hours a day, they either withdraw from the labour force or perform a casual independent job.

consequently increases the likelihood of an intermittent participation due to the fact that they have to alternate between periods of being openly unemployed, a discouraged worker, or sporadically employed.

Two main types of labour trajectories can be distinguished among married women living in poor households: *intermittent but predominately in the labour force* and intermittent *but predominately out of the labour force.*

Labour trajectories of poor women are particularly unstable. As expected, this is partly due to their limited human capital and their great difficulty in combining paid and domestic work. However, another important factor that affects their trajectories that could not be assessed before is the hardship in gaining access to jobs. These difficulties are not only due to their low level of education but also to their concentration in geographically and economically segregated areas. Occupational opportunities in local labour markets are scarce. Thus, the opportunity cost of finding a job when paying for domestic help is not an option is particularly high. Consequently, poor women are more frequently employed in informal-type activities—in particular domestic services—either because they provide flexibility or because they are the only job opportunities available.

A great deal of labour force instability among poor women with children at home is related to the way job opportunities arise and the sorts of domestic arrangements they must make to be able to work. If an opportunity arises in a very difficult moment, when money is desperately needed, women will tend to accept the job, making provisional domestic arrangements, such as leaving the kids with a relative who is only temporarily out of the labour force. The problem is that most of the time those arrangements are not stable and the workload is harder than expected for women who do most of the domestic chores; therefore, they have to quit. As was initially suggested, intermittent participation in the labour force appears then as an income-generating strategy for married women with children in economically disadvantaged households.

Married women who *work intermittently but who are most of the time in the labour force* did not spend much time as domestic servants. They have been able to work in other types of occupations such as salespersons in small but formally established retail stores, low-skill administrative jobs, and semi-skilled and skilled jobs in manufacturing. Also, they have a few more years of education than those in the previous group. All of them are currently working and make substantial contributions to the family budget; those with small children had access to stable childcare from relatives or pre-schools. Though they consider their most important role taking care of their children, they consider that bringing money home is also their responsibility. In none of these cases does it seem that working outside the home has generated any real conflict with their husbands.

Heads of households

Labour trajectories of middle-class single parent heads of household are significantly different from those of married women with children. Because they are usually the main economic providers, they are not only more likely to be employed than married women, but also to work for longer periods. Their labour force patterns, thus, are almost exclusively affected by job availability and wage levels and not by family considerations. Some of them have changed several jobs during a short period of time, however they never stop working. All middle-class female heads had worked most of their lives. A few only interrupted for a relatively short period when their children were born. Interestingly, most of these women were economically independent before getting separated or divorced. Though causal relationships between economic independence, a characteristic that is strongly connected to women's commitment to work and to their labour trajectories, and spousal separation are very difficult to establish, there is no doubt that there is a strong relationship.

Labour trajectories of single parent heads of low socio-economic households are generally more unstable and heterogeneous than those of their middle-class counterparts. There are mainly two types of labour trajectories and the most significant factor affecting them is women's work experience before spousal separation. Women who were abandoned by their husbands and had worked only sporadically when they were married are more likely to be intermittently employed. Their labour force instability is strongly related to their lack of human and social capital and also their low commitment to work.

In contrast, those who gained work experience and economic independence before spouse separation perceived working as a central part of their lives. They feel that having economic independence through their work allowed them to finish unsatisfactory conjugal relations. Thus, they have worked most of their lives. In any case, it should be emphasized that even for those with stable careers, survival for single parent heads of low socio-economic households is particularly hard. They generally do not receive any kind of support from their husbands and have a large number of children.

Daughters

Finally, regarding labour force behaviours of daughters, I found in my interviews that intermittent employment is common among young women independent of their socio-economic backgrounds. Middle-class daughters differ from their counterparts who live in poor households in several aspects. They start to work later in life and they have access to better jobs. The main purpose of work is to cover their personal expenses, something very common among those studying at college. They made explicit references that they started working due to the recent deterioration of their families standards of living. By working, they were able to release some of the pressure on their family budgets.[16] However, despite their short labour careers, most of them have worked in a large number of jobs, as many as nine.

There is a close relation between the commitment these middle-class young women have with their current job and the commitment they have as college students. Those

[16] In the metropolitan area of Buenos Aires, labour supply of young daughters increased during recent years. They are the ones with the highest unemployment rates. In 1994, for those aged 15–19 and 20–24 the unemployment rates were close to 40 per cent and 20 per cent, respectively (Cerrutti, 2000*a*).

with more stable jobs are the ones who have experienced more interruptions at school. The ones with more unstable labour careers are more committed to study. Women who have spent longer periods in the labour force are older and work in administrative jobs in the public sector.

Middle-class daughters, who were intermittently employed, have worked during the last two years in several jobs: vendors or managers in stores, secretaries or receptionists in small professional and social service offices, employees in promotions, interviewers for marketing firms, and manual workers at home. An important factor that was overlooked in the quantitative analysis and only became apparent during the interviews was the fact that employers frequently take advantage of youth by offering lower wages and casual employment. From the experiences of these women, it was often clear that employers were profiting from having an amenable labour force willing to work, which could be easily hired and fired. Most of those with very unstable trajectories did not receive labour benefits in their jobs, among other factors, because labour legislation allowed employers to hire them as temporary trainees. Young interviewees argued that they stopped working because the jobs were temporary, the pay was poor, or the labour conditions were unfavourable. Thus, even though it is true that in the process of entering the labour force young women tend to have been less committed to their jobs, it is also true that they felt a great deal of dissatisfaction with meagre salaries and labour conditions.

Daughters in poor households started working mainly to contribute to family maintenance. They also dropped out of high school more frequently and started working earlier than their middle-class counterparts. All started working relatively young (ages 13–15) in very precarious or casual occupations. Despite their short labour careers they have worked intermittently as domestic servants, vendors in street markets or small commerce, jobs in personal services—such as hairdresser's assistant or babysitter—and manual workers in small workshops.

Their expectations regarding working after marriage are particularly interesting and differ from those expressed by middle-class daughters. All answered that they would only work if there were economic necessity. Otherwise, they will stay at home taking care of their children. It is therefore clear that, from their own experiences, working is not necessarily seen as a rewarding activity.

CONCLUSIONS

In this chapter, I examined a relatively unexplored dimension of women's employment in Latin America, that is the determinants and consequences of short-term movements into and out of the labour force. In so doing, the study focused on the case of the metropolitan area of Buenos Aires, the third largest metropolitan area in Latin America. The study combined qualitative and quantitative data in order to present a more comprehensive analysis of the factors associated to different patterns of labour force behaviour over time.

A point of departure of this research was that working intermittently negatively affects women's careers, since it prevents the accumulation of work experience, undermines promotions (internal labour markets) and decreases the chances of obtaining other benefits acquired from a stable job (especially social security and health insurance).

I found that intermittent employment arises from both the conflict in combining paid and domestic work and from the nature of the labour opportunities available for women, particularly for those with relatively low education and children at home.

Labour force mobility is strongly related to individual and family characteristics, as well as types of jobs and labour conditions. It is more likely for a woman to work intermittently if either she is very young or is closer to retirement; if she is married and has young children at home; and if she has low levels of formal education.

The influence of family composition on women's labour careers is mediated, among other factors, by the socio-economic level of the household. Besides the fact that middle-class women have smaller families, have a less traditional view regarding gender roles, and have higher levels of education which allow them to obtain more rewarding jobs, they are also able to afford domestic and childcare services. Middle class women have, therefore, a more stable labour force participation because they are more committed to their jobs and are able to establish stable domestic arrangements in order to work.

Besides individual and family factors, there are also labour factors associated with female labour force stability. It is more likely for a woman to work intermittently if she works part time, in informal activities, such as being self-employed or a wage-worker in a small firm, or a wage worker who does not receive fringe benefits. The associations between these characteristics hold even after accounting for individual and household characteristics.

Bringing women's own experiences and perspectives into the analysis served two purposes. One was to grant interpretations and support for the quantitative findings, and the other was to suggest qualifications and to introduce several possible caveats to the more general results provided by survey data. The qualitative analysis was useful to draw attention to factors that also have an influence on women's labour force mobility. Two important factors were the existence of labour force 'arrangements' between husbands and wives, and the difficulties in obtaining affordable childcare. The interviews also clearly showed the negative influence of the lack of occupational opportunities (in particular part-time regular white collar jobs), the geographical segregation of job opportunities and the impact of economic restructuring on women's labour careers. Finally, another important factor that was recurrently pointed out by interviewees was the detrimental effect of employers' practices, in particular discrimination against married women with children.

From this study, four areas for public policy intervention appear to be central in order to improve the conditions for a more stable participation in the labour force. One is the improvement in the provision of affordable and reliable childcare services. Second is the promotion of women's higher education. The effect of education showed itself to be crucial throughout my study. The more educated women are not only more likely to work, but they are also more likely to stay in the labour force for longer periods, and to express greater commitment to their jobs, partly because they have access to more rewarding jobs. Finally, the third and fourth aspects are related to job access. One is the need for the enforcement of anti-discriminatory regulations that will guarantee equal opportunity access to jobs for women in different family situations; and the other is the promotion of more flexible regular formal jobs, in terms of hours and days, through labour legislation.

References

Barata Bivar, W. (1993), *Aspectos da Estrutua do Deseprego no Brasil: Composicao por Sexo e Duracao*, Rio de Janeiro: BNDES, FINAME BNDESPAR.

Beechey, V. and Perkins, T. (1987), '*A Matter of Hours. Women, Part-time Work and Labour the Market*', Minneapolis: University of Minnesota Press.

Cerrutti, M. (1997), 'Coping with Opposing Pressures: A Comparative Analysis of Women's Intermittent Participation in the Labour Force in Buenos Aires and Mexico City', Ph.D. Dissertation, The University of Texas at Austin.

—— (2000*a*), 'Economic Reform, Structural Adjustment and Female Participation in the Labour Force in Buenos Aires, Argentina', *World Development*, 28(5).

—— (2000*b*). 'Intermittent Employment among Married Women: A Comparative Study of Buenos Aires and Mexico City', *Journal of Comparative Family Studies*, 31(1): 19–43.

——. and Zenteno, R. (2000), 'Cambios en el Papel Económico de las Mujeres entre las Parejas Mexicanas', *Estudios Demográficos y Urbanos*, 15(1).

Clark, K. and Summers, L. (1981), 'Demographic Differences in Cyclical Employment Variation', *The Journal of Human Resources*, 16(11): 61–77.

Clogg, C., Elison, S., and Wahl, R. (1990), 'Labor Market Experiences and Labor Force Outcomes', *American Journal of Sociology*, 95(6): 1536–76.

Corcoran, M. and Hill, M. (1984), 'Recurrence of Unemployment Among Adult Men', *The Journal of Human Resources*, 20(2): 165–83.

Cruz, R. (1995), 'Inestabilidad y Volatilidad en el Empleo de la Fuerza de Trabajo Fronteriza', *Estudios Demográficos y Urbanos*, 10(3): 523–44.

Desai, S. and Waite, L. (1991), 'Women's Employment During Pregnancy and After the First Birth: Occupational Characteristics and Work Commitment', *American Sociological Review*, 56: 551–66.

Devens, R. (1986), 'Displaced Workers: One Year Later', *Monthly Labour Review*, July: 40–43.

Donohoe, (1998), 'Women's Work in Egypt: Measuring Activity and Highlighting Diversity' paper presented at the 1998 Annual Meeting of the American Sociological Association (ASA), San Francisco.

Felmlee, D. (1982), 'Women's Job Mobility Processes Within and Between Employers', *American Sociological Review*, 47: 142–51.

—— (1984), 'A Dynamic Analysis of Women's Employment Exits', *Demography*, 21(2): 171–83.

Gallart. M. A., Moreno, M., and Cerrutti, M. (1991), *Los Trabajadores por Cuenta Propia del Gran Buenos Aires: Sus Estrategias Educativas y Ocupacionales*. Buenos Aires: Centro de Estudios de Población, CENEP. Cuadernos del CENEP No. 45.

García, B. and Oliveira, O. (1994), *Trabajo Femenino y Vida Familiar en Mexico*, Mexico City: El Colegio de México.

Geldstein, R. (1994), *Los Roles de Genero en la Crisis. Mujeres como Principal Sostén Económico del Hogar*, Buenos Aires: Centro de Estudios de Población, CENEP. Cuadernos del CENEP No. 50.

González de la Rocha, M. (1994), *The Resources of Poverty. Women and Survival in a Mexican City*, Oxford: Blackwell.

Hill, A. (1990), 'Intercohort Differences in Women's Labour Market Transitions', *The American Economic Review*, 80(2): 289–92.

—— and O'Neill, J. (1992), 'Intercohort Changes in Women's Labour Market Status', *Research in Labour Economics*, 1992: 215–86

Junsay, A. and Heaton. (1989), *Women Working. Comparative Perspectives in Developing Areas*, New York: Greenwood Press

Marshall, A. (1990), 'Contrataciones Flexibles o Trabajo Precario? El Empleo Temporario y a Tiempo Parcial', in Galín, P. and Novick, M. (eds) *La Precarización del Empleo en la Argentina*. Buenos Aires: Centro Editor de America Latina, ILO-CIAT, CLACSO.

—— (1998), *Empleo en la Argentina, 1991–1997: Nuevas pautas de comportamiento despúes de la liberalización económica*? Santiago: OIT-ETM 79, OIT (Oficina Internacional del Trabajo-Equipo Técnico Multidisciplinario)

Nakamura, A. and Nakamura, M. (1994), 'Predicting Female Labour Supply. The Effects of Children and Recent Work Experience', *The Journal of Human Resources*, 29(2): 304–27.

Pacheco Gomez, E. and Parker, S. (1997), 'Male and Female Labour Market Mobility in Urban Mexico. Longitudinal Evidence from Two Periods of Crisis', paper presented at the Annual Meeting of the Population Association of America, Washington, March 27–9.

Parker, S. and Knaul, F. (1996), 'Employment and Child Care Strategies Among Women with Young Children: The Mexican Case', paper presented at the Annual Meeting of the Population Association of America, New Orleans, May 9–11.

Phang, H. (1994), *Labour Market Transitions of Young Women Over the Early Life Course: Age Pattern: Life-Cycle Variation, and Racial Differences*, Center for Demography and Ecology, University of Wisconsin-Madison, Working Paper 94–19.

Portes, A. and Benton. L. (1984), 'Industrial Development and Labour Absorption: A Reinterpretation', *Population and Development Review*, 10(4): 589–611.

—— Castells, M., and Benton, L. (1989), *The Informal Economy: Studies in Advanced and Less Developed Countries*, Baltimore: The John Hopkins University.

—— and Schauffler, R. (1993), 'Competing Perspectives on the Latin American Informal Sector', *Population and Development Review*, 9(1): 33–60.

—— and Walton, J. (1981), *Labour Class and the International System*, New York: Academic Press.

Psacharopoulos, G. and Tzannatos, Z. (1993), *Case Studies on Women's Employment and Pay in Latin America*. Washington: The World Bank.

Roberts, B. (1993), 'The Dynamics of Informal Employment in Mexico' in US Department of Labour *Work Without Protection: Case Studies of Informal Sector in Developing Countries*. Washington: Bureau of International Affairs.

Rosenfeld, R. (1992), 'Job Mobility and Career Processes', *Annual Review in Sociology*, 18: 39–61.

Sautu, R. (2000), 'Marketización y Feminización del Mercado de Trabajo: Perspectivas Macro y Microsociales'. *Estudios Demográficos y Urbanos*, 15(1).

Shapiro, D. and Mott, F. (1994), 'Long-term Employment and Earnings of Women in Relation to Employment Behavior Surrounding the First Birth', *Journal of Human Resources*, 29(2): 248–76.

Suarez, A. L. (1998), 'Cambios en las Estrategias Ocupacionales de Hogares de Bajos Ingresos del Gran Buenos Aires. 1985–95, Profundización de la Exclusión', paper presented at the XXI International Congress of the Latin American Studies Association (LASA), Chicago, September 24–26, 1998.

Wainerman, C. (1995), 'Las Mujeres y el Trabajo en la Argentina', paper prepared to elaborate the National Argentine Report presented in the IV International Conference on Women. Beijing, China, 1995.

——(2000), 'La División del Trabajo en Familias de Dos Provedores. Relato desde Ambos Géneros y Dos Generaciones', *Estudios Demográficos y Urbanos*, 15(1).

——and Giusti, A. (1994), 'Crecimiento Real o Aparente? La Fuerza de Trabajo en la Argentina en la Ultima Década', *Desarrollo Económico*, 34(135): 379–95.

14

The Influence of Female Employment and Autonomy on Reproductive Behaviour in Egypt

ANDRZEJ KULCZYCKI AND LUCÍA JUÁREZ

INTRODUCTION

The 1994 International Conference on Population and Development (ICPD) held in Cairo, Egypt, emphasized the importance of improving access to employment for women in order to promote their empowerment and to enhance demographic change. Female labour force participation has often been used as a marker of women's status, on the assumption that an earning capacity empowers women and increases their autonomy. Yet the implications of women's work for their general well-being and empowerment are, in fact, not always so clear. Economic development, often assumed to give women a more active role in the society and economy, may equally lead to the marginalization and exploitation of poorer urban and rural women in non-competitive sectors. Meanwhile, women participating in the modern sector may be disproportionately selected from privileged backgrounds or working in gender-segregated fields. With so many economic, social, political, ideological, and legal forces impacting on women's roles and position, it may be simplistic to assume that women's labour force participation automatically leads to their empowerment.

Although no uniform relationship exists between a woman's employment, family size, and autonomy, analysts tend to agree that women's work experience is likely to lead to higher age at first marriage, increased modern contraceptive use, and reductions in desired family size and the number of children ever born. Many studies have shown higher levels of contraceptive use among educated women than among those who have received fewer years of schooling (Cochrane 1979; Jejeebhoy 1995). But the linkages between other aspects of women's socio-economic position and their reproductive behaviour are less well established. This is despite considerable efforts made towards conceptualizing and measuring women's socio-economic position and its linkages to fertility transition (Mason 1993).

In contrast to the situation pertaining in wealthy regions, research in developing countries has produced ambiguous findings about the relationship between women's economic activity and fertility. This is evident from analyses based on several rounds of international surveys, including the World Fertility Surveys (WFS) programme of the 1970s (Sathar and Chidambaram 1984; Lloyd 1991) and the Demographic and

Health Surveys (DHS) programmes of the 1980s and 1990s. In the Middle East and North Africa, women have made gains in health and education, but fertility levels remain high relative to other major world regions, and women continue to lag far behind in their economic and social participation and decision-making (UN 1995, 1997).

In this Chapter, we investigate the characteristics of women who are employed and who are financially empowered, and ask to what extent employment status is related to the use of modern contraception. We do so using the case of Egypt, a country at the heart of the Middle East and North Africa region. It is a predominantly Islamic society with a relatively rigid gender system, moderate fertility (though there are marked differentials), and high adult illiteracy. Its population is by far the largest among Arab states, though the level of economic development is low. The female labour force participation rate, estimated at 21.2 per cent in 1995 (ILO 1997), is about average for North Africa which has a lower proportion of economically active women aged 15 and over than any other major region (UN 1995). These figures are underestimates, but as shall be discussed, they reflect a situation that presents a timely and instructive context to this study. Additionally the 1995 Egyptian Demographic and Health Survey (EDHS95) provides rich information on employment, what women do with their earnings, and on their status more broadly defined.

Egypt has witnessed modest changes in social and economic factors that may be associated with women's status. These include urbanization, an expansion of female labour force participation, an increase in female education levels and a decline in the illiteracy rate among women aged 15 and over. However, analyses of how these changes are related to reproductive change remain inconclusive. Birth rates began to fall in Egypt earlier than in most of the Arab world, but by the mid-1990s, this decline appeared to have slowed, with contraceptive prevalence plateauing at a moderately high level and improvements in the position of women uncertain.

Women's entry into the formal labour force depends on structural conditions, including the macroeconomic and demographic setting, the general situation of women in society and the relative importance of female labour outside the family or household unit to their domestic work. This emphasizes the importance of studying women's financial independence at different stages of family formation, how this may affect the participation of women in the formal labour force, and the impact of this participation on women's familial role including, *prima facie*, that of reproduction. Our analysis begins with a consideration of the demographic and economic context that shapes women's lives in Egypt. This includes changes in demographic, economic, and labour market conditions, together with a review of existing work on the concept of autonomy and its linkages to demographic behaviour in Egypt.

THE DEMOGRAPHIC AND ECONOMIC CONTEXT

Demographic and economic conditions in Egypt

Egypt is divided into 26 governorates. The four Urban Governorates (Cairo, Alexandria, Port Said, and Suez) have no rural population. Nine of the other governorates are

Table 14.1. *Trends in Fertility and Current Contraceptive Use, by Place of Residence, Egypt, 1992–95*

	Total fertility rate		Current use of contraception		
	1992	1995	1992	1995	Change %
Urban/Rural residence					
Urban	2.91	3.01	57.0	56.4	−1.1
Rural	4.91	4.19	38.4	40.5	5.5
Place of Residence					
Urban Governorates	2.69	2.82	59.1	58.1	−1.7
Lower Egypt	3.70	3.22	53.5	55.4	3.6
Urban	2.80	2.66	60.5	59.1	−2.3
Rural	4.10	3.45	50.5	53.8	6.5
Upper Egypt	5.17	4.73	31.4	32.1	2.2
Urban	3.58	3.80	48.1	49.9	3.7
Rural	5.97	5.19	24.3	24.0	−1.2
Frontier Governorates	Unknown	4.00	Unknown	44.0	—
(Total) Egypt	3.9	3.6	47.1	47.9	1.7

Source: El-Zanaty *et al.* 1996.

located in the Nile delta (Lower Egypt), eight in the Nile valley (Upper Egypt), and five in the eastern and western margins of the country, the so-called Frontier Governorates, that account for 1 per cent of the population. Upper Egypt occupies half of Egypt's territory and is less exposed to external influences.

By the year 2000, Egypt's population was expected to total 68.5 million and to be growing at a rate of just under 2 per cent per annum, down from 2.5 per cent during 1985–90 (UN 1999). The economically active population is reported officially at almost 18 million and the working age population continues to grow as millions of young people come of age. In 1995, the total fertility rate (TFR) equalled 3.6 (El-Zanaty *et al.* 1996), almost half its 1960 value of 7.1 children per woman. The TFR ranged from 3.0 in urban areas to 4.2 in rural regions, and from 2.7 in urban Lower Egypt to 5.2 in rural Upper Egypt (Table 14.1). The TFR in rural Lower Egypt (3.5 births) is lower than that for urban Upper Egypt (3.8). However, whereas fertility has continued to fall in rural areas, fertility decline stalled in urban regions in the early 1990s. As shown in Table 14.1, small increases in fertility were recorded for the Urban Governorates and urban Upper Egypt over the 3-year period between 1992 and 1995 Demographic and Health Surveys. These birth rates were sustained by an overall contraceptive prevalence rate of only 48 per cent for currently married women aged 15–49 and high rates of adult illiteracy, especially among women in rural areas and among the urban poor. The urban share of the population (46 per cent) is expanding and about half of all urban residents live in the four Urban Governorates.

Despite registering economic growth rates of around 5 per cent in the mid- and late-1990s, Egypt remains a low-income country. In 1996, the GNP per capita stood at $1,080 (World Bank 1998), with a real GDP per capita of $3,829 (after allowing for purchasing power parity in US dollars). According to 1995 data, Egypt ranked

112 among 174 countries in terms of its index of human development value (UNDP 1998). Only 51.4 per cent of all adults and 38.8 per cent of adult women were literate in 1995, but school enrollments and the mean number of years of schooling have increased. Between 1960 and 1990, adult literacy rose from 30 to 48 per cent and primary and secondary enrollment rose from 55 to 89 percent (Ibrahim *et al.* 1998). By 1990, women constituted 37 per cent of total enrollments at the tertiary level (ESCWA 1999). While these developments have not been accompanied by an increase in educational quality (Moghadam 1998), some authors attribute much of the recent fertility decline to the expansion of female education and the changes in household economic conditions linked to the economic liberalization (Fargues 1997). This has included cutbacks in subsidies for social services, including health and schooling, directly affecting the cost of children.

The measurement of female labour force participation in Egypt

Official labour force statistics collected by international agencies suggest that Arab countries have the lowest female economic participation rates in the world (UN 1995, 1997; UNDP 1998). Political, economic, and cultural conditions continue to discourage formal employment by women and to reproduce a family system that preferences their domestic roles and seclusion. But the official figures also severely underestimate female labour force activity. In particular, they undercount second jobs and work in the informal sector where women are very active, as well as in subsistence activities. At the same time, existing definitions of employment undervalue service work and suggest that women stay at home. As a result, women's traditional roles are not looked upon as productive. The low levels of female participation in the labour market are also attributable to the relatively early age at marriage, high fertility, and the low literacy and education levels of many women.

For Egypt, estimates of the employment status of women vary owing to definitional differences used by the census and the labour force sample survey (LFSS).[1] Until the early 1980s, both sources reported that only some 5 per cent of Egyptian women were in the labour force. Although the 1992 Egyptian census estimated a crude female labour force participation of 6.2 per cent, the LFSS suggested that the crude female activity rate had risen to 12 per cent by 1983 and to an estimated 22 per cent in 1993 (Arab Republic of Egypt 1995). In fact, casual observation, in-depth studies of farm families, and refined methods of data collection suggest that female activity rates are significantly higher.[2] In particular, the size of the female labour force in

[1] The LFSS conducted by the Central Agency for Public Mobilization and Statistics (CAPMAS) counts women in the urban informal sector (which includes many in sales occupations) and in agriculture (which includes many unpaid family workers). It therefore indicates higher percentages of non-salaried female workers in the traditional sectors than census data which suggest fewer women workers and a higher share salaried and employed in the modern sector.

[2] Results from the ILO/CAPMAS Labour Force Methods Test survey suggested that female activity rates are significantly higher and that improved definition and data collection may account for much of the underestimation of the size of the female labour force in rural Egypt (Anker and Anker 1995).

rural Egypt is consistently underreported. Privatization, the expansion of the services sector, and economic need are thought to have pushed more women into the labour force and into services and tourist-related occupations.

As in other Arab countries (ESCWA 1999), Egyptian women who are economically active are more likely to be found in clerical, sales, and services jobs (18.2 per cent) and in the agricultural sector (35.2 per cent). In addition, one in five working women (19.7 per cent) in 1994 were employed in more skilled professional, technical, administrative, and managerial positions. However, little is known about the real contribution of women in the workforce, especially those working in the informal sector and in small-scale industries. Available statistics generally underestimate women's contribution to the labour market for several reasons. First, they tend to overlook most unpaid employment, which accounts for a significant portion of women's work. Second, women and poor men may have to devise more complex strategies to get by than those captured by questionnaires that assume a person has only one occupation and a household has only one head. Interviewers may further assume that women do not contribute to the economy.

In addition to these and other deficiencies of survey procedures, social attitudes undervalue the significance of women's social life in general. Women themselves may not apply the term 'work' to the economic activities they carry out within the family household or enterprise. In contrast to the restrictive definition of work found in national labour force surveys, in-depth microsurveys and anthropological studies show that women engage in a range of income-generating activities apart from wage labour (Hoodfar 1997). Common examples include craft production, inter-household cooperative tasks, and economic activities that are conducted within the household or within the family enterprise. Nevertheless, women are undoubtedly disadvantaged in the labour market. They suffer greater unemployment and are more likely to be laid off as a result of structural adjustment programmes.[3] Their greater dependence on the informal sector implies lower pay and greater vulnerability to discrimination and exploitation. Also, recent Islamist pressure that a woman's 'natural' place is in the home has strengthened barriers to the entry of women into the labour force.

Conceptualizing and measuring women's autonomy and demographic behaviour in Egypt

As is the case with female labour force participation, women's autonomy and its linkages with demographic change are notoriously difficult concepts to measure. The concept of autonomy is itself multifaceted and context-dependent. It may, however, be gauged through its various dimensions such as decision-making within the household or family unit, personal independence of judgement and action, physical mobility and

[3] Open unemployment, reported at 11.3 per cent for both sexes in 1995, was as high as 24.1 per cent for women (Arab Republic of Egypt 1995), among whom it was higher in Lower Egypt (27.6 per cent) than in either Upper Egypt (19.6 per cent) or the Urban Governorates (21.5 per cent).

interaction with the outside world, or economic independence, access to and control over economic resources.

The EDHS95 contained a special module on women's status, unlike other DHS surveys held in the Arab states. Women were asked about the extent to which they had, either alone or jointly with their husbands, the last word in eight aspects of household decision-making. The responses given show that women alone rarely have a final say in household decisions except concerning the food cooked in the house (69 per cent) and medical attention for children (26 per cent). Only 7.8 per cent and 14.1 per cent of currently married women reported having the final say in decisions about visits to friends and relatives and on the household budget. Few women have the final say about having another child (3.6 per cent) or contraceptive use (13.3 per cent), though as many as 74 per cent and 65 per cent, respectively, say they make such decisions jointly with their husbands. The input of women in household decisions rises with age, level of education, exposure to non-domestic work, and urban residence.

Several authors have developed indices of decision-making based on such measures for Egypt (Nawar *et al.* 1995; Govindasamy and Malhotra 1996; Kishor 1995, 1999). However, the indices of female autonomy used by these studies are problematic. For example, not all the dimensions of decision-making utilized seem to be equally relevant to the Egyptian context, such as the responses to questions about children's marriage and the food cooked in the house. In addition, research investigating the association between contraceptive use and women's status in Egypt has proved indeterminate (Kishor 1995; Govindasamy and Malhotra 1996). Moreover, existing multivariate studies on the determinants of contraceptive use in Egypt have neglected to specify employment as an explanatory variable (e.g. El-Zanaty 1995). The dimensions of domestic power explored in the present chapter are directly relevant to Egypt where women have had traditionally little say in household decisions, especially in the financial sphere, and their say in the reproductive arena has been heavily culturally delimited. We investigate the hypothesis that women's employment status is a measure of female autonomy, and further analyse how female employment and financial autonomy affect reproductive outcomes at different stages of the life course.

Ethnographic research in low-income neighbourhoods of Cairo shows that women working for wages have an elevated status within their families, and are granted better treatment and more say in financial affairs (Hoodfar 1997). This observation needs to be qualified, however, because women working for wages at the lower end of the social scale may not have the 'elevated status' of those working in professional occupations. Nonetheless, wage employment can enhance women's economic independence and their access to and control over resources. It also gives women access to non-kin settings and exposure to the world outside the home. Employment, particularly if it is wage-related, can be taken as a measure of autonomy therefore, to which it may directly or indirectly contribute. The EDHS95 collected information on working women and the cash they earned. Examination of women's participation in the formal labour market, whether they worked for cash, and contraceptive use, may give important insights into how women's employment, autonomy, life course and fertility are linked in Egypt.

DATA AND METHODOLOGY

This study makes use of the EDHS95, the third DHS survey conducted in Egypt.[4] It included a special module on women's status administered to a total of 7,121 ever-married women, 5,477 of whom were currently married and of age 20–44. All these women constituted a sub-sample of the 14,779 ever-married women aged 15–49 interviewed in the whole survey (El Zanaty *et al.* 1996). Whereas the profiles of working women developed below are based on data available for all currently married women aged 20–44, the multivariate analyses exclude women who are either currently pregnant or who want to be pregnant. A further 14 records were excluded owing to missing values in one or more of the explanatory variables. This means that the multivariate analyses are based on approximately 4,162 currently married women, or 76 per cent of all the currently married women interviewed in the women's status questionnaire.

The focus on currently married women is considered appropriate because of the concern with women's employment status and financial position relative to men. Marriage remains the most significant social event in the lives of Egyptian women, notwithstanding the rise in the mean age at first marriage from 15.7 years for women who married before 1970 to 20.2 years for those who first married between 1989 and 1995. Analysis of the EDHS95 further reveals that about nine of every ten women in the peak child-bearing years of 25–34 are currently married. Also, women engaging in non-marital sexual relations may suffer strict sanctions (including honour killings) and non-marital childbearing is to all practical purposes non-existent. A further reason for focusing on currently married women is that a number of measures of household decision-making used in this analysis were asked only of currently married women; this enables us to further understand how women fare in the context of the wider gender system.

Outcome variable

The outcome variable is current use of any modern contraceptive method, which is highly correlated with fertility in Egypt (El-Zanaty *et al.* 1996). Among currently married women aged 20–44, one in five were pregnant or seeking to have children at the time of the survey; of the rest, 50 per cent reported using modern contraception, with prevalence rates ranging from 33 per cent in rural Upper Egypt to 69 per cent in the Urban Governorates.

On average, women using modern contraceptives have completed 5.7 years of education, 1.6 years more than non-users. Traditional method users account for only two per cent of currently married women aged 15–49 and do not constitute an adequate number of sample cases for a separate analysis. It should be noted, though, that such

[4] The first such survey, conducted in 1988, remains a restricted dataset unavailable to most researchers. The second, held in 1992, asked more in-depth questions about women's roles and status than did most DHS-II surveys. However, both surveys lacked a women's status module and their questions differ from those posed in the EDHS95 women's status questionnaire. For these reasons, we cannot readily compare our findings with EDHS data from either the 1988 or the 1992 surveys.

users are more than twice as likely to be non-Muslim (11.7 per cent) as the general population. In addition, they have on average almost 8 years of schooling, substantially more than those using either modern methods or not using any methods at all. Those not using any methods include women who are pregnant or who want more children, that is, women who are more likely to be young and to have completed more years of education than older cohorts of women.

Independent variables

We considered variables related to women's socio-economic position, cultural background, life course variables, autonomy, husband's characteristics, and household living conditions. The background variables were selected with due consideration to their anticipated association with contraceptive outcomes, based on related research and an awareness of conditions in Egypt. The type of employment sector could not be used as a variable due to the small number of employed women in the subsample. Table 14.2 provides descriptives for the variables included in the analyses. There are only 3 variables with less than 5,477 cases, as noted in Table 14.2. Age, number of children, years since first marriage, and education, are treated here essentially as control variables because they are basic to contraceptive decision-making and a large literature exists on the impacts of these individual characteristics (e.g. Mulhuri *et al.* 1994).

A new index of assets has been proposed by Filmer and Pritchett (1999) in an analysis of educational attainment across countries using DHS data. A similar approach is adopted in this study, with a principal components analysis applied to housing characteristics and asset ownership. These variables include the type of toilet, main source of drinking water, number of sleeping rooms, presence of a separate room for cooking, and ownership of 12 assets. We refer to this measure, therefore, as an index of wealth with households classified according to their value on this index. Ranking households using the first principal component score is a good proxy for long-run household wealth, as argued by Filmer and Pritchett (1999). Here, we are looking at Egypt alone and our findings differ somewhat from those of Filmer and Pritchett (1999) who included only four of the 14 household assets available in the EDHS95 questionnaire and ignored several household characteristics.[5]

Profiling Egyptian working women

A gross picture of the situation of Egyptian working women can be constructed from the data, in spite of the non-availability of working histories. Only a small minority of women report being employed both before and after marriage. Barely one in five

[5] Whereas Filmer and Pritchett (1999) attempted to construct an index whose main objective was to make cross-country comparisons, we include more assets and housing characteristics in order to utilize as much of the useful data available in the EDHS95. The results of a more detailed index should provide better information for comparing sub-groups of women within Egypt.

Table 14.2. *Percentage Distribution of Currently Married Women Aged 20–44 by Selected Background Characteristics, According to Sub-sample, Egypt, 1995*

Categorical variables	%	Categorical variables	%
Region		Ever work before marriage	21.5
Urban Governorates	23.0	*Current working status*	
Lower Egypt urban	12.9	Cash work	16.6
Lower Egypt rural	30.7	Non-cash work	3.9
Upper Egypt urban	10.1	Not working	79.5
Upper Egypt rural	22.3	*Current contraceptive use*	
Frontier Governorates	1.0	Using modern contraception	49.1
		Not using modern contraception	30.4
		Pregnant or wanting children	20.5
Age			
20–24	18.1	Continuous variables	Mean(SD)
25–29	23.1		
		Education in years	5.3 (6.0)
30–34	21.7	Spousal educational gap[b]	1.7 (4.4)
35–39	21.7	Spousal age difference[c]	7.1 (5.8)
40–44	15.4	Number of living children	3.1 (1.9)
Childhood in rural area[a]	56.0	Years since first marriage	12.0 (7.2)
Respondent is Muslim	94.6		
Nuclear household	68.4		
Chose first husband	25.8		
Husband is a blood relative	39.9	$N = 5{,}477$	

Notes: The percentages presented are those calculated for weighted data and may not add to 100 per cent due to rounding. The number of cases refers to the actual number of women interviewed.

[a] $N = 5{,}471$.

[b] $N = 5{,}470$.

[c] $N = 5{,}476$.

Source: Own calculations based on EDHS-95.

women (20.5 per cent) had ever worked before marriage, of whom 81 per cent had received cash as payment and just over half (54 per cent) continued to work after marriage. In the sample studied here, 20.5 per cent of women were working in the 12-month period before the survey. The lowest proportion of working women is found in rural Upper Egypt (10 per cent). Unpaid work is more common in rural areas where there are also higher proportions of uneducated and poor women (Table 14.3).

The proportion of women working for cash is significantly greater in the 20 per cent of households that score highest on the wealth index. By contrast, women from the least well-off households are more likely to be engaged in non-cash work, if at all. Non-cash workers tend to be the least educated women in each region. The more privileged backgrounds of cash workers suggests that the acquisition of paid employment may be chiefly a function of having access to education and other resources. These findings justify a closer examination of the effects of female employment and education as predictors of contraceptive use.

Table 14.3. *Percentage Distribution of Women Aged 20–44 by Working Status and Selected Characteristics, Egypt, 1995*

Variable	Working status		
	Not working	Non-cash work	Cash work
Region			
Urban Governorates	77.4	0.9	21.7
Lower Egypt—urban	71.5	1.7	26.9
Lower Egypt—rural	77.6	6.9	15.5
Upper Egypt—urban	80.0	1.2	18.8
Upper Egypt—rural	88.7	5.6	5.7
Frontier Governorates	74.2	1.0	24.8
Wealth index			
Bottom 40%	83.7	7.8	8.5
Mid 40%	83.8	2.6	13.6
Top 20%	65.5	0.0	34.5
Household decision-making			
Joint say in household budget	48.3	33.7	71.2
Having influence in having a child	81.3	75.0	89.3
Education			
Average years of education	4.4	1.1	10.7
Age			
Average age	30.9	32.1	33.6

Source: Own calculations based on EDHS-95.

Table 14.4. *Percentage Distribution of Currently Working Women, Aged 20–44 by Reason for Working, Egypt, 1995*

	Working status		
	Non-cash work	Cash work	All workers
External reasons	90.5	64.2	69.2
Family needs	47.9	57.9	56.0
Help family business	42.6	6.3	13.3
Personal reasons	9.5	35.5	30.5
Use educational skills	2.9	10.9	9.4
Get social status	0.0	9.2	7.5
Financial independence	4.4	7.4	6.9
Use free time	2.2	3.7	3.4
To be herself	0.0	2.9	2.3
Pursue profession	0.0	1.3	1.1

Source: Own calculations based on EDHS-95.

Almost seven out of ten (69.2 per cent) of all working women in our sample said they worked for family needs or to help their family business (Table 14.4). This proportion reached as high as 90.5 per cent among non-cash workers, only 9.5 per cent of whom worked for personal reasons as compared to almost half (35.5 per cent) of all cash workers. One in ten (10.9 per cent) cash workers said they worked to use their educational skills and 24.6 per cent worked to gain social status, financial independence, or for other personal reasons. After controlling for region, there were no significant differences in age among either cash or non-cash workers as to their reasons for working.

The most commonly reported reasons for not working were the absence of skills or education (35.6 per cent), followed by family reasons such as taking care of the household and children (29.3 per cent). Younger and urban women were more likely to face opposition from their husbands or elder relatives to their employment; rural women were more likely to encounter difficulties in finding work. These results clearly suggest that most women are not sufficiently qualified to hold formal labour market occupations, especially in the modern sector, or are prevented from doing so.

Multivariate analyses

Model description

Since many of these covariates of contraceptive use are interrelated, a multivariate analysis of the determinants of modern contraceptive use was undertaken. Four logistic regression models are considered. The initial model (Model 1) treats contraceptive use as a function of regional, educational, and religious backgrounds, as well as the influences of spousal choice, life course and living conditions. Model 2 additionally considers working status and its interaction with marital duration. Models 3 and 4 include variables that account for women's financial and reproductive positions, respectively, so as to determine their contributions to predicting the likelihood that women currently use modern contraceptives, after controlling for all other variables. Women's financial decision power is measured by having a final say in the household budget; reproductive decision power is measured by the ability to exercise an influence in the decision to have an extra child.

An interaction term consisting of employment with marital duration was introduced to account for differences among type of workers and their stage of family formation. Quadratic terms were tested for all continuous variables (especially the life course variables) in order to allow for the fact that most women would like to have children at an early stage of their family formation. Accordingly, a quadratic term for number of children was included in the model. Regarding the respondent's age, 5-year age groups were used for ease of interpretation.

RESULTS

Table 14.5 presents the results of four logistic regression models predicting the likelihood that women currently use a modern method of contraception. The inclusion of working status variables and their interaction terms with years since first marriage is statistically significant ($p = 0.01$).

Table 14.5. *Logistic Regression Coefficients for the Effects of Employment and Women's Characteristics on Modern Contraceptive Use, Egypt 1995*

Variable	Model 1	Model 2	Model 3	Model 4
Region				
Urban Governorates (r)				
Lower Egypt Urban	−0.010	−0.013	−0.010	−0.033
Lower Egypt Rural	−0.187	−0.186	−0.183	−0.212[a]
Upper Egypt Urban	−0.799[c]	−0.806[c]	−0.785[c]	−0.795[c]
Upper Egypt Rural	−1.406[c]	−1.419[c]	−1.399[c]	−1.422[c]
Frontier Governorates	−0.639[a]	−0.643[a]	−0.622[a]	−0.583[a]
Years of education	0.021[b]	0.025[c]	0.023[b]	0.022[b]
Ever worked before marriage	−0.020	−0.005	−0.002	−0.001
Working status				
Cash work		0.265	0.236	0.234
Non-cash work		0.952[b]	0.972[b]	1.096[b]
Not working (r)				
Interaction term				
Cash work*Years since first marriage		−0.035[b]	−0.034[b]	−0.032[b]
Non-cash work*Years since first marriage		−0.050[a]	−0.051[a]	−0.058[b]
Decision-making variable			0.157[b]	0.564[c]
Wealth index				
Bottom 40% (r)				
Mid 40%	0.219[b]	0.207[b]	0.201[b]	0.210[b]
Top 20%	0.546[c]	0.552[c]	0.550[c]	0.534[c]
Childhood in rural area	−0.138	−0.140	−0.142	−0.115
Nuclear household	0.089	0.087	0.052	0.081
Age of respondent				
20–24	0.580[c]	0.554[b]	0.538[b]	0.558[c]
25–29	0.518[c]	0.482[c]	0.471[c]	0.504[c]
30–34	0.427[c]	0.396[c]	0.383[c]	0.403[c]
35–39	0.498[c]	0.472[c]	0.465[c]	0.464[c]
40–44 (r)				
Religion (Muslim)	−0.396[b]	−0.426[c]	−0.412[c]	−0.384[b]
Spousal choice				
Chose first husband	−0.026	−0.028	−0.031	−0.018
Husband is blood relative	−0.124[a]	−0.128	−0.124	−0.127[a]
Spousal educational gap (years)	0.013	0.014[a]	0.013	0.012
Spousal age difference	−0.026[c]	−0.027[c]	−0.027[c]	−0.026[c]
Other life course variables				
Number of children	0.326[c]	0.326[c]	0.329[c]	0.336[c]
Number of children squared	−0.061[c]	−0.062[c]	−0.063[c]	−0.060[c]
Years since first marriage	0.003	0.008	0.006	0.007
Chi-Square for Covariates (DF)	598.7 (23)	611.7(27)	614.9(28)	653.3(28)
N	4162	4162	4160	4162

(r) = Reference category.
[a] $p<0.10$.
[b] $p<0.05$.
[c] $p<0.01$.
Source: Own calculations based on EDHS-9.5.

Region. Model 2 reveals three levels of modern contraceptive use. Women living in the Frontier Governorates and in urban Upper Egypt occupy an intermediate level. They are half as likely to be using contraception as their counterparts in the Urban Governorates which, with higher living standards on average than the rest of the country, is used as the reference category for the analyses. The lowest level occurs in rural Upper Egypt, where women are about one quarter as likely to be using modern contraceptives as women in the Urban Governorates. By contrast, women from the Urban Governorates and Lower Egypt are more likely to be using contraception.

Education. As expected, education is positively associated with contraceptive use, but its effect is modest. For every 5 extra years of education, the odds of using modern contraception rise by 13 per cent. There is no evidence of a non-linear relationship between years of education and modern contraceptive use. The effect of education is slightly smaller when life course and living conditions variables are accounted for, but it remains positive and significant.

Work status and its interaction with years since first marriage. Having work experience prior to marriage was not a significant variable in the model. Instead, it is the interaction of current working status with the stage of the woman's reproductive career (measured by years from first marriage) which helps explain the effect of working status on the use of modern contraception. On average, the odds of using modern contraceptives decline with years of marriage for working women, whereas they increase marginally for non-working women. In fact, during the first 18 years of marriage, the effect of working status is highest for non-cash workers than for all other women. Results from a cross-sectional analysis like this however, can only suggest the existence of a relationship; a longitudinal analysis relating working histories to reproductive histories could shed more light on this.

Index of wealth. The index of wealth, a rough marker of socio-economic status, is one of the most significant variables in the model. Compared to women living in the poorest 40 per cent of households, women who belong to an intermediate wealth status are 1.2 times more likely to be using modern contraception. Those in the top 20 per cent are 1.7 times more likely to be using contraceptives as women from the least well-off households.

Rural childhood. The chances that a woman is using modern contraception are reduced by 0.9 if she spent the first 12 years of life in a rural area. This variable was included because although most of the women who had a rural childhood were still living in a rural area, 15.4 per cent of them were now living in some urban area.

Living arrangements. Women living in nuclear type of household (i.e., without any relatives) were not significantly more likely to be using contraception than those living in any other type of household arrangement.

Age of respondent. After controlling for all other variables, women aged 20–24 are the most likely to be using a modern contraceptive method. The likelihood of using a modern contraceptive method is at least 1.5 times higher in every age group compared to women aged 40–44.

Muslim. The odds that a Muslim woman is currently using a modern method of contraception are 0.7 times those for a non-Muslim woman. In other words, not being a Muslim increases the odds of using contraception 1.4 times. As discussed earlier, women using traditional methods of contraception were also more likely to be non-Muslim. Moreover, Muslim women were disproportionately likely to think that contraception was forbidden by their religion (14 per cent of Muslim women thought so, as compared to 6 per cent of non-Muslims).

Spousal choice. Neither choosing one's first husband, nor marrying a blood relative, significantly influences the likelihood of using modern contraceptives. This result is not altogether unexpected given that in our sub-sample, only one in four (26 per cent) women said they had chosen their husbands while 40 per cent said their husband was a blood relative. These statistics indicate that arranged marriages are still the norm in Egypt. However, richer women tend to choose their husbands; one in three women from the wealthiest group chose their husbands compared to 12 per cent from the poorest 40 per cent of households. The educational gap between husbands and wives proved to be marginally significant, indicating that the woman's education is a more important determinant of modern contraceptive use than the level of education attained by her husband. In addition, large differences in age between husband and wife were found to have a negative impact on contraceptive use. For every 2 extra years of spousal age difference, the odds of using modern contraception decrease by 5 per cent. A woman who is the same age as her husband is 1.2 times more likely to be using modern contraception than if she was in a marriage characterized by the mean spousal age difference of 7.1 years. This is significant given that in Egypt, traditional norms continue to favour an age difference of 5 or more years between husbands and wives.

Number of children. The number of living children assumes an inverted U-shape. Compared to a childless woman, a woman with one child is 1.1 times more likely to be using a modern contraceptive method. The odds are 2.7 times greater should she have three children and 4.2 times more if she has six children, after which the likelihood of using modern contraception start to decrease with each extra child that a woman may have.

Models 3 and 4

The models investigating how the exercise of power in different aspects of decision-making affects contraceptive use, in the presence of life course and living conditions variables, reveal that both the financial and reproductive dimensions of autonomy are significant predictors of contraceptive use. As expected, having more influence in the decision to have an extra child has the largest effect. Women who reported having equal or more influence than their husbands in having an extra child are 1.8 times as likely to be using a modern contraceptive than those without any say in the matter. The inclusion of the variable in the model is also significant as judged by the increase in the chi-squared value for covariates. Although the measure of financial influence likewise proved significant and positive (an odds ratio of 1.2), the inclusion of this variable scarcely adds to the model, producing only a minimal change in the model chi-squared value.

DISCUSSION

This has examined the effects of employment and other aspects of female autonomy on current use of modern contraception in Egypt. In 1995, women made up 29 per cent of the adult labour force (UNDP 1998), a level comparable to the average for the Middle East and North Africa region. Almost one in two (49 per cent) currently married women aged 20–44 were using modern contraceptives. Since the early 1980s, declining economic conditions and changes in the labour market, as well as the substantial increase in contraceptive prevalence, have all affected gender roles in Egypt. Economic reforms and structural adjustment programmes have underpinned a fundamental departure from past policies toward a more market-oriented economy. Within this changing context, both sexes realize that expanding women's work opportunities may affect their power and participation in household decision-making, including choices about fertility and family planning.

Although women frequently encounter opposition from their husbands about leaving the house to work, consent is typically given, however grudgingly, in situations of economic need (Hoodfar 1997; El Dawla *et al.* 1998). Earning an income is, *ceteris paribus*, likely to improve the position of women in the household through giving them more power and resources with which to negotiate both their relations with husbands and relatives, and their status in the community. However, economic involvement is not the same as economic equality and the economic dimension is but one facet of gender relations, albeit a very important one. And whereas an increasing number of women work for wages, they are doing so primarily to supplement family income rather than for their empowerment. Moreover, notwithstanding an overall rise in reported female work activity, only one in five Egyptian women were found to work before marriage, with barely one in two of those continuing to work after marriage.

Until the early 1990s, contraceptive prevalence rates rose steadily among Egyptian women, despite their relatively low levels of autonomy overall. But the results of this study suggest that not all indicators of women's autonomy and position are significant predictors of reproductive behaviour. Regarding women's employment, this analysis confirms the significance of women's economic power for the increased uptake of modern contraceptive use. However, the results do not suggest in a straightforward manner that working women are significantly more likely to use modern contraceptives than other women.

It is the interaction of employment status with the stage of family formation that helps explain the relationship between employment and contraceptive use. While the odds of using contraception are highest among working women during their first years of marriage and decrease thereafter, the odds for a non-working woman increase slightly. This suggests that working women tend to begin using modern contraception earlier in their marital lives than do non-working women. However, this finding needs to be interpreted with caution because of the non-availability of working histories and the cross-sectional nature of the data. These caveats notwithstanding, the findings of this paper are important, not least because they add to the growing literature on the evidence concerning the relationship between female employment and contraceptive use in low-income countries, and because Egypt accounts for one-quarter of the population of the Arab world.

Debate continues in Egypt about the role of women as housewives and workers. Although further research is warranted, the evidence presented here indicates that empowering women in the workplace may contribute to changes in contraceptive and fertility behaviour in Egypt. However, the evidence is indirect as the relationship between female employment and contraceptive use is confounded with the stage of family formation. Though cash-earning opportunities may improve the autonomy of women and promote their participation in reproductive decision-making, it is possible that additional programmes may be needed to improve women's economic security. These in turn could have a greater net impact on their reproductive behaviour.

References

Anker, R. and Anker M. (1995), 'Measuring Female Labour Force with Emphasis on Egypt', in N. F. Khoury and V. M. Moghadam (eds), *Gender and Development in the Arab World—Women's Economic Participation: Patterns and Policies*, London: Zed Books, 148–176.

Arab Republic of Egypt (1995), *Egypt Human Development Report 1995*, Institute of National Planning, Cairo.

Cochrane, S. H. (1979), *Fertility and Education: What Do We Really Know?*, Baltimore, MD: Johns Hopkins University Press.

ESCWA (1999), *The ESCWA Region: Twenty Five Years 1974–1999*, New York: Economic and Social Commission for Western Asia.

El Dawla, A. S., Abdel Hadi, A., and Wahab, N. A. (1998), 'Women's Wit over Men's: Trade-offs and Strategic Accommodations in Egyptian Women's Reproductive Lives', in R. Petchesky and K. Judd (eds), *Negotiating Reproductive Rights*, London: Zed Books, 69–107.

El-Zanaty, F. (1995), 'Contraceptive Use in Egypt: Trends and Determinants', in M. Mahran, F. El-Zanaty, and A. A. Way (eds), *Perspectives on Fertility and Family Planning in Egypt: Results of Further Analysis of the 1992 Egypt Demographic and Health Survey*, Calverton, MD: Macro International, 1–29.

—— Hussein, E. M., Shawky, G. A., Way A., and Kishor S. (1996), *Egypt Demographic and Health Survey 1995*, Cairo and Calverton, MD: National Population Council and Macro International.

Fargues, P. (1997), 'State Policies and the Birth Rate in Egypt: From Socialism to Liberalism', *Population and Development Review*, 23, 115–38.

Filmer, D. and Pritchett, L. (1999), 'The Effect of Household Wealth on Educational Attainment: Evidence from 35 Countries', *Population and Development Review*, 25, 85–120.

Govindasamy, P. and Malhotra, A. (1996), 'Women's Position and Family Planning in Egypt', *Studies in Family Planning*, 27, 328–40.

Hoodfar, H. (1997), *Between Marriage and the Market: Intimate Politics and Survival in Cairo*, University of California, Berkeley.

Ibrahim, S. E. and Ibrahim, B. L. (1998), 'Egypt's Population Policy: The Long March of State and Civil Society', in A. Jain (ed.) *Do Population Policies Matter? Fertility and Politics in Egypt, India, Kenya, and Mexico*, New York: Population Council, 19–52.

ILO (1997), *Yearbook of Labour Statistics 1997* Geneva: International Labour Organization.

Jejeebhoy, S. J. (1995), *Women's Education, Autonomy, and Reproductive Behaviour: Experience from Developing Countries*, Oxford: Clarendon Press.

Kishor, S. (1995), 'Autonomy and Egyptian Women: Findings from the 1988 Egypt Demographic and Health Survey', *Demographic and Health Surveys Occasional Papers 2*, Calverton, MD: Macro International.

Kishor, S. (1999), 'Women's Empowerment and Contraceptive Use in Egypt', paper presented at the Annual Meeting of the Population Association of America, New York, March.

Lloyd, C. B. (1991), 'The Contribution of the World Fertility Surveys to an Understanding of the Relationship between Women's Work and Fertility', *Studies in Family Planning*, 22, 144–61.

Mason, K. O (1993), 'The Impact of Women's Position on Demographic Change during the Course of Development', in N. Federici, K. O. Mason, and S. Sogner (eds), *Women's Position and Demographic Change*, Oxford: Clarendon Press, pp. 19–42.

Moghadam, V. M. (1998), *Women, Work, and Economic Reform in the Middle East and North Africa*, Lynne Rienner, London.

Mulhori, P., Blanc, A., and Rutstein, S. (1994), 'Socioeconomic differentials in fertility', *DHS Comparative Studies No. 13*, Calverton, MD: Macro International.

Nawar, L., Lloyd C. B., and Ibrahim, B. (1995), 'Women's Autonomy and Gender Roles in Egyptian Families', in C. M. Obermeyer (ed.), *Family, Gender, and Population in the Middle East: Policies in Context*, Cairo: American University in Cairo Press, 147–78.

Sathar, Z. A. and Chidambaram, V. C. (1984), 'Differentials in contraceptive use', *WFS Comparative Studies No. 36*, Voorburg, Netherlands: International Statistical Institute.

UN (1995), *The World's Women 1995: Trends and Statistics*, New York: United Nations.

—— (1997), *Arab Women 1995*, New York: United Nations.

—— (1999), *World Population Prospects: The 1998 Revision. Volume 1: Comprehensive Tables*, New York: United Nations.

UNDP (1998), *Human Development Report, 1998*, New York: Oxford University Press.

World Bank (1998), *World Development Report 1998*, New York: Oxford University Press.

Index

The manufacturer's authorised representative in the EU for product safety is Oxford University Press España S.A. of el Parque Empresarial San Fernando de Henares, Avenida de Castilla, 2 – 28830 Madrid (www.oup.es/en or product.safety@oup.com). OUP España S.A. also acts as importer into Spain of products made by the manufacturer.

www.ingramcontent.com/pod-product-compliance
Lightning Source LLC
LaVergne TN
LVHW011910200926
848484LV00002B/583
* 9 7 8 0 1 9 9 2 6 1 1 2 3 *